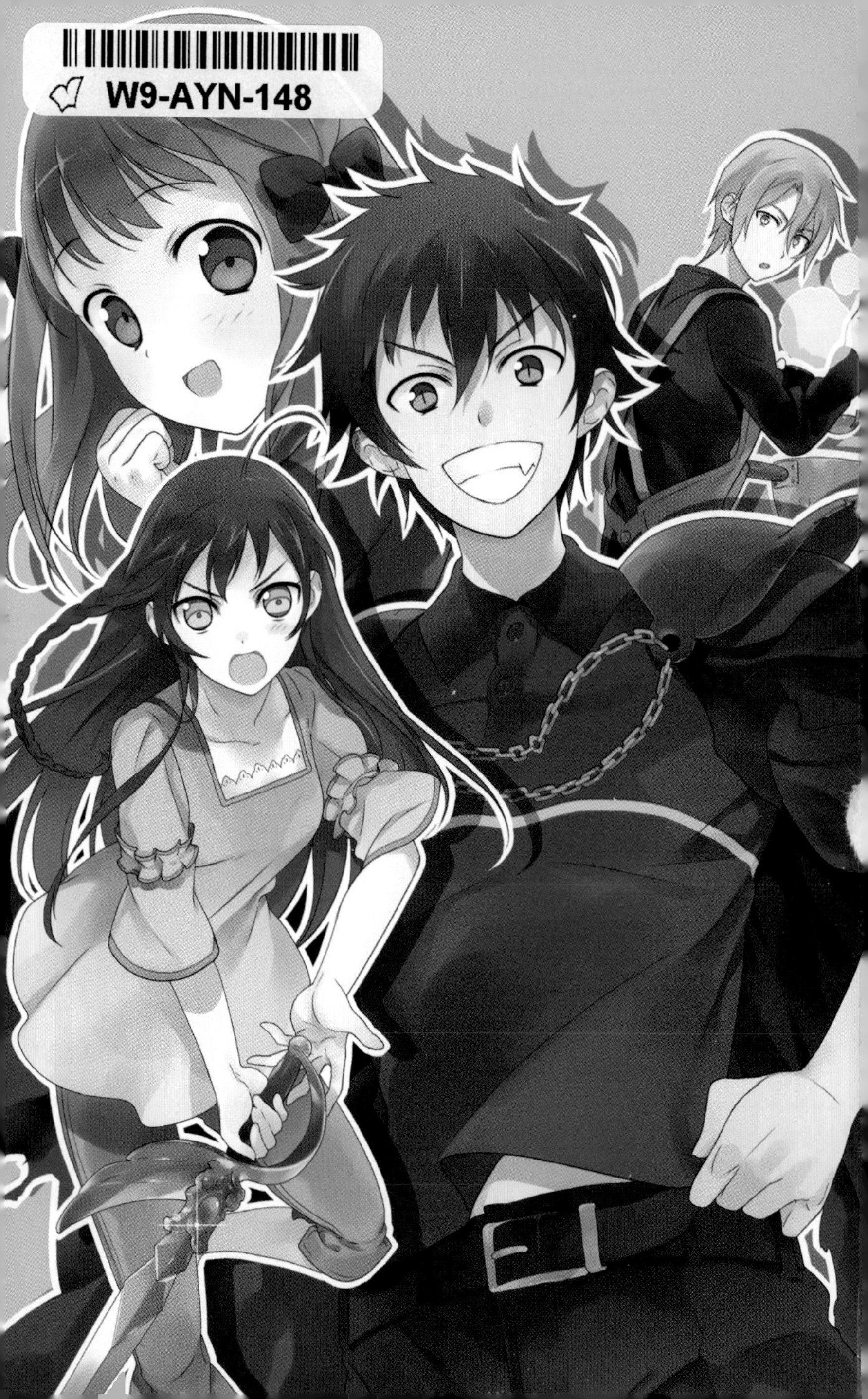

Chapter 1: The Devil Works Part-Time in Sasazuka ············· p3
Chapter 2: The Devil Receives an Ominous Text Message ········· p46
Chapter 3: The Devil Goes on a Date with This Girl from Work ····· p79
Chapter 4: The Devil and the Hero Are Trapped ················· p110
Chapter 5: The Hero Experiences a Little Human Kindness ········· p139
Bonus Manga & Afterword·· p173

THE DEVIL IS A PART-TIMER! ①

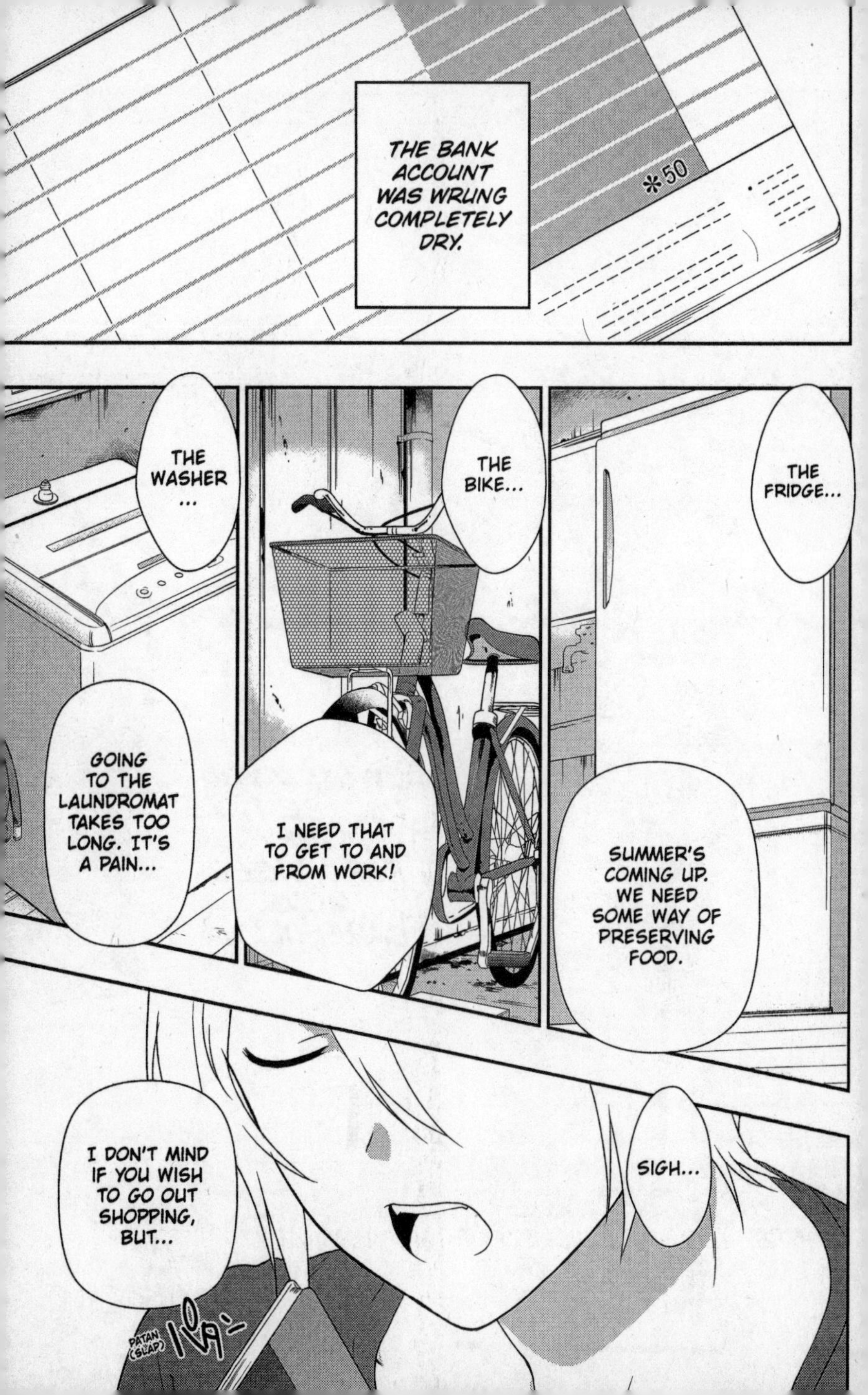
THE BANK ACCOUNT WAS WRUNG COMPLETELY DRY.
*50
THE FRIDGE...
SUMMER'S COMING UP. WE NEED SOME WAY OF PRESERVING FOOD.
THE BIKE...
I NEED THAT TO GET TO AND FROM WORK!
THE WASHER ...
GOING TO THE LAUNDROMAT TAKES TOO LONG. IT'S A PAIN...
SIGH...
I DON'T MIND IF YOU WISH TO GO OUT SHOPPING, BUT...
PATAN (SLAP)

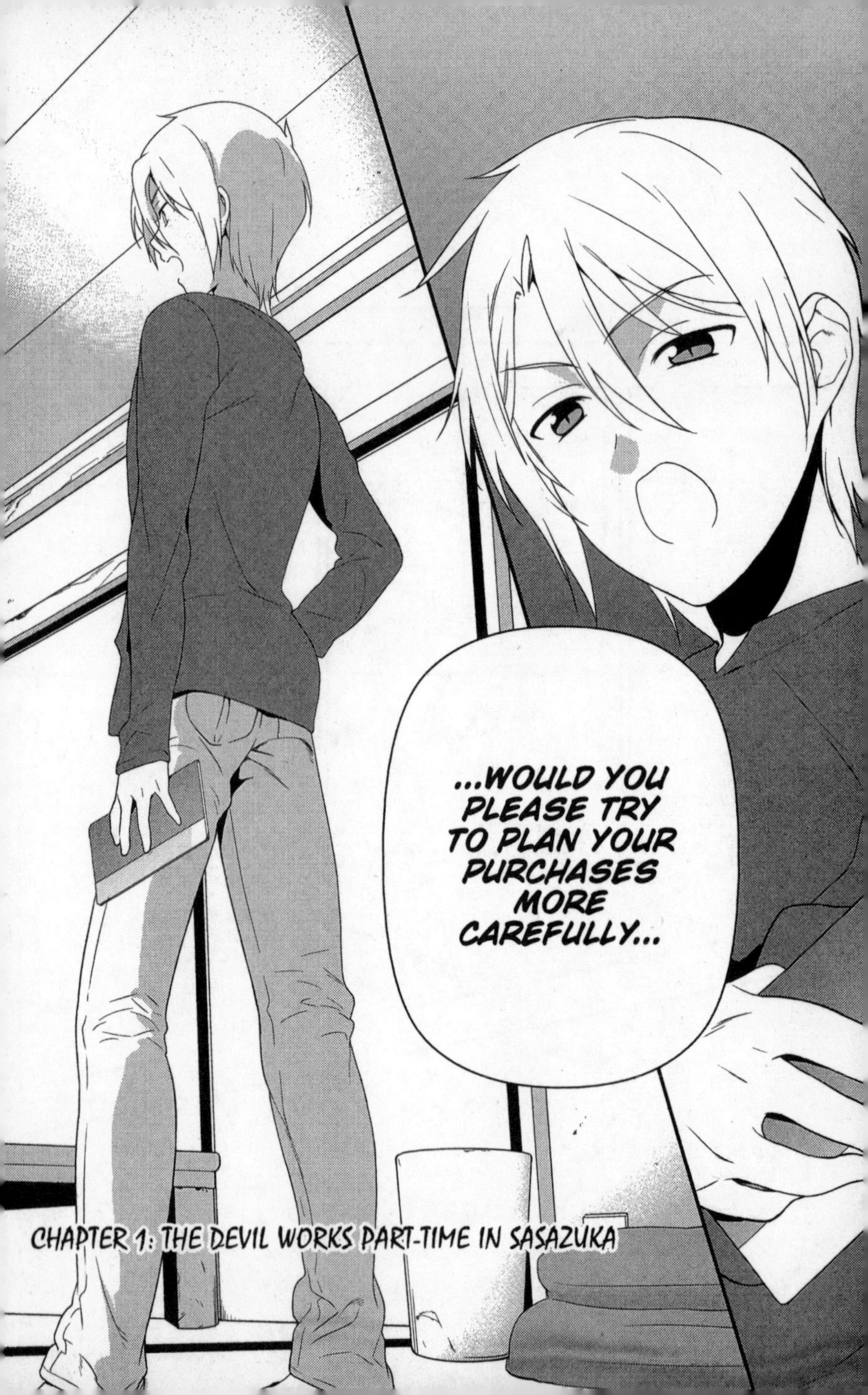
...WOULD YOU PLEASE TRY TO PLAN YOUR PURCHASES MORE CAREFULLY...
CHAPTER 1: THE DEVIL WORKS PART-TIME IN SASAZUKA

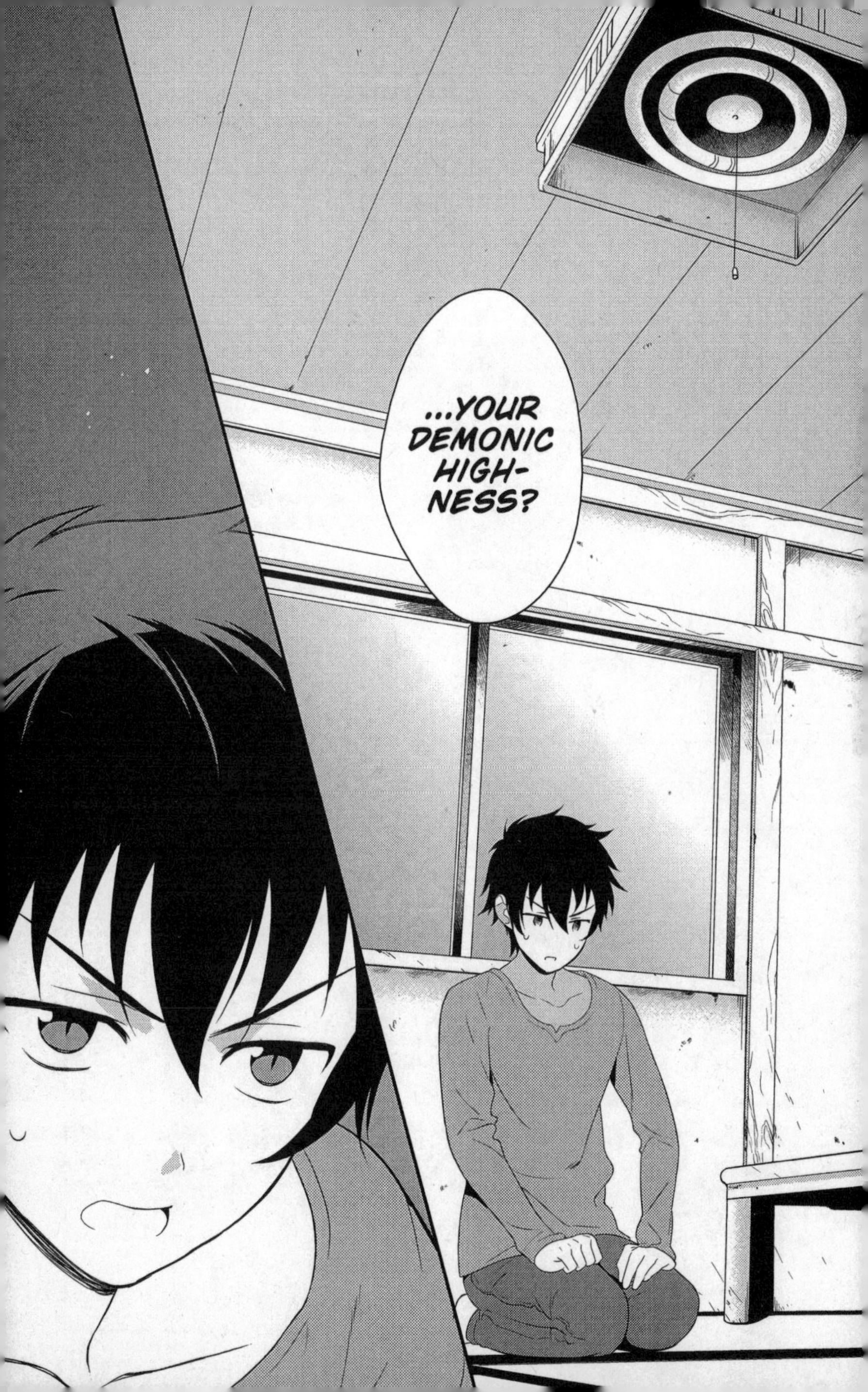
...YOUR DEMONIC HIGH-NESS?

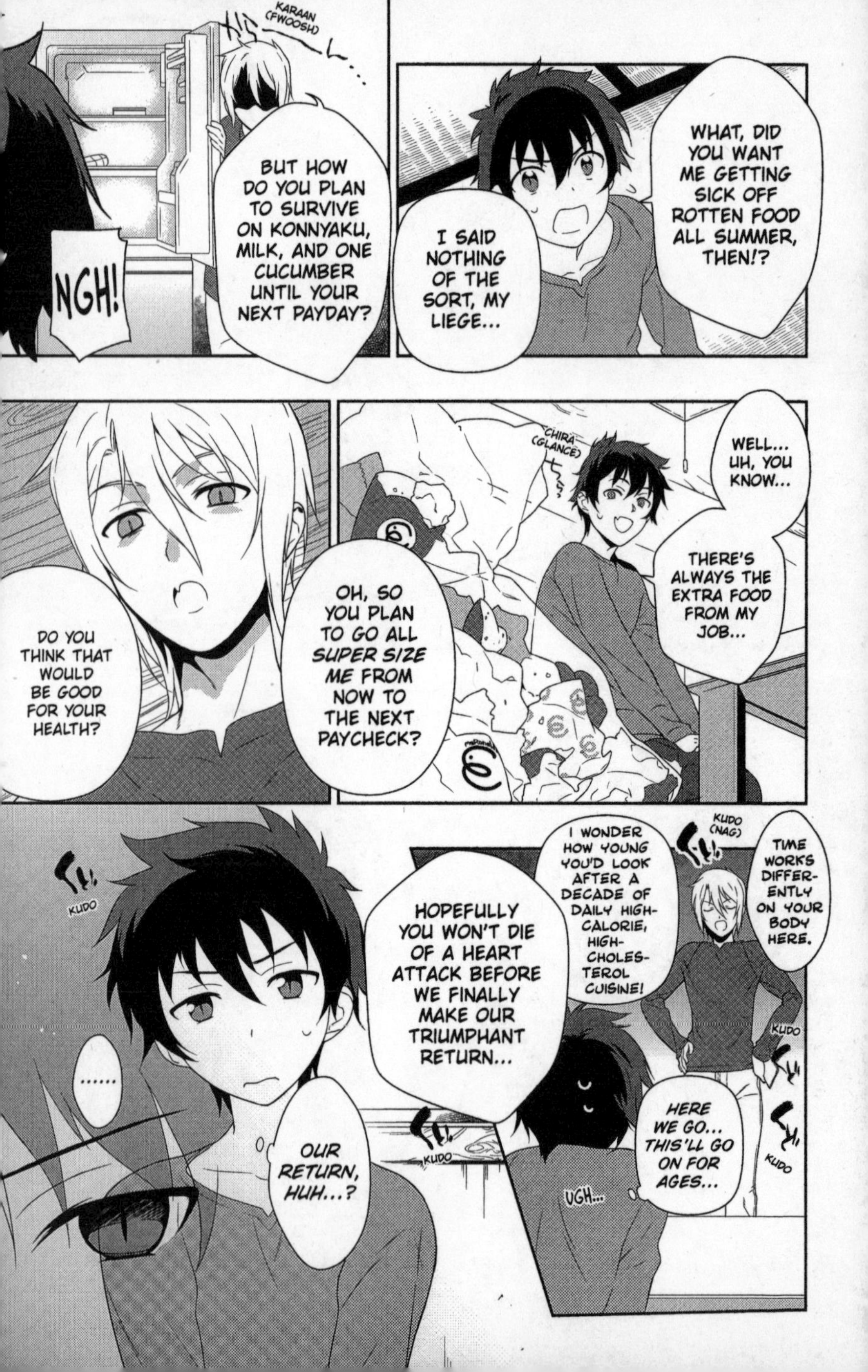
WHAT, DID YOU WANT ME GETTING SICK OFF ROTTEN FOOD ALL SUMMER, THEN!?
I SAID NOTHING OF THE SORT, MY LIEGE...
KARAAN (FWOOSH)
BUT HOW DO YOU PLAN TO SURVIVE ON KONNYAKU, MILK, AND ONE CUCUMBER UNTIL YOUR NEXT PAYDAY?
NGH!
CHIRA (GLANCE)
WELL... UH, YOU KNOW...
THERE'S ALWAYS THE EXTRA FOOD FROM MY JOB...
OH, SO YOU PLAN TO GO ALL SUPER SIZE ME FROM NOW TO THE NEXT PAYCHECK?
DO YOU THINK THAT WOULD BE GOOD FOR YOUR HEALTH?
KUDO (NAG)
TIME WORKS DIFFERENTLY ON YOUR BODY HERE.
I WONDER HOW YOUNG YOU'D LOOK AFTER A DECADE OF DAILY HIGH-CALORIE, HIGH-CHOLESTEROL CUISINE!
KUDO
KUDO
HERE WE GO... THIS'LL GO ON FOR AGES...
UGH...
KUDO
KUDO
HOPEFULLY YOU WON'T DIE OF A HEART ATTACK BEFORE WE FINALLY MAKE OUR TRIUMPHANT RETURN...
......
OUR RETURN, HUH...?

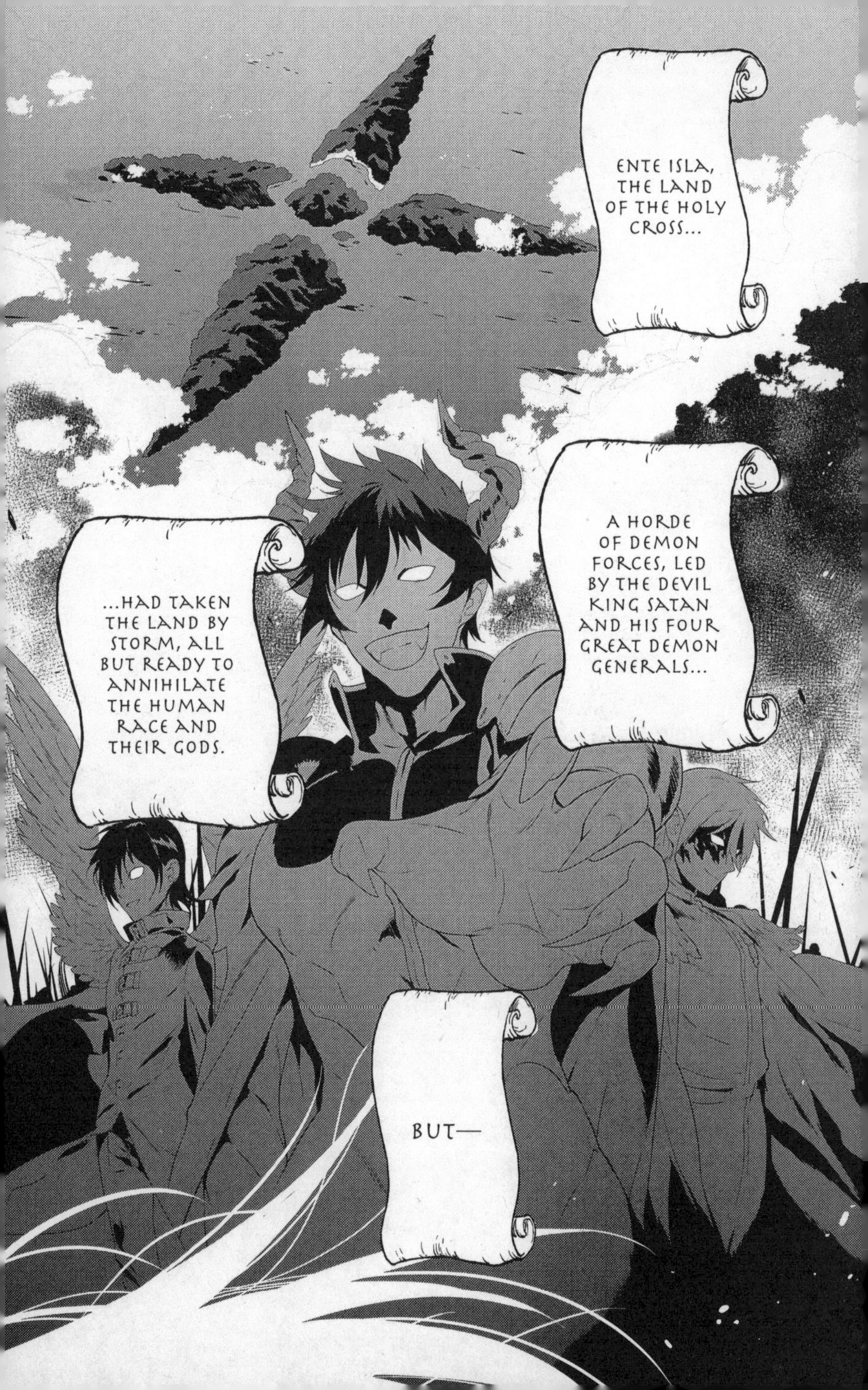
ENTE ISLA, THE LAND OF THE HOLY CROSS...
A HORDE OF DEMON FORCES, LED BY THE DEVIL KING SATAN AND HIS FOUR GREAT DEMON GENERALS...
...HAD TAKEN THE LAND BY STORM, ALL BUT READY TO ANNIHILATE THE HUMAN RACE AND THEIR GODS.
BUT—

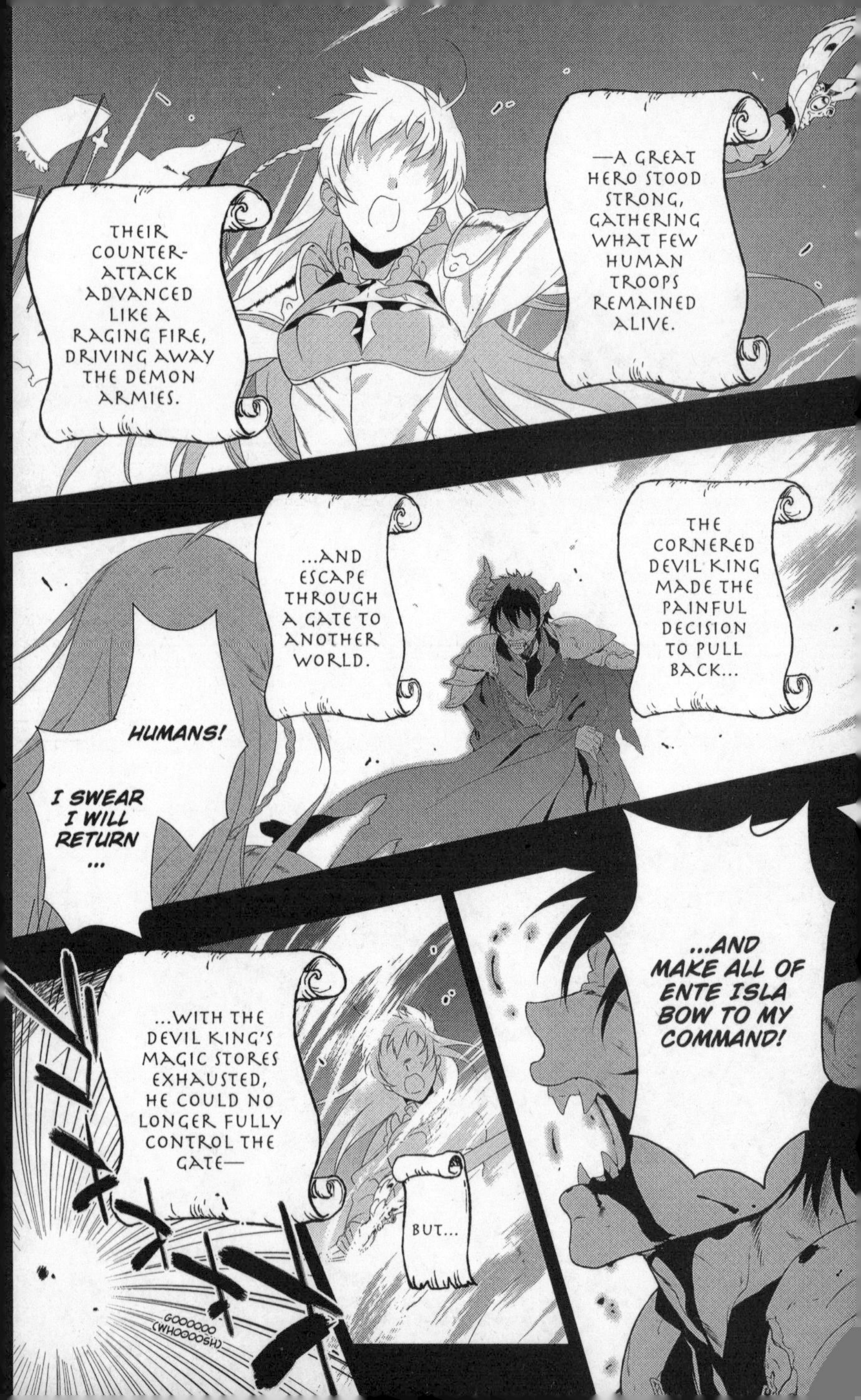
—A GREAT HERO STOOD STRONG, GATHERING WHAT FEW HUMAN TROOPS REMAINED ALIVE.
THEIR COUNTER-ATTACK ADVANCED LIKE A RAGING FIRE, DRIVING AWAY THE DEMON ARMIES.
THE CORNERED DEVIL KING MADE THE PAINFUL DECISION TO PULL BACK...
...AND ESCAPE THROUGH A GATE TO ANOTHER WORLD.
HUMANS!
I SWEAR I WILL RETURN ...
...AND MAKE ALL OF ENTE ISLA BOW TO MY COMMAND!
BUT...
...WITH THE DEVIL KING'S MAGIC STORES EXHAUSTED, HE COULD NO LONGER FULLY CONTROL THE GATE—
GOOOOOO (WHOOOOSH)

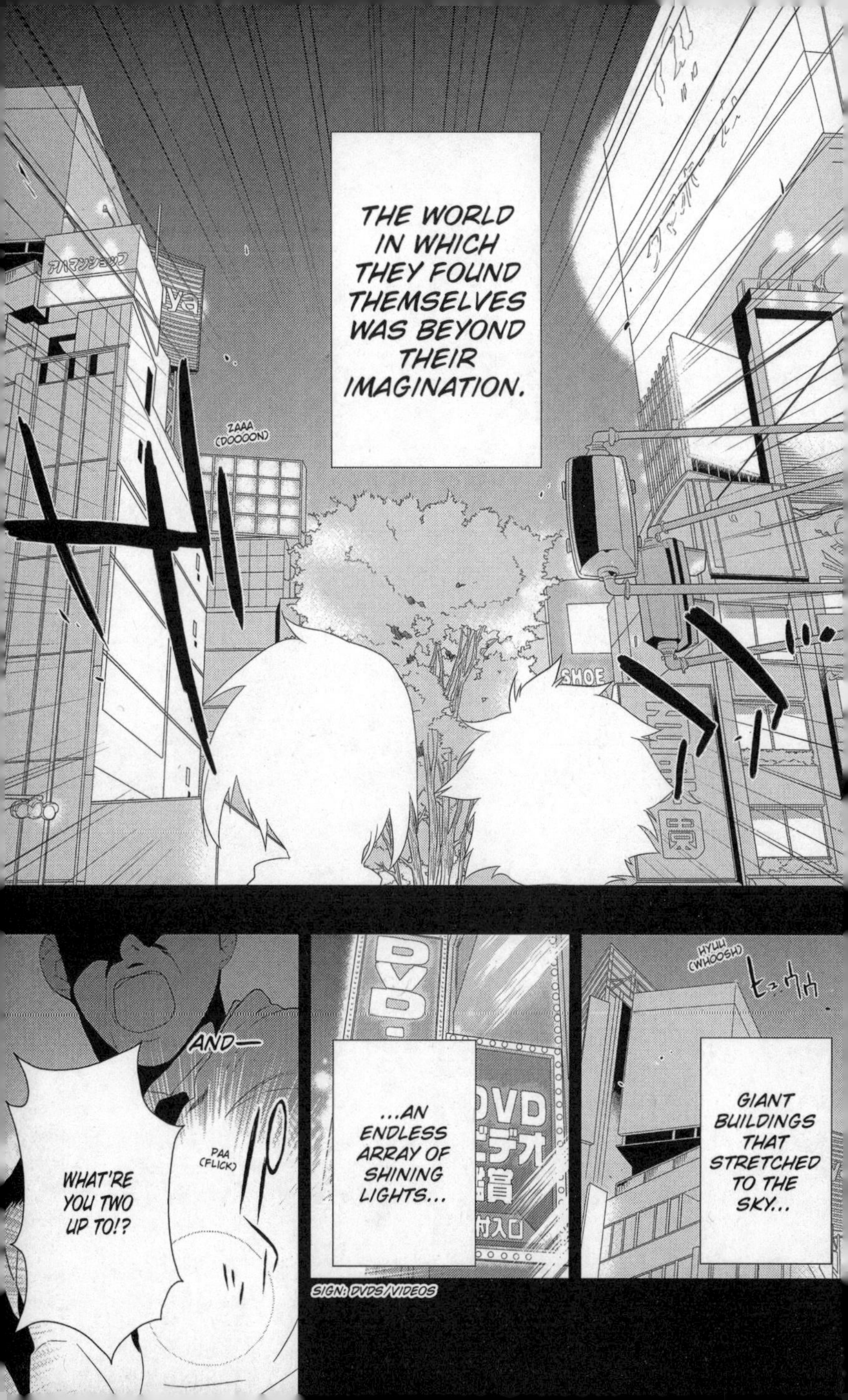
THE WORLD IN WHICH THEY FOUND THEMSELVES WAS BEYOND THEIR IMAGINATION.
ZAAA (DOOOON)
SHOE
HYUU (WHOOSH)
GIANT BUILDINGS THAT STRETCHED TO THE SKY...
DVD
...AN ENDLESS ARRAY OF SHINING LIGHTS...
DVD
SIGN: DVDS/VIDEOS
AND—
PAA (FLICK)
WHAT'RE YOU TWO UP TO!?

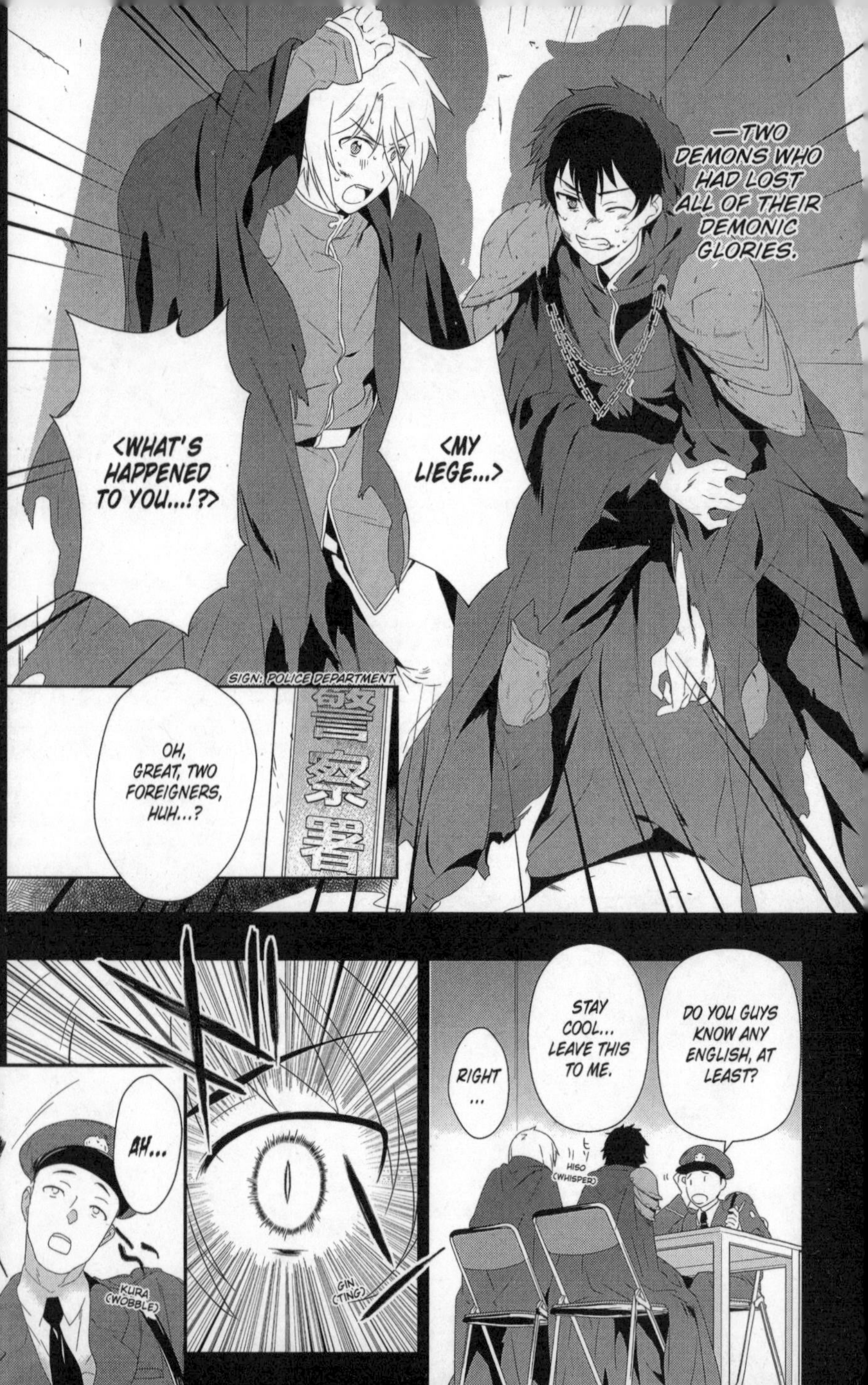
—TWO DEMONS WHO HAD LOST ALL OF THEIR DEMONIC GLORIES.
<MY LIEGE...>
<WHAT'S HAPPENED TO YOU...!?>
SIGN: POLICE DEPARTMENT
警察署
OH, GREAT, TWO FOREIGNERS, HUH...?
DO YOU GUYS KNOW ANY ENGLISH, AT LEAST?
STAY COOL... LEAVE THIS TO ME.
RIGHT ...
HISO (WHISPER)
GIN (TING)
AH...
KURA (WOBBLE)

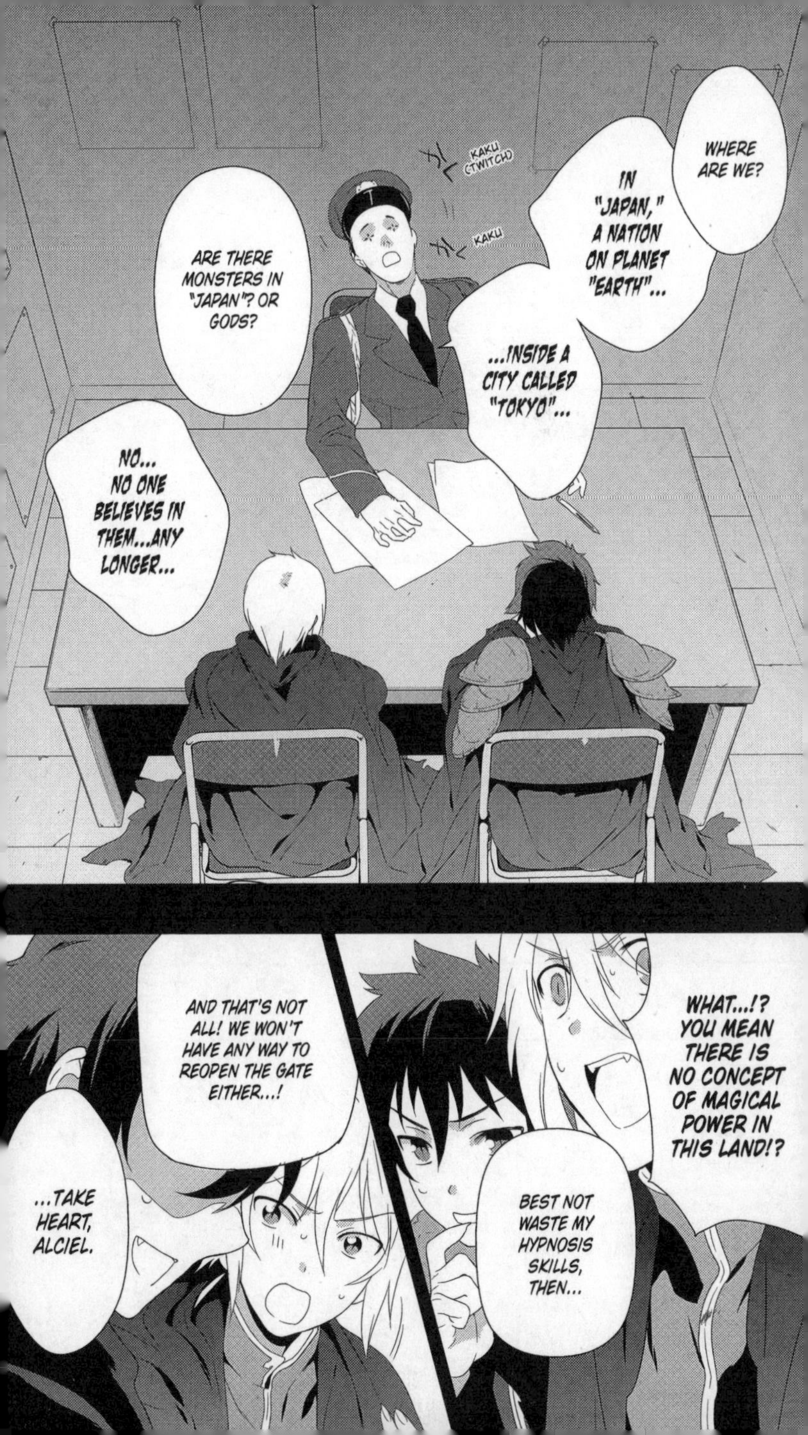
WHERE ARE WE?
IN "JAPAN," A NATION ON PLANET "EARTH"...
...INSIDE A CITY CALLED "TOKYO"...
KAKU (TWITCH)
KAKU
ARE THERE MONSTERS IN "JAPAN"? OR GODS?
NO... NO ONE BELIEVES IN THEM...ANY LONGER...
WHAT...!? YOU MEAN THERE IS NO CONCEPT OF MAGICAL POWER IN THIS LAND!?
BEST NOT WASTE MY HYPNOSIS SKILLS, THEN...
AND THAT'S NOT ALL! WE WON'T HAVE ANY WAY TO REOPEN THE GATE EITHER...!
...TAKE HEART, ALCIEL.

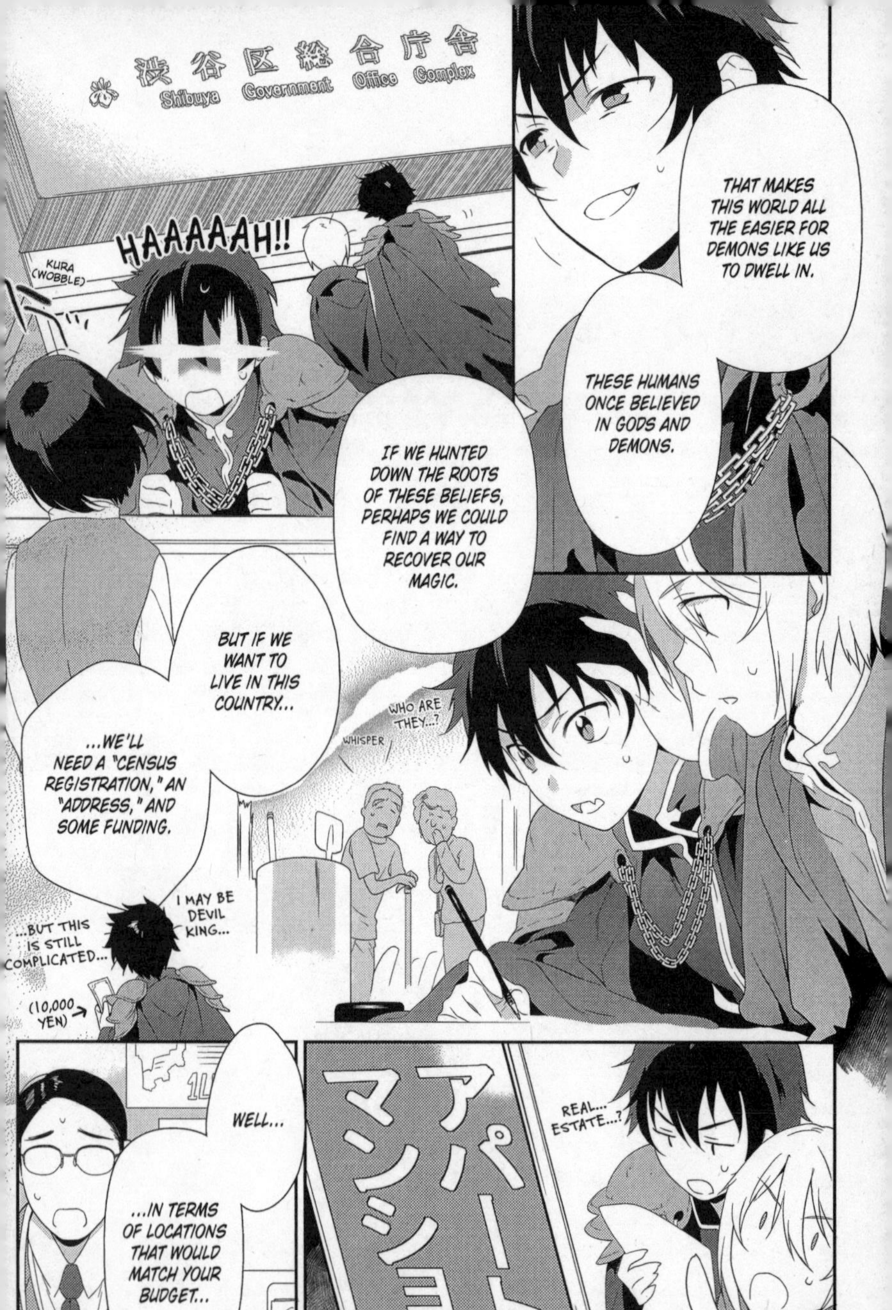
THAT MAKES THIS WORLD ALL THE EASIER FOR DEMONS LIKE US TO DWELL IN.
THESE HUMANS ONCE BELIEVED IN GODS AND DEMONS.
IF WE HUNTED DOWN THE ROOTS OF THESE BELIEFS, PERHAPS WE COULD FIND A WAY TO RECOVER OUR MAGIC.
渋谷区総合庁舎
Shibuya Government Office Complex
HAAAAAH!!
KURA (WOBBLE)
WHO ARE THEY...?
WHISPER
BUT IF WE WANT TO LIVE IN THIS COUNTRY...
...WE'LL NEED A "CENSUS REGISTRATION," AN "ADDRESS," AND SOME FUNDING.
I MAY BE DEVIL KING...
...BUT THIS IS STILL COMPLICATED...
(10,000 YEN)
アパート
マンション
REAL... ESTATE...?
WELL...
...IN TERMS OF LOCATIONS THAT WOULD MATCH YOUR BUDGET...
SIGN: APARTMENTS/CONDOMINIUMS

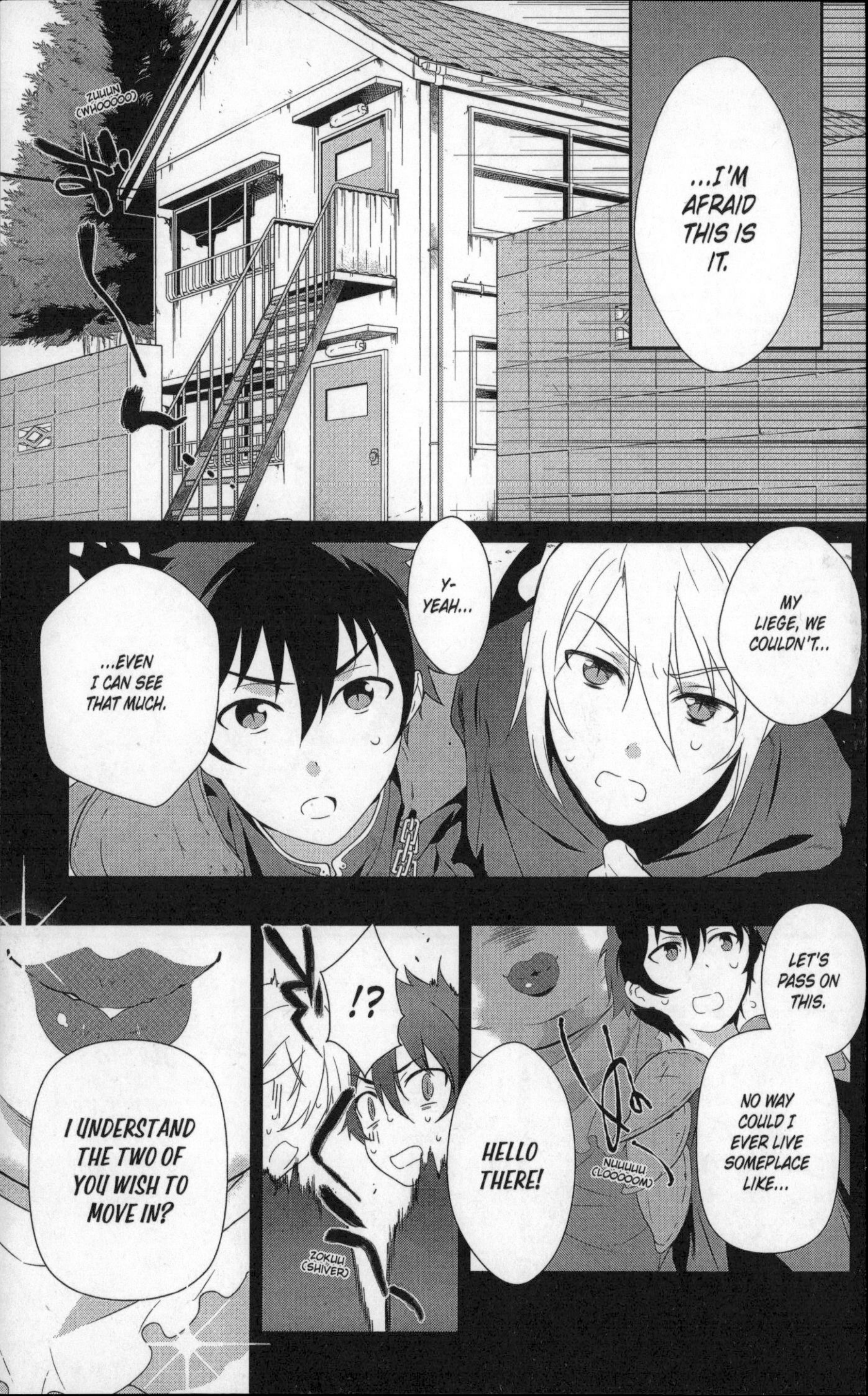
...I'M AFRAID THIS IS IT.
ZUUUN (WHOOOOO)
MY LIEGE, WE COULDN'T...
Y-YEAH...
...EVEN I CAN SEE THAT MUCH.
LET'S PASS ON THIS.
NO WAY COULD I EVER LIVE SOMEPLACE LIKE...
NUUUUU (LOOOOOM)
HELLO THERE!
!?
ZOKUU (SHIVER)
I UNDERSTAND THE TWO OF YOU WISH TO MOVE IN?

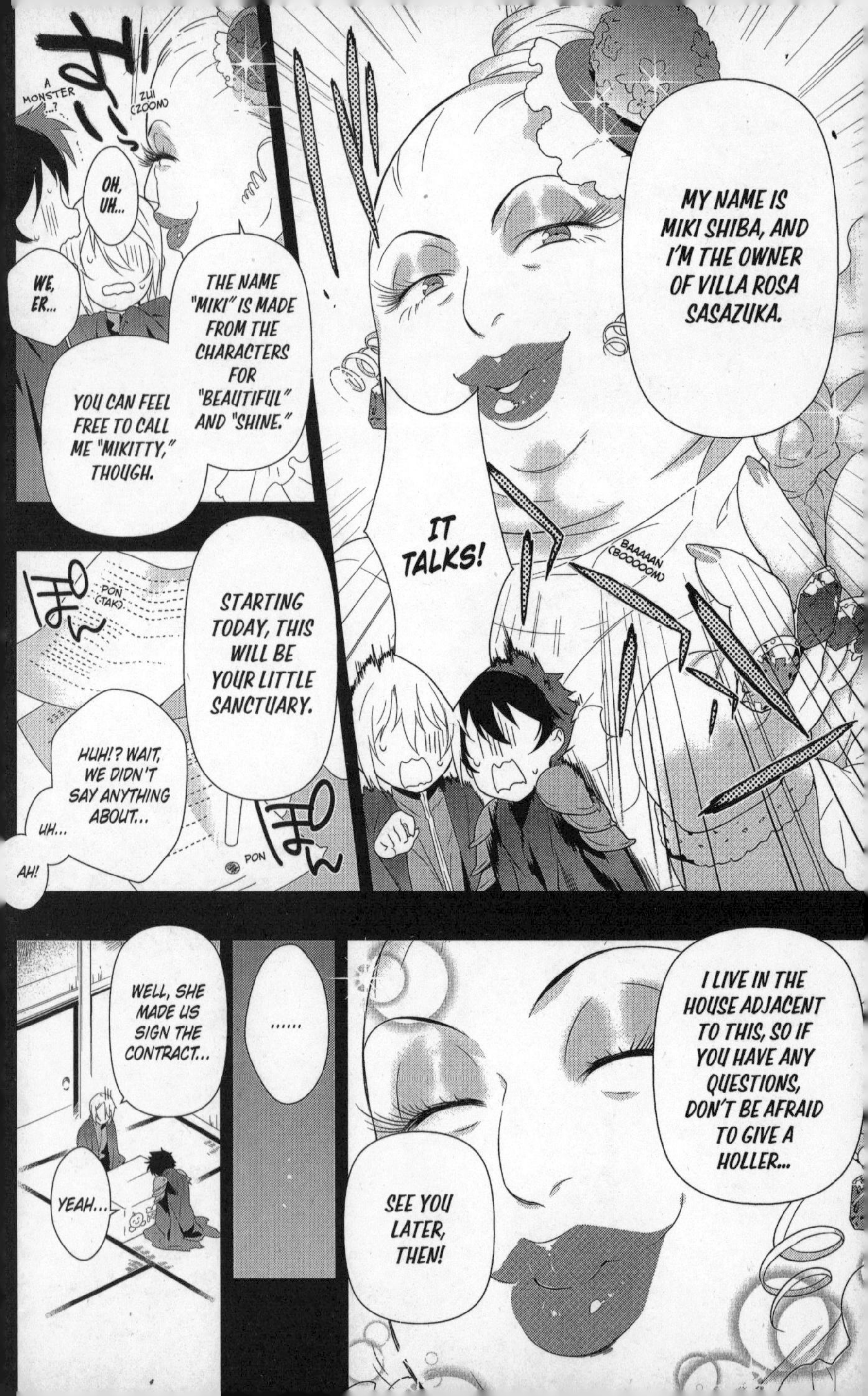
MY NAME IS MIKI SHIBA, AND I'M THE OWNER OF VILLA ROSA SASAZUKA.
IT TALKS!
BAAAAAN (BOOOOOM)
ZUI (ZOOM)
A MONSTER ...?
OH, UH...
WE, ER...
THE NAME "MIKI" IS MADE FROM THE CHARACTERS FOR "BEAUTIFUL" AND "SHINE."
YOU CAN FEEL FREE TO CALL ME "MIKITTY," THOUGH.
STARTING TODAY, THIS WILL BE YOUR LITTLE SANCTUARY.
PON (TAK)
HUH!? WAIT, WE DIDN'T SAY ANYTHING ABOUT...
UH...
PON
AH!
I LIVE IN THE HOUSE ADJACENT TO THIS, SO IF YOU HAVE ANY QUESTIONS, DON'T BE AFRAID TO GIVE A HOLLER...
SEE YOU LATER, THEN!
......
WELL, SHE MADE US SIGN THE CONTRACT...
YEAH...

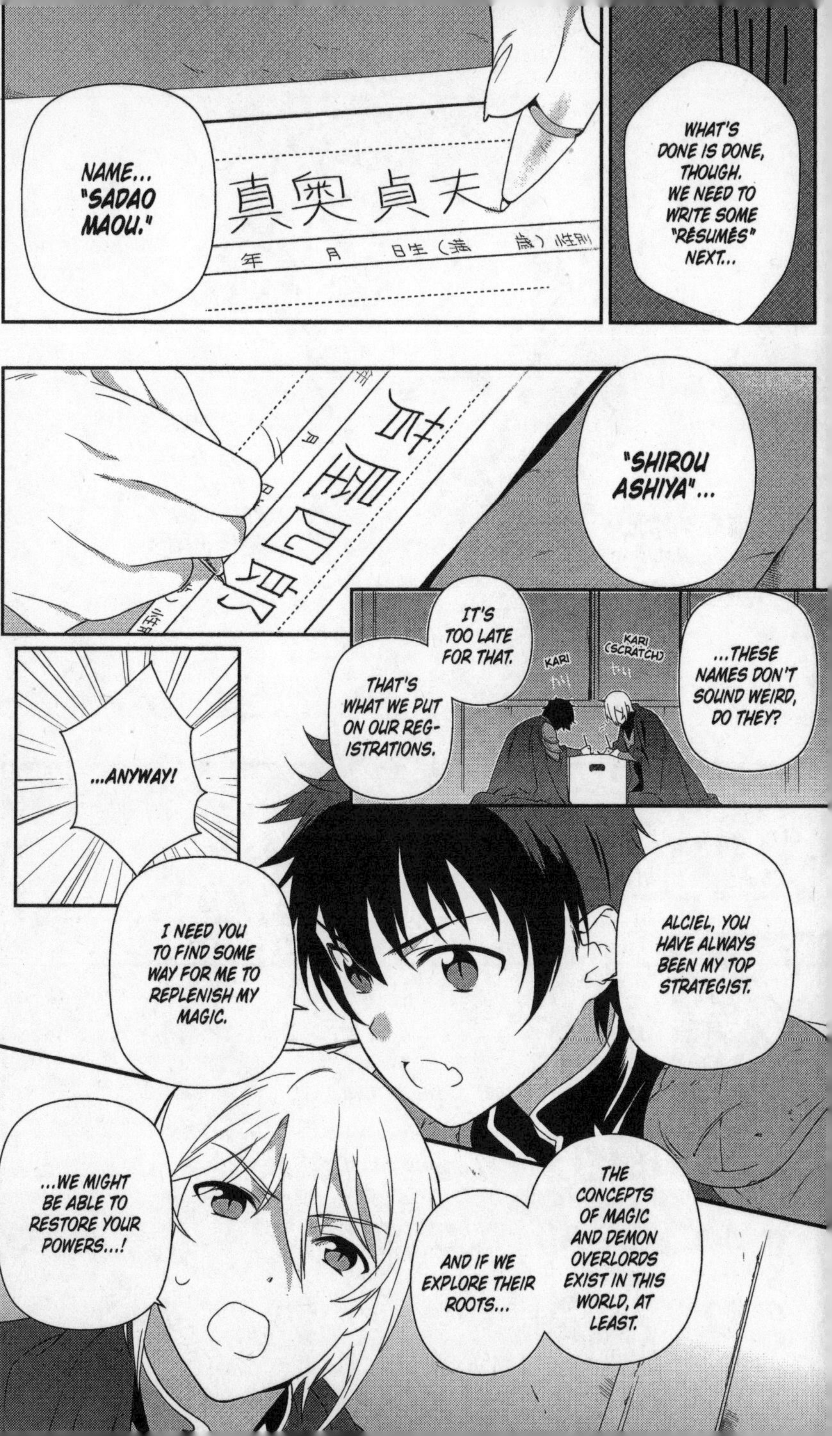
WHAT'S DONE IS DONE, THOUGH. WE NEED TO WRITE SOME "RÉSUMÉS" NEXT...
NAME... "SADAO MAOU."
真奥 貞夫
"SHIROU ASHIYA"...
...THESE NAMES DON'T SOUND WEIRD, DO THEY?
KARI (SCRATCH)
KARI
IT'S TOO LATE FOR THAT.
THAT'S WHAT WE PUT ON OUR REG-ISTRATIONS.
...ANYWAY!
ALCIEL, YOU HAVE ALWAYS BEEN MY TOP STRATEGIST.
I NEED YOU TO FIND SOME WAY FOR ME TO REPLENISH MY MAGIC.
THE CONCEPTS OF MAGIC AND DEMON OVERLORDS EXIST IN THIS WORLD, AT LEAST.
AND IF WE EXPLORE THEIR ROOTS...
...WE MIGHT BE ABLE TO RESTORE YOUR POWERS...!

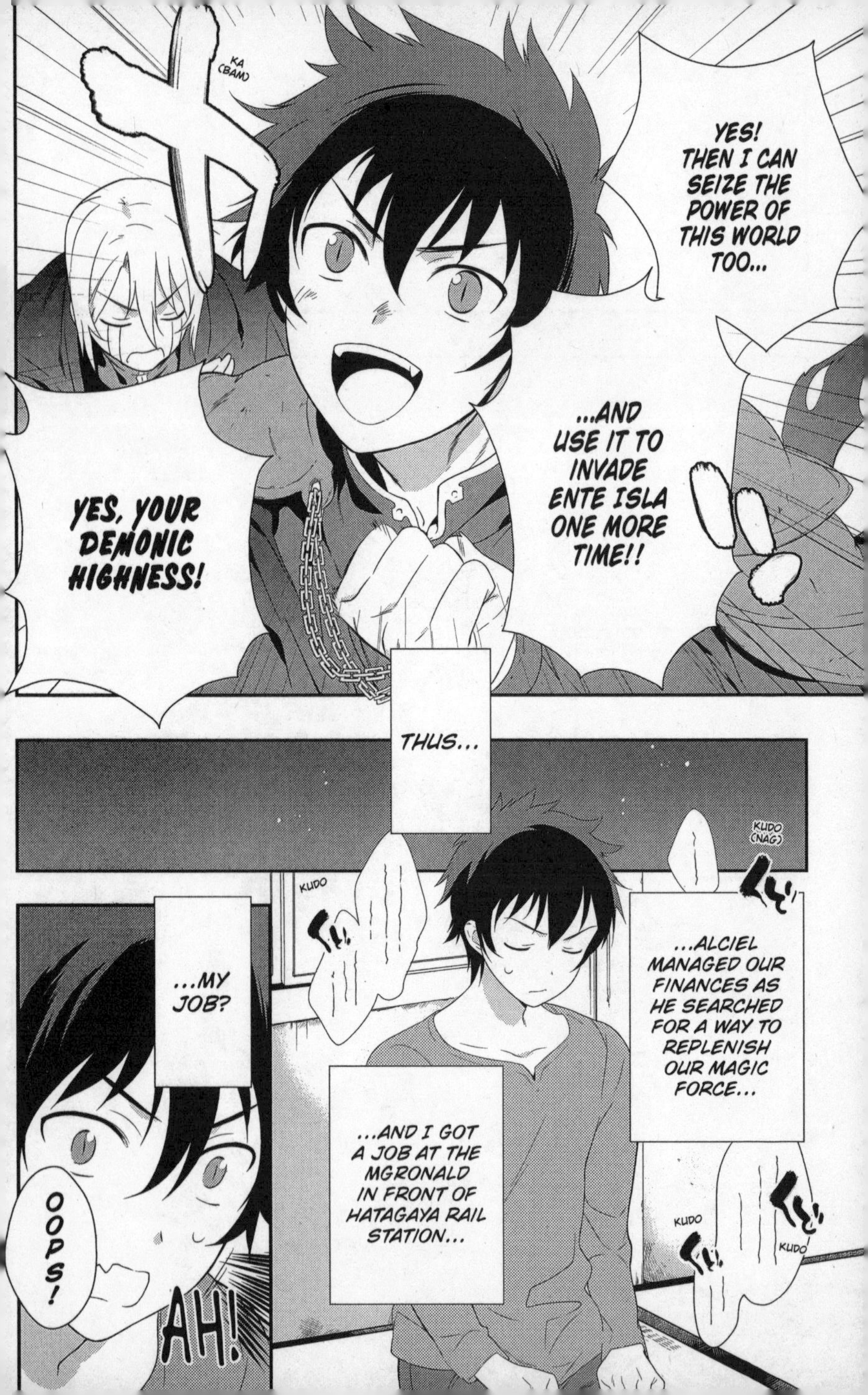
YES! THEN I CAN SEIZE THE POWER OF THIS WORLD TOO...
...AND USE IT TO INVADE ENTE ISLA ONE MORE TIME!!
KA (BAM)
YES, YOUR DEMONIC HIGHNESS!
THUS...
KUDO (NAG)
...ALCIEL MANAGED OUR FINANCES AS HE SEARCHED FOR A WAY TO REPLENISH OUR MAGIC FORCE...
KUDO
...AND I GOT A JOB AT THE MGRONALD IN FRONT OF HATAGAYA RAIL STATION...
KUDO
KUDO
...MY JOB?
OOPS!
AH!

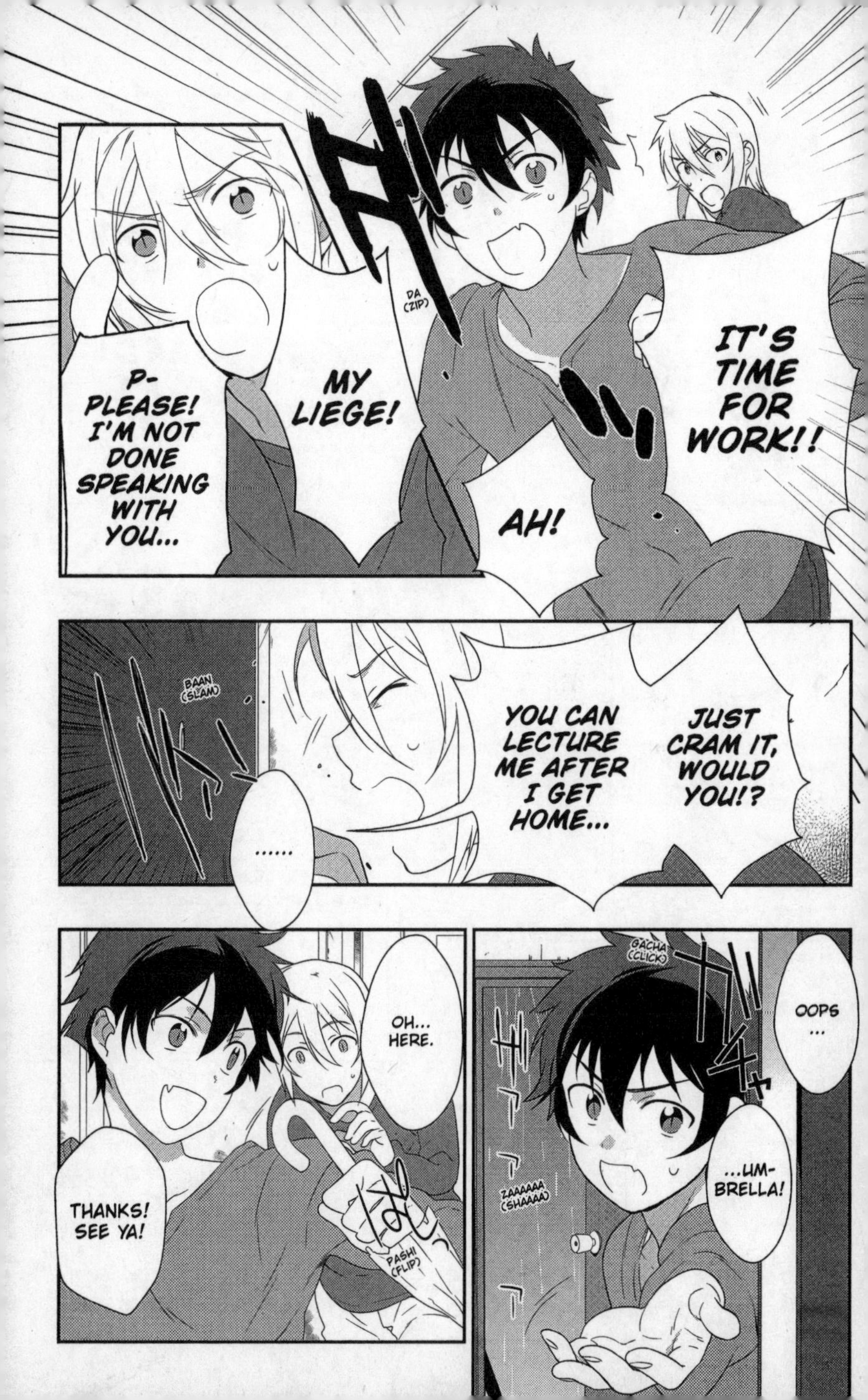
IT'S TIME FOR WORK!!
AH!
DA (ZIP)
MY LIEGE!
P-PLEASE! I'M NOT DONE SPEAKING WITH YOU...
JUST CRAM IT, WOULD YOU!?
YOU CAN LECTURE ME AFTER I GET HOME...
BAAN (SLAM)
......
GACHA (CLICK)
OOPS ...
...UM-BRELLA!
ZAAAAAA (SHAAAA)
OH... HERE.
THANKS! SEE YA!
PASHI (FLIP)

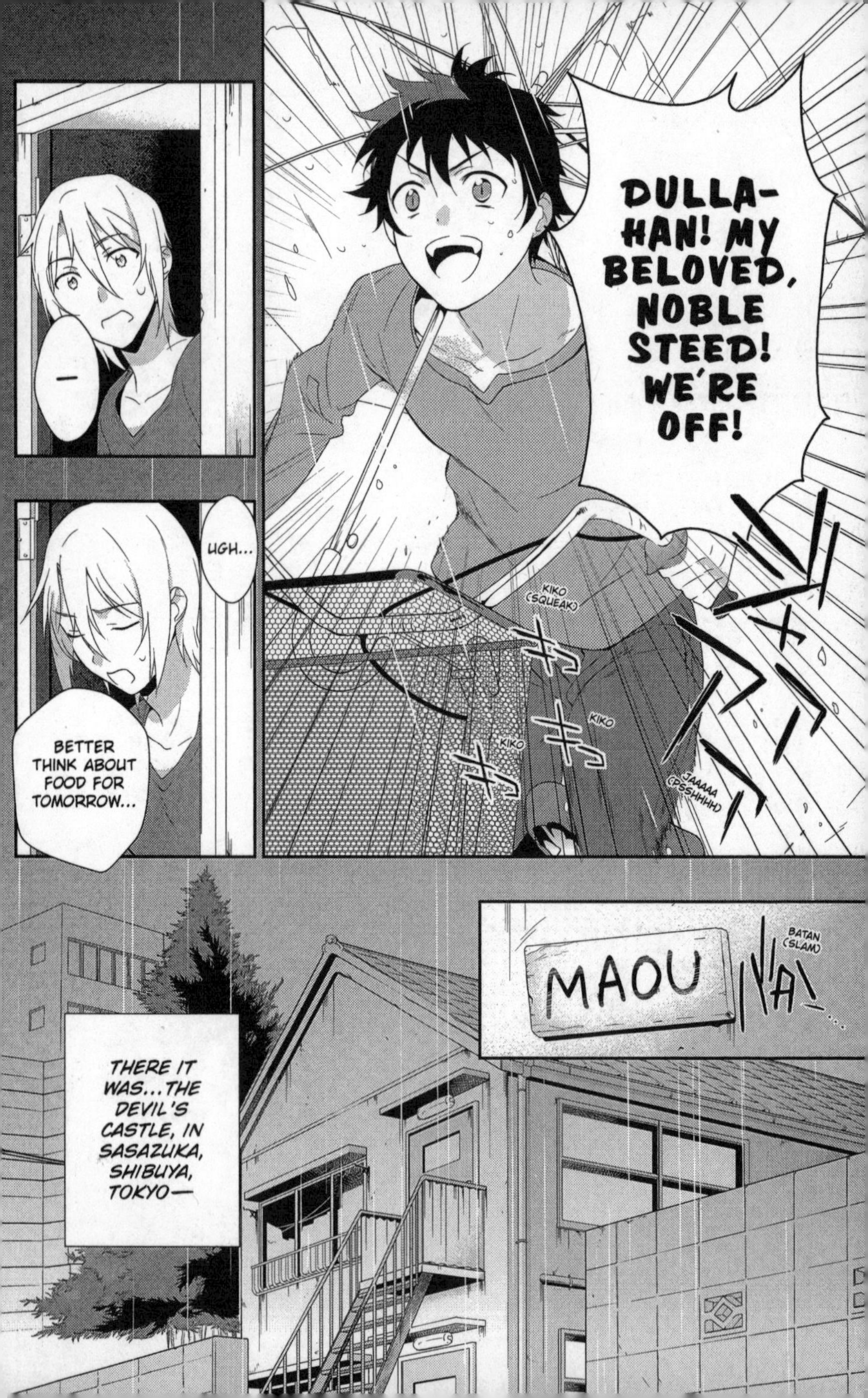
DULLA-HAN! MY BELOVED, NOBLE STEED! WE'RE OFF!
KIKO (SQUEAK)
KIKO
KIKO
JAAAAA (PSSHHHH)
—
UGH...
BETTER THINK ABOUT FOOD FOR TOMORROW...
MAOU
BATAN (SLAM)
THERE IT WAS...THE DEVIL'S CASTLE, IN SASAZUKA, SHIBUYA, TOKYO—

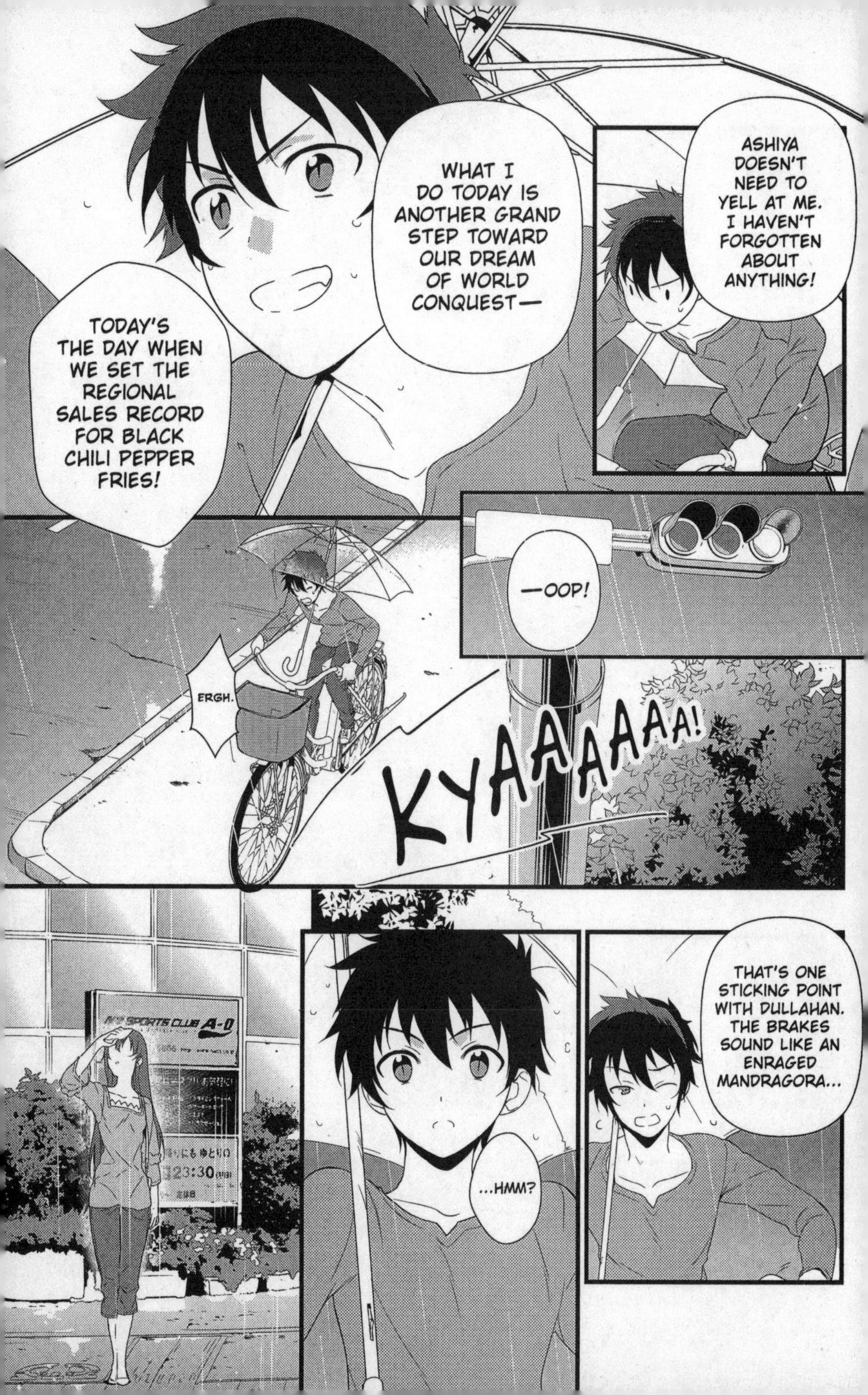
ASHIYA DOESN'T NEED TO YELL AT ME. I HAVEN'T FORGOTTEN ABOUT ANYTHING!
WHAT I DO TODAY IS ANOTHER GRAND STEP TOWARD OUR DREAM OF WORLD CONQUEST—
TODAY'S THE DAY WHEN WE SET THE REGIONAL SALES RECORD FOR BLACK CHILI PEPPER FRIES!
—OOP!
ERGH.
KYAAAAAAA!
THAT'S ONE STICKING POINT WITH DULLAHAN. THE BRAKES SOUND LIKE AN ENRAGED MANDRAGORA...
...HMM?

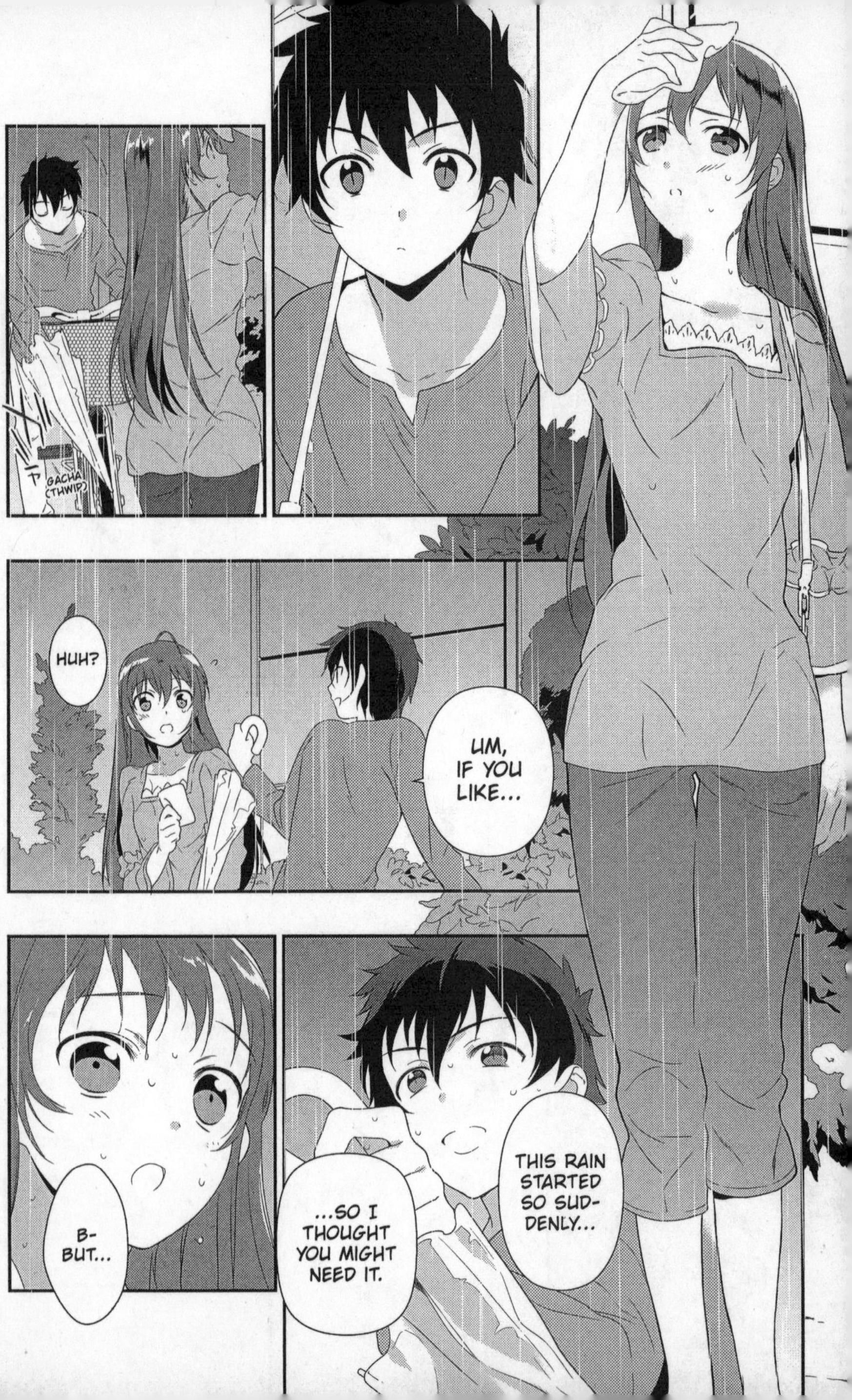

GACHA (THWIP)
UM, IF YOU LIKE...
HUH?
THIS RAIN STARTED SO SUD-DENLY...
...SO I THOUGHT YOU MIGHT NEED IT.
B-BUT...

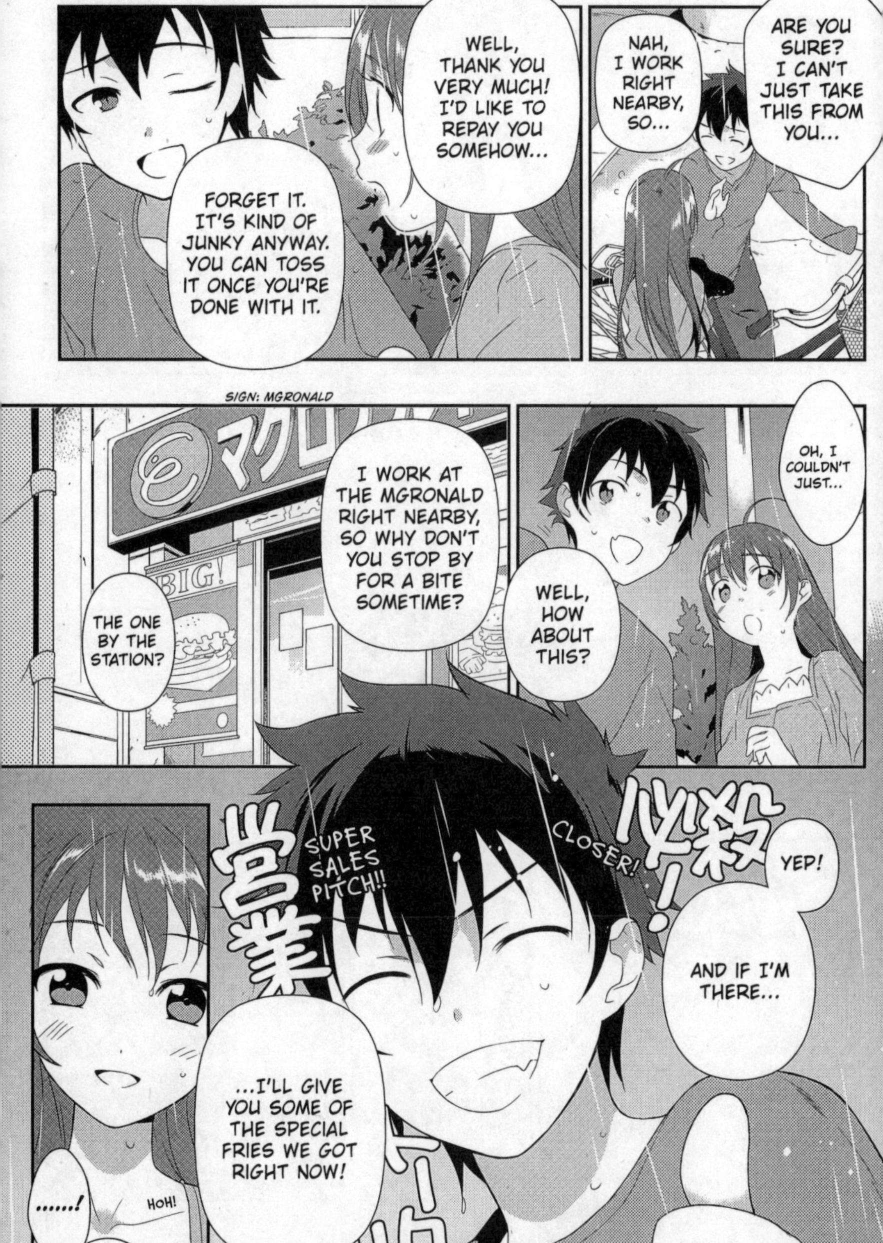
ARE YOU SURE? I CAN'T JUST TAKE THIS FROM YOU...
NAH, I WORK RIGHT NEARBY, SO...
WELL, THANK YOU VERY MUCH! I'D LIKE TO REPAY YOU SOMEHOW...
FORGET IT. IT'S KIND OF JUNKY ANYWAY. YOU CAN TOSS IT ONCE YOU'RE DONE WITH IT.
OH, I COULDN'T JUST...
WELL, HOW ABOUT THIS?
SIGN: MGRONALD
マクロ
BIG!
I WORK AT THE MGRONALD RIGHT NEARBY, SO WHY DON'T YOU STOP BY FOR A BITE SOMETIME?
THE ONE BY THE STATION?
YEP!
必殺
CLOSER!
AND IF I'M THERE...
営業
SUPER SALES PITCH!!
...I'LL GIVE YOU SOME OF THE SPECIAL FRIES WE GOT RIGHT NOW!
HOH!
......!

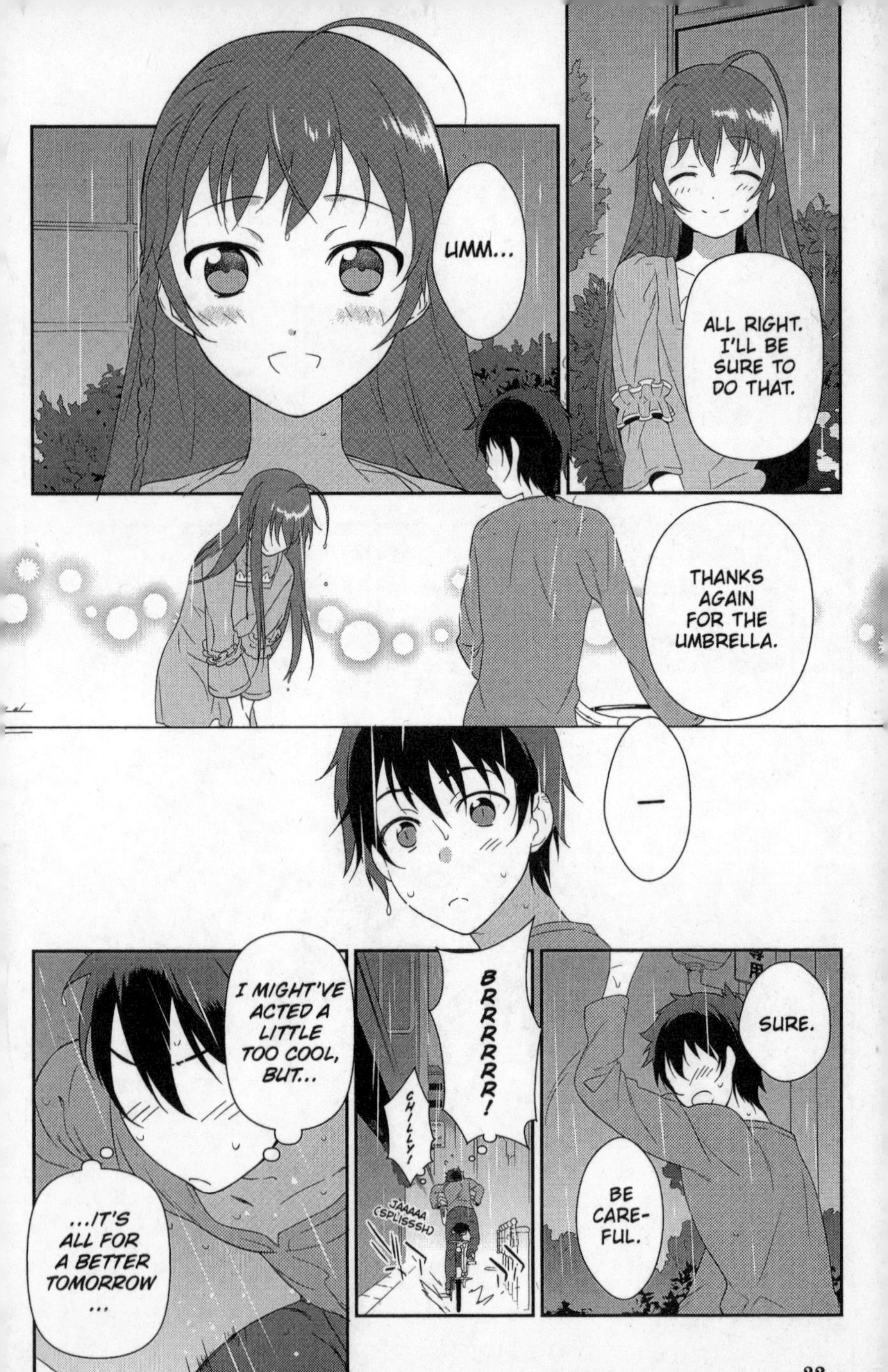
ALL RIGHT. I'LL BE SURE TO DO THAT.
UMM...
THANKS AGAIN FOR THE UMBRELLA.
—
SURE.
BE CARE-FUL.
BRRRRRR!
CHILLY!
JAAAAA (SPLISSSH)
I MIGHT'VE ACTED A LITTLE TOO COOL, BUT...
...IT'S ALL FOR A BETTER TOMORROW ...

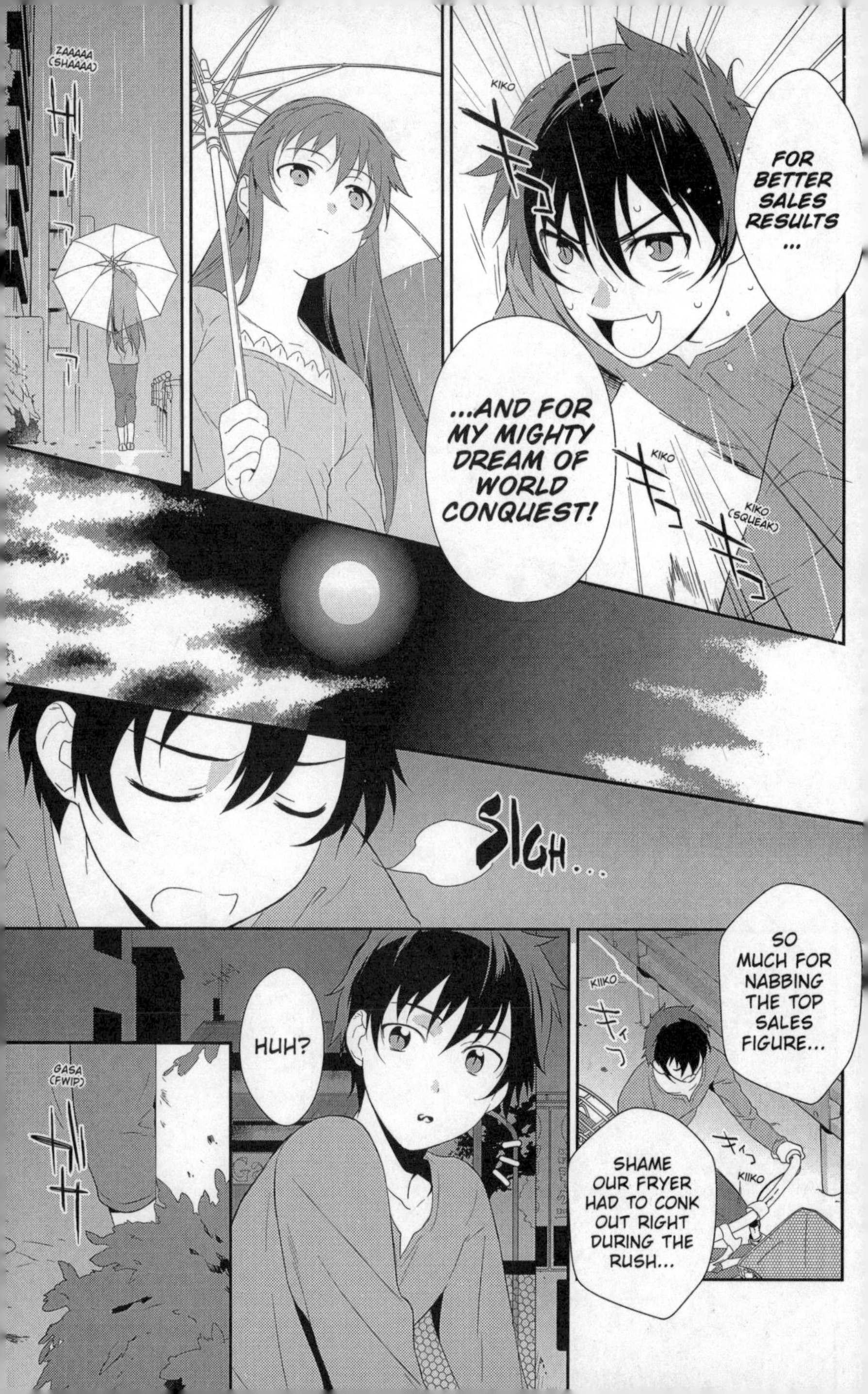
KIKO
FOR BETTER SALES RESULTS ...
...AND FOR MY MIGHTY DREAM OF WORLD CONQUEST!
KIKO
KIKO (SQUEAK)
ZAAAAA (SHAAAA)
SIGH...
SO MUCH FOR NABBING THE TOP SALES FIGURE...
KIIKO
SHAME OUR FRYER HAD TO CONK OUT RIGHT DURING THE RUSH...
KIIKO
HUH?
GASA (FWIP)

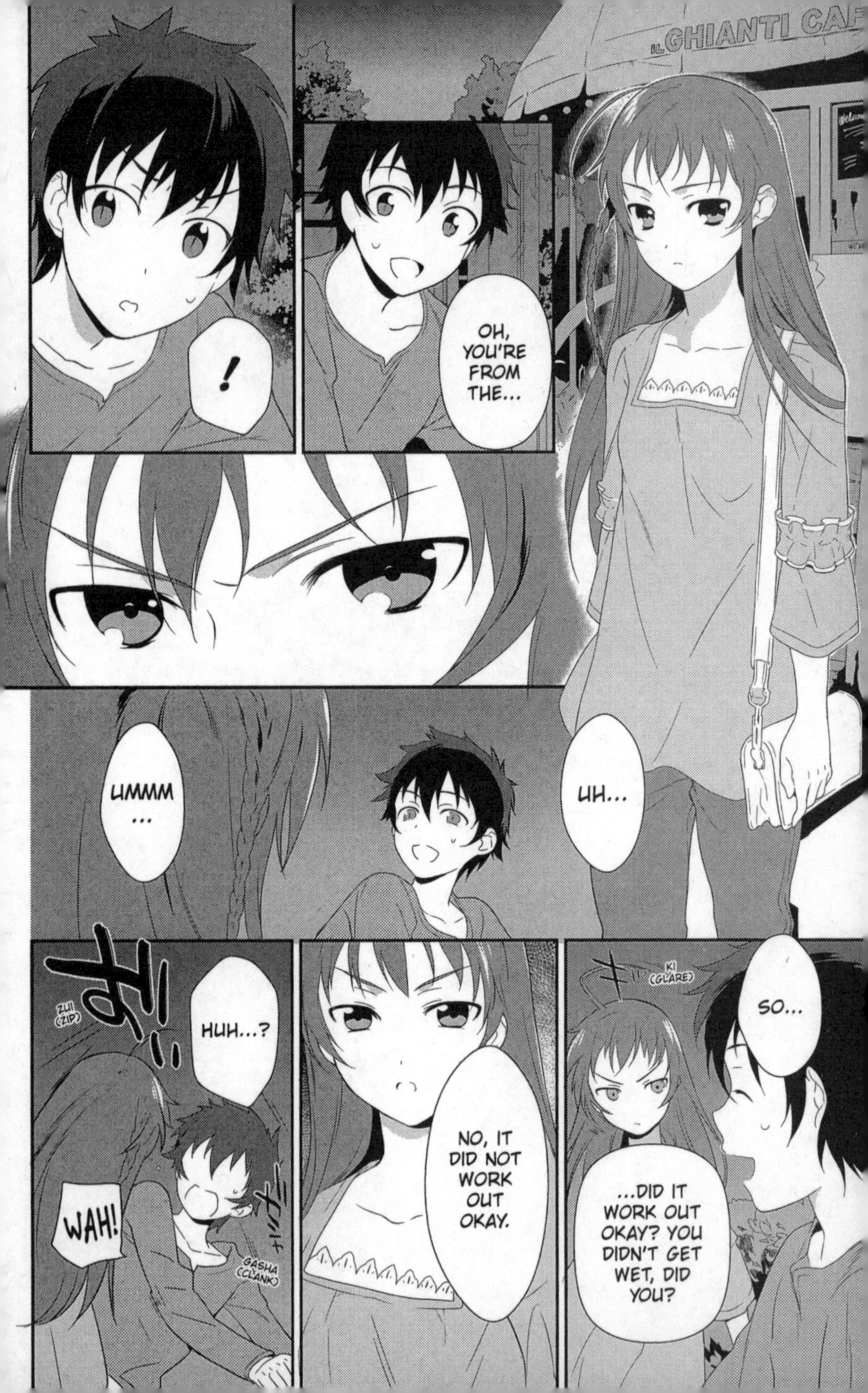
IL GHIANTI CAF
UH...
OH, YOU'RE FROM THE...
!
UMMM...
SO...
KI (GLARE)
...DID IT WORK OUT OKAY? YOU DIDN'T GET WET, DID YOU?
NO, IT DID NOT WORK OUT OKAY.
HUH...?
ZUI (ZIP)
WAH!
GASHA (CLANK)

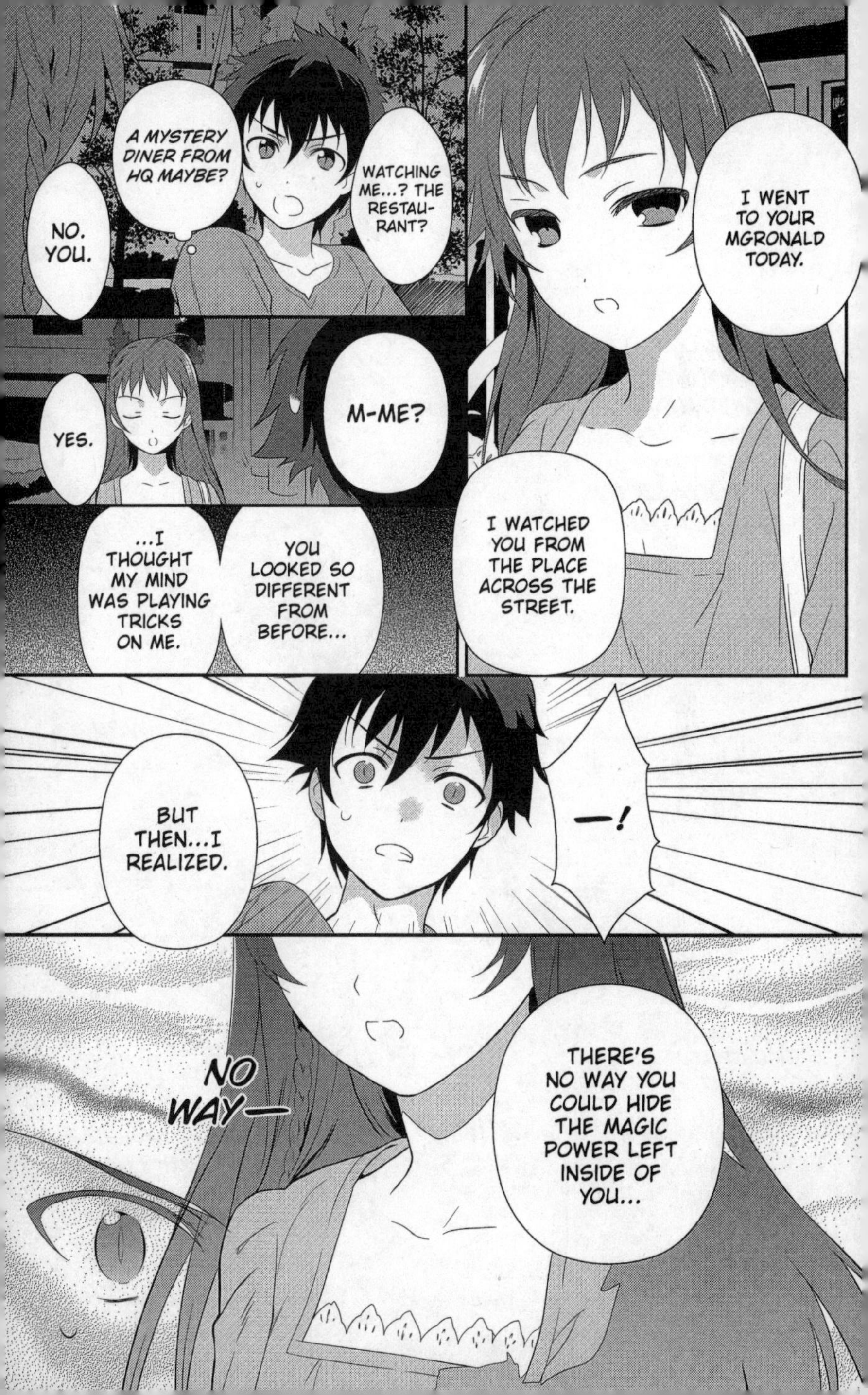
I WENT TO YOUR MGRONALD TODAY.
I WATCHED YOU FROM THE PLACE ACROSS THE STREET.
WATCHING ME...? THE RESTAU-RANT?
A MYSTERY DINER FROM HQ MAYBE?
NO. YOU.
M-ME?
YES.
YOU LOOKED SO DIFFERENT FROM BEFORE...
...I THOUGHT MY MIND WAS PLAYING TRICKS ON ME.
—!
BUT THEN...I REALIZED.
THERE'S NO WAY YOU COULD HIDE THE MAGIC POWER LEFT INSIDE OF YOU...
NO WAY—

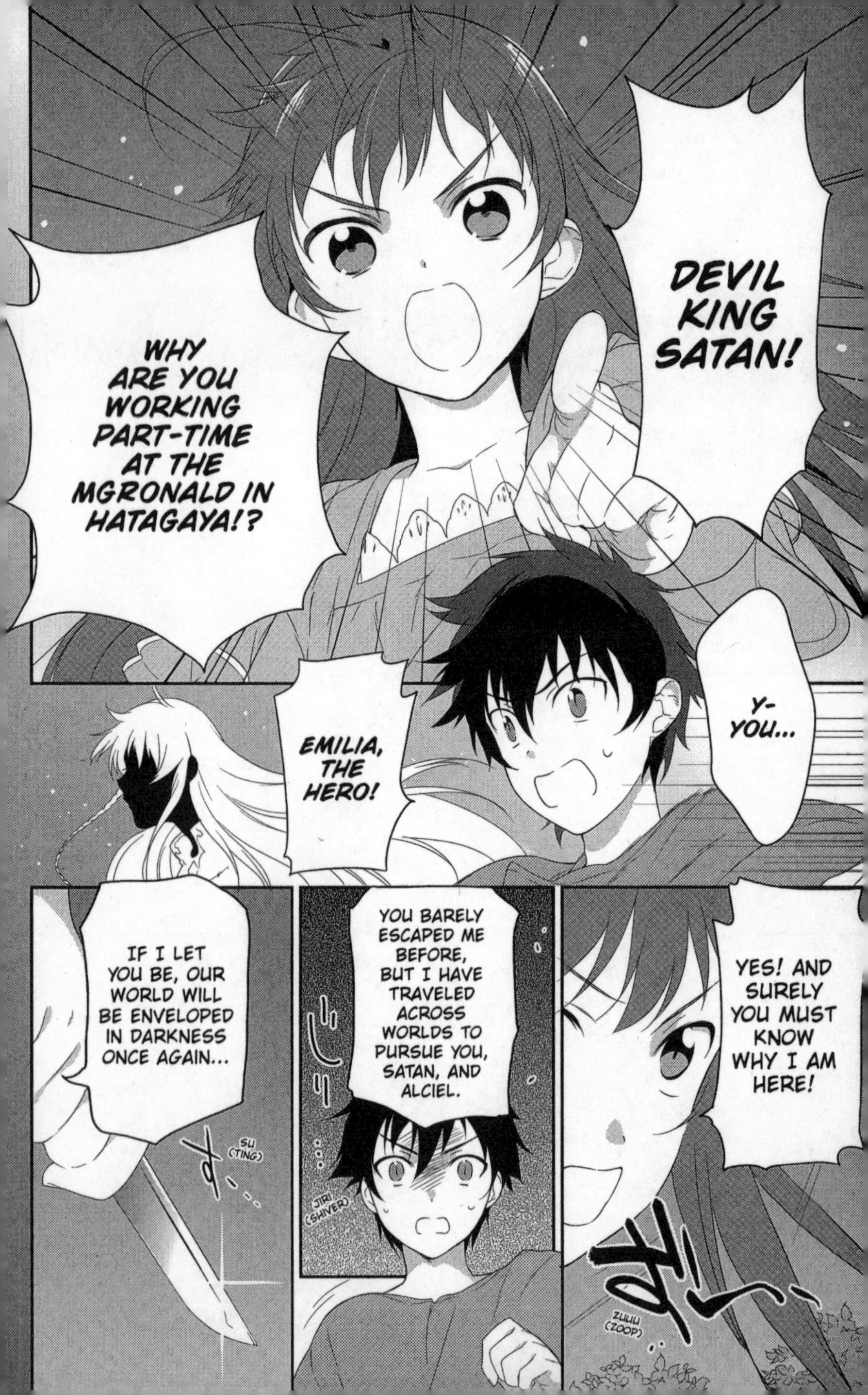
DEVIL KING SATAN!
WHY ARE YOU WORKING PART-TIME AT THE MGRONALD IN HATAGAYA!?
Y-YOU...
EMILIA, THE HERO!
YES! AND SURELY YOU MUST KNOW WHY I AM HERE!
ZUUU (ZOOP)
YOU BARELY ESCAPED ME BEFORE, BUT I HAVE TRAVELED ACROSS WORLDS TO PURSUE YOU, SATAN, AND ALCIEL.
JIRI (SHIVER)
IF I LET YOU BE, OUR WORLD WILL BE ENVELOPED IN DARKNESS ONCE AGAIN...
SU (TING)

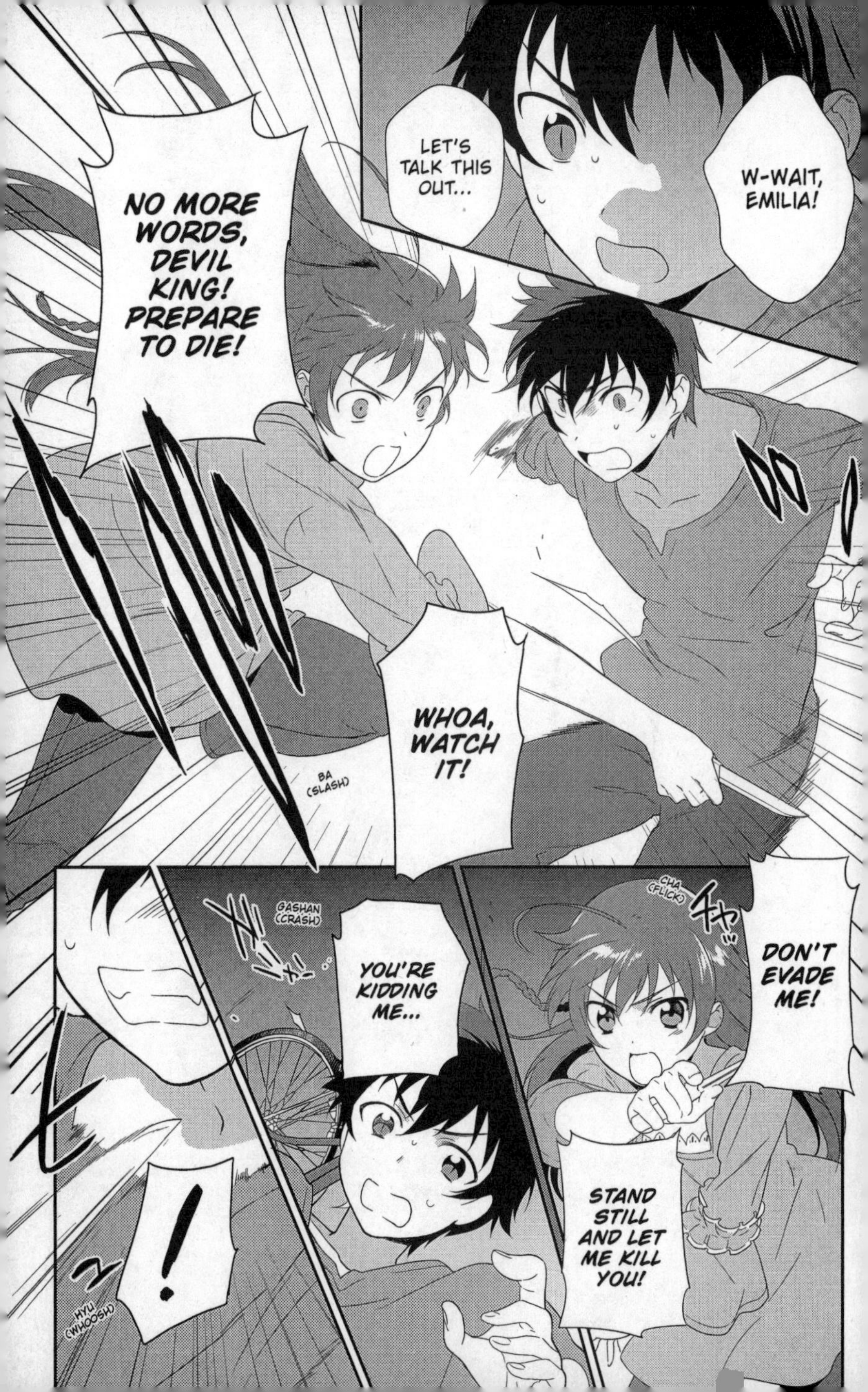
W-WAIT, EMILIA!
LET'S TALK THIS OUT...
NO MORE WORDS, DEVIL KING! PREPARE TO DIE!
WHOA, WATCH IT!
BA (SLASH)
CHA (FLICK)
DON'T EVADE ME!
STAND STILL AND LET ME KILL YOU!
GASHAN (CRASH)
YOU'RE KIDDING ME...
!
HYU (WHOOSH)

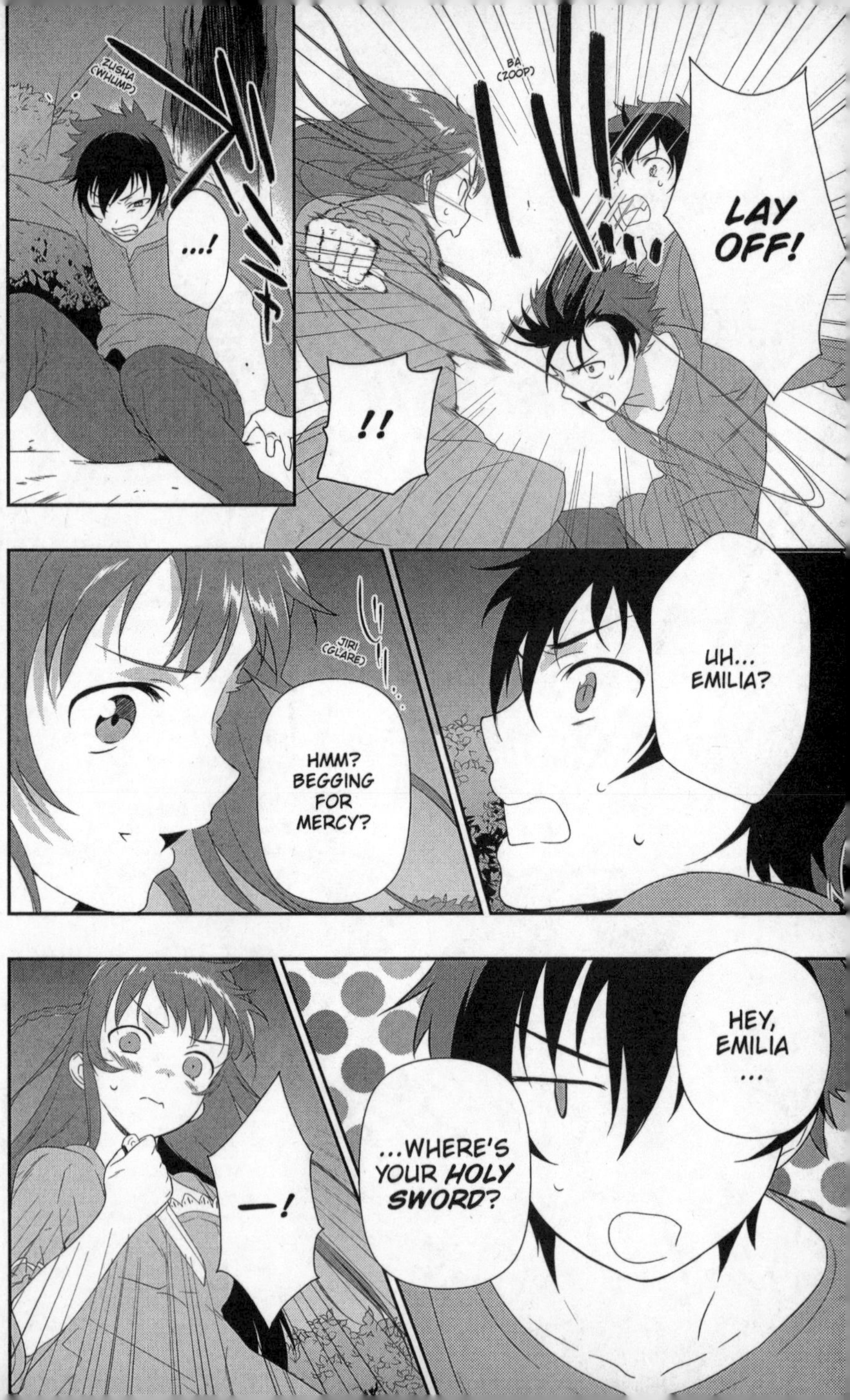
LAY OFF!
BA (ZOOP)
!!
ZUSHA (WHUMP)
...!
UH... EMILIA?
JIRI (GLARE)
HMM? BEGGING FOR MERCY?
HEY, EMILIA ...
...WHERE'S YOUR *HOLY SWORD*?
—!

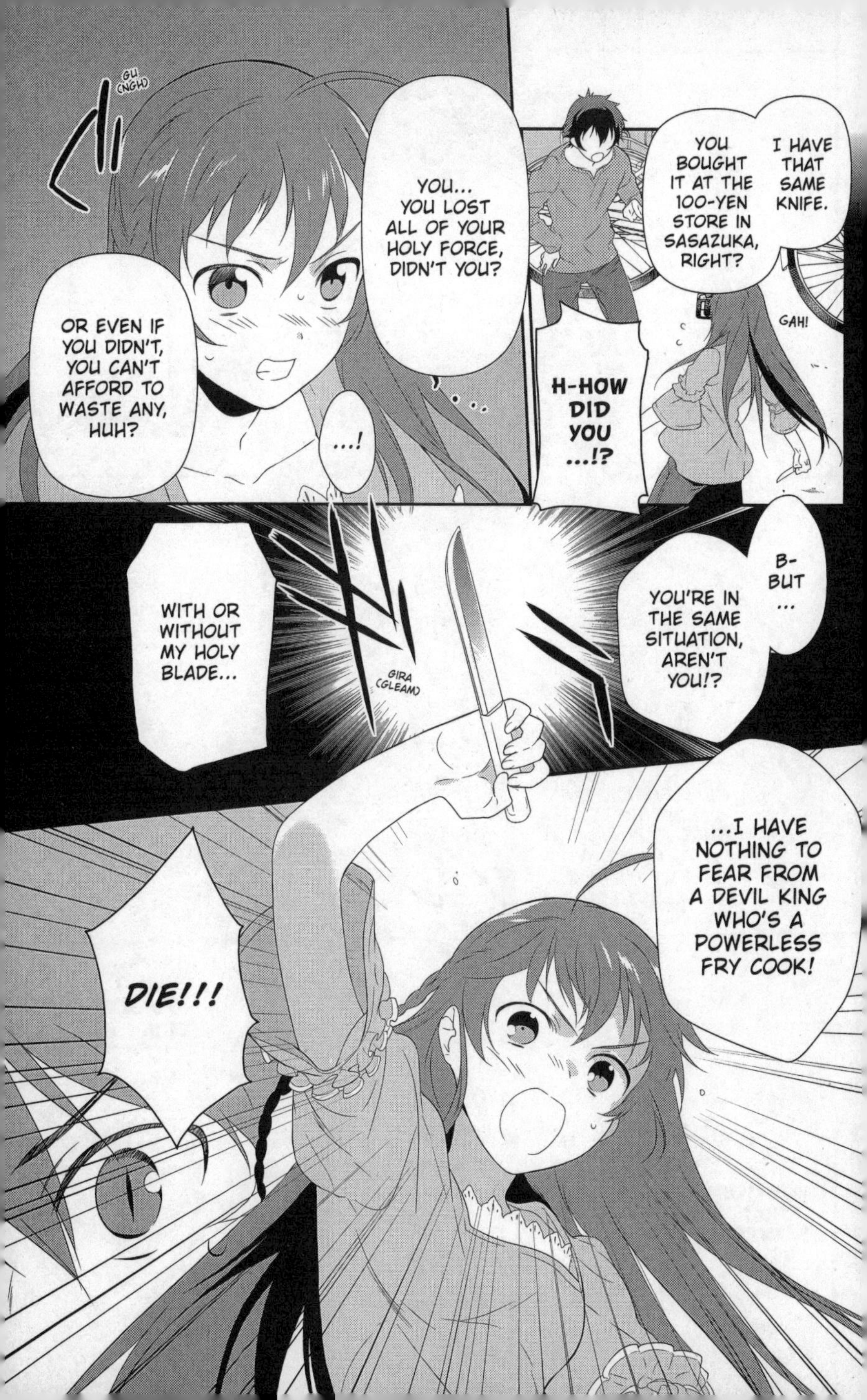
I HAVE THAT SAME KNIFE.
YOU BOUGHT IT AT THE 100-YEN STORE IN SASAZUKA, RIGHT?
GAH!
H-HOW DID YOU ...!?
YOU... YOU LOST ALL OF YOUR HOLY FORCE, DIDN'T YOU?
GU (NGH)
OR EVEN IF YOU DIDN'T, YOU CAN'T AFFORD TO WASTE ANY, HUH?
...!
B-BUT ...
YOU'RE IN THE SAME SITUATION, AREN'T YOU!?
GIRA (GLEAM)
WITH OR WITHOUT MY HOLY BLADE...
...I HAVE NOTHING TO FEAR FROM A DEVIL KING WHO'S A POWERLESS FRY COOK!
DIE!!!

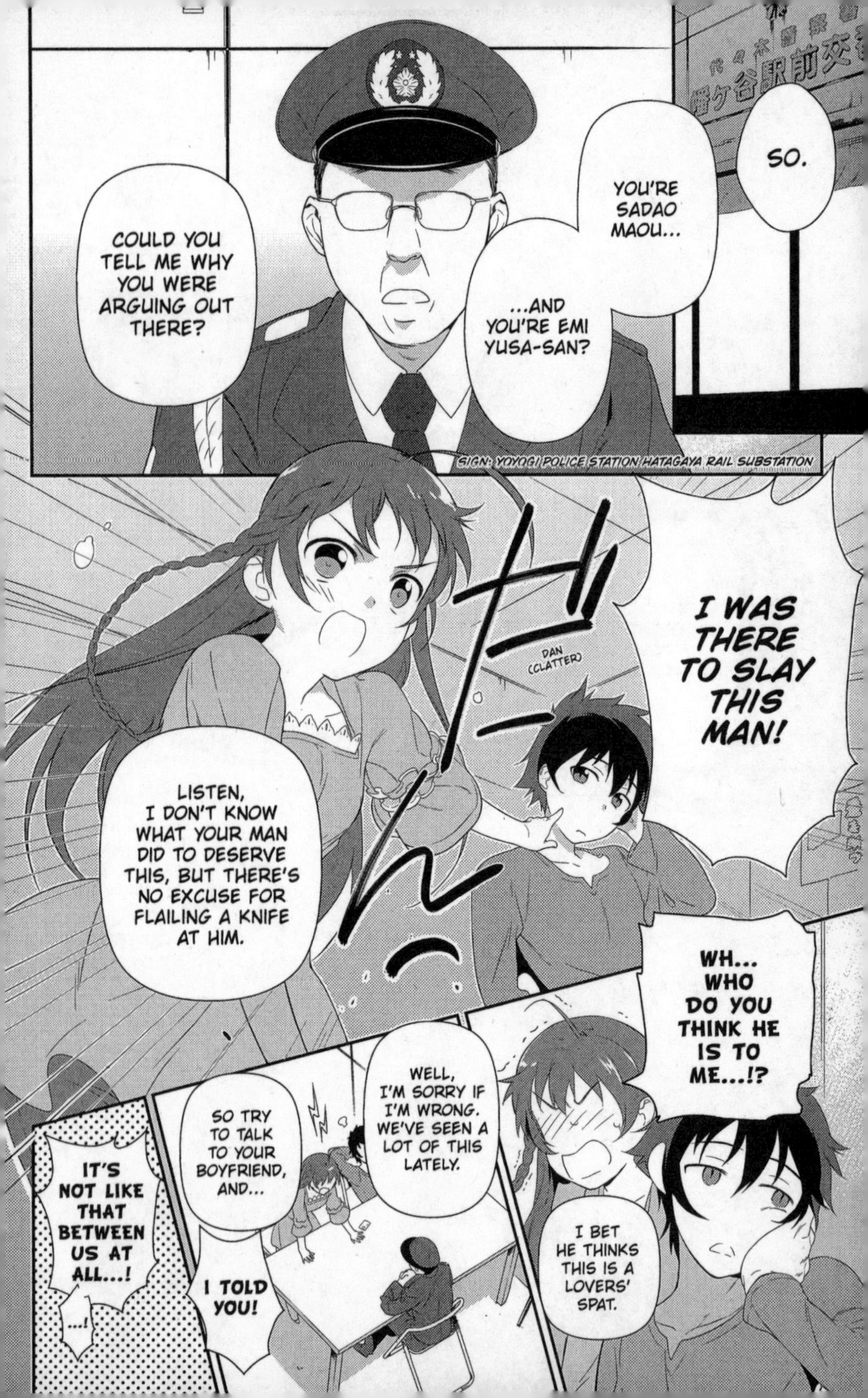
SO.
YOU'RE SADAO MAOU...
...AND YOU'RE EMI YUSA-SAN?
COULD YOU TELL ME WHY YOU WERE ARGUING OUT THERE?
SIGN: YOYOGI POLICE STATION HATAGAYA RAIL SUBSTATION
I WAS THERE TO SLAY THIS MAN!
DAN (CLATTER)
LISTEN, I DON'T KNOW WHAT YOUR MAN DID TO DESERVE THIS, BUT THERE'S NO EXCUSE FOR FLAILING A KNIFE AT HIM.
WH... WHO DO YOU THINK HE IS TO ME...!?
I BET HE THINKS THIS IS A LOVERS' SPAT.
WELL, I'M SORRY IF I'M WRONG. WE'VE SEEN A LOT OF THIS LATELY.
SO TRY TO TALK TO YOUR BOYFRIEND, AND...
I TOLD YOU!
IT'S NOT LIKE THAT BETWEEN US AT ALL...!
...!

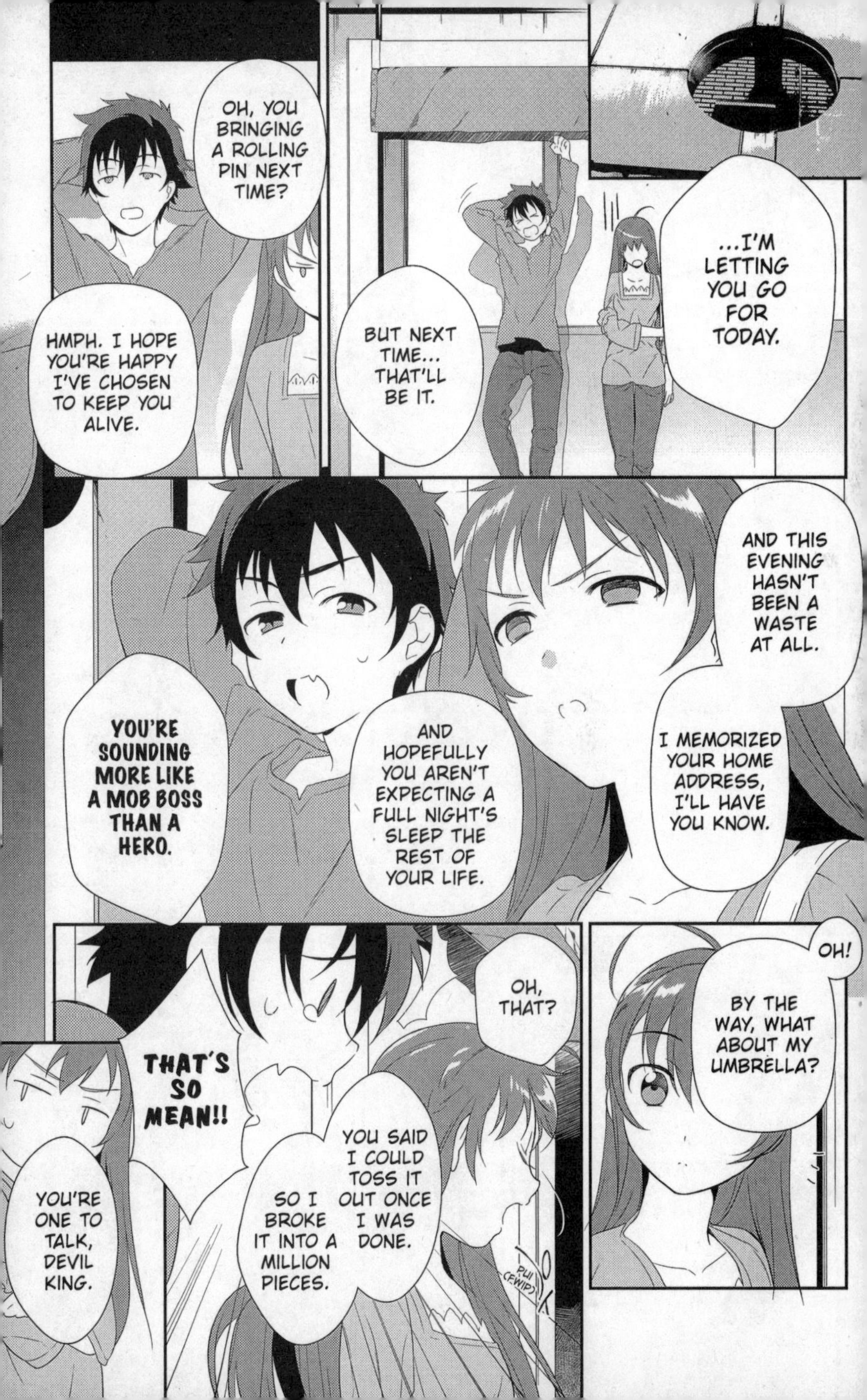
...I'M LETTING YOU GO FOR TODAY.
BUT NEXT TIME... THAT'LL BE IT.
OH, YOU BRINGING A ROLLING PIN NEXT TIME?
HMPH. I HOPE YOU'RE HAPPY I'VE CHOSEN TO KEEP YOU ALIVE.
AND THIS EVENING HASN'T BEEN A WASTE AT ALL.
I MEMORIZED YOUR HOME ADDRESS, I'LL HAVE YOU KNOW.
AND HOPEFULLY YOU AREN'T EXPECTING A FULL NIGHT'S SLEEP THE REST OF YOUR LIFE.
YOU'RE SOUNDING MORE LIKE A MOB BOSS THAN A HERO.
OH!
BY THE WAY, WHAT ABOUT MY UMBRELLA?
OH, THAT?
YOU SAID I COULD TOSS IT OUT ONCE I WAS DONE.
SO I BROKE IT INTO A MILLION PIECES.
PUI (FWIP)
THAT'S SO MEAN!!
YOU'RE ONE TO TALK, DEVIL KING.

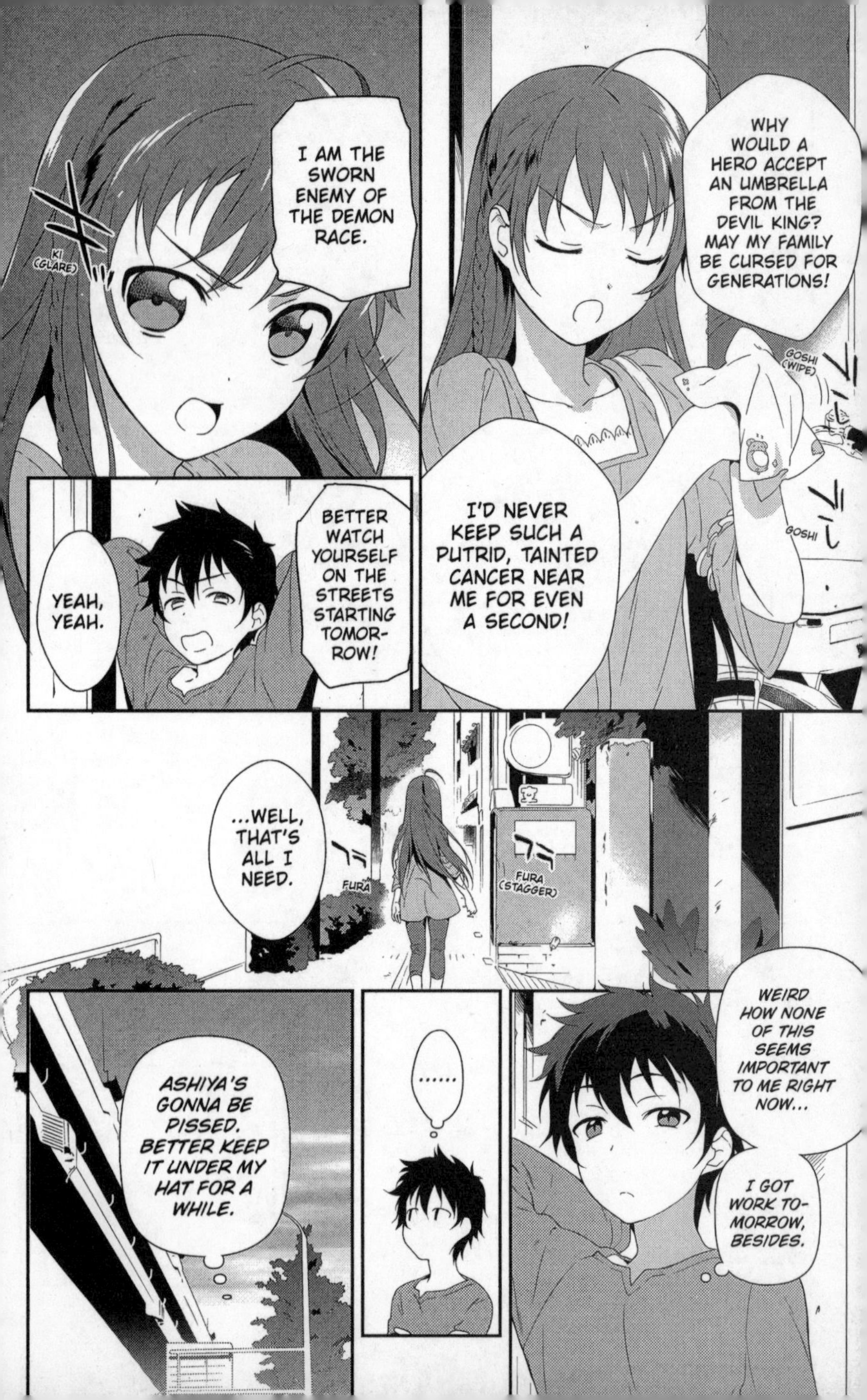
WHY WOULD A HERO ACCEPT AN UMBRELLA FROM THE DEVIL KING? MAY MY FAMILY BE CURSED FOR GENERATIONS!
GOSHI (WIPE)
GOSHI
I'D NEVER KEEP SUCH A PUTRID, TAINTED CANCER NEAR ME FOR EVEN A SECOND!
I AM THE SWORN ENEMY OF THE DEMON RACE.
KI (GLARE)
BETTER WATCH YOURSELF ON THE STREETS STARTING TOMOR-ROW!
YEAH, YEAH.
FURA (STAGGER)
FURA
...WELL, THAT'S ALL I NEED.
WEIRD HOW NONE OF THIS SEEMS IMPORTANT TO ME RIGHT NOW...
I GOT WORK TO-MORROW, BESIDES.
....
ASHIYA'S GONNA BE PISSED. BETTER KEEP IT UNDER MY HAT FOR A WHILE.

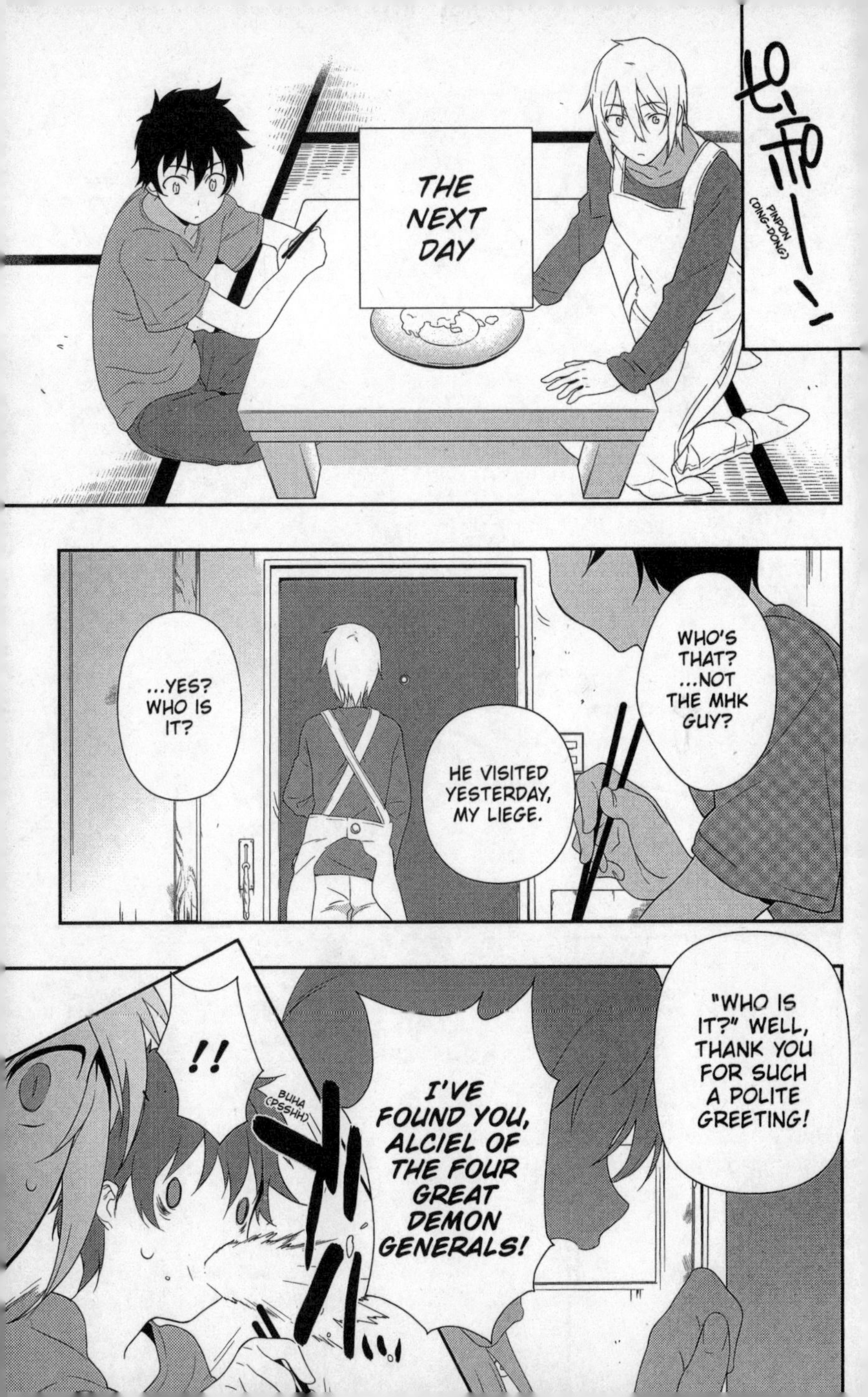
ピンポーン!
PINPON (DING-DONG)
THE NEXT DAY
WHO'S THAT? ...NOT THE MHK GUY?
HE VISITED YESTERDAY, MY LIEGE.
...YES? WHO IS IT?
"WHO IS IT?" WELL, THANK YOU FOR SUCH A POLITE GREETING!
I'VE FOUND YOU, ALCIEL OF THE FOUR GREAT DEMON GENERALS!
BUHA (PSSHH)
!!

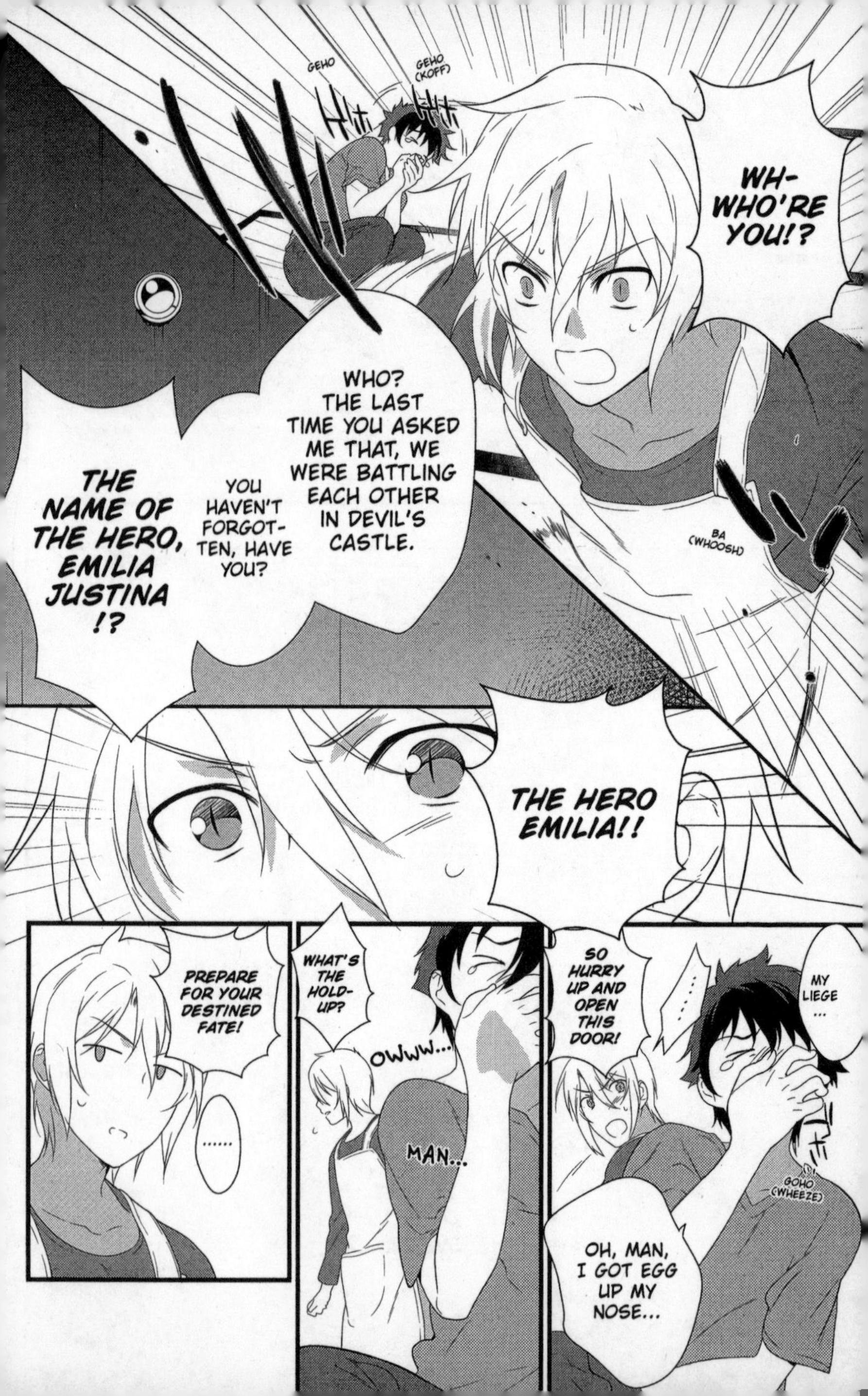
WH-WHO'RE YOU!?
GEHO (KOFF)
GEHO
BA (WHOOSH)
WHO? THE LAST TIME YOU ASKED ME THAT, WE WERE BATTLING EACH OTHER IN DEVIL'S CASTLE.
YOU HAVEN'T FORGOT-TEN, HAVE YOU?
THE NAME OF THE HERO, EMILIA JUSTINA!?
THE HERO EMILIA!!
MY LIEGE ...
......
SO HURRY UP AND OPEN THIS DOOR!
GOHO (WHEEZE)
OH, MAN, I GOT EGG UP MY NOSE...
WHAT'S THE HOLD-UP?
OWWW...
MAN...
PREPARE FOR YOUR DESTINED FATE!
......

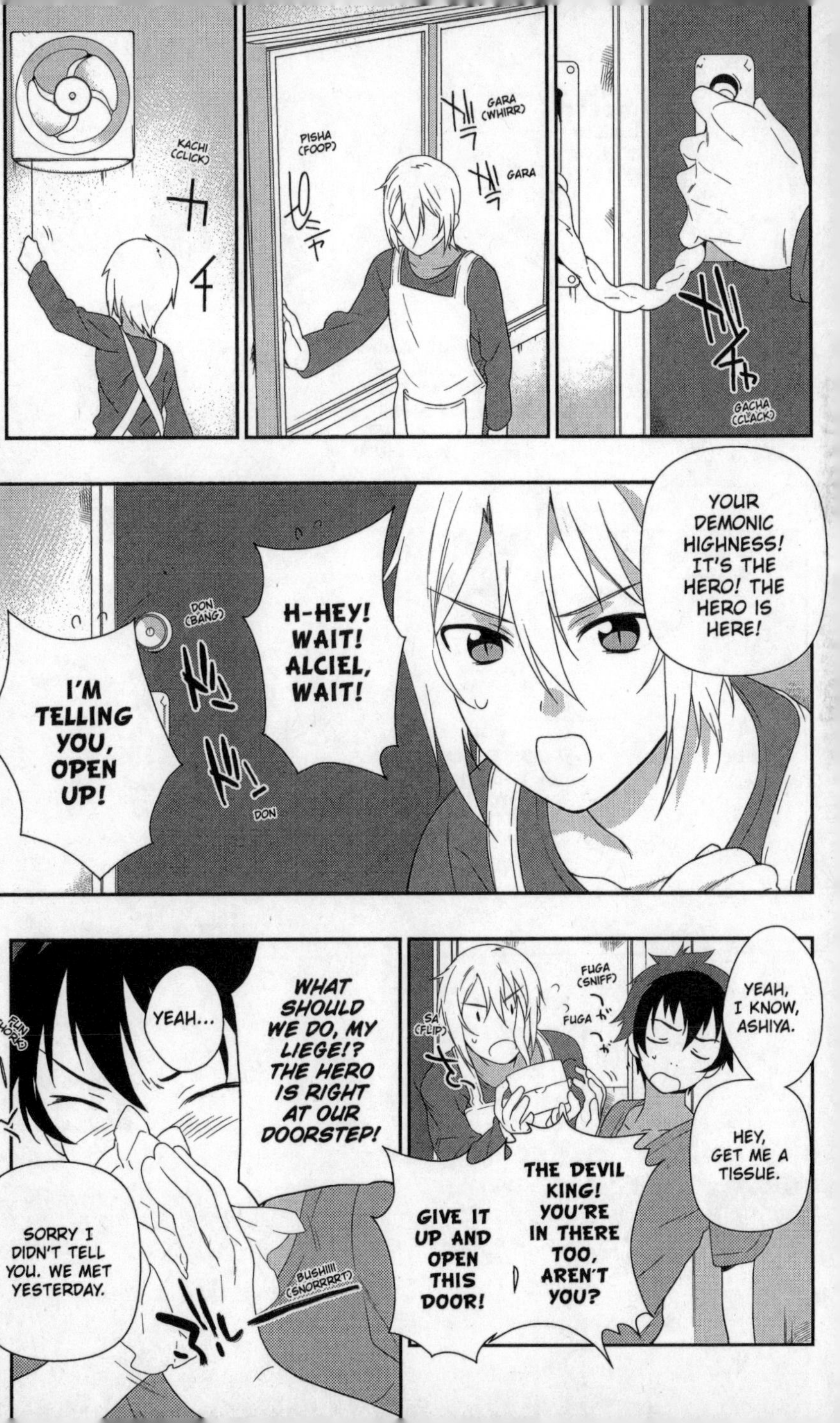
GACHA (CLACK)
GARA (WHIRR)
GARA
PISHA (FOOP)
KACHI (CLICK)
YOUR DEMONIC HIGHNESS! IT'S THE HERO! THE HERO IS HERE!
H-HEY! WAIT! ALCIEL, WAIT!
DON (BANG)
DON
I'M TELLING YOU, OPEN UP!
YEAH, I KNOW, ASHIYA.
HEY, GET ME A TISSUE.
FUGA (SNIFF)
FUGA
SA (FLIP)
THE DEVIL KING! YOU'RE IN THERE TOO, AREN'T YOU?
GIVE IT UP AND OPEN THIS DOOR!
WHAT SHOULD WE DO, MY LIEGE!? THE HERO IS RIGHT AT OUR DOORSTEP!
YEAH...
FUN (CHORK)
BUSHIIII (SNORRRRT)
SORRY I DIDN'T TELL YOU. WE MET YESTERDAY.

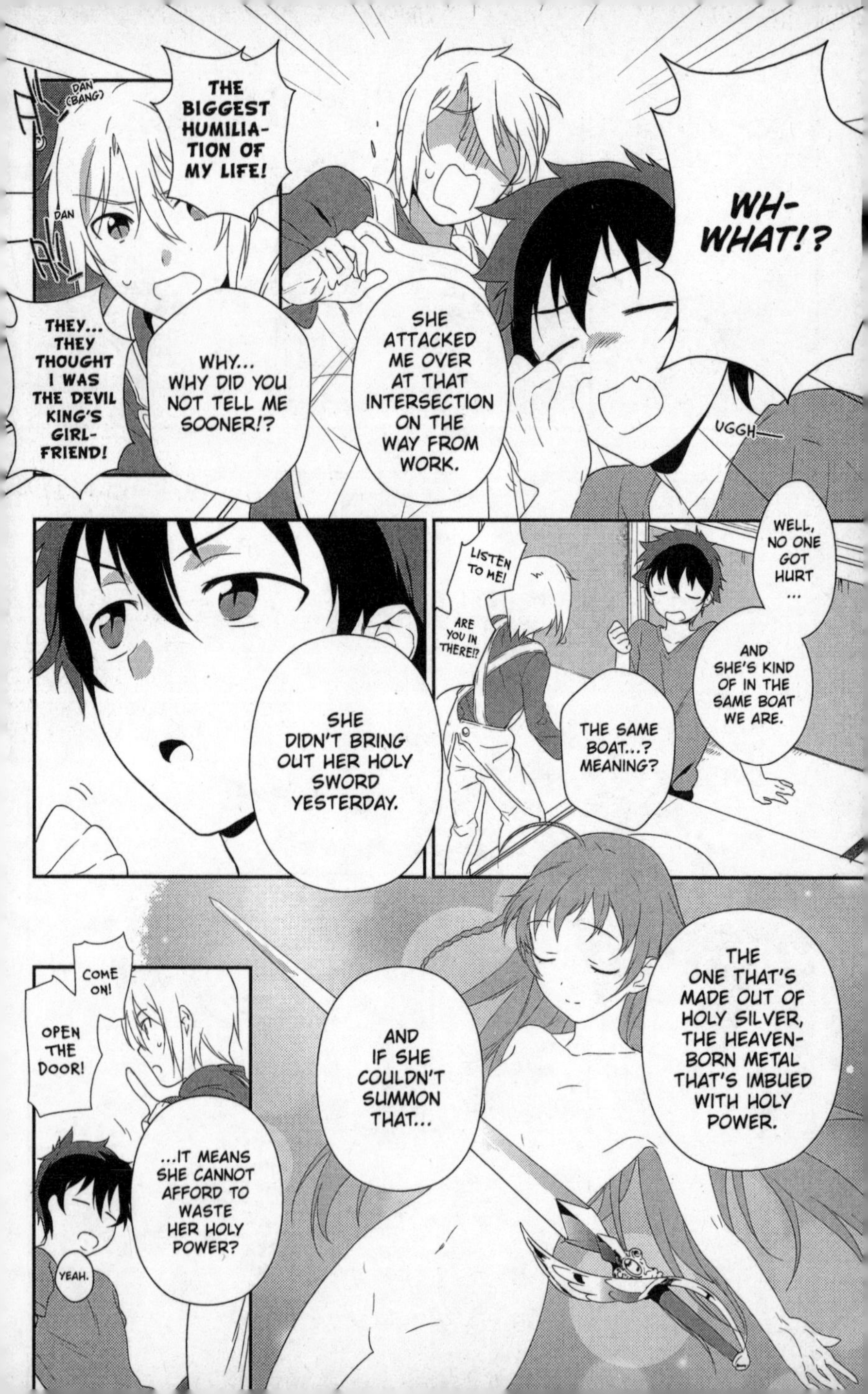
WH-WHAT!?
UGGH—
SHE ATTACKED ME OVER AT THAT INTERSECTION ON THE WAY FROM WORK.
WHY... WHY DID YOU NOT TELL ME SOONER!?
DAN (BANG)
THE BIGGEST HUMILIATION OF MY LIFE!
DAN
THEY... THEY THOUGHT I WAS THE DEVIL KING'S GIRLFRIEND!
WELL, NO ONE GOT HURT ...
AND SHE'S KIND OF IN THE SAME BOAT WE ARE.
LISTEN TO ME!
ARE YOU IN THERE!?
THE SAME BOAT...? MEANING?
SHE DIDN'T BRING OUT HER HOLY SWORD YESTERDAY.
THE ONE THAT'S MADE OUT OF HOLY SILVER, THE HEAVEN-BORN METAL THAT'S IMBUED WITH HOLY POWER.
AND IF SHE COULDN'T SUMMON THAT...
COME ON!
OPEN THE DOOR!
...IT MEANS SHE CANNOT AFFORD TO WASTE HER HOLY POWER?
YEAH.

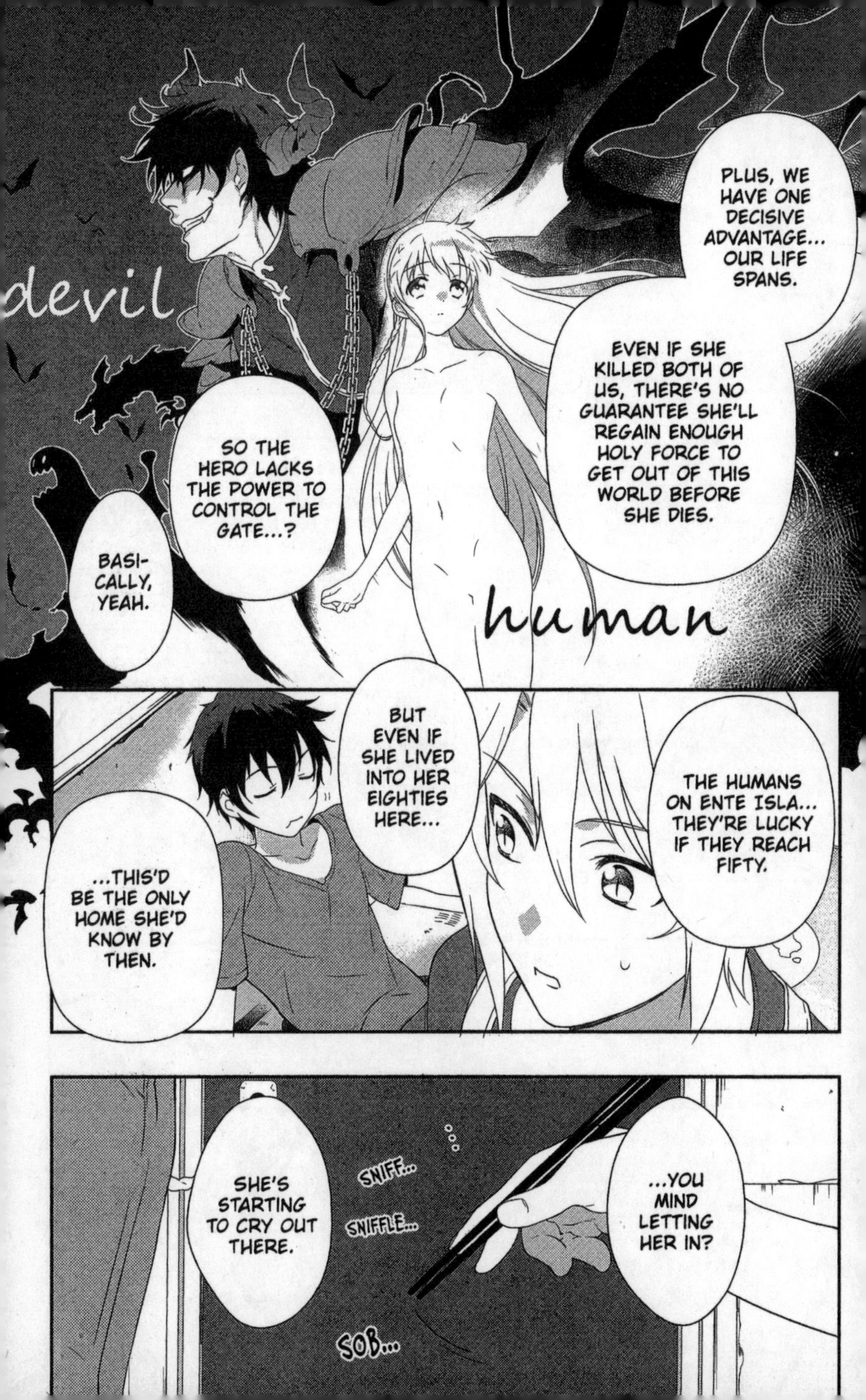
PLUS, WE HAVE ONE DECISIVE ADVANTAGE... OUR LIFE SPANS.
EVEN IF SHE KILLED BOTH OF US, THERE'S NO GUARANTEE SHE'LL REGAIN ENOUGH HOLY FORCE TO GET OUT OF THIS WORLD BEFORE SHE DIES.
devil
SO THE HERO LACKS THE POWER TO CONTROL THE GATE...?
BASI-CALLY, YEAH.
human
THE HUMANS ON ENTE ISLA... THEY'RE LUCKY IF THEY REACH FIFTY.
BUT EVEN IF SHE LIVED INTO HER EIGHTIES HERE...
...THIS'D BE THE ONLY HOME SHE'D KNOW BY THEN.
...YOU MIND LETTING HER IN?
...
SNIFF...
SNIFFLE...
SHE'S STARTING TO CRY OUT THERE.
SOB...

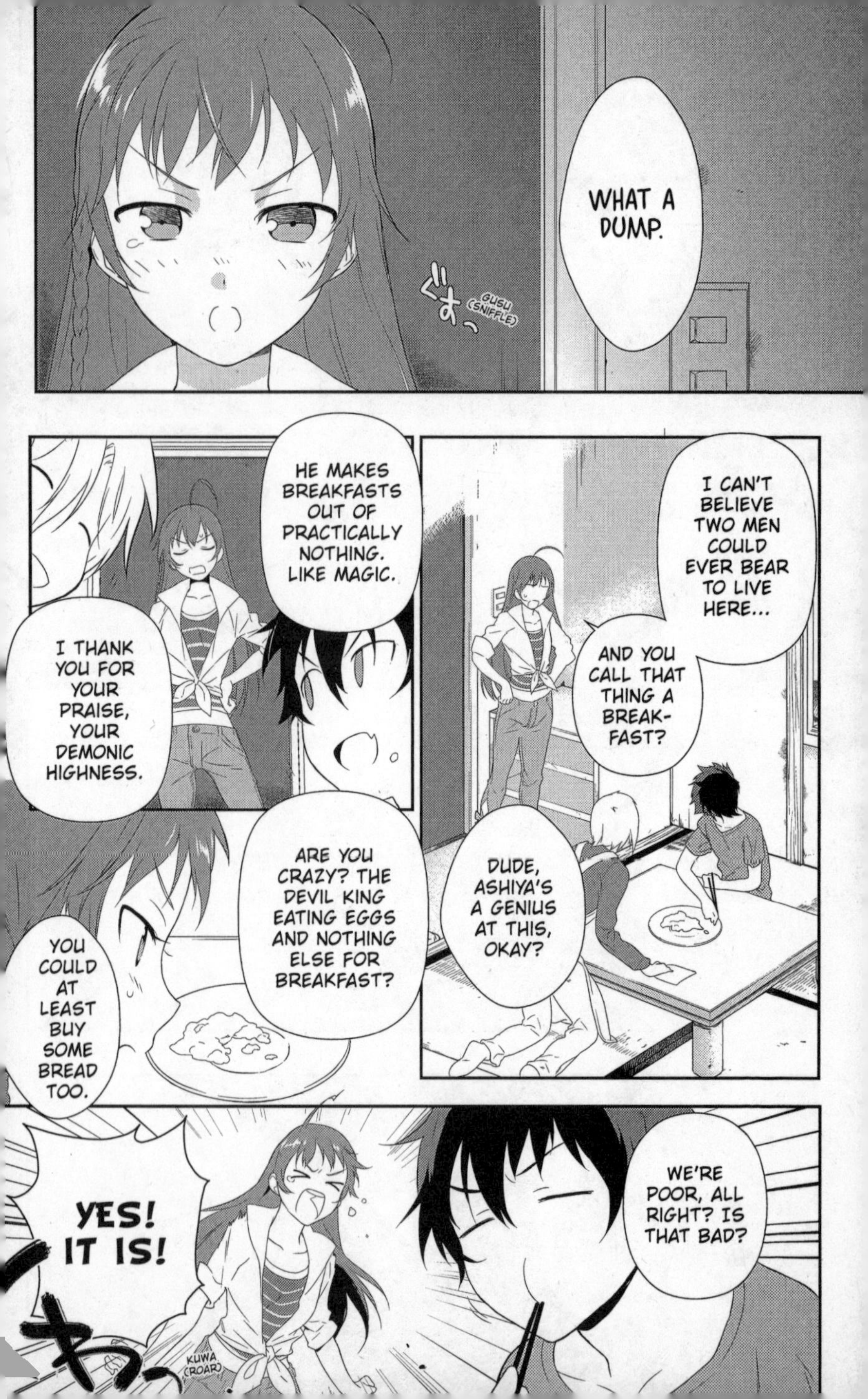
WHAT A DUMP.
GUSU (SNIFFLE)
I CAN'T BELIEVE TWO MEN COULD EVER BEAR TO LIVE HERE...
AND YOU CALL THAT THING A BREAK-FAST?
DUDE, ASHIYA'S A GENIUS AT THIS, OKAY?
HE MAKES BREAKFASTS OUT OF PRACTICALLY NOTHING. LIKE MAGIC.
I THANK YOU FOR YOUR PRAISE, YOUR DEMONIC HIGHNESS.
ARE YOU CRAZY? THE DEVIL KING EATING EGGS AND NOTHING ELSE FOR BREAKFAST?
YOU COULD AT LEAST BUY SOME BREAD TOO.
WE'RE POOR, ALL RIGHT? IS THAT BAD?
YES! IT IS!
KUWA (ROAR)

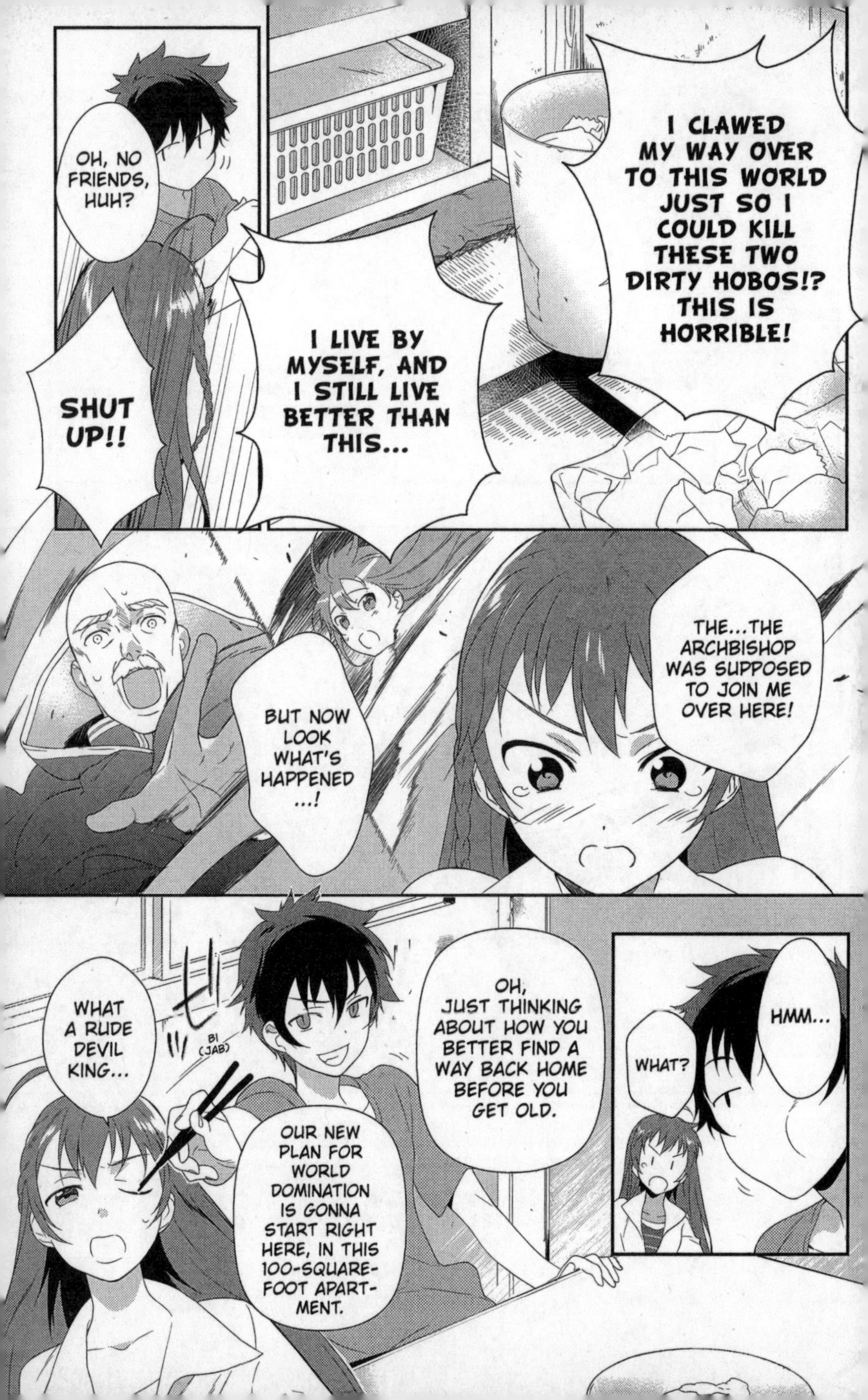

I CLAWED MY WAY OVER TO THIS WORLD JUST SO I COULD KILL THESE TWO DIRTY HOBOS!? THIS IS HORRIBLE!
I LIVE BY MYSELF, AND I STILL LIVE BETTER THAN THIS...
OH, NO FRIENDS, HUH?
SHUT UP!!
THE...THE ARCHBISHOP WAS SUPPOSED TO JOIN ME OVER HERE!
BUT NOW LOOK WHAT'S HAPPENED...!
HMM...
WHAT?
OH, JUST THINKING ABOUT HOW YOU BETTER FIND A WAY BACK HOME BEFORE YOU GET OLD.
OUR NEW PLAN FOR WORLD DOMINATION IS GONNA START RIGHT HERE, IN THIS 100-SQUARE-FOOT APARTMENT.
BI (JAB)
WHAT A RUDE DEVIL KING...

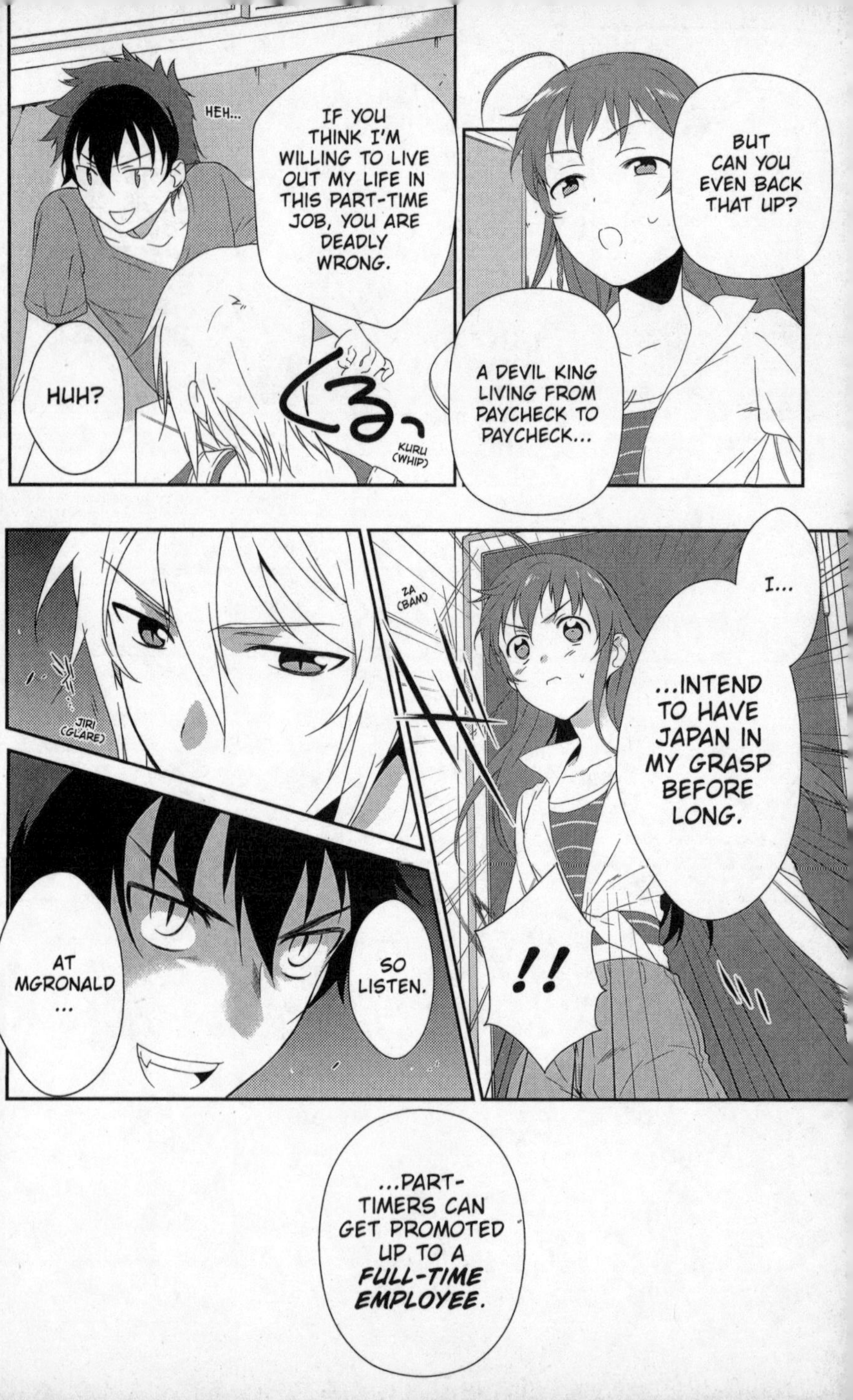
BUT CAN YOU EVEN BACK THAT UP?
A DEVIL KING LIVING FROM PAYCHECK TO PAYCHECK...
IF YOU THINK I'M WILLING TO LIVE OUT MY LIFE IN THIS PART-TIME JOB, YOU ARE DEADLY WRONG.
HEH...
HUH?
KURU (WHIP)
I...
...INTEND TO HAVE JAPAN IN MY GRASP BEFORE LONG.
ZA (BAM)
!!
JIRI (GLARE)
SO LISTEN.
AT MGRONALD ...
...PART-TIMERS CAN GET PROMOTED UP TO A *FULL-TIME EMPLOYEE*.

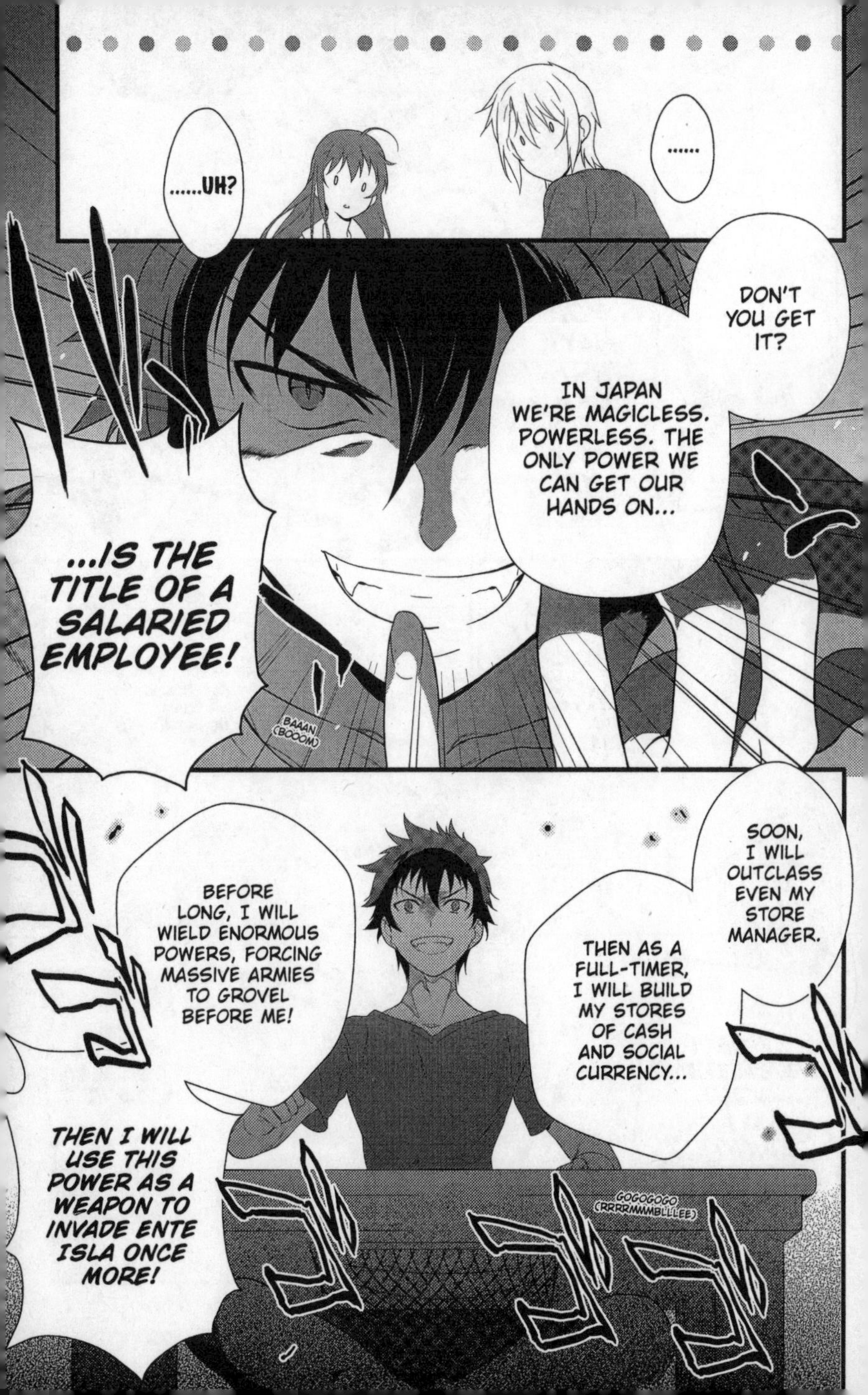
......
......UH?
DON'T YOU GET IT?
IN JAPAN WE'RE MAGICLESS. POWERLESS. THE ONLY POWER WE CAN GET OUR HANDS ON...
...IS THE TITLE OF A SALARIED EMPLOYEE!
BAAAN (BOOOM)
SOON, I WILL OUTCLASS EVEN MY STORE MANAGER.
THEN AS A FULL-TIMER, I WILL BUILD MY STORES OF CASH AND SOCIAL CURRENCY...
BEFORE LONG, I WILL WIELD ENORMOUS POWERS, FORCING MASSIVE ARMIES TO GROVEL BEFORE ME!
GOGOGOGO (RRRRMMMBLLLEE)
THEN I WILL USE THIS POWER AS A WEAPON TO INVADE ENTE ISLA ONCE MORE!

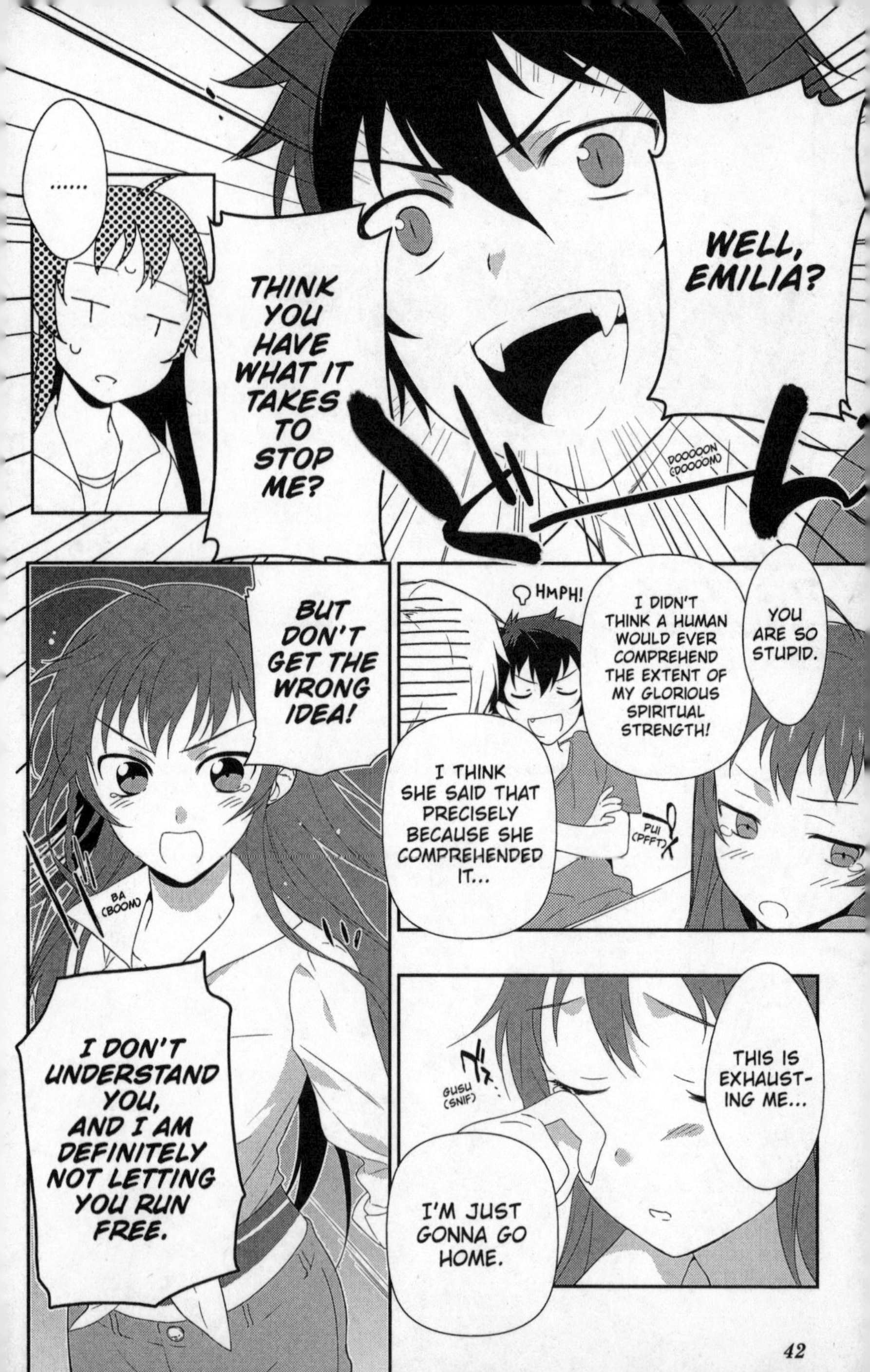
WELL, EMILIA?
THINK YOU HAVE WHAT IT TAKES TO STOP ME?
DOOOOON (DOOOOOM)
......
YOU ARE SO STUPID.
I DIDN'T THINK A HUMAN WOULD EVER COMPREHEND THE EXTENT OF MY GLORIOUS SPIRITUAL STRENGTH!
HMPH!
PUI (PFFFT)
I THINK SHE SAID THAT PRECISELY BECAUSE SHE COMPREHENDED IT...
THIS IS EXHAUST-ING ME...
GUSU (SNIF)
I'M JUST GONNA GO HOME.
BUT DON'T GET THE WRONG IDEA!
BA (BOOM)
I DON'T UNDERSTAND YOU, AND I AM DEFINITELY NOT LETTING YOU RUN FREE.

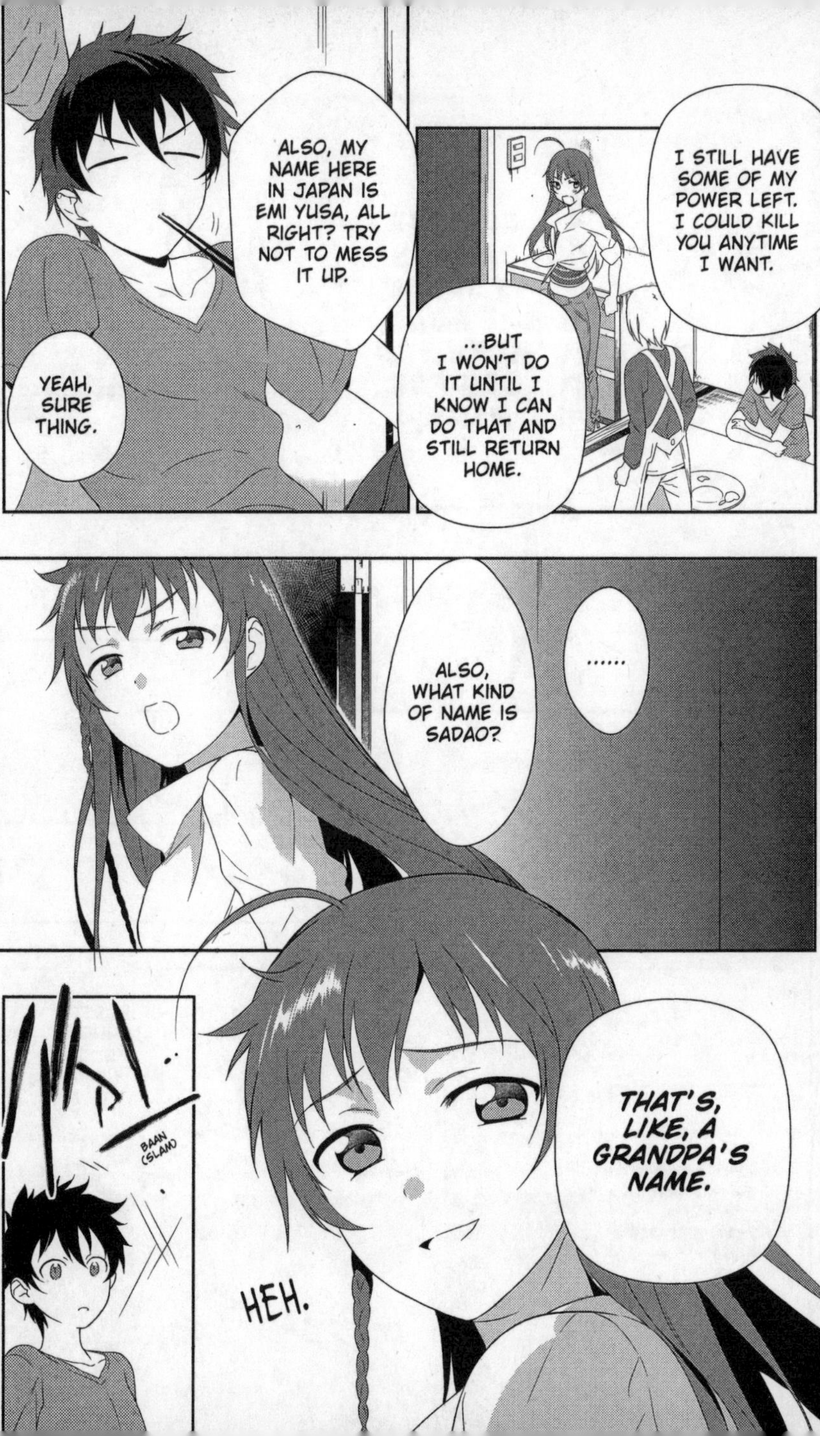
I STILL HAVE SOME OF MY POWER LEFT. I COULD KILL YOU ANYTIME I WANT.
...BUT I WON'T DO IT UNTIL I KNOW I CAN DO THAT AND STILL RETURN HOME.
ALSO, MY NAME HERE IN JAPAN IS EMI YUSA, ALL RIGHT? TRY NOT TO MESS IT UP.
YEAH, SURE THING.
......
ALSO, WHAT KIND OF NAME IS SADAO?
THAT'S, LIKE, A GRANDPA'S NAME.
HEH.
BAAN (SLAM)

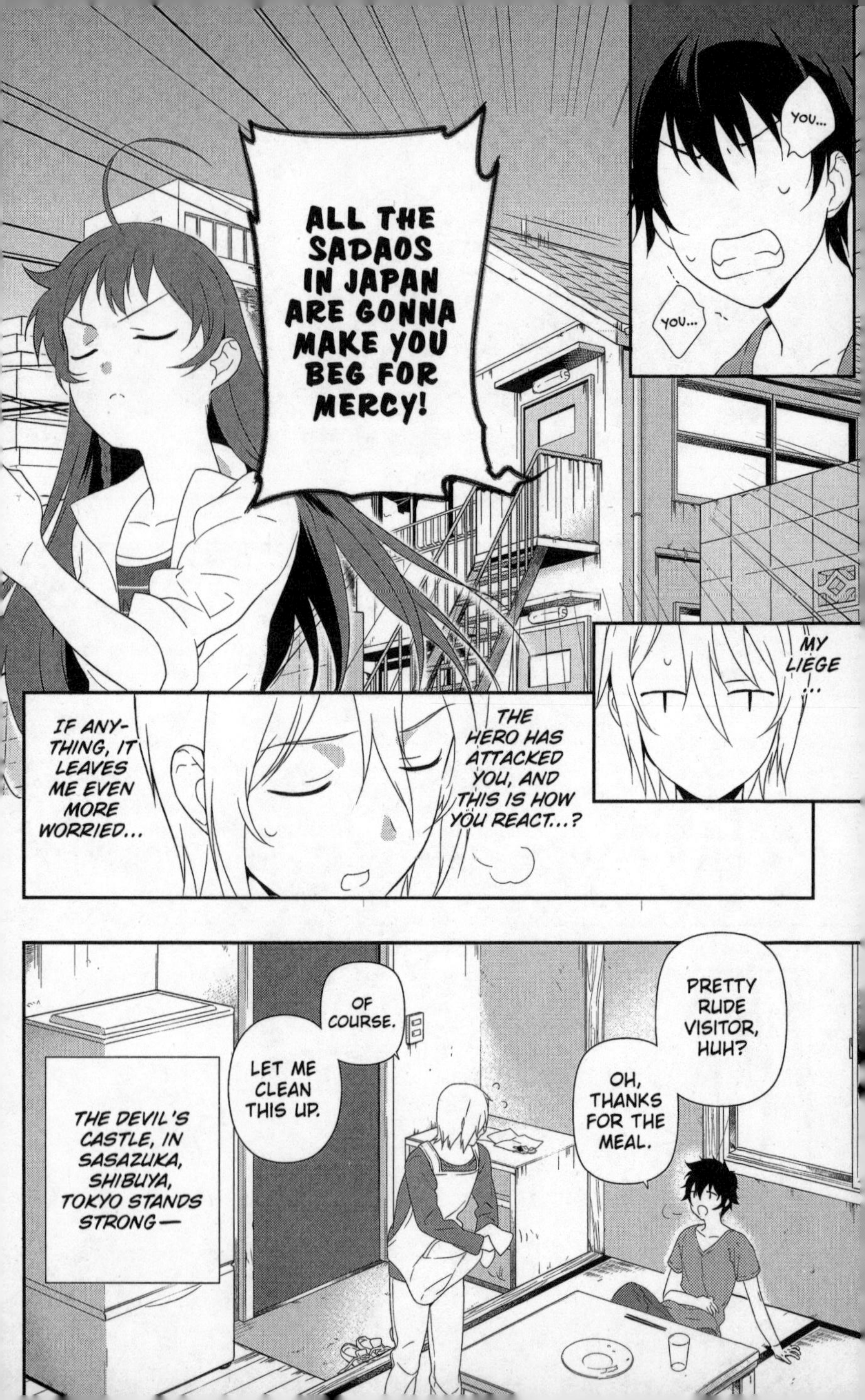
YOU...
YOU...
ALL THE SADAOS IN JAPAN ARE GONNA MAKE YOU BEG FOR MERCY!
MY LIEGE...
THE HERO HAS ATTACKED YOU, AND THIS IS HOW YOU REACT...?
IF ANYTHING, IT LEAVES ME EVEN MORE WORRIED...
PRETTY RUDE VISITOR, HUH?
OH, THANKS FOR THE MEAL.
OF COURSE.
LET ME CLEAN THIS UP.
THE DEVIL'S CASTLE, IN SASAZUKA, SHIBUYA, TOKYO STANDS STRONG—

Sadao
Maou

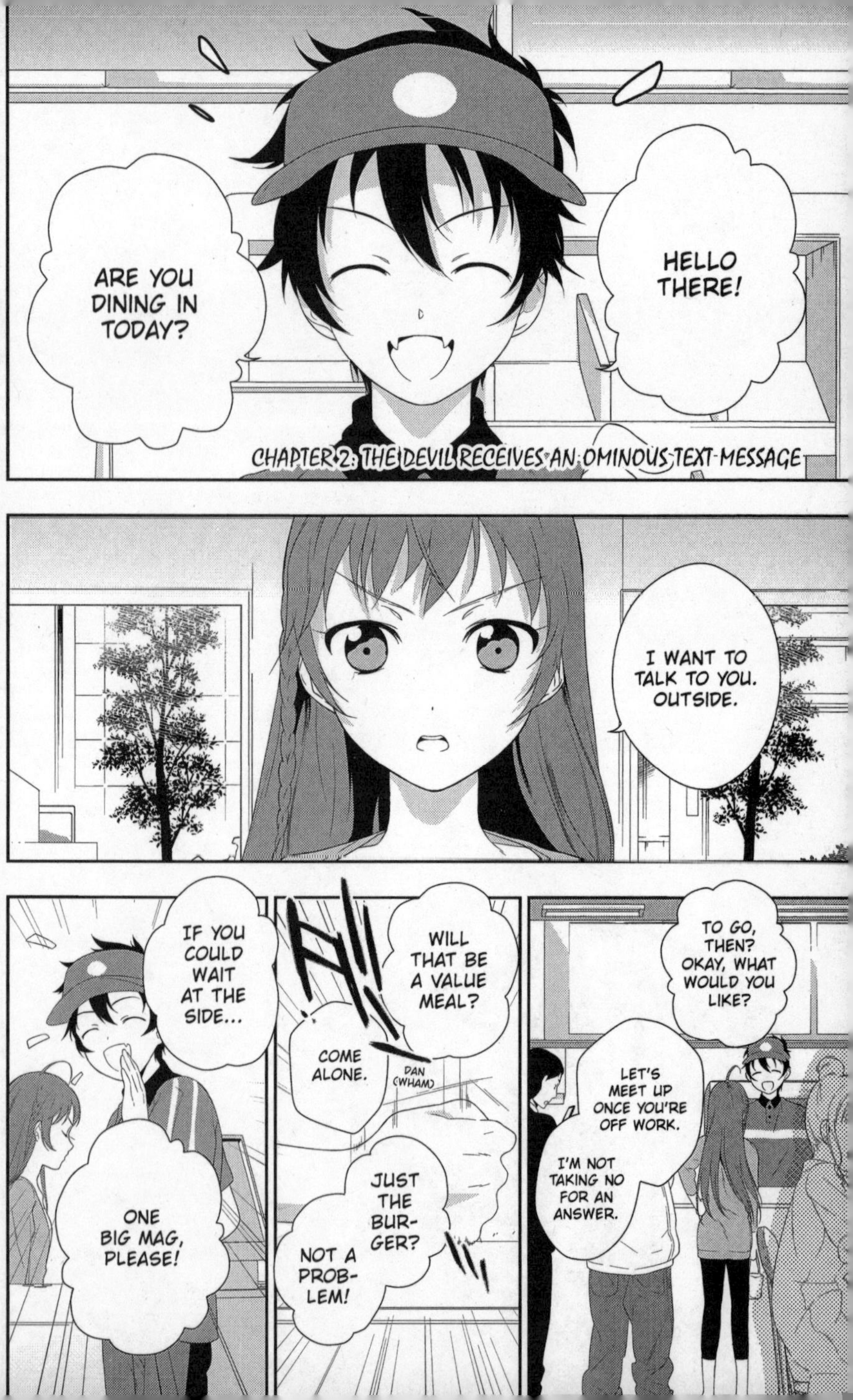
HELLO THERE!
ARE YOU DINING IN TODAY?
CHAPTER 2: THE DEVIL RECEIVES AN OMINOUS TEXT MESSAGE
I WANT TO TALK TO YOU. OUTSIDE.
TO GO, THEN? OKAY, WHAT WOULD YOU LIKE?
LET'S MEET UP ONCE YOU'RE OFF WORK.
I'M NOT TAKING NO FOR AN ANSWER.
WILL THAT BE A VALUE MEAL?
COME ALONE.
DAN (WHAM)
JUST THE BURGER?
NOT A PROB-LEM!
IF YOU COULD WAIT AT THE SIDE...
ONE BIG MAG, PLEASE!

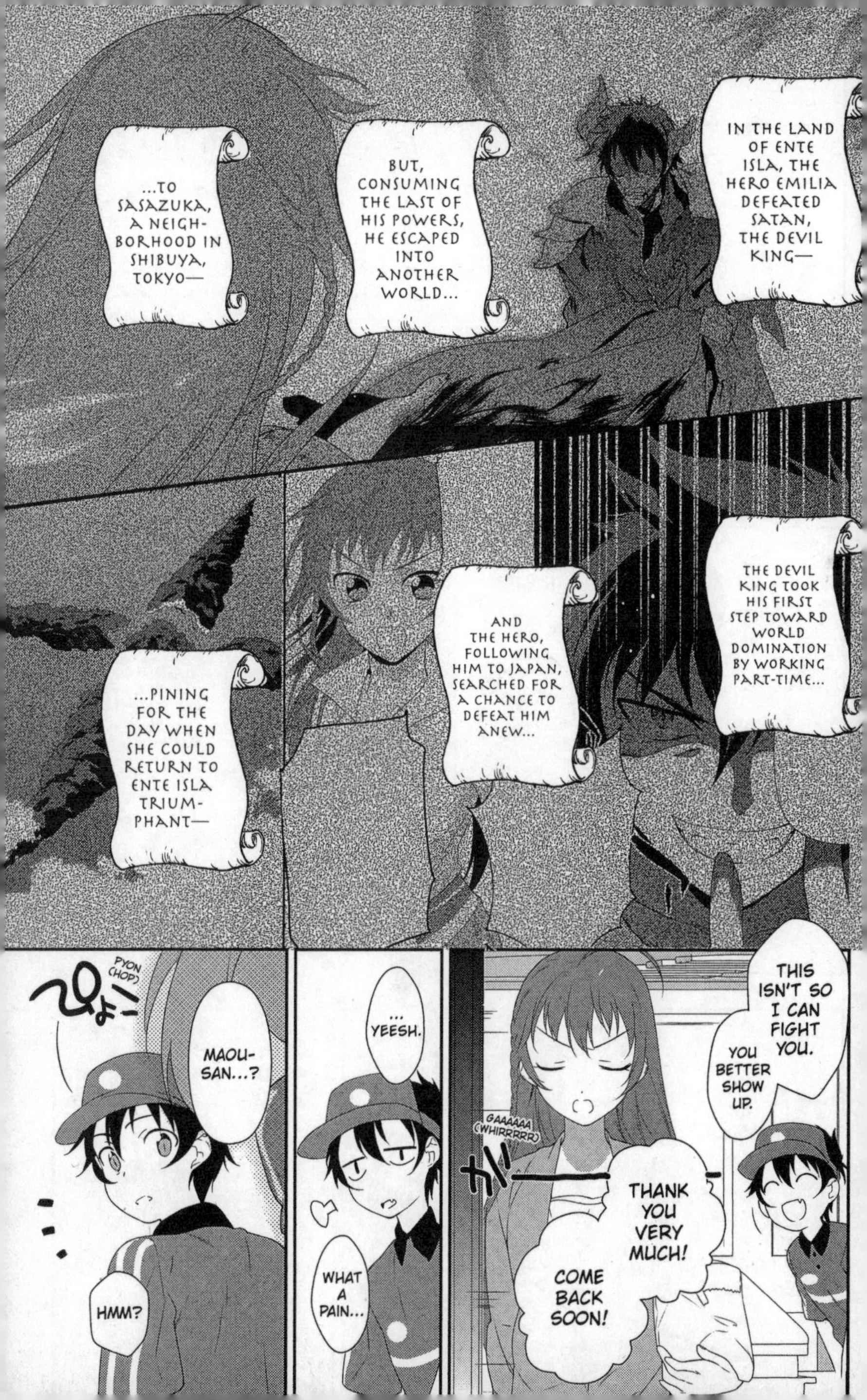
IN THE LAND OF ENTE ISLA, THE HERO EMILIA DEFEATED SATAN, THE DEVIL KING—
BUT, CONSUMING THE LAST OF HIS POWERS, HE ESCAPED INTO ANOTHER WORLD...
...TO SASAZUKA, A NEIGHBORHOOD IN SHIBUYA, TOKYO—
THE DEVIL KING TOOK HIS FIRST STEP TOWARD WORLD DOMINATION BY WORKING PART-TIME...
AND THE HERO, FOLLOWING HIM TO JAPAN, SEARCHED FOR A CHANCE TO DEFEAT HIM ANEW...
...PINING FOR THE DAY WHEN SHE COULD RETURN TO ENTE ISLA TRIUMPHANT—
THIS ISN'T SO I CAN FIGHT YOU.
YOU BETTER SHOW UP.
GAAAAAA (WHIRRRRR)
THANK YOU VERY MUCH!
COME BACK SOON!
...YEESH.
WHAT A PAIN...
PYON (HOP)
MAOU-SAN...?
HMM?

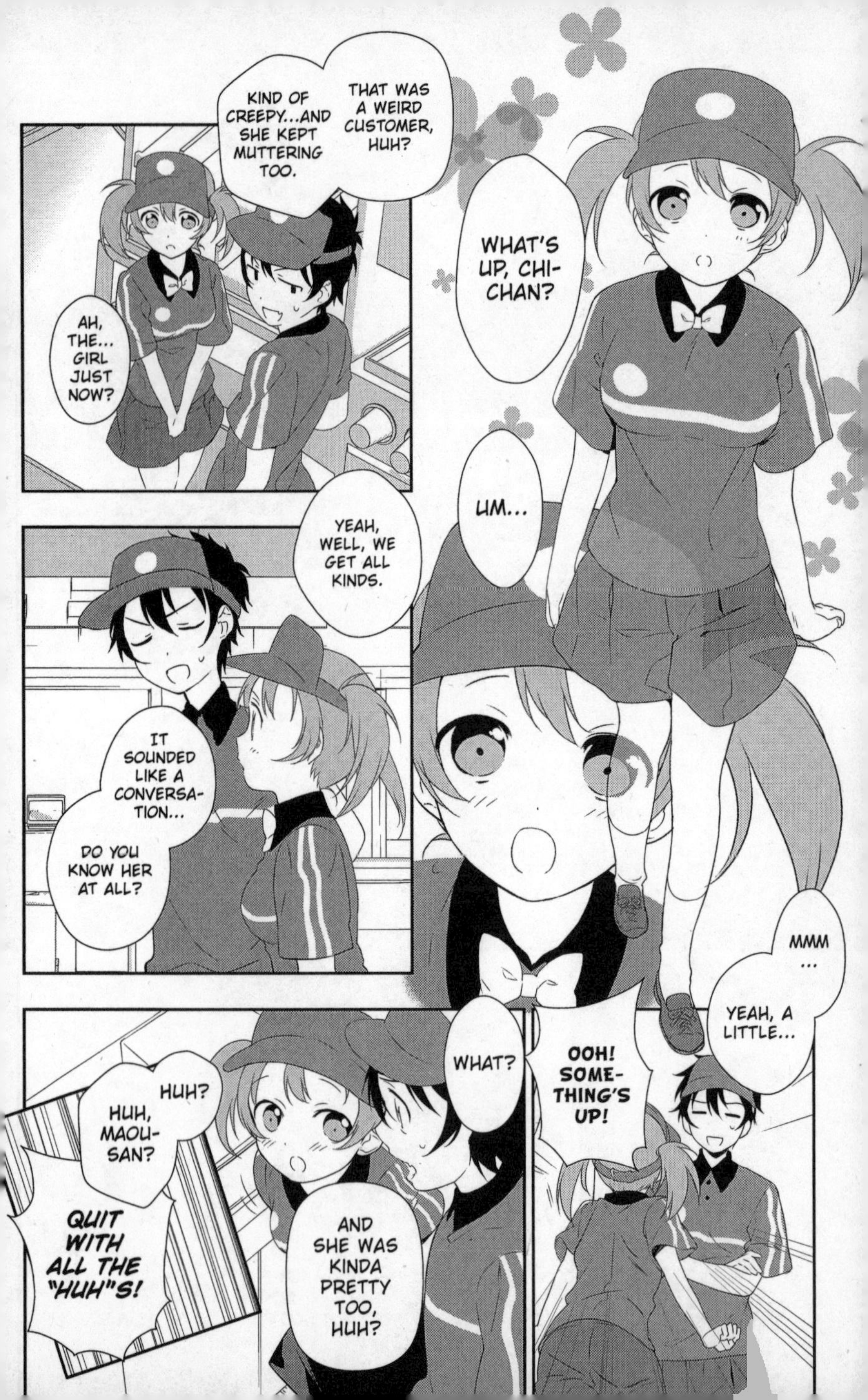
WHAT'S UP, CHI-CHAN?
UM...
THAT WAS A WEIRD CUSTOMER, HUH?
KIND OF CREEPY...AND SHE KEPT MUTTERING TOO.
AH, THE... GIRL JUST NOW?
YEAH, WELL, WE GET ALL KINDS.
IT SOUNDED LIKE A CONVERSATION...
DO YOU KNOW HER AT ALL?
MMM...
YEAH, A LITTLE...
OOH! SOMETHING'S UP!
WHAT?
AND SHE WAS KINDA PRETTY TOO, HUH?
HUH?
HUH, MAOU-SAN?
QUIT WITH ALL THE "HUH"S!

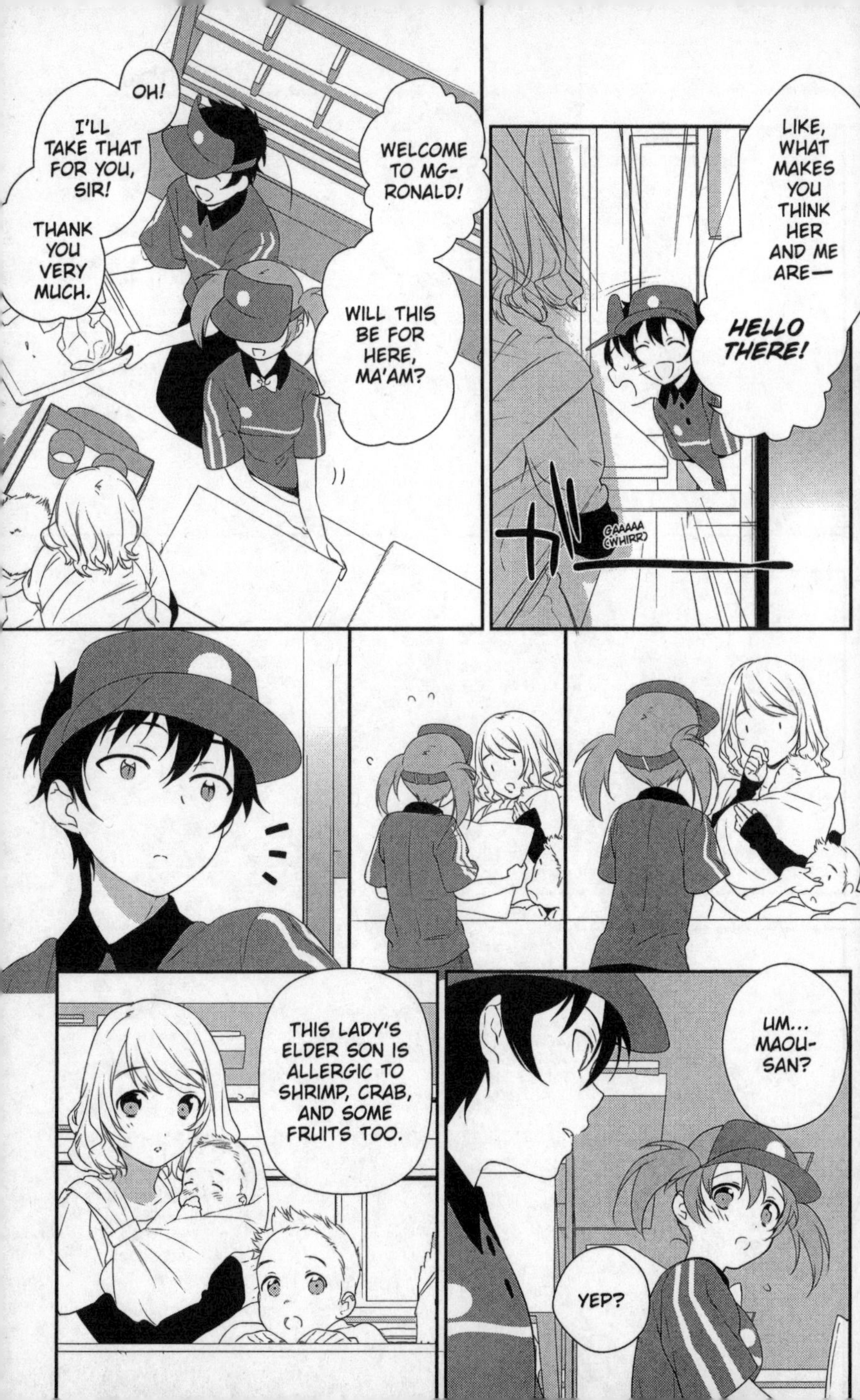
LIKE, WHAT MAKES YOU THINK HER AND ME ARE—
HELLO THERE!
GAAAAA (WHIRR)
WELCOME TO MG-RONALD!
OH!
I'LL TAKE THAT FOR YOU, SIR!
THANK YOU VERY MUCH.
WILL THIS BE FOR HERE, MA'AM?
UM... MAOU-SAN?
YEP?
THIS LADY'S ELDER SON IS ALLERGIC TO SHRIMP, CRAB, AND SOME FRUITS TOO.

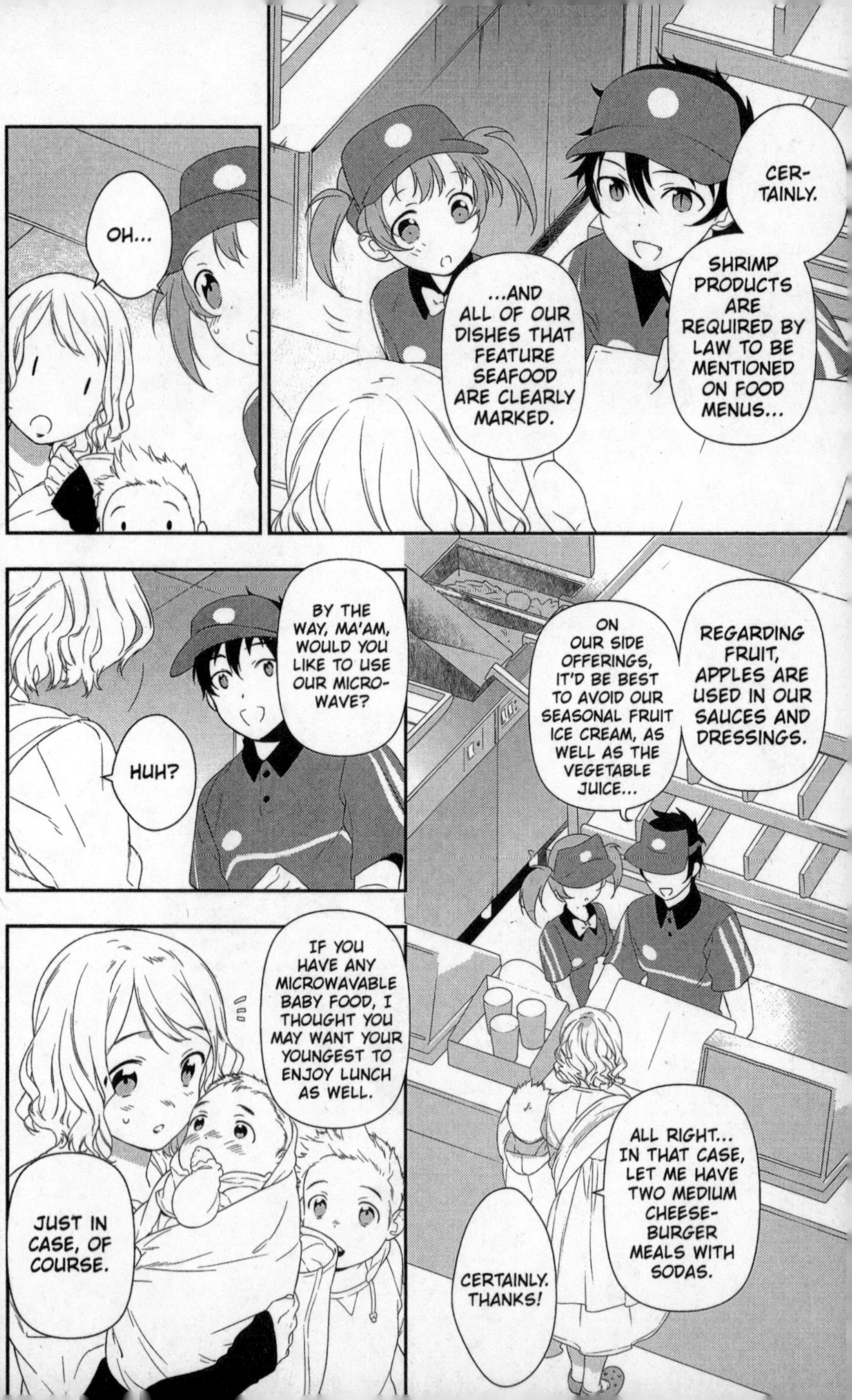
CER-TAINLY.
SHRIMP PRODUCTS ARE REQUIRED BY LAW TO BE MENTIONED ON FOOD MENUS...
...AND ALL OF OUR DISHES THAT FEATURE SEAFOOD ARE CLEARLY MARKED.
OH...
REGARDING FRUIT, APPLES ARE USED IN OUR SAUCES AND DRESSINGS.
ON OUR SIDE OFFERINGS, IT'D BE BEST TO AVOID OUR SEASONAL FRUIT ICE CREAM, AS WELL AS THE VEGETABLE JUICE...
ALL RIGHT... IN THAT CASE, LET ME HAVE TWO MEDIUM CHEESE-BURGER MEALS WITH SODAS.
CERTAINLY. THANKS!
BY THE WAY, MA'AM, WOULD YOU LIKE TO USE OUR MICRO-WAVE?
HUH?
IF YOU HAVE ANY MICROWAVABLE BABY FOOD, I THOUGHT YOU MAY WANT YOUR YOUNGEST TO ENJOY LUNCH AS WELL.
JUST IN CASE, OF COURSE.

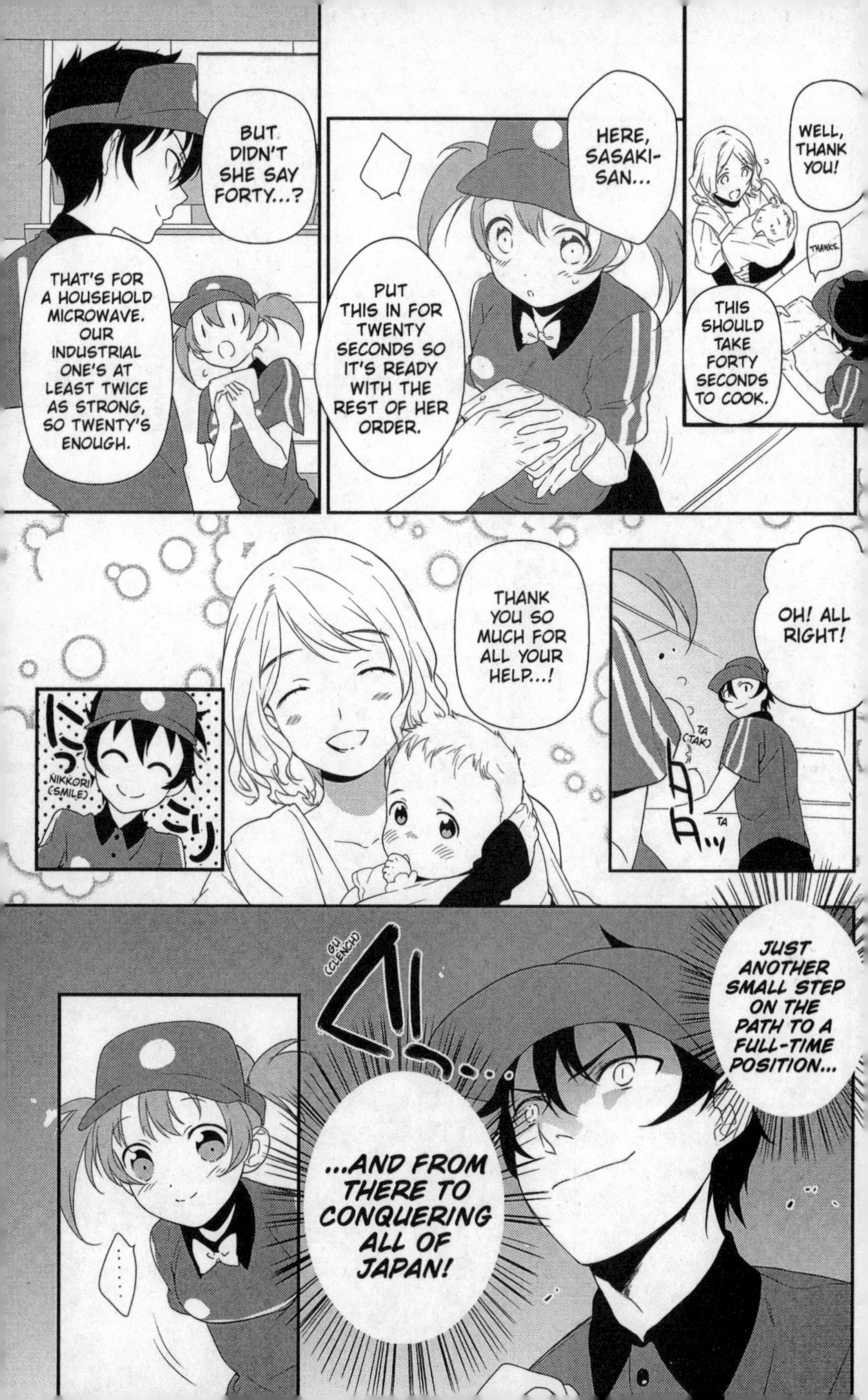
WELL, THANK YOU!
THANKS.
THIS SHOULD TAKE FORTY SECONDS TO COOK.
HERE, SASAKI-SAN...
PUT THIS IN FOR TWENTY SECONDS SO IT'S READY WITH THE REST OF HER ORDER.
BUT DIDN'T SHE SAY FORTY...?
THAT'S FOR A HOUSEHOLD MICROWAVE. OUR INDUSTRIAL ONE'S AT LEAST TWICE AS STRONG, SO TWENTY'S ENOUGH.
OH! ALL RIGHT!
TA (TAK)
TA
THANK YOU SO MUCH FOR ALL YOUR HELP...!
NIKKORI (SMILE)
JUST ANOTHER SMALL STEP ON THE PATH TO A FULL-TIME POSITION...
GU (CLENCH)
...AND FROM THERE TO CONQUERING ALL OF JAPAN!
......

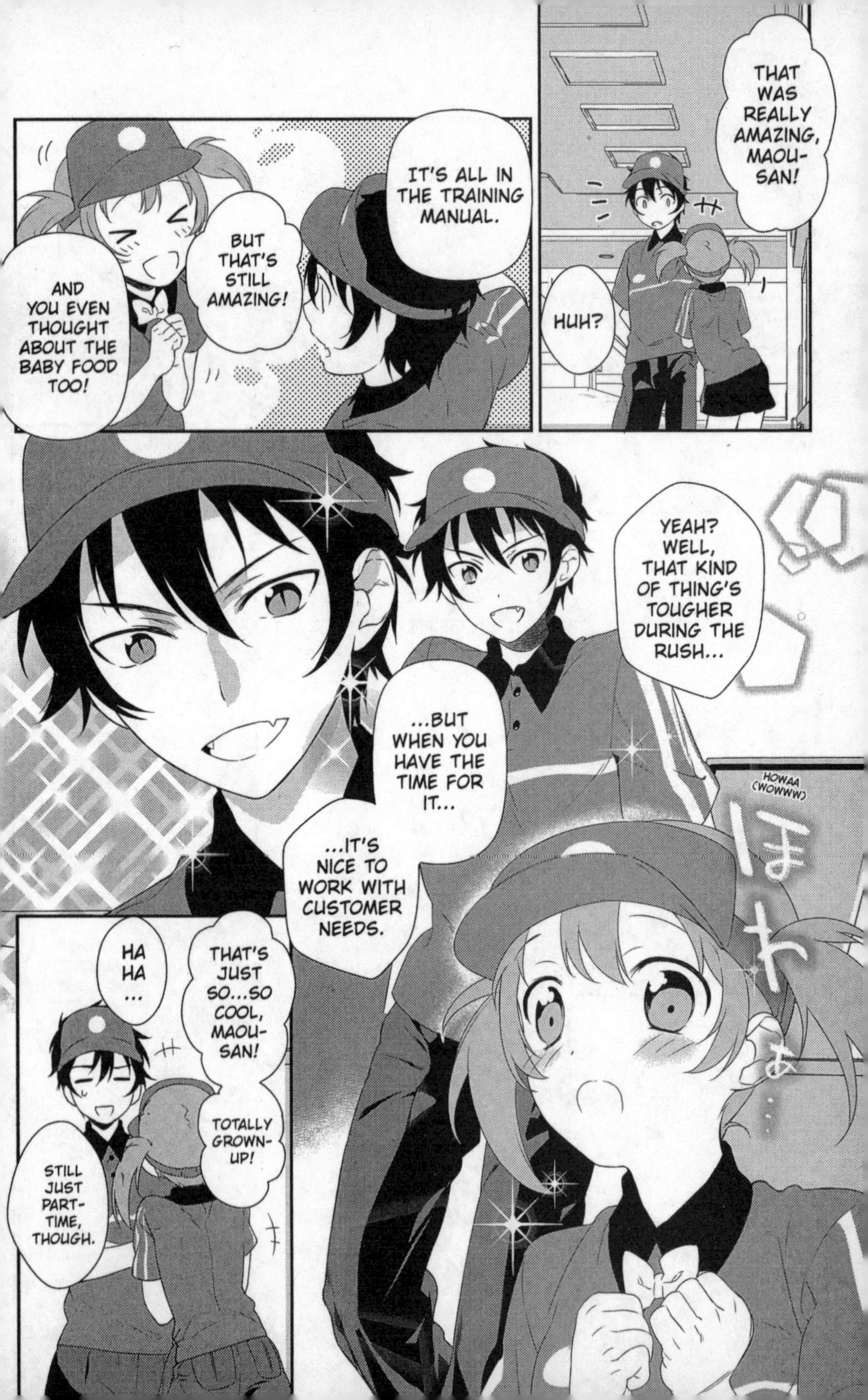
THAT WAS REALLY AMAZING, MAOU-SAN!
HUH?
IT'S ALL IN THE TRAINING MANUAL.
BUT THAT'S STILL AMAZING!
AND YOU EVEN THOUGHT ABOUT THE BABY FOOD TOO!
YEAH? WELL, THAT KIND OF THING'S TOUGHER DURING THE RUSH...
...BUT WHEN YOU HAVE THE TIME FOR IT...
...IT'S NICE TO WORK WITH CUSTOMER NEEDS.
HOWAA (WOWWW)
ほわぁ…
THAT'S JUST SO...SO COOL, MAOU-SAN!
HA HA ...
TOTALLY GROWN-UP!
STILL JUST PART-TIME, THOUGH.

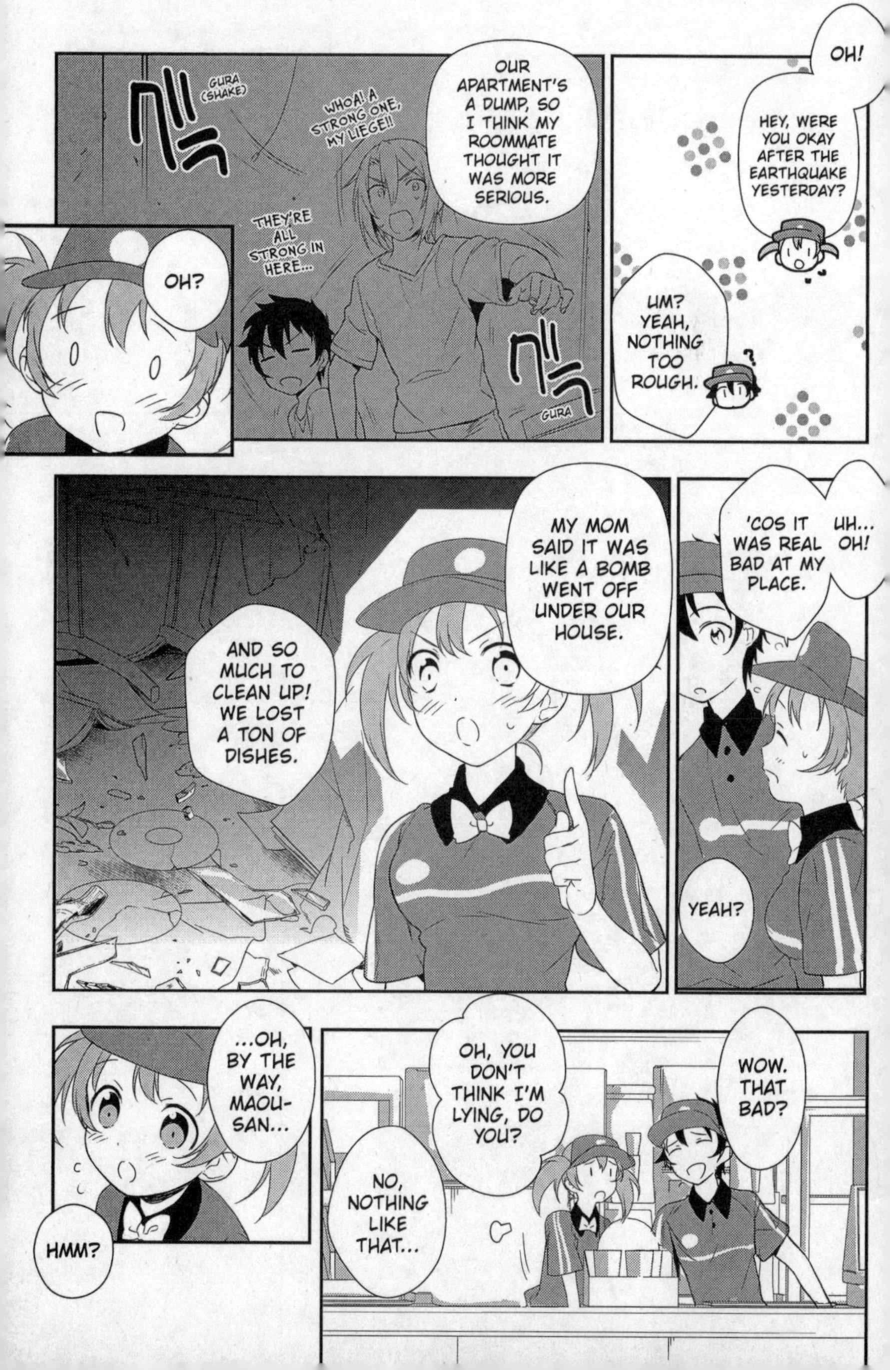
OH!
HEY, WERE YOU OKAY AFTER THE EARTHQUAKE YESTERDAY?
UM? YEAH, NOTHING TOO ROUGH.
OUR APARTMENT'S A DUMP, SO I THINK MY ROOMMATE THOUGHT IT WAS MORE SERIOUS.
WHOA! A STRONG ONE, MY LIEGE!!
GURA (SHAKE)
THEY'RE ALL STRONG IN HERE...
GURA
OH?
UH... OH!
'COS IT WAS REAL BAD AT MY PLACE.
YEAH?
MY MOM SAID IT WAS LIKE A BOMB WENT OFF UNDER OUR HOUSE.
AND SO MUCH TO CLEAN UP! WE LOST A TON OF DISHES.
WOW. THAT BAD?
OH, YOU DON'T THINK I'M LYING, DO YOU?
NO, NOTHING LIKE THAT...
...OH, BY THE WAY, MAOU-SAN...
HMM?

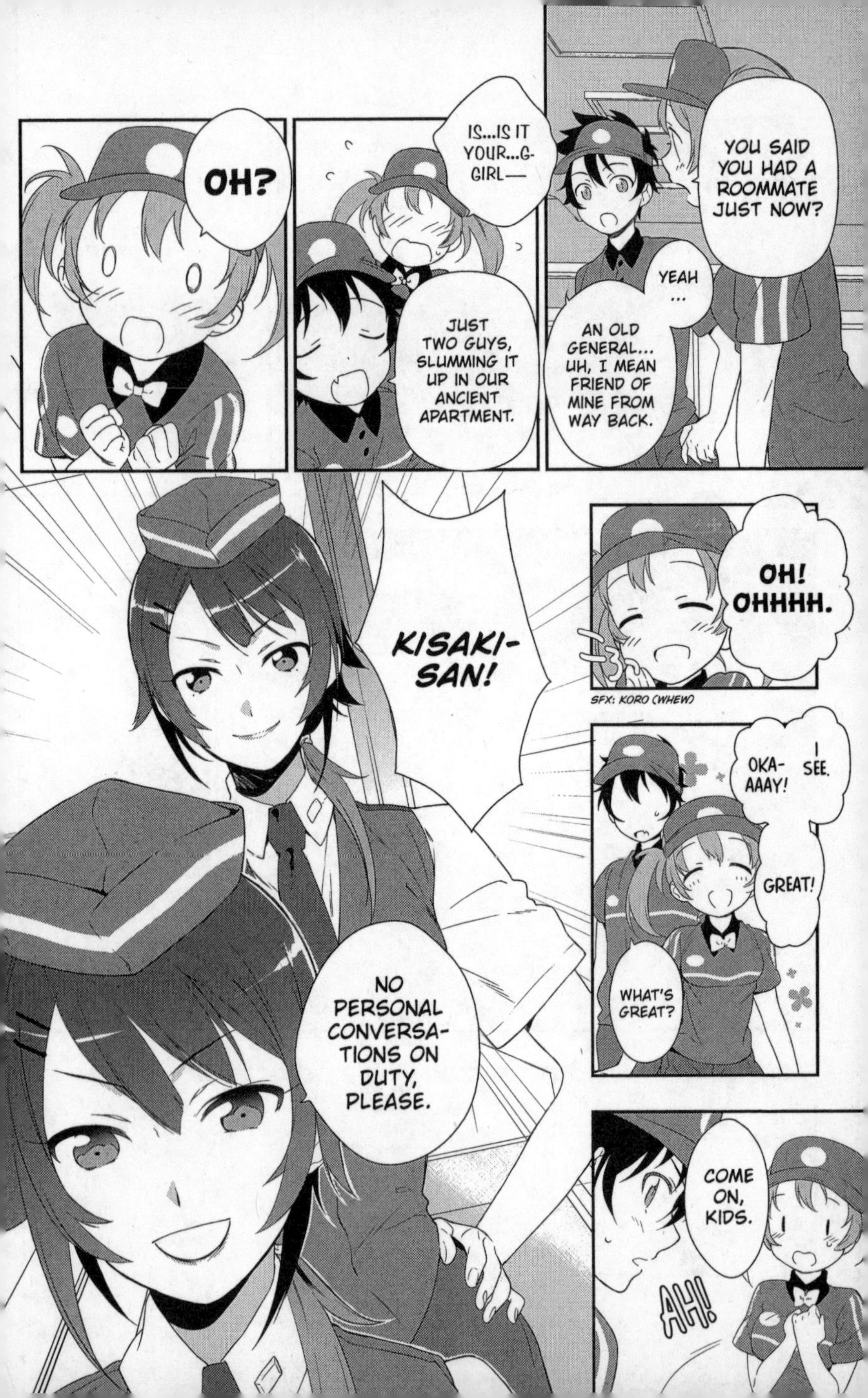
YOU SAID YOU HAD A ROOMMATE JUST NOW?
YEAH ...
AN OLD GENERAL... UH, I MEAN FRIEND OF MINE FROM WAY BACK.
IS...IS IT YOUR...G-GIRL—
JUST TWO GUYS, SLUMMING IT UP IN OUR ANCIENT APARTMENT.
OH?
OH! OHHHH.
SFX: KORO (WHEW)
I SEE.
OKA-AAAY!
GREAT!
WHAT'S GREAT?
COME ON, KIDS.
AH!
KISAKI-SAN!
NO PERSONAL CONVERSATIONS ON DUTY, PLEASE.

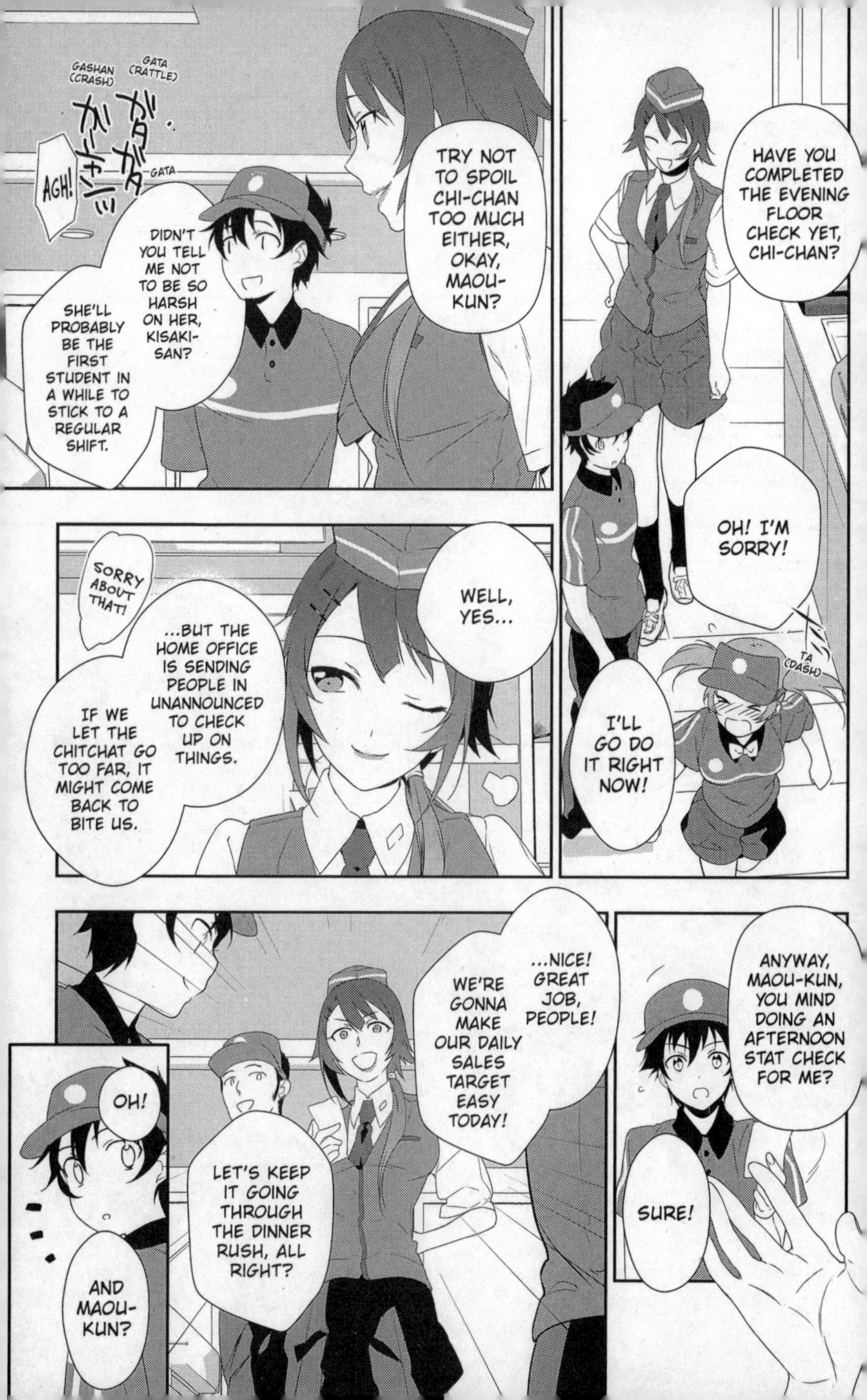
HAVE YOU COMPLETED THE EVENING FLOOR CHECK YET, CHI-CHAN?
OH! I'M SORRY!
TA (DASH)
I'LL GO DO IT RIGHT NOW!
GATA (RATTLE)
GASHAN (CRASH)
GATA
AGH!
TRY NOT TO SPOIL CHI-CHAN TOO MUCH EITHER, OKAY, MAOU-KUN?
DIDN'T YOU TELL ME NOT TO BE SO HARSH ON HER, KISAKI-SAN?
SHE'LL PROBABLY BE THE FIRST STUDENT IN A WHILE TO STICK TO A REGULAR SHIFT.
WELL, YES...
...BUT THE HOME OFFICE IS SENDING PEOPLE IN UNANNOUNCED TO CHECK UP ON THINGS.
SORRY ABOUT THAT!
IF WE LET THE CHITCHAT GO TOO FAR, IT MIGHT COME BACK TO BITE US.
ANYWAY, MAOU-KUN, YOU MIND DOING AN AFTERNOON STAT CHECK FOR ME?
SURE!
...NICE! GREAT JOB, PEOPLE!
WE'RE GONNA MAKE OUR DAILY SALES TARGET EASY TODAY!
LET'S KEEP IT GOING THROUGH THE DINNER RUSH, ALL RIGHT?
AND MAOU-KUN?
OH!

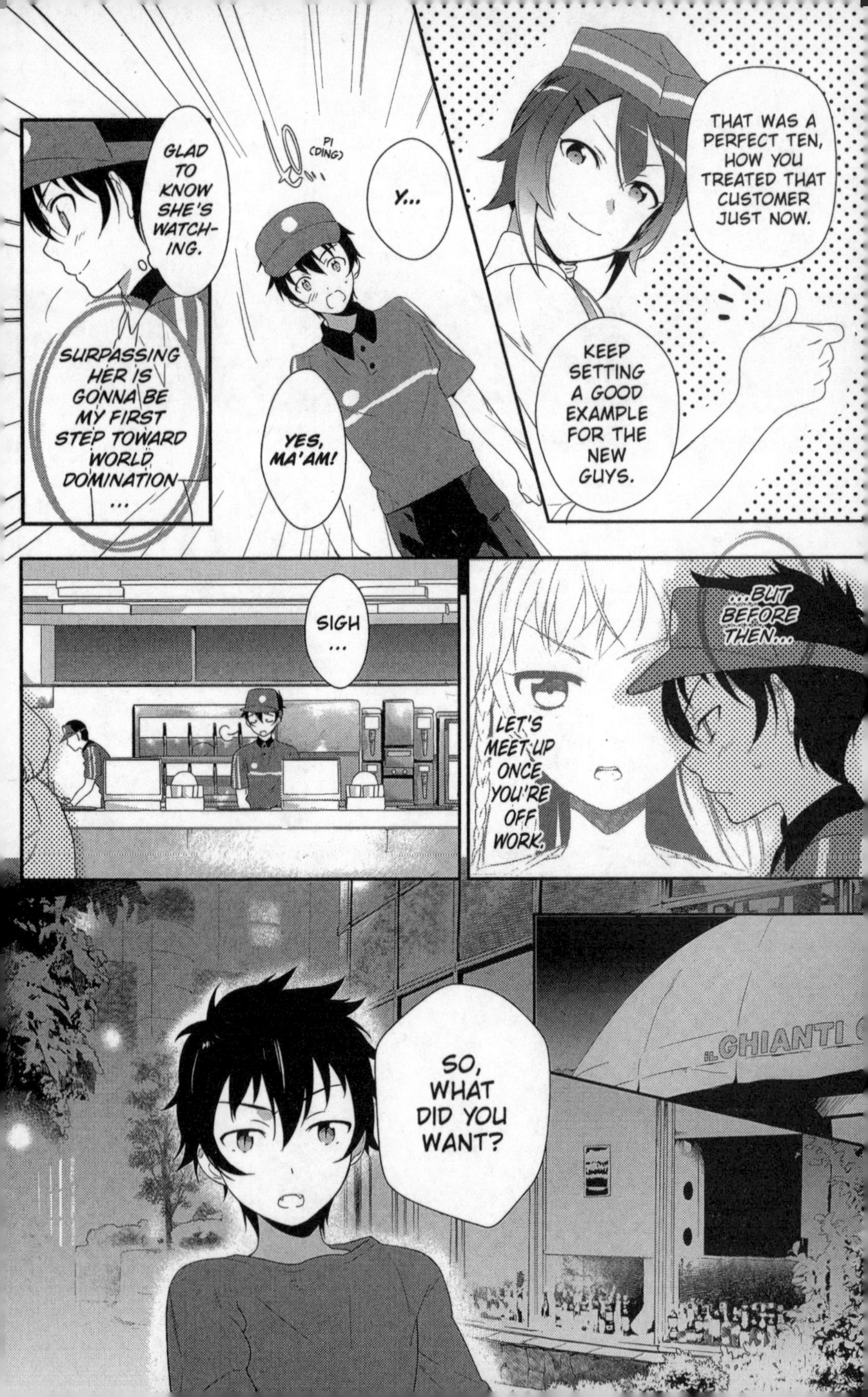

THAT WAS A PERFECT TEN, HOW YOU TREATED THAT CUSTOMER JUST NOW.
KEEP SETTING A GOOD EXAMPLE FOR THE NEW GUYS.
PI (DING)
Y...
YES, MA'AM!
GLAD TO KNOW SHE'S WATCH-ING.
SURPASSING HER IS GONNA BE MY FIRST STEP TOWARD WORLD DOMINATION...
...BUT BEFORE THEN...
LET'S MEET UP ONCE YOU'RE OFF WORK.
SIGH...
SO, WHAT DID YOU WANT?
GHIANTI

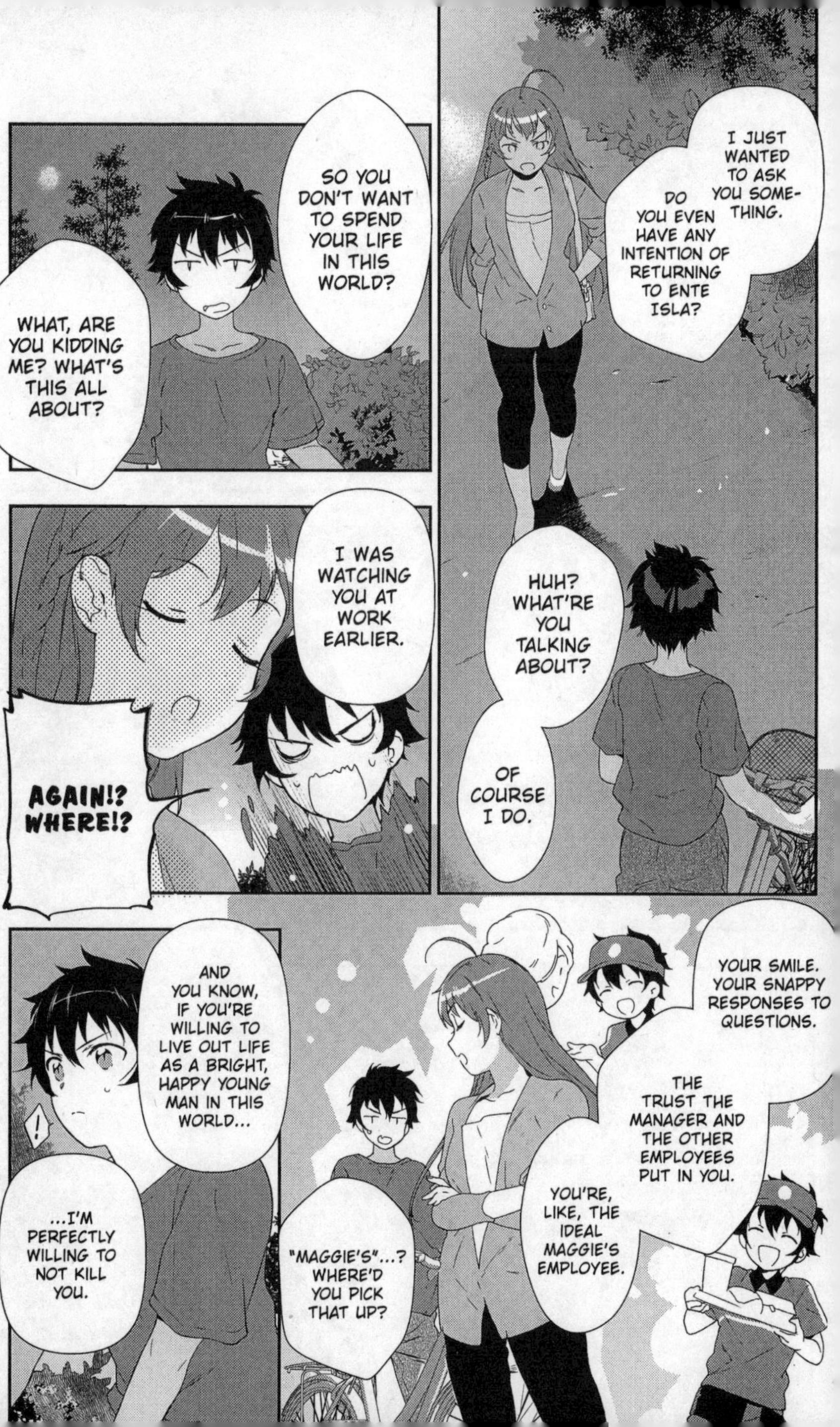
I JUST WANTED TO ASK YOU SOME-THING.
DO YOU EVEN HAVE ANY INTENTION OF RETURNING TO ENTE ISLA?
HUH? WHAT'RE YOU TALKING ABOUT?
OF COURSE I DO.
SO YOU DON'T WANT TO SPEND YOUR LIFE IN THIS WORLD?
WHAT, ARE YOU KIDDING ME? WHAT'S THIS ALL ABOUT?
I WAS WATCHING YOU AT WORK EARLIER.
AGAIN!? WHERE!?
YOUR SMILE. YOUR SNAPPY RESPONSES TO QUESTIONS.
THE TRUST THE MANAGER AND THE OTHER EMPLOYEES PUT IN YOU.
YOU'RE, LIKE, THE IDEAL MAGGIE'S EMPLOYEE.
"MAGGIE'S"...? WHERE'D YOU PICK THAT UP?
AND YOU KNOW, IF YOU'RE WILLING TO LIVE OUT LIFE AS A BRIGHT, HAPPY YOUNG MAN IN THIS WORLD...
!
...I'M PERFECTLY WILLING TO NOT KILL YOU.

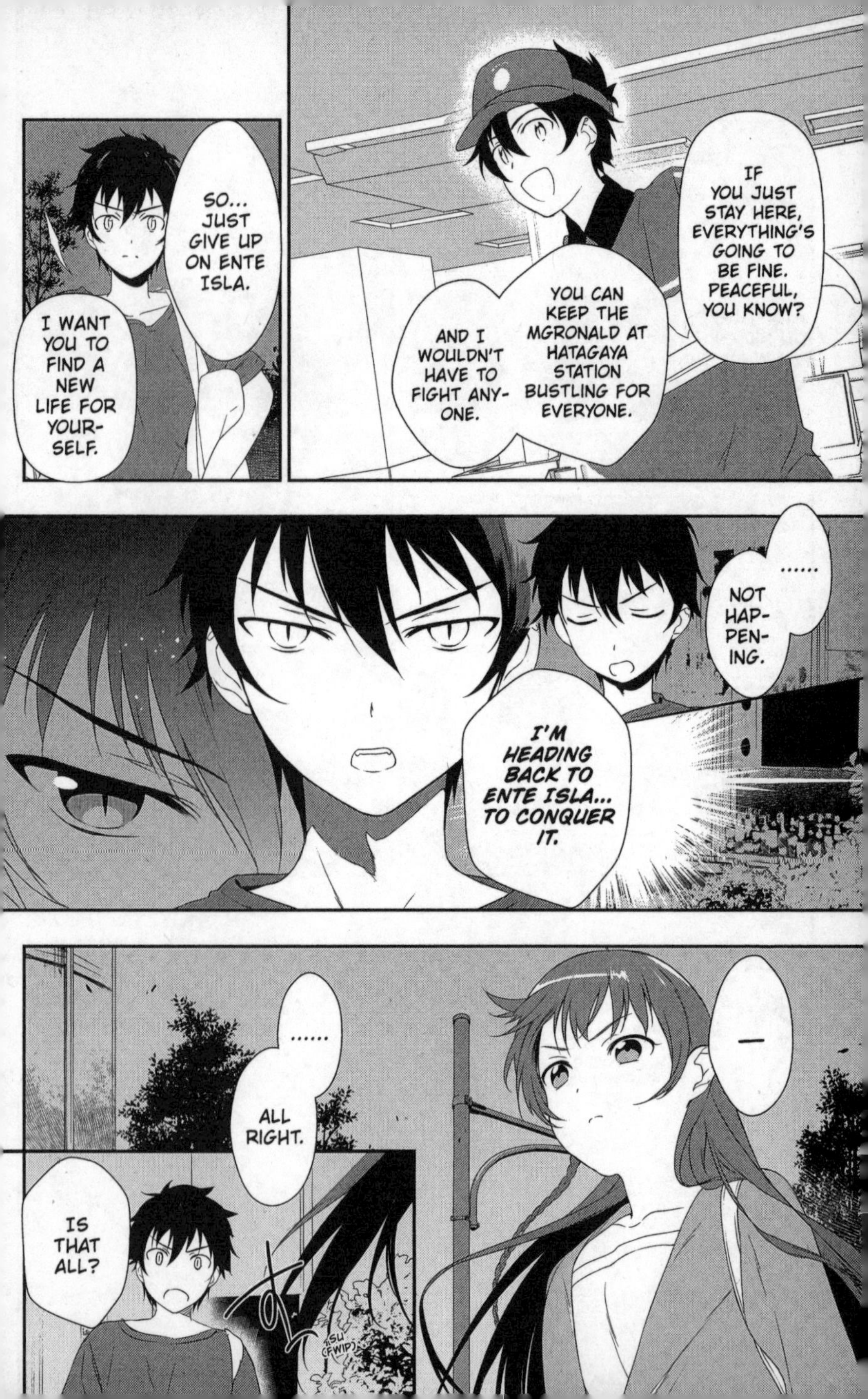
IF YOU JUST STAY HERE, EVERYTHING'S GOING TO BE FINE. PEACEFUL, YOU KNOW?
YOU CAN KEEP THE MGRONALD AT HATAGAYA STATION BUSTLING FOR EVERYONE.
AND I WOULDN'T HAVE TO FIGHT ANYONE.
SO... JUST GIVE UP ON ENTE ISLA.
I WANT YOU TO FIND A NEW LIFE FOR YOURSELF.
......
NOT HAPPENING.
I'M HEADING BACK TO ENTE ISLA... TO CONQUER IT.
—
......
ALL RIGHT.
IS THAT ALL?
SU (FWIP)

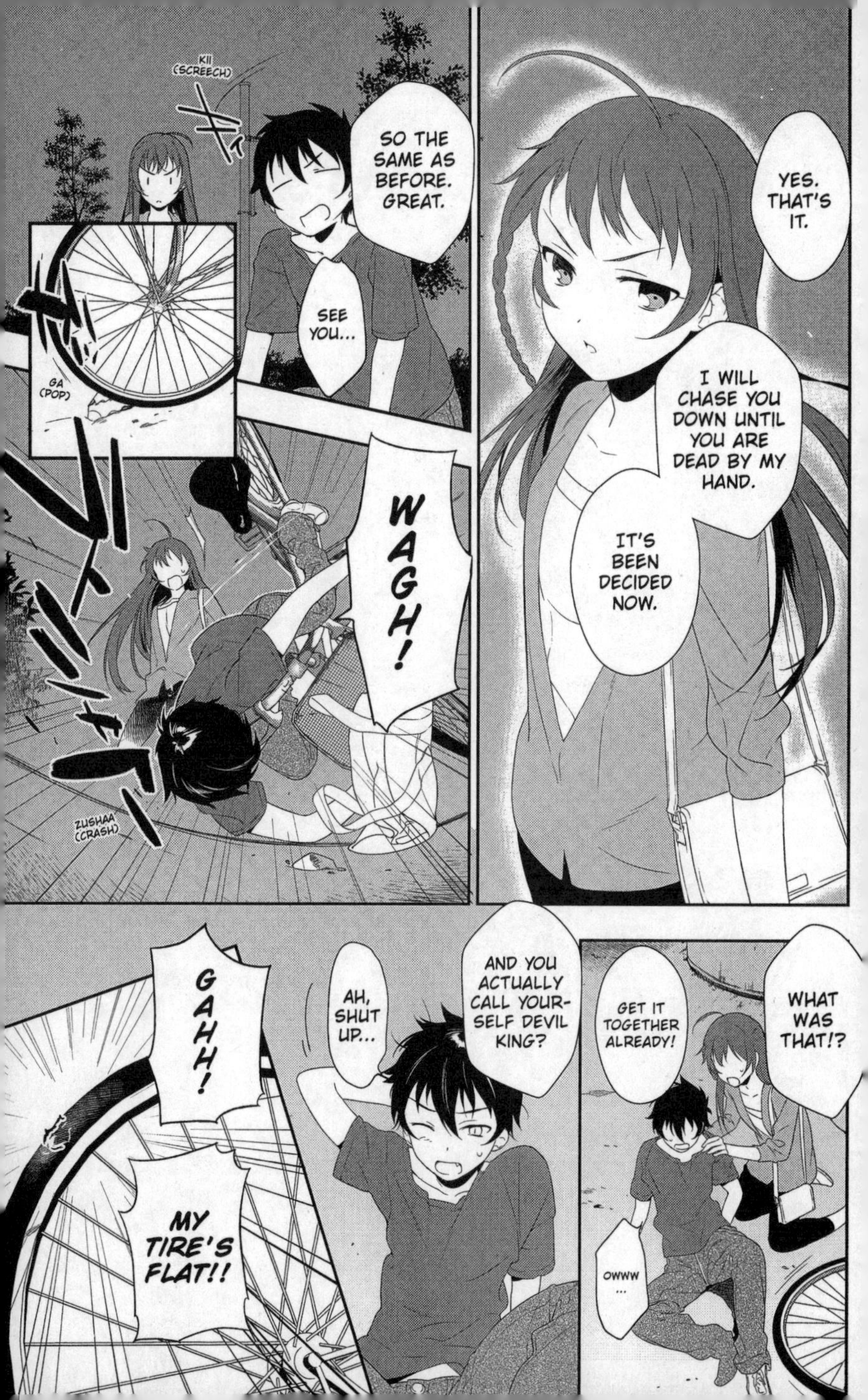
YES. THAT'S IT.
I WILL CHASE YOU DOWN UNTIL YOU ARE DEAD BY MY HAND.
IT'S BEEN DECIDED NOW.
SO THE SAME AS BEFORE. GREAT.
KII (SCREECH)
SEE YOU...
GA (POP)
WAGH!
ZUSHAA (CRASH)
WHAT WAS THAT!?
GET IT TOGETHER ALREADY!
OWWW ...
AND YOU ACTUALLY CALL YOURSELF DEVIL KING?
AH, SHUT UP...
GAHH!
MY TIRE'S FLAT!!

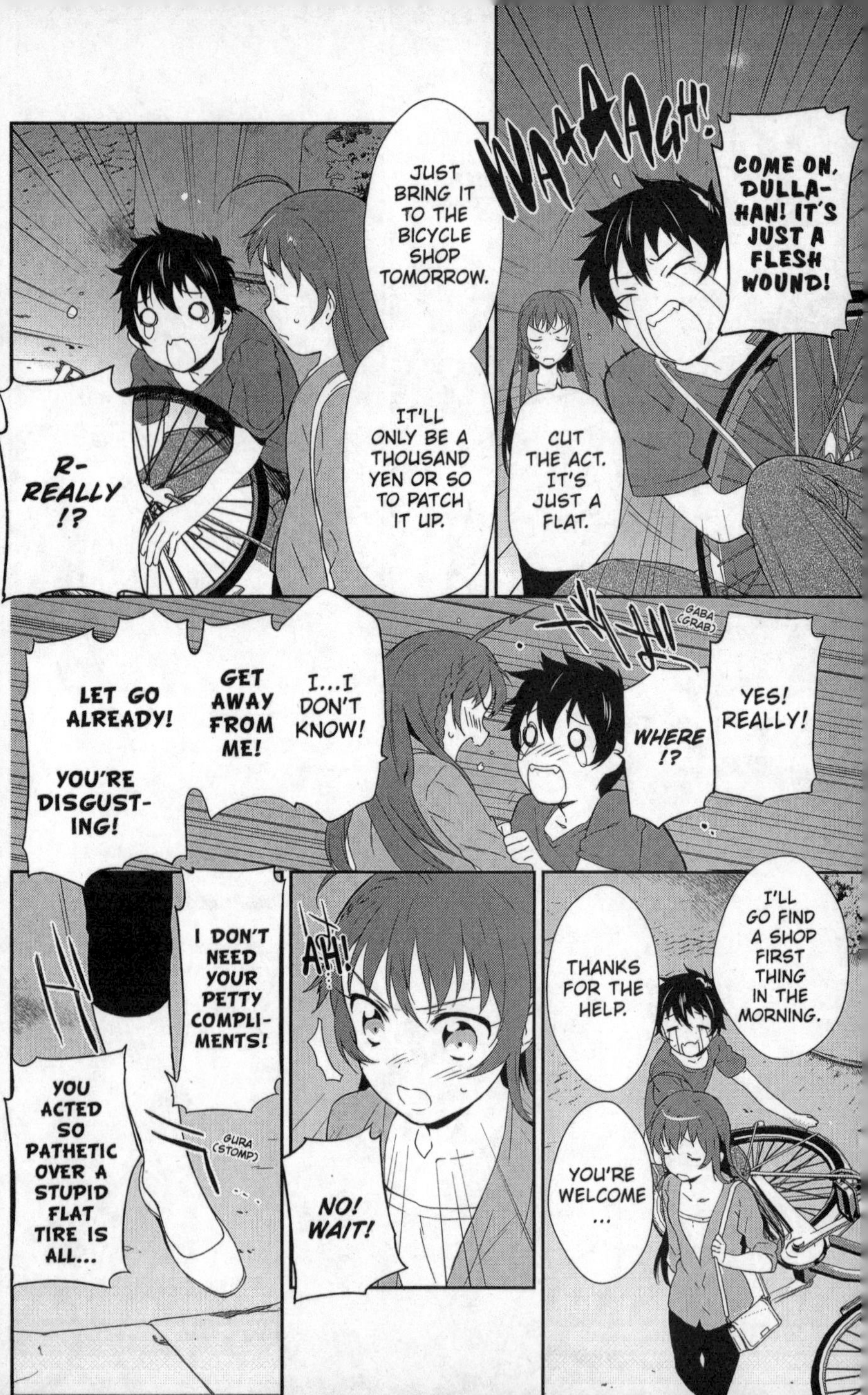
WAAAAGH!
COME ON, DULLA-HAN! IT'S JUST A FLESH WOUND!
CUT THE ACT. IT'S JUST A FLAT.
JUST BRING IT TO THE BICYCLE SHOP TOMORROW.
IT'LL ONLY BE A THOUSAND YEN OR SO TO PATCH IT UP.
R-REALLY!?
GABA (GRAB)
YES! REALLY!
WHERE!?
I...I DON'T KNOW!
GET AWAY FROM ME!
LET GO ALREADY!
YOU'RE DISGUST-ING!
I'LL GO FIND A SHOP FIRST THING IN THE MORNING.
THANKS FOR THE HELP.
YOU'RE WELCOME...
AH!
NO! WAIT!
I DON'T NEED YOUR PETTY COMPLI-MENTS!
GURA (STOMP)
YOU ACTED SO PATHETIC OVER A STUPID FLAT TIRE IS ALL...

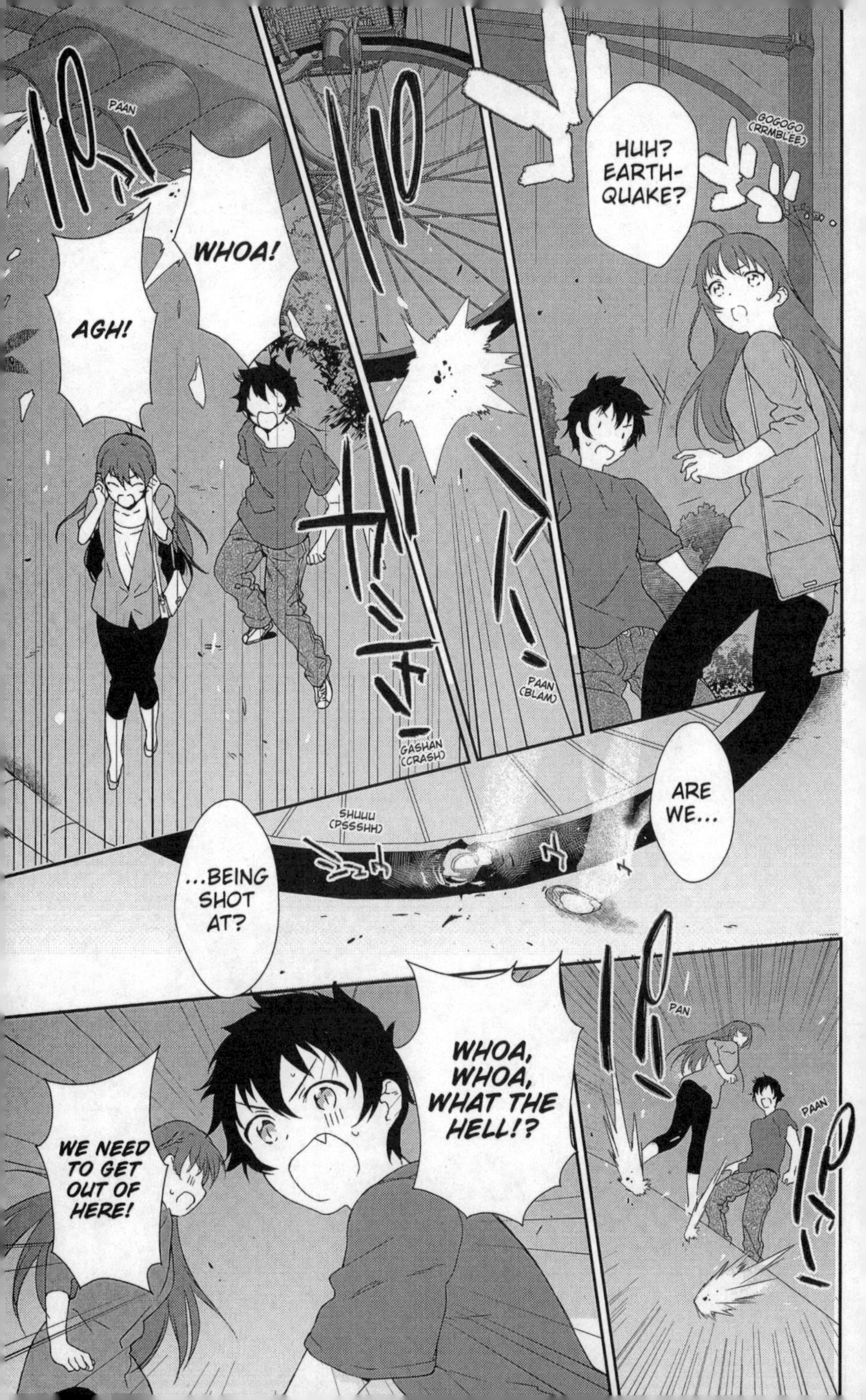
GOGOGO (RRMBLEE)
HUH? EARTH-QUAKE?
PAAN (BLAM)
GASHAN (CRASH)
PAAN
WHOA!
AGH!
ARE WE...
SHUUU (PSSSHH)
...BEING SHOT AT?
PAAN
PAN
WHOA, WHOA, WHAT THE HELL!?
WE NEED TO GET OUT OF HERE!

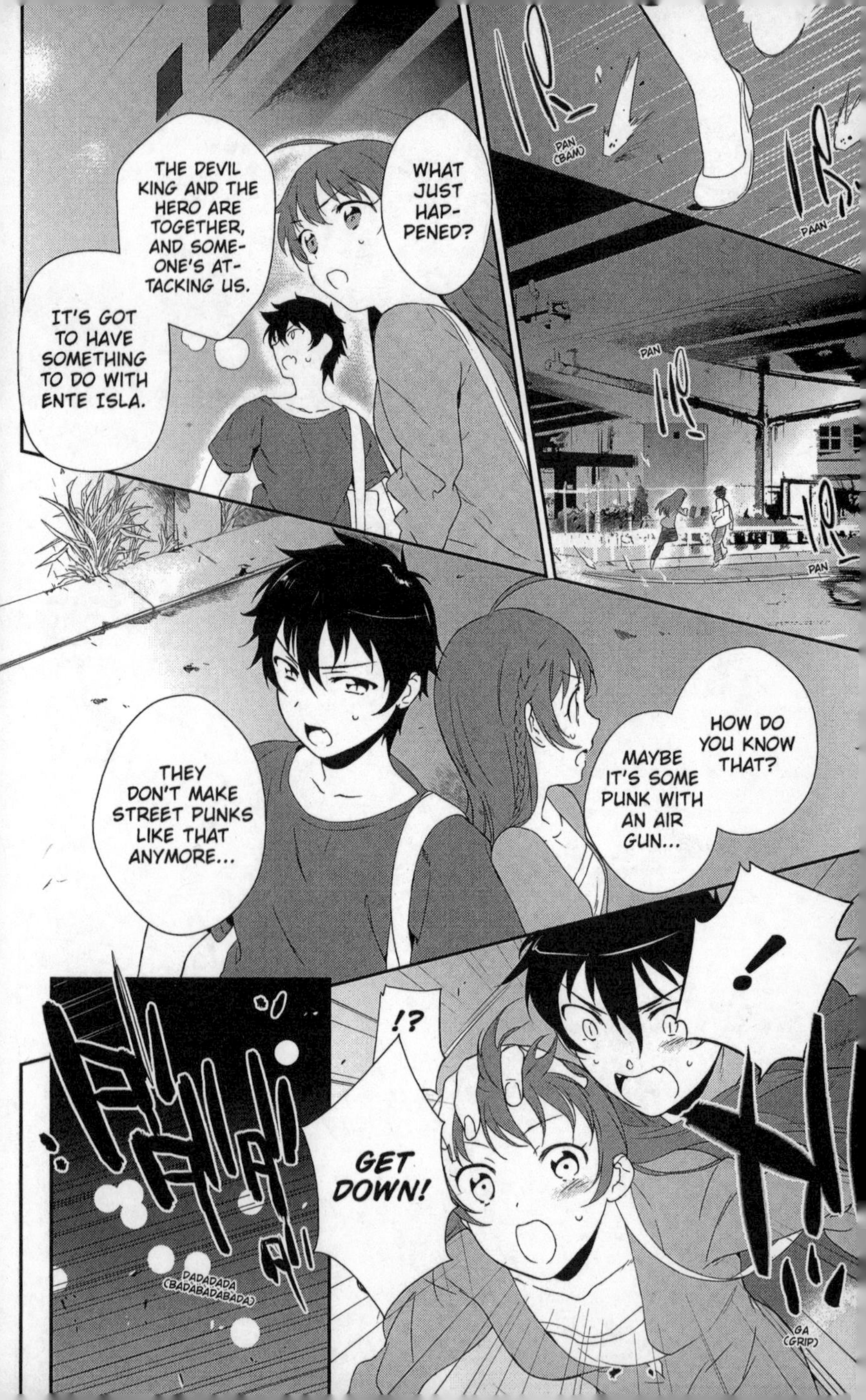
PAN (BAM)
PAAN
PAN
PAN
WHAT JUST HAP-PENED?
THE DEVIL KING AND THE HERO ARE TOGETHER, AND SOME-ONE'S AT-TACKING US.
IT'S GOT TO HAVE SOMETHING TO DO WITH ENTE ISLA.
HOW DO YOU KNOW THAT?
MAYBE IT'S SOME PUNK WITH AN AIR GUN...
THEY DON'T MAKE STREET PUNKS LIKE THAT ANYMORE...
!
GA (GRIP)
!?
GET DOWN!
DADADADA (BADABADABADA)

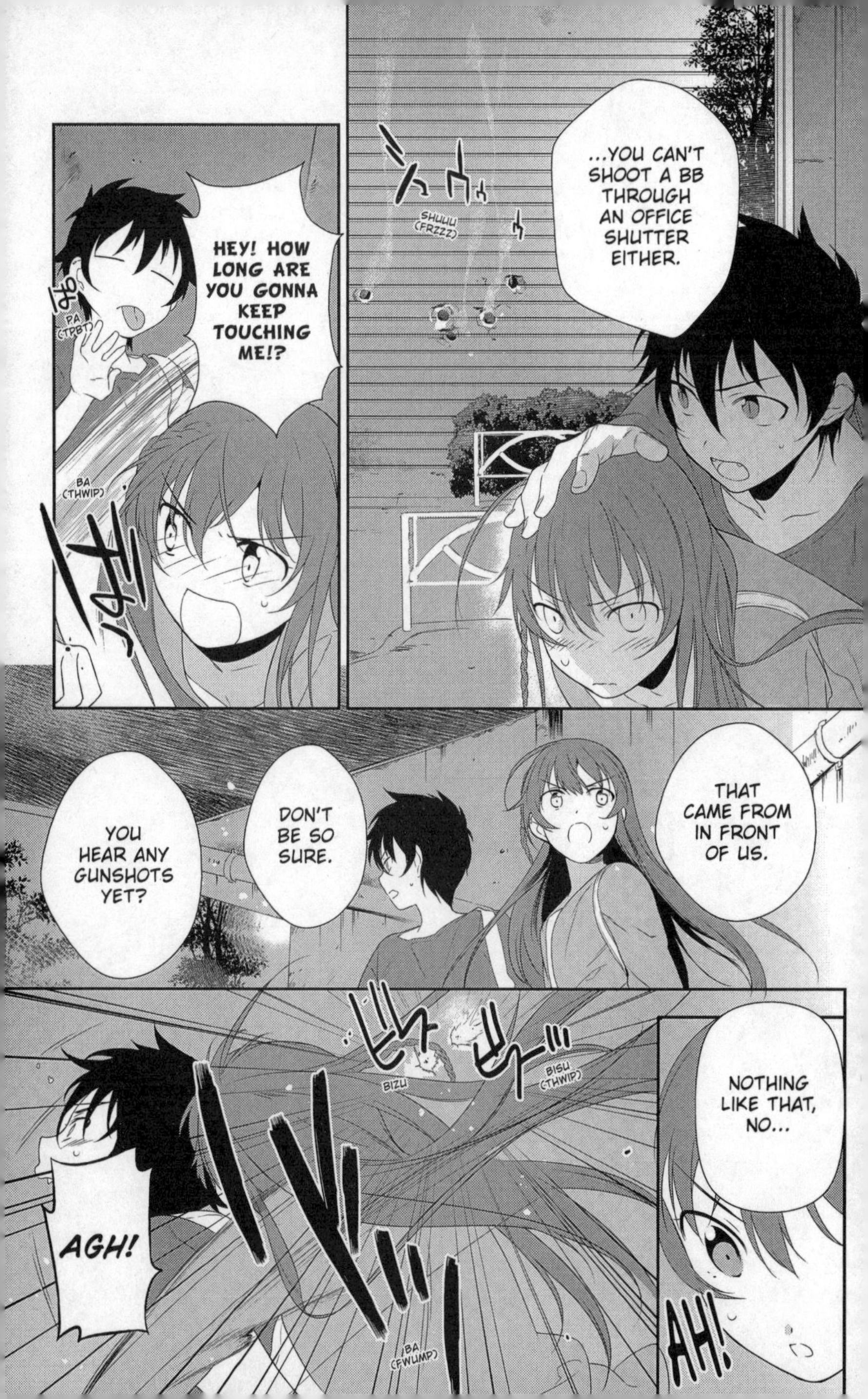
...YOU CAN'T SHOOT A BB THROUGH AN OFFICE SHUTTER EITHER.
SHUUU (FRZZZ)
HEY! HOW LONG ARE YOU GONNA KEEP TOUCHING ME!?
PA (TPBT)
BA (THWIP)
THAT CAME FROM IN FRONT OF US.
DON'T BE SO SURE.
YOU HEAR ANY GUNSHOTS YET?
NOTHING LIKE THAT, NO...
AH!
BISU (THWIP)
BIZU
BA (FWUMP)
AGH!

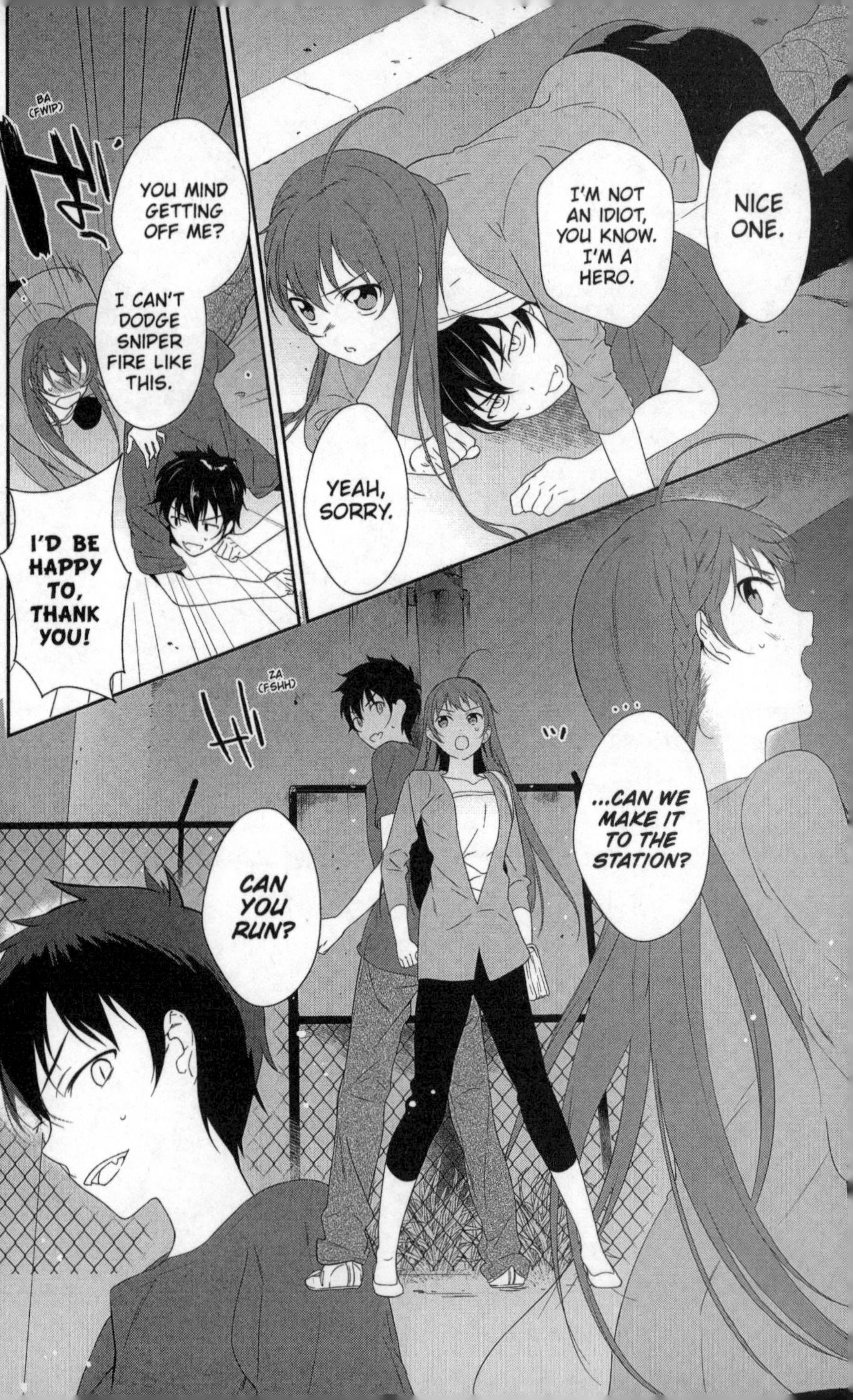
NICE ONE.
I'M NOT AN IDIOT, YOU KNOW. I'M A HERO.
YEAH, SORRY.
BA (FWIP)
YOU MIND GETTING OFF ME?
I CAN'T DODGE SNIPER FIRE LIKE THIS.
I'D BE HAPPY TO, THANK YOU!
ZA (FSHH)
...CAN WE MAKE IT TO THE STATION?
CAN YOU RUN?

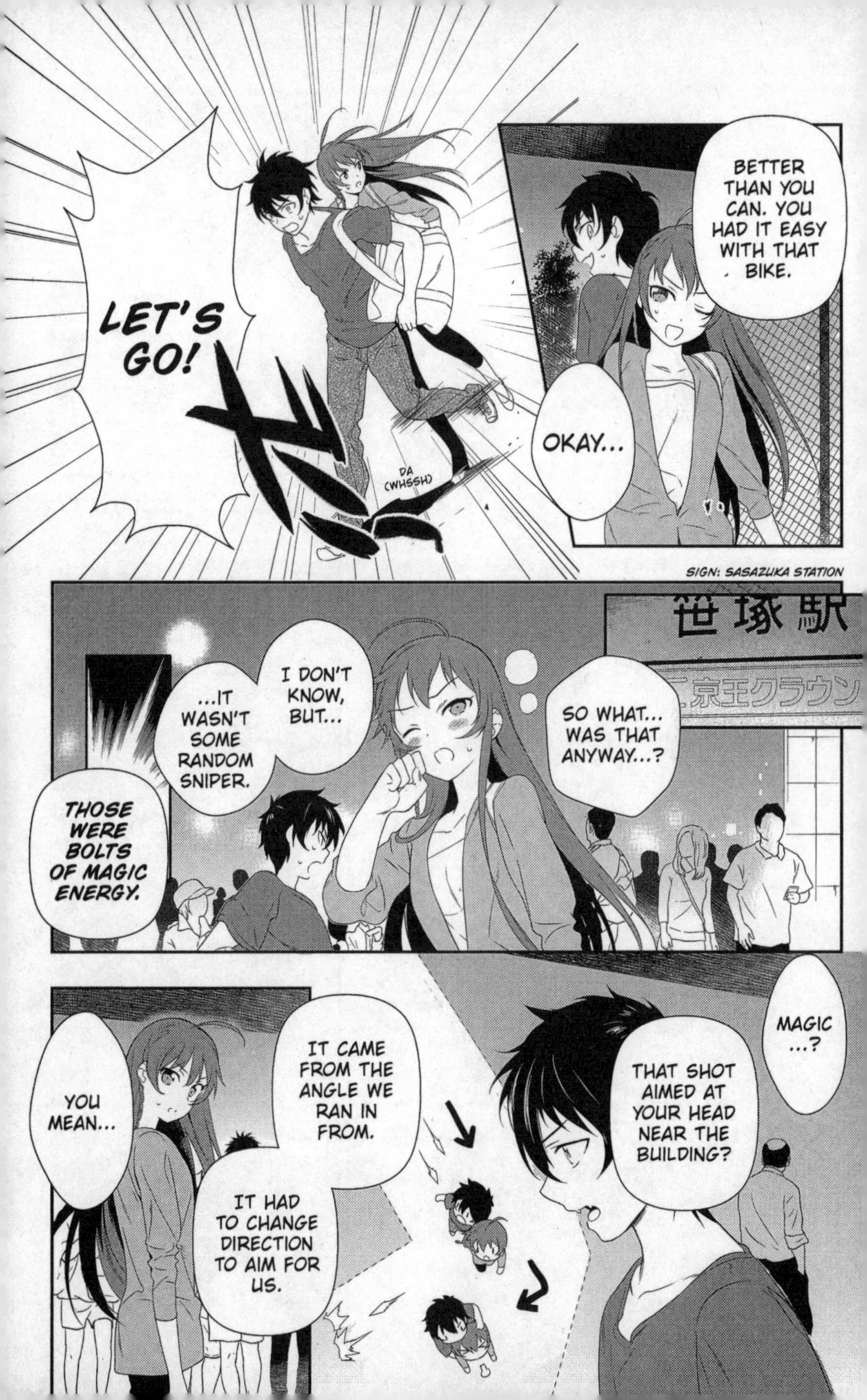
BETTER THAN YOU CAN. YOU HAD IT EASY WITH THAT BIKE.
OKAY...
LET'S GO!
DA (WHSSH)
SIGN: SASAZUKA STATION
笹塚駅
京王クラウン
SO WHAT... WAS THAT ANYWAY...?
I DON'T KNOW, BUT...
...IT WASN'T SOME RANDOM SNIPER.
THOSE WERE BOLTS OF MAGIC ENERGY.
MAGIC ...?
THAT SHOT AIMED AT YOUR HEAD NEAR THE BUILDING?
IT CAME FROM THE ANGLE WE RAN IN FROM.
YOU MEAN...
IT HAD TO CHANGE DIRECTION TO AIM FOR US.

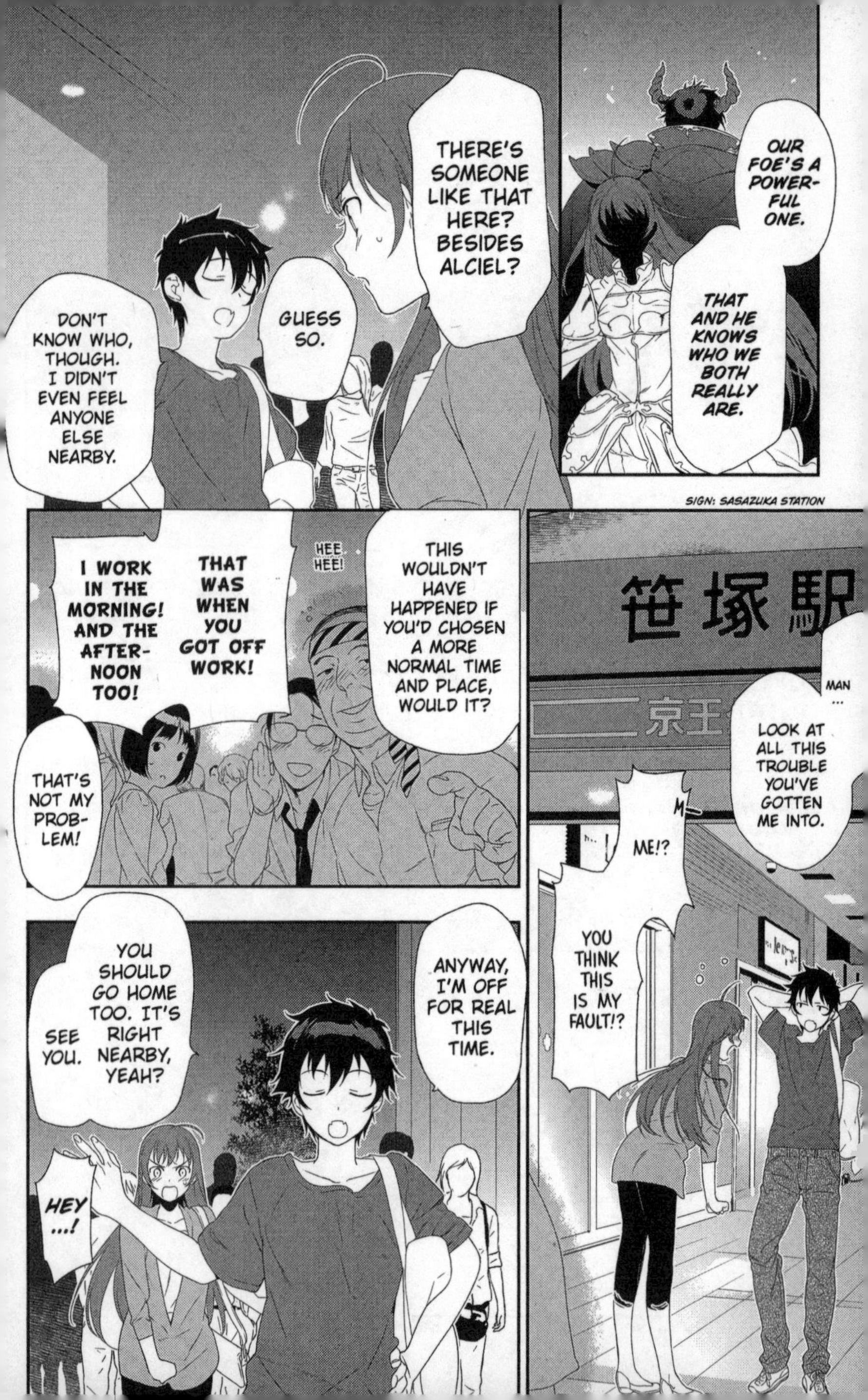
OUR FOE'S A POWER-FUL ONE.
THAT AND HE KNOWS WHO WE BOTH REALLY ARE.
THERE'S SOMEONE LIKE THAT HERE? BESIDES ALCIEL?
GUESS SO.
DON'T KNOW WHO, THOUGH. I DIDN'T EVEN FEEL ANYONE ELSE NEARBY.
SIGN: SASAZUKA STATION
笹塚駅
京王
MAN...
LOOK AT ALL THIS TROUBLE YOU'VE GOTTEN ME INTO.
M-ME!?
YOU THINK THIS IS MY FAULT!?
THIS WOULDN'T HAVE HAPPENED IF YOU'D CHOSEN A MORE NORMAL TIME AND PLACE, WOULD IT?
HEE HEE!
THAT WAS WHEN YOU GOT OFF WORK!
I WORK IN THE MORNING! AND THE AFTER-NOON TOO!
THAT'S NOT MY PROB-LEM!
ANYWAY, I'M OFF FOR REAL THIS TIME.
YOU SHOULD GO HOME TOO. IT'S RIGHT NEARBY, YEAH?
SEE YOU.
HEY...!

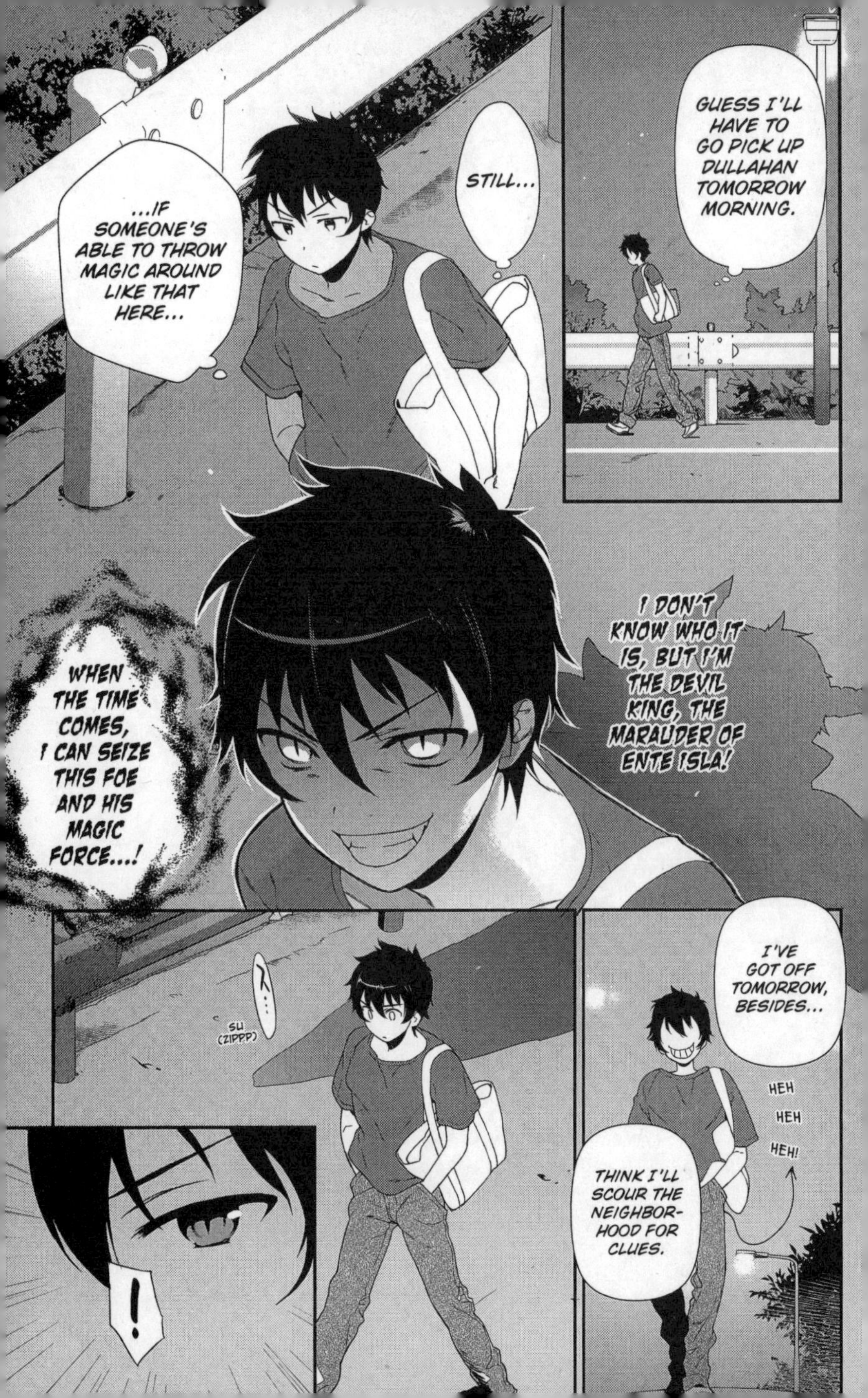
GUESS I'LL HAVE TO GO PICK UP DULLAHAN TOMORROW MORNING.
STILL...
...IF SOMEONE'S ABLE TO THROW MAGIC AROUND LIKE THAT HERE...
I DON'T KNOW WHO IT IS, BUT I'M THE DEVIL KING, THE MARAUDER OF ENTE ISLA!
WHEN THE TIME COMES, I CAN SEIZE THIS FOE AND HIS MAGIC FORCE...!
I'VE GOT OFF TOMORROW, BESIDES...
HEH HEH HEH!
THINK I'LL SCOUR THE NEIGHBOR-HOOD FOR CLUES.
ス...
SU (ZIPPP)
!

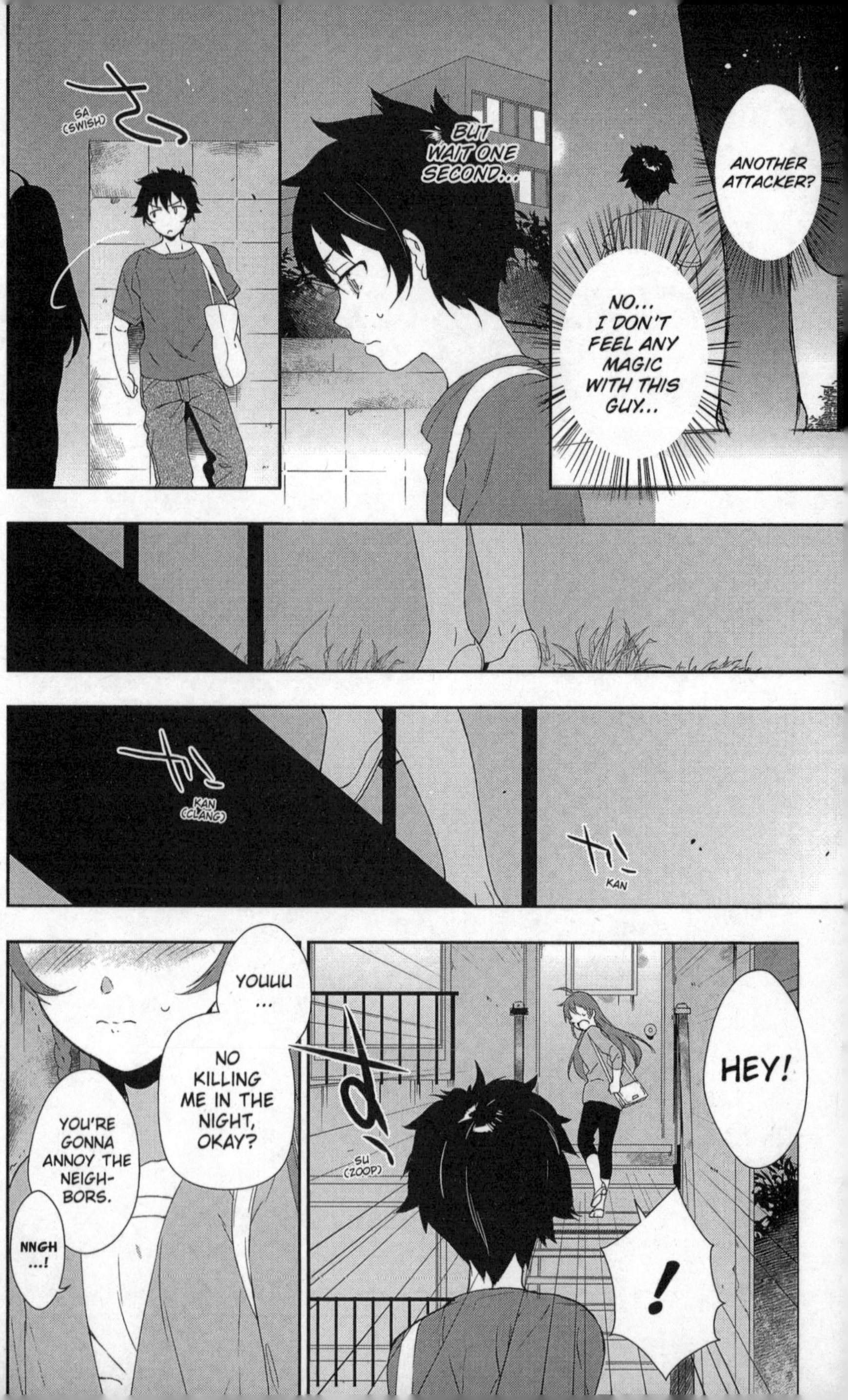
ANOTHER ATTACKER?
NO... I DON'T FEEL ANY MAGIC WITH THIS GUY...
BUT WAIT ONE SECOND...
SA (SWISH)
KAN
KAN (CLANG)
HEY!
!
SU (ZOOP)
YOUUU ...
NO KILLING ME IN THE NIGHT, OKAY?
YOU'RE GONNA ANNOY THE NEIGH-BORS.
NNGH ...!

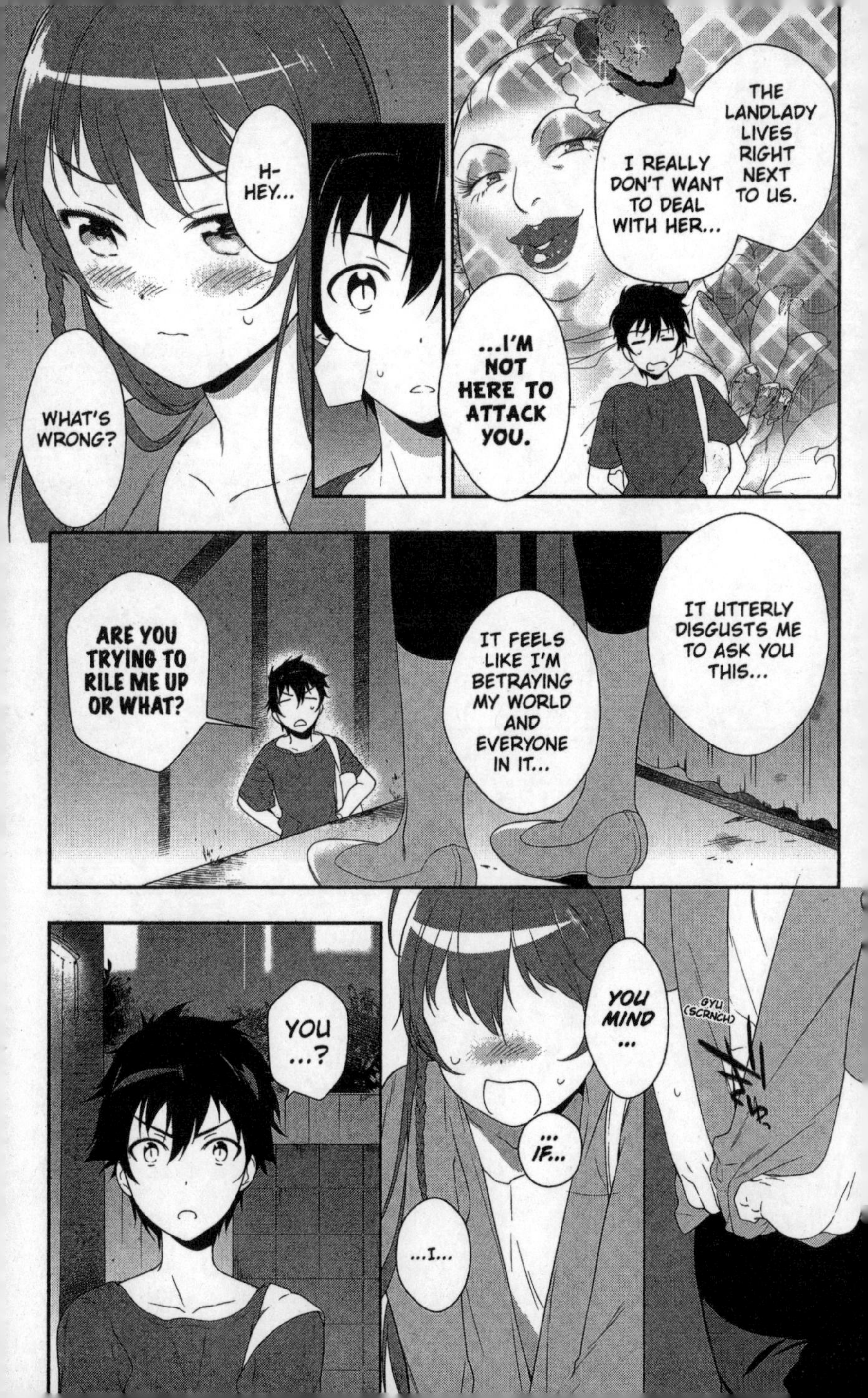
THE LANDLADY LIVES RIGHT NEXT TO US.
I REALLY DON'T WANT TO DEAL WITH HER...
...I'M NOT HERE TO ATTACK YOU.
H-HEY...
WHAT'S WRONG?
IT UTTERLY DISGUSTS ME TO ASK YOU THIS...
IT FEELS LIKE I'M BETRAYING MY WORLD AND EVERYONE IN IT...
ARE YOU TRYING TO RILE ME UP OR WHAT?
GYU (SCRNCH)
YOU MIND ...
... IF...
...I...
YOU ...?

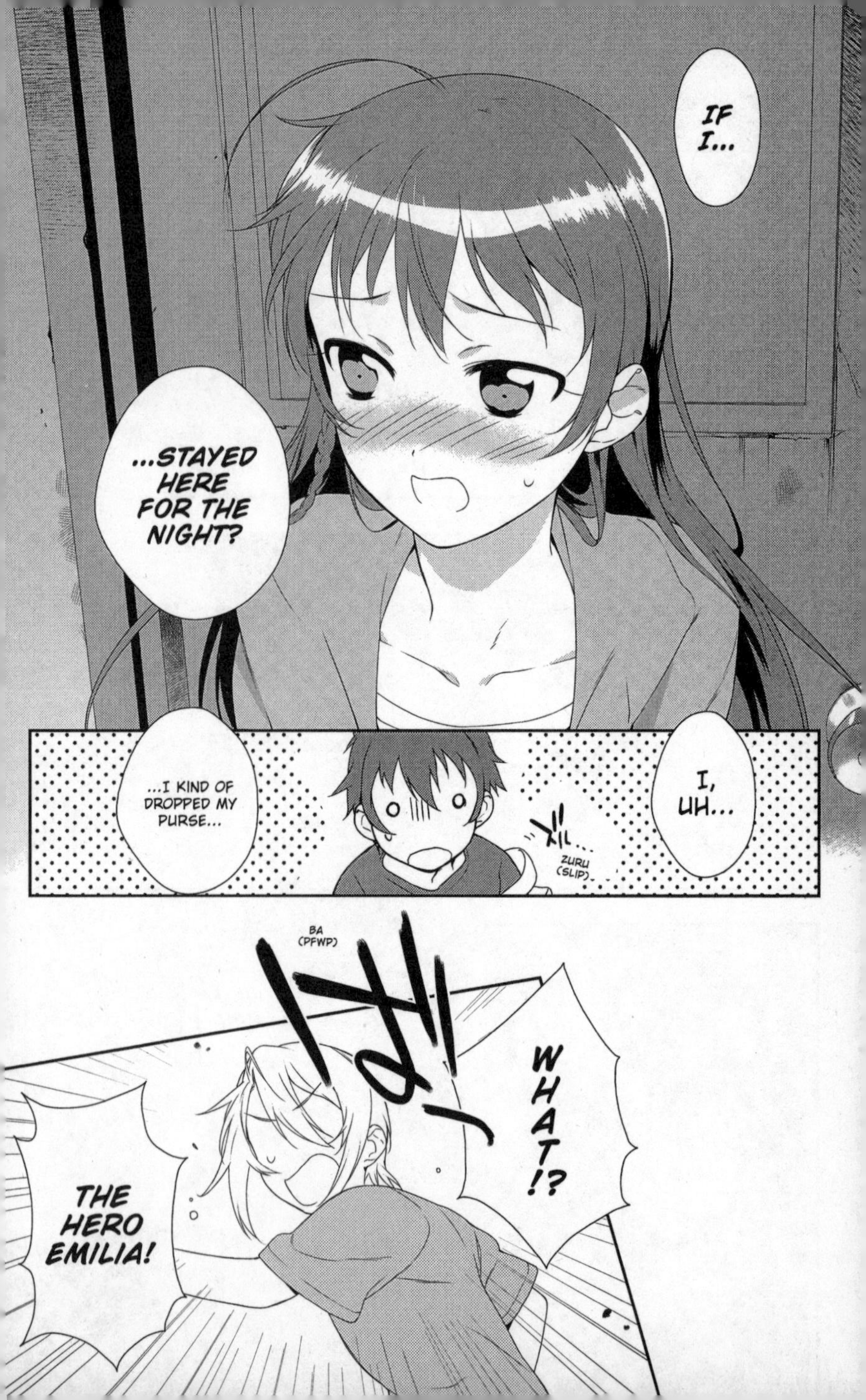
IF I...
...STAYED HERE FOR THE NIGHT?
I, UH...
ZURU (SLIP)
...I KIND OF DROPPED MY PURSE...
BA (PFWP)
WHAT!?
THE HERO EMILIA!

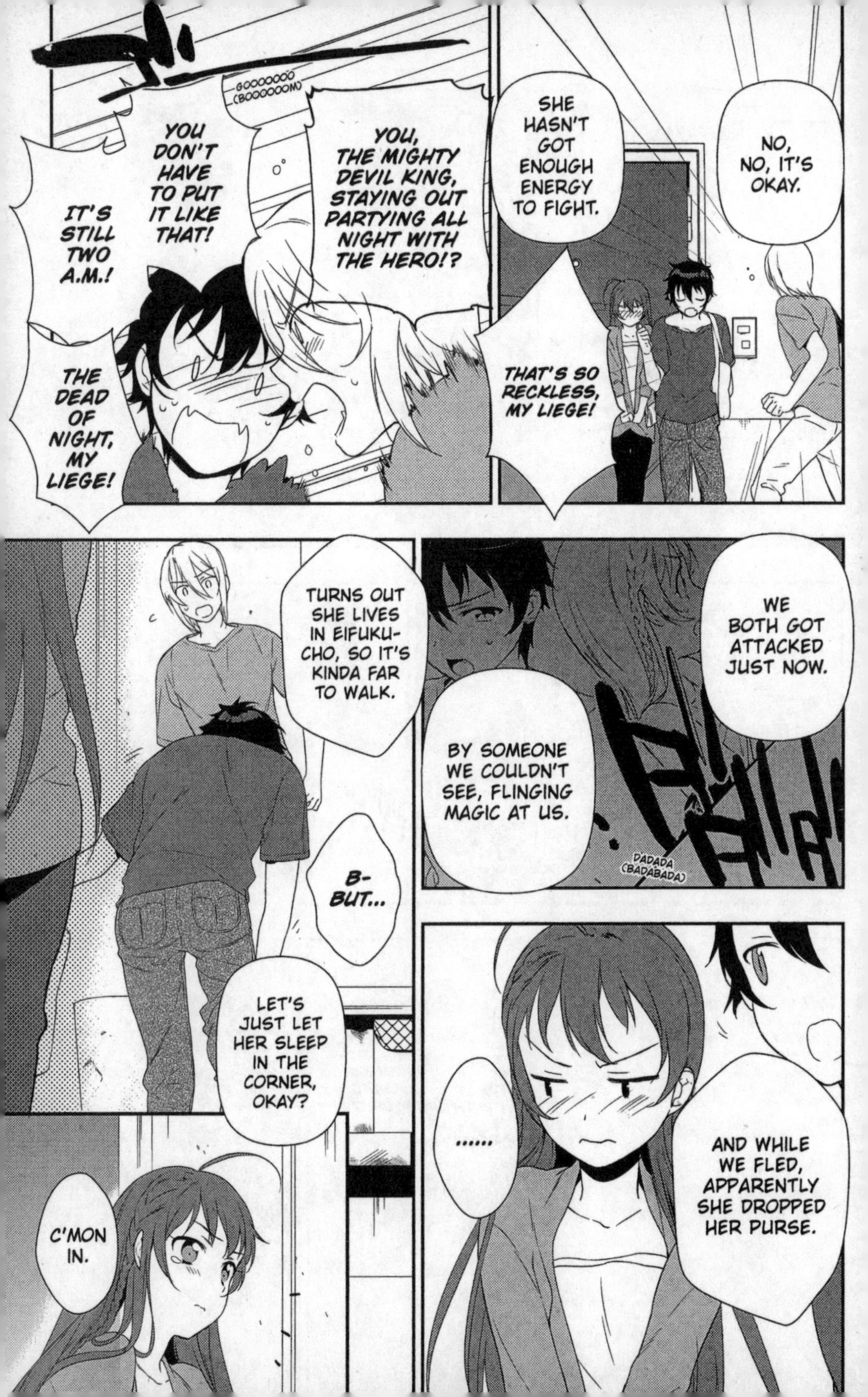
NO, NO, IT'S OKAY.
SHE HASN'T GOT ENOUGH ENERGY TO FIGHT.
THAT'S SO RECKLESS, MY LIEGE!
GOOOOOOOO (BOOOOOOOM)
YOU, THE MIGHTY DEVIL KING, STAYING OUT PARTYING ALL NIGHT WITH THE HERO!?
YOU DON'T HAVE TO PUT IT LIKE THAT!
IT'S STILL TWO A.M.!
THE DEAD OF NIGHT, MY LIEGE!
WE BOTH GOT ATTACKED JUST NOW.
BY SOMEONE WE COULDN'T SEE, FLINGING MAGIC AT US.
DADADA (BADABADA)
AND WHILE WE FLED, APPARENTLY SHE DROPPED HER PURSE.
......
TURNS OUT SHE LIVES IN EIFUKU-CHO, SO IT'S KINDA FAR TO WALK.
B-BUT...
LET'S JUST LET HER SLEEP IN THE CORNER, OKAY?
C'MON IN.

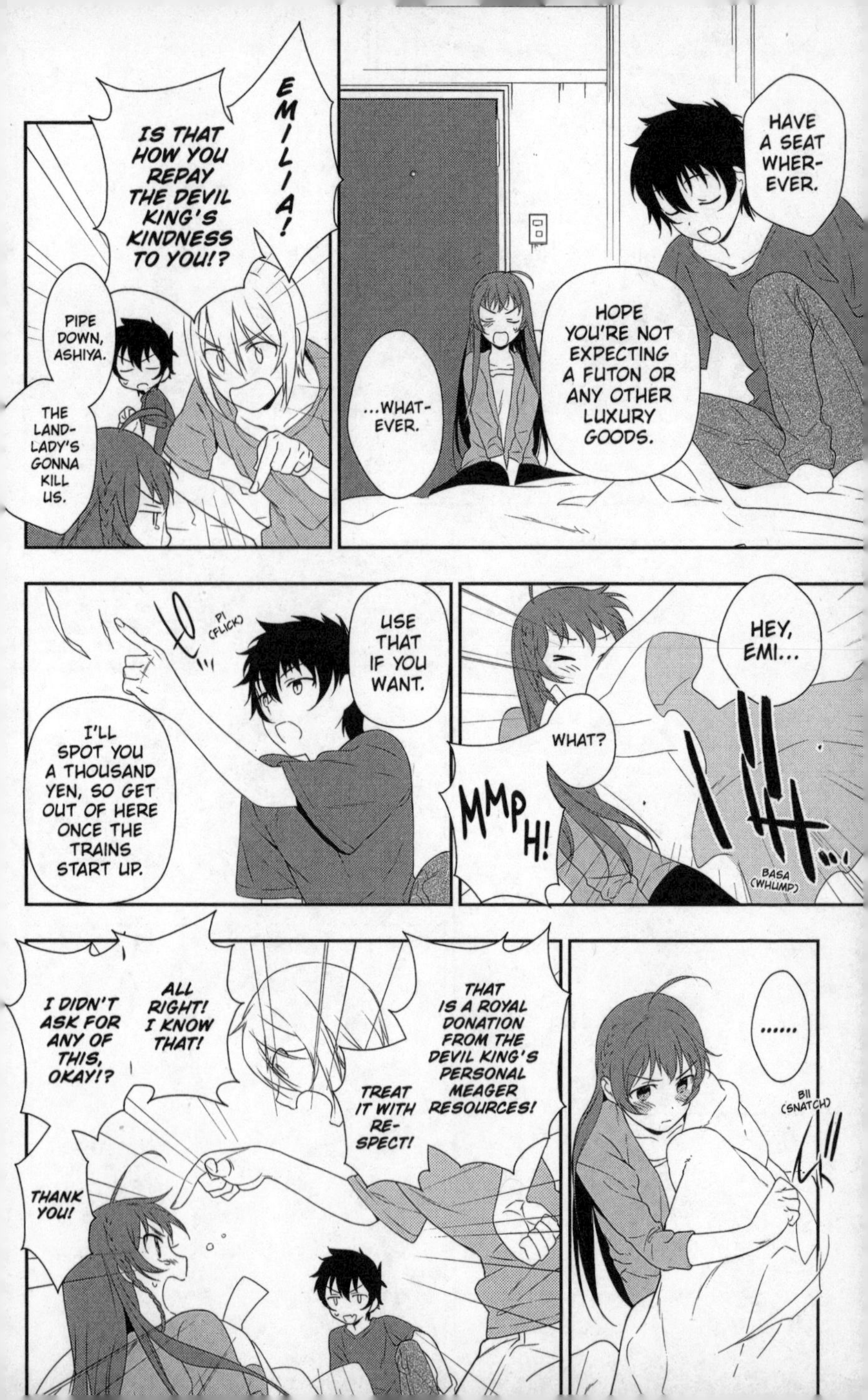
HAVE A SEAT WHEREVER.
HOPE YOU'RE NOT EXPECTING A FUTON OR ANY OTHER LUXURY GOODS.
...WHATEVER.
EMILIA!
IS THAT HOW YOU REPAY THE DEVIL KING'S KINDNESS TO YOU!?
PIPE DOWN, ASHIYA.
THE LANDLADY'S GONNA KILL US.
HEY, EMI...
WHAT?
BASA (WHUMP)
MMPH!
PI (FLICK)
USE THAT IF YOU WANT.
I'LL SPOT YOU A THOUSAND YEN, SO GET OUT OF HERE ONCE THE TRAINS START UP.
......
BII (SNATCH)
THAT IS A ROYAL DONATION FROM THE DEVIL KING'S PERSONAL MEAGER RESOURCES!
TREAT IT WITH RESPECT!
ALL RIGHT! I KNOW THAT!
I DIDN'T ASK FOR ANY OF THIS, OKAY!?
THANK YOU!

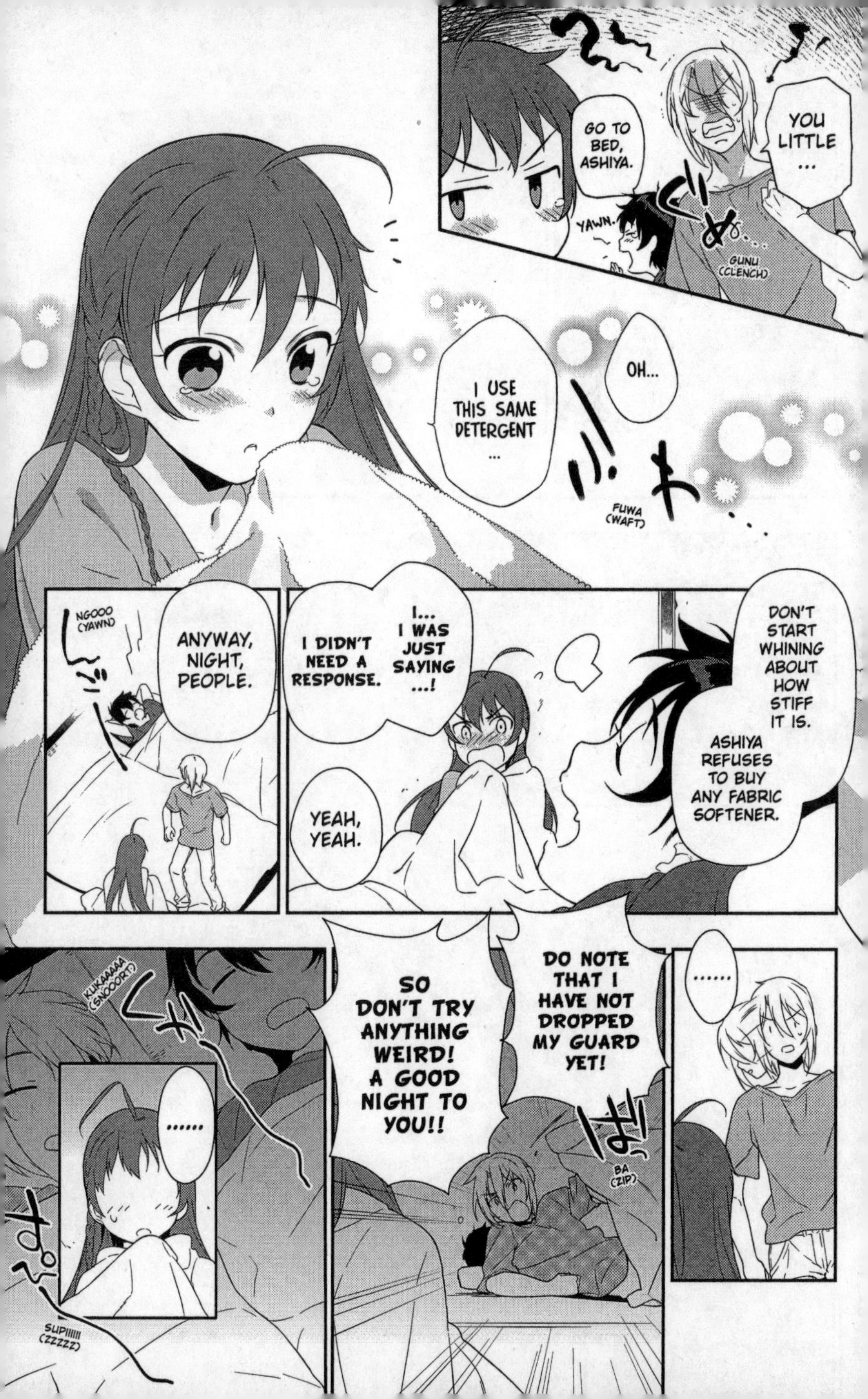
YOU LITTLE ...
GO TO BED, ASHIYA.
GUNU (CLENCH)
YAWN.
OH...
I USE THIS SAME DETERGENT ...
FUWA (WAFT)
DON'T START WHINING ABOUT HOW STIFF IT IS.
ASHIYA REFUSES TO BUY ANY FABRIC SOFTENER.
I... I WAS JUST SAYING ...!
I DIDN'T NEED A RESPONSE.
YEAH, YEAH.
ANYWAY, NIGHT, PEOPLE.
NGOOO (YAWN)
......
DO NOTE THAT I HAVE NOT DROPPED MY GUARD YET!
SO DON'T TRY ANYTHING WEIRD! A GOOD NIGHT TO YOU!!
BA (ZIP)
KUKAAAAA (SNOOORT)
......
SUPIIIII (ZZZZZ)

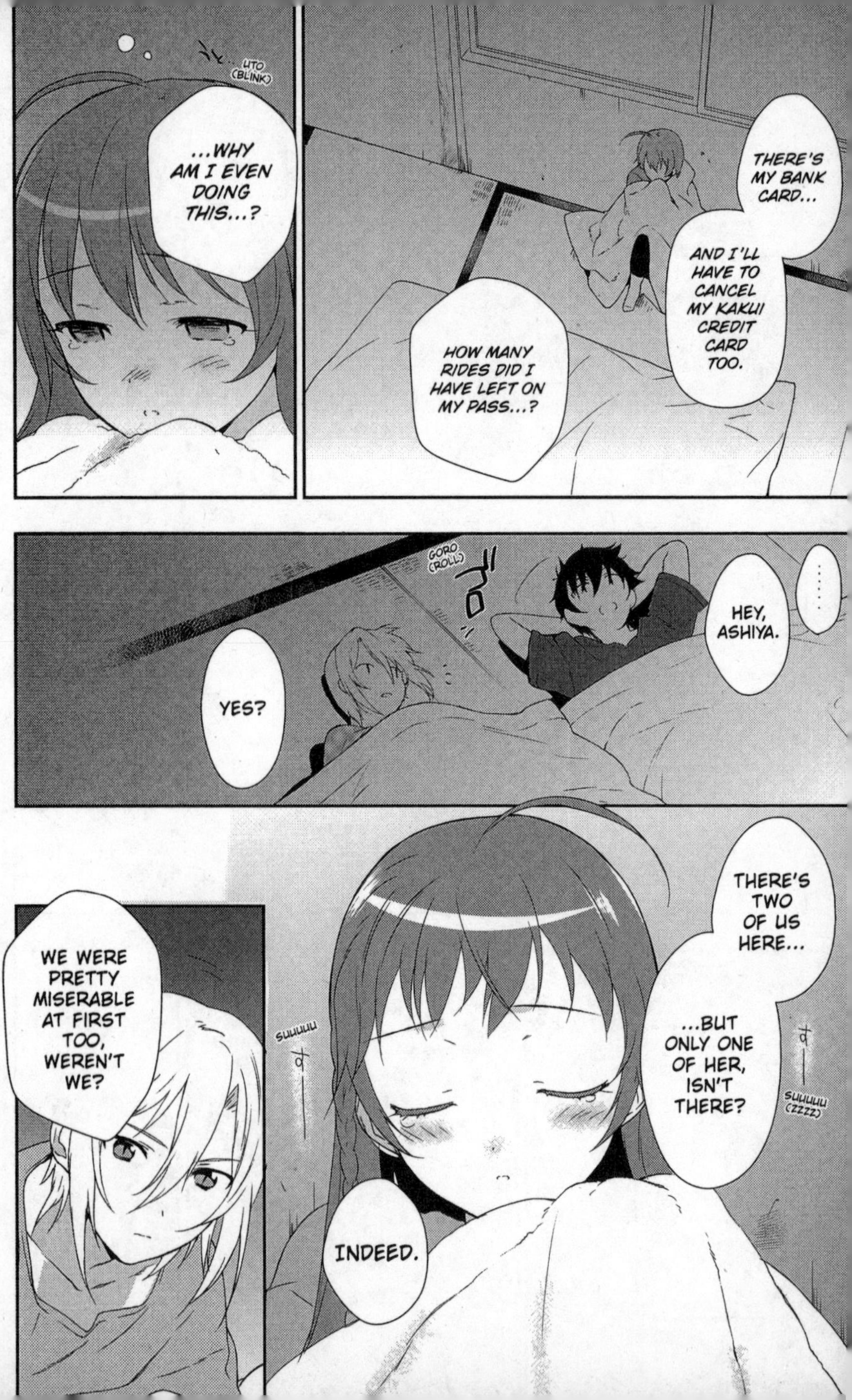
THERE'S MY BANK CARD...
AND I'LL HAVE TO CANCEL MY KAKUI CREDIT CARD TOO.
HOW MANY RIDES DID I HAVE LEFT ON MY PASS...?
UTO (BLINK)
...WHY AM I EVEN DOING THIS...?
......
HEY, ASHIYA.
GORO (ROLL)
YES?
THERE'S TWO OF US HERE...
...BUT ONLY ONE OF HER, ISN'T THERE?
SUUUUU (ZZZZ)
WE WERE PRETTY MISERABLE AT FIRST TOO, WEREN'T WE?
SUUUUU
INDEED.

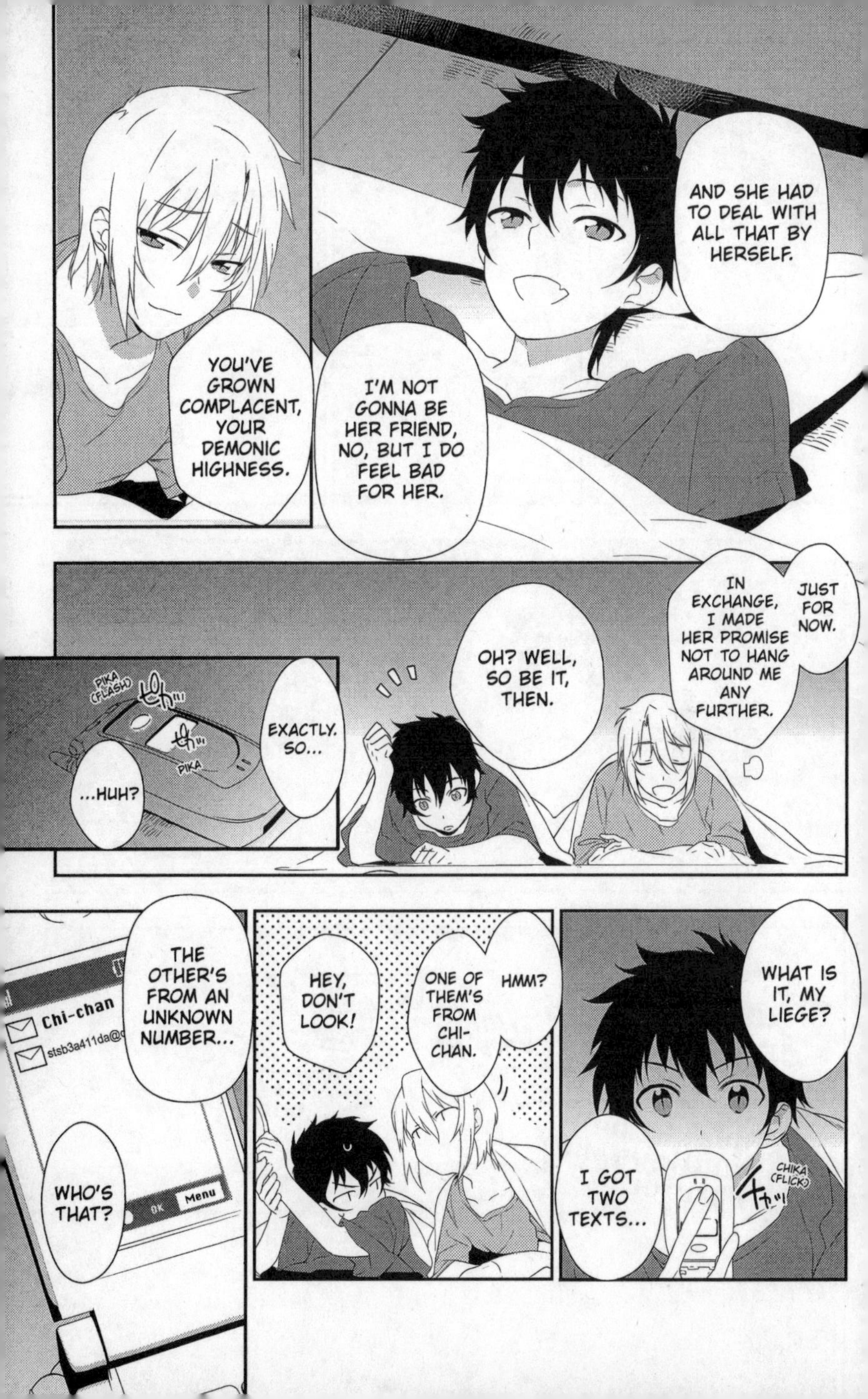
AND SHE HAD TO DEAL WITH ALL THAT BY HERSELF.
I'M NOT GONNA BE HER FRIEND, NO, BUT I DO FEEL BAD FOR HER.
YOU'VE GROWN COMPLACENT, YOUR DEMONIC HIGHNESS.
IN EXCHANGE, I MADE HER PROMISE NOT TO HANG AROUND ME ANY FURTHER.
JUST FOR NOW.
OH? WELL, SO BE IT, THEN.
EXACTLY. SO...
PIKA (FLASH)
PIKA
...HUH?
WHAT IS IT, MY LIEGE?
I GOT TWO TEXTS...
CHIKA (FLICK)
HMM?
ONE OF THEM'S FROM CHI-CHAN.
HEY, DON'T LOOK!
THE OTHER'S FROM AN UNKNOWN NUMBER...
Chi-chan
stsb3a411da@
OK
Menu
WHO'S THAT?

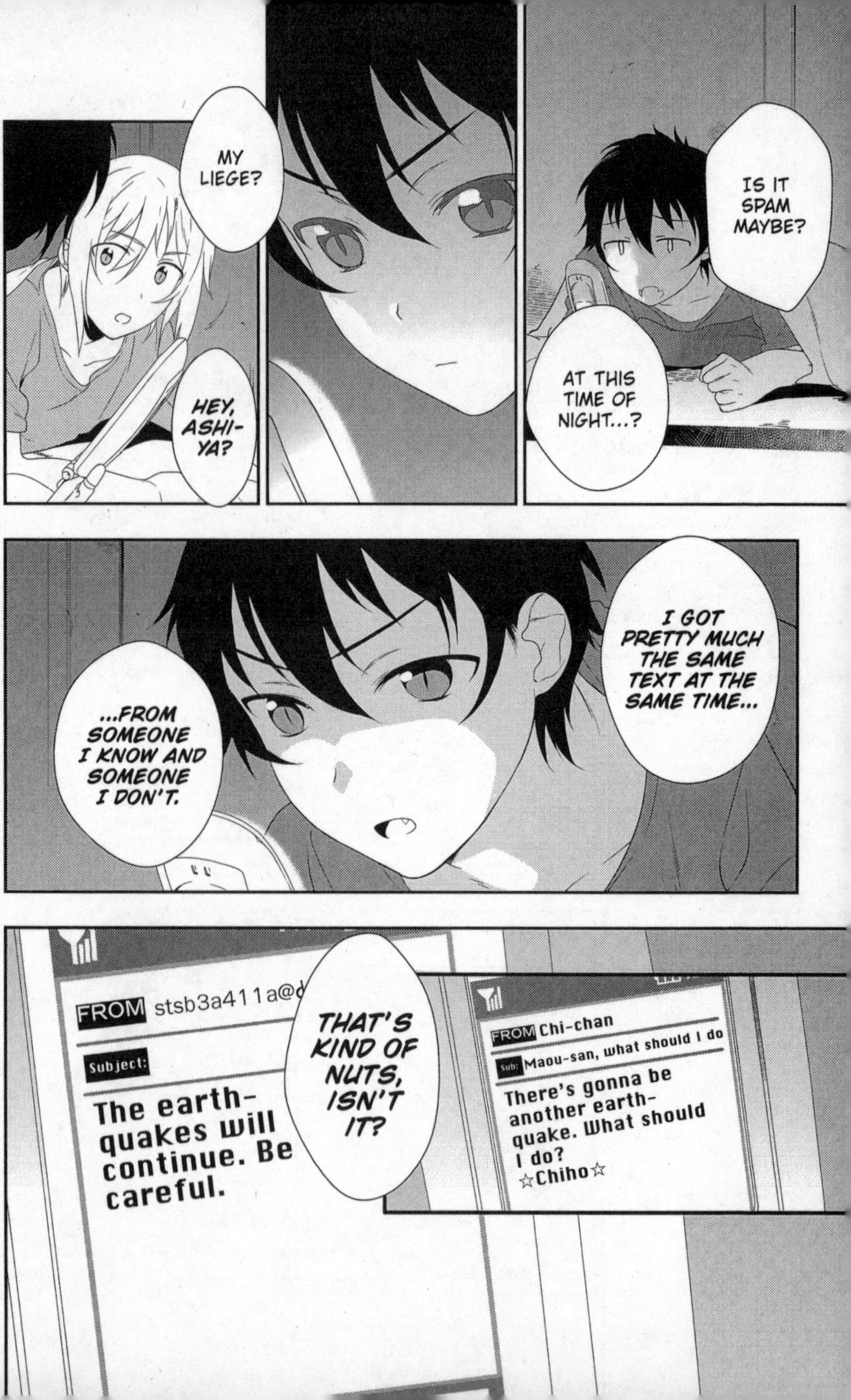
IS IT SPAM MAYBE?
AT THIS TIME OF NIGHT...?
MY LIEGE?
HEY, ASHI-YA?
I GOT PRETTY MUCH THE SAME TEXT AT THE SAME TIME...
...FROM SOMEONE I KNOW AND SOMEONE I DON'T.
FROM Chi-chan
Sub: Maou-san, what should I do
There's gonna be another earth-quake. What should I do?
☆Chiho☆
THAT'S KIND OF NUTS, ISN'T IT?
FROM stsb3a411a@
Subject:
The earth-quakes will continue. Be careful.

Kisaki
Mayumi

THE DEVIL IS A PART-TIMER!

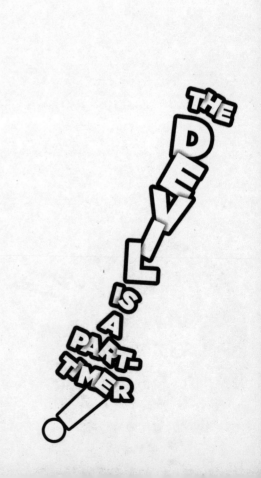

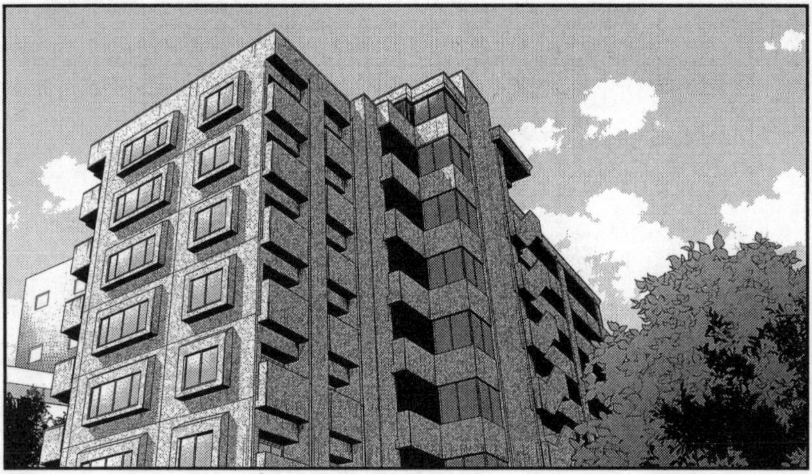

CHAPTER 3: THE DEVIL GOES ON A DATE WITH THIS GIRL FROM WORK

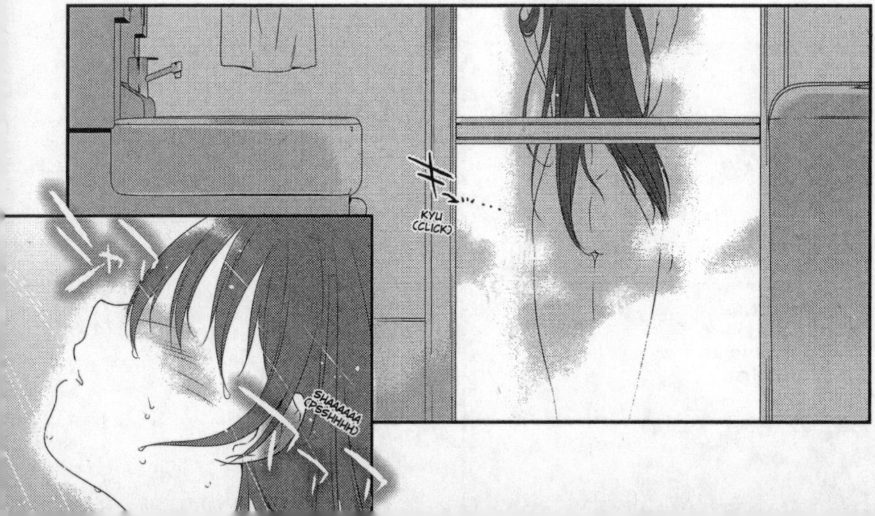
KYU
(CLICK)
SHAAAAAA
(PSSHHHH)

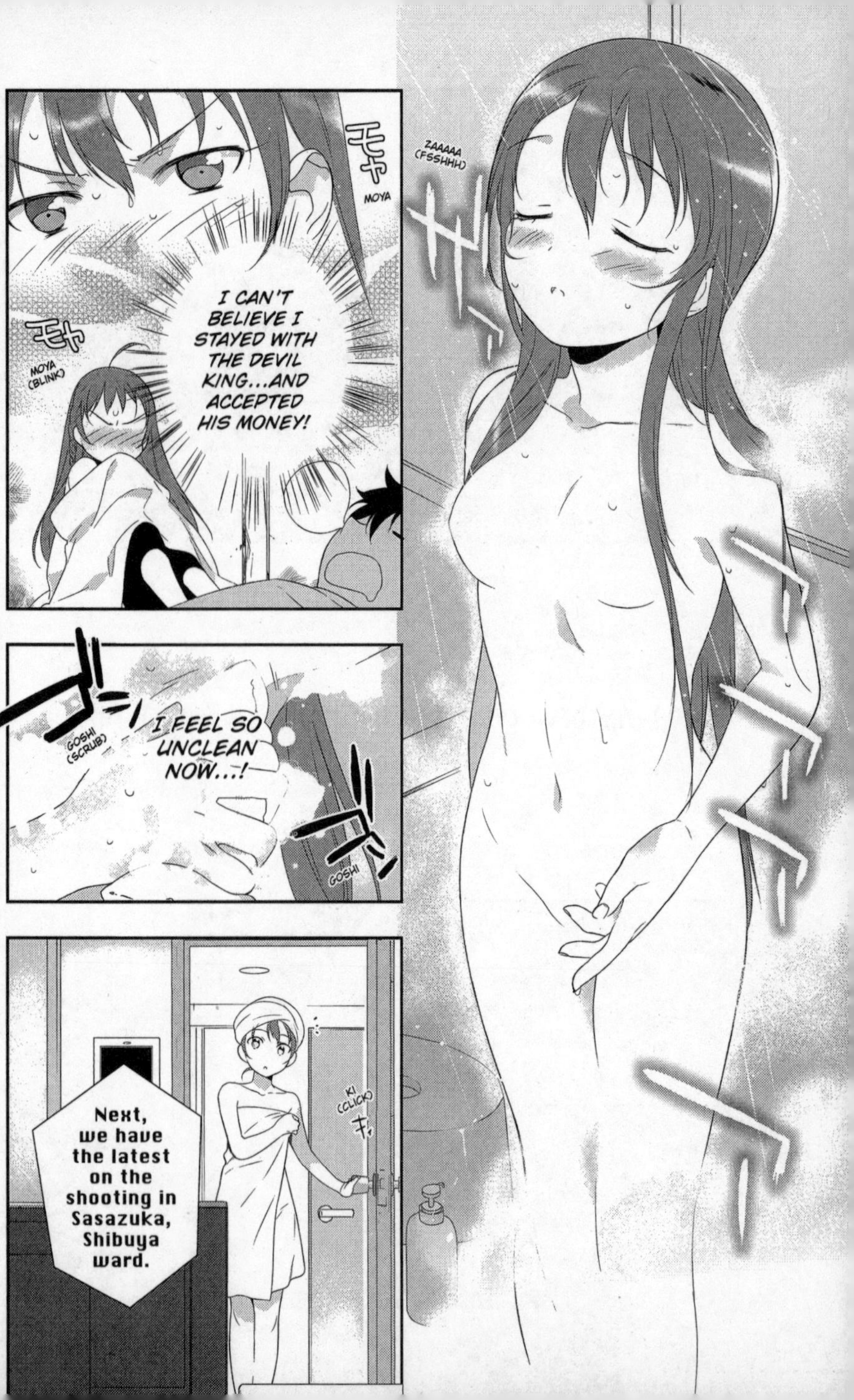
ZAAAAA (FSSHHH)
MOYA
I CAN'T BELIEVE I STAYED WITH THE DEVIL KING...AND ACCEPTED HIS MONEY!
MOYA (BLINK)
GOSHI (SCRUB)
I FEEL SO UNCLEAN NOW...!
GOSHI
KI (CLICK)
Next, we have the latest on the shooting in Sasazuka, Shibuya ward.

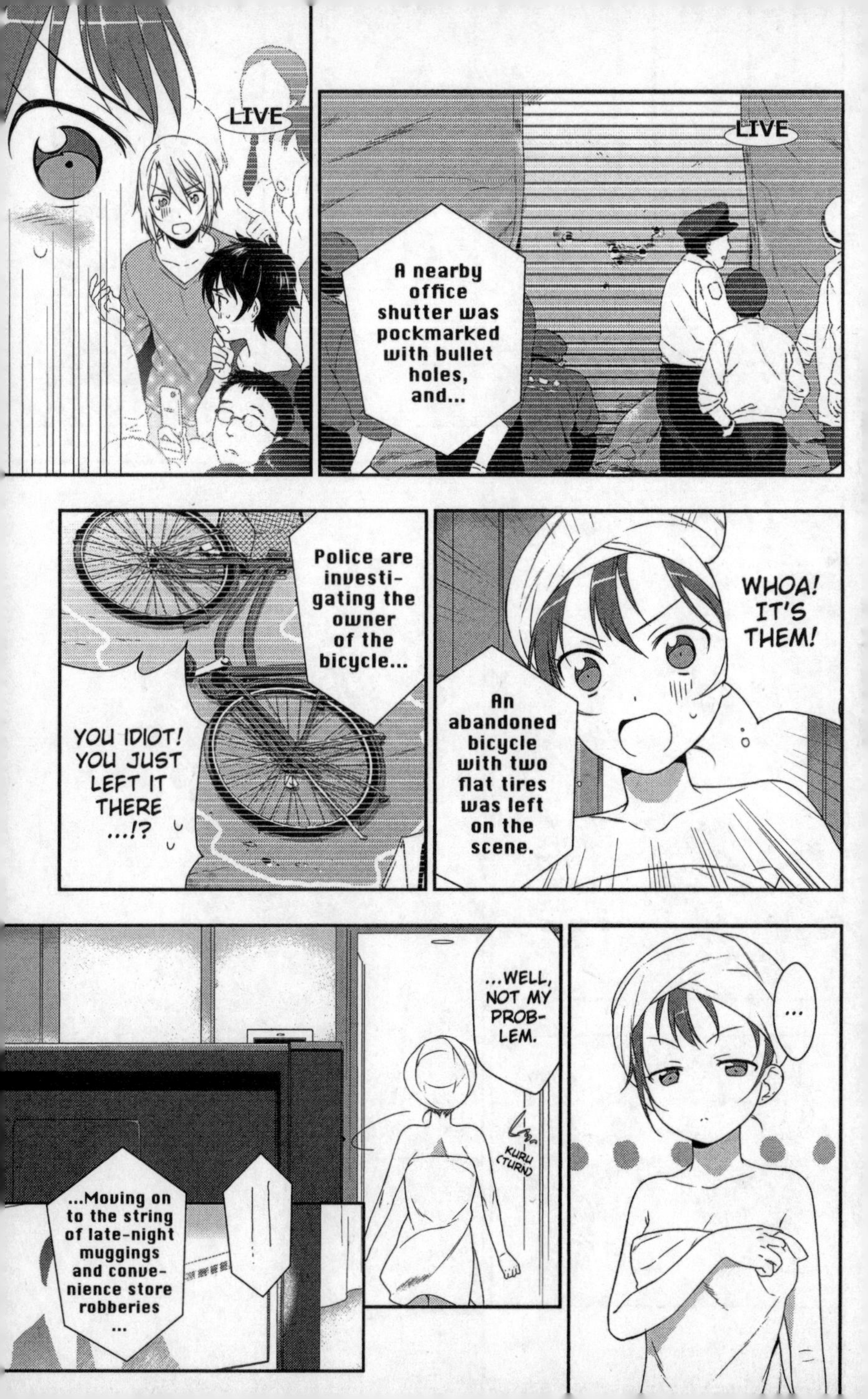
LIVE
A nearby office shutter was pockmarked with bullet holes, and...
LIVE
WHOA! IT'S THEM!
An abandoned bicycle with two flat tires was left on the scene.
Police are investi-gating the owner of the bicycle...
YOU IDIOT! YOU JUST LEFT IT THERE ...!?
...
...WELL, NOT MY PROB-LEM.
KURU (TURN)
...
...Moving on to the string of late-night muggings and conve-nience store robberies ...

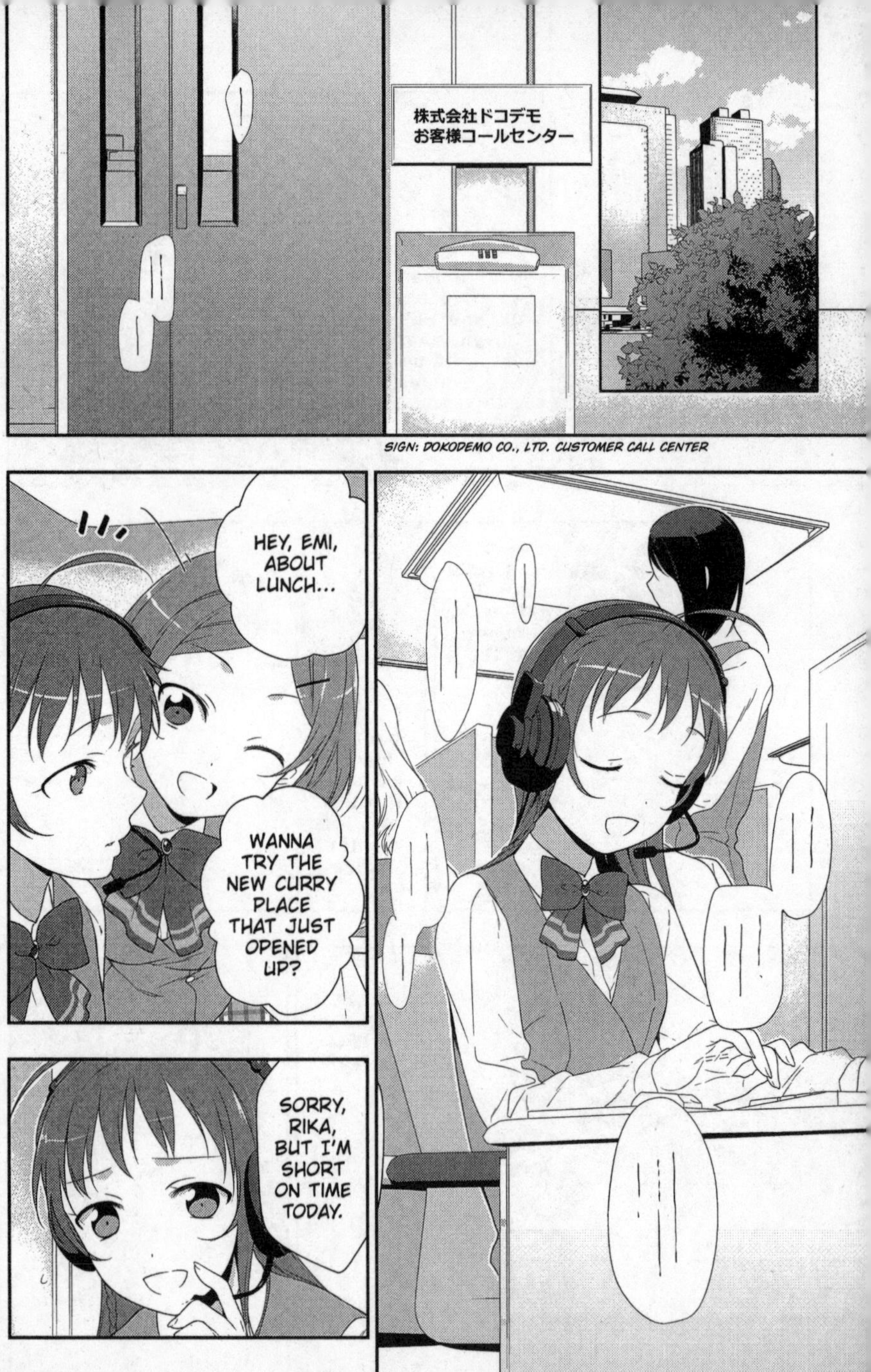
株式会社ドコデモ
お客様コールセンター
SIGN: DOKODEMO CO., LTD. CUSTOMER CALL CENTER
HEY, EMI, ABOUT LUNCH...
WANNA TRY THE NEW CURRY PLACE THAT JUST OPENED UP?
SORRY, RIKA, BUT I'M SHORT ON TIME TODAY.

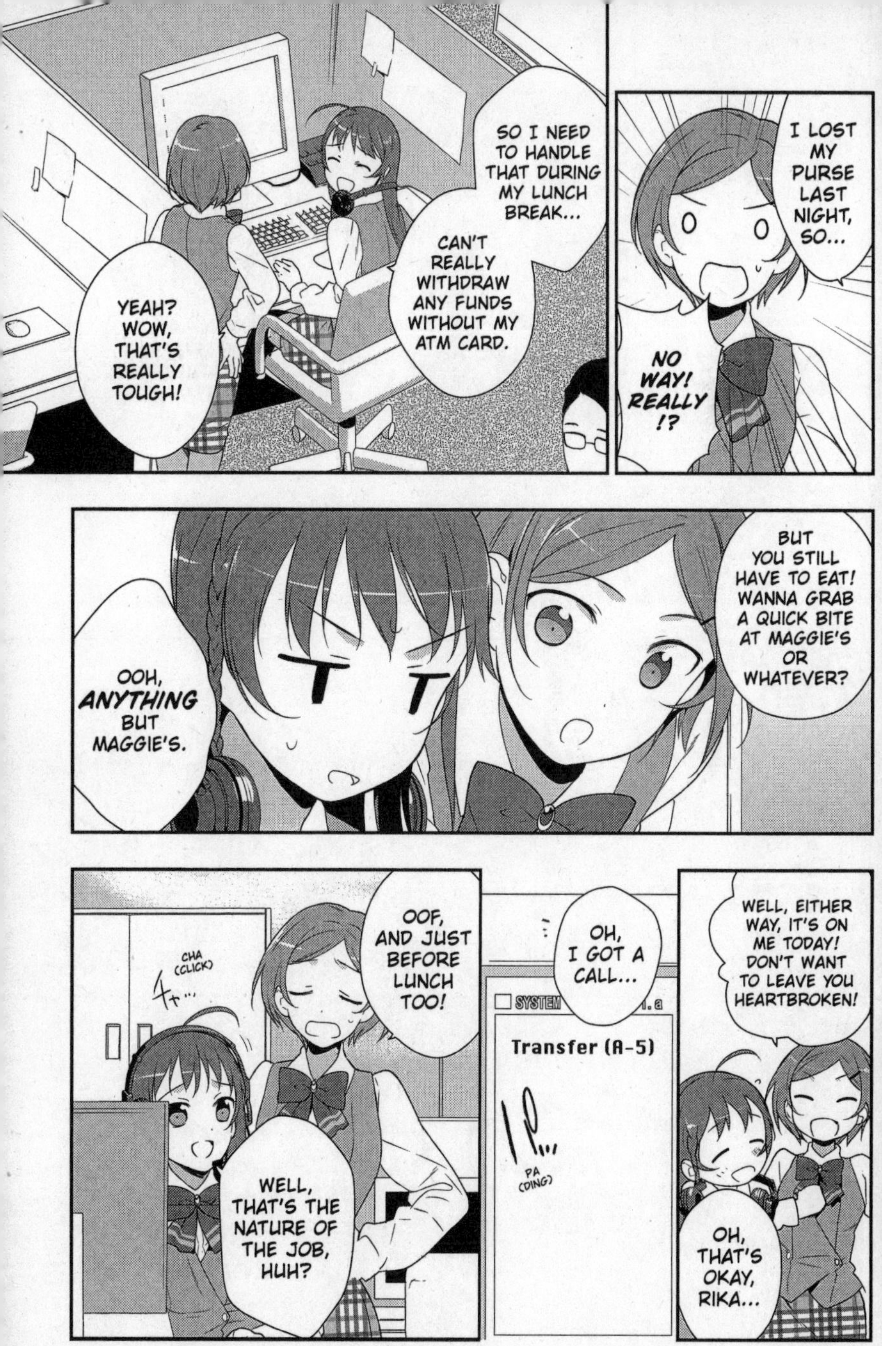
I LOST MY PURSE LAST NIGHT, SO...
NO WAY! REALLY!?
SO I NEED TO HANDLE THAT DURING MY LUNCH BREAK...
CAN'T REALLY WITHDRAW ANY FUNDS WITHOUT MY ATM CARD.
YEAH? WOW, THAT'S REALLY TOUGH!
BUT YOU STILL HAVE TO EAT! WANNA GRAB A QUICK BITE AT MAGGIE'S OR WHATEVER?
OOH, ANYTHING BUT MAGGIE'S.
WELL, EITHER WAY, IT'S ON ME TODAY! DON'T WANT TO LEAVE YOU HEARTBROKEN!
OH, THAT'S OKAY, RIKA...
OH, I GOT A CALL...
Transfer (A-5)
PA (DING)
OOF, AND JUST BEFORE LUNCH TOO!
CHA (CLICK)
WELL, THAT'S THE NATURE OF THE JOB, HUH?

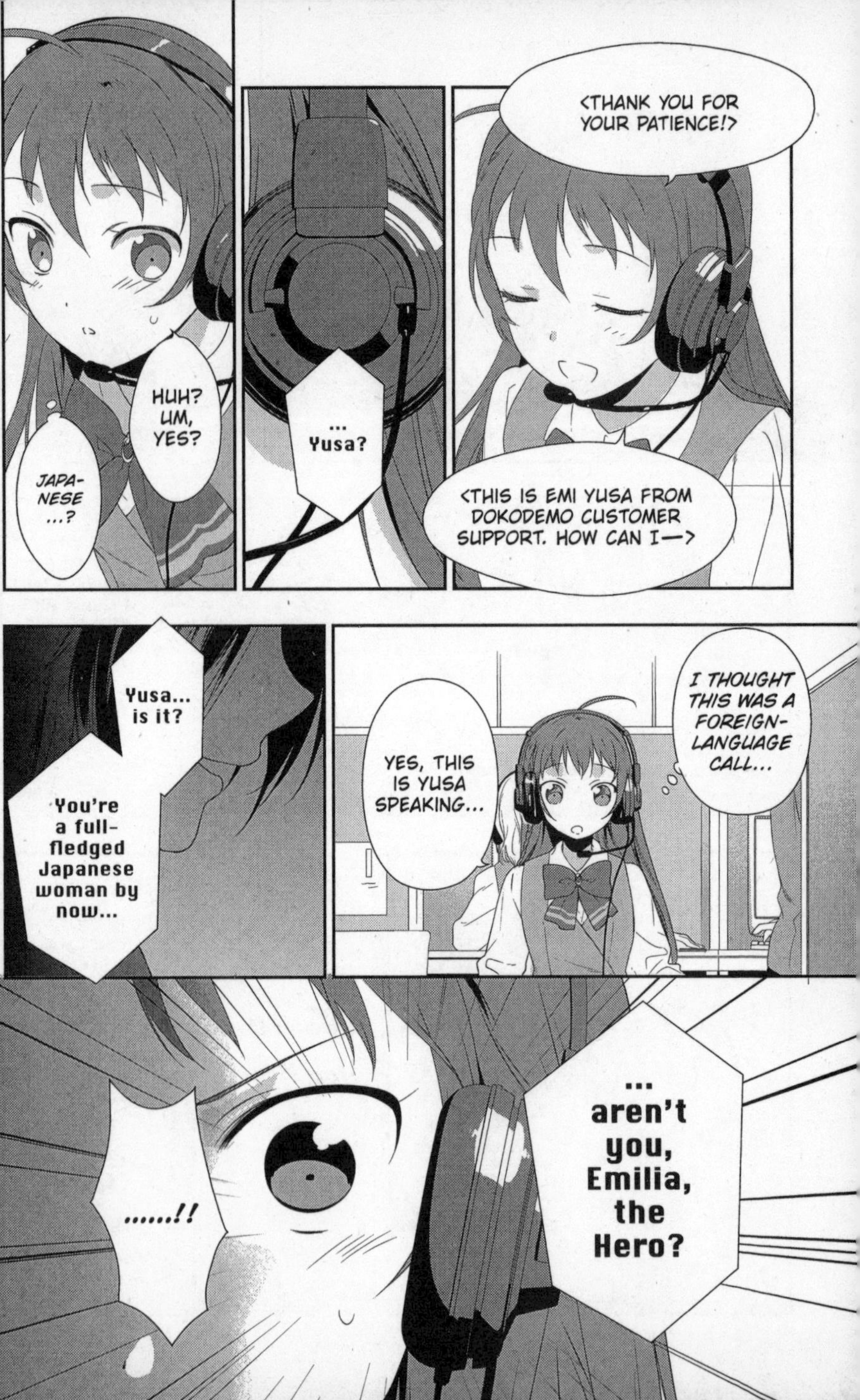

<THANK YOU FOR YOUR PATIENCE!>
<THIS IS EMI YUSA FROM DOKODEMO CUSTOMER SUPPORT. HOW CAN I—>
... Yusa?
HUH? UM, YES?
JAPANESE...?
I THOUGHT THIS WAS A FOREIGN-LANGUAGE CALL...
YES, THIS IS YUSA SPEAKING...
Yusa... is it?
You're a full-fledged Japanese woman by now...
... aren't you, Emilia, the Hero?
......!!

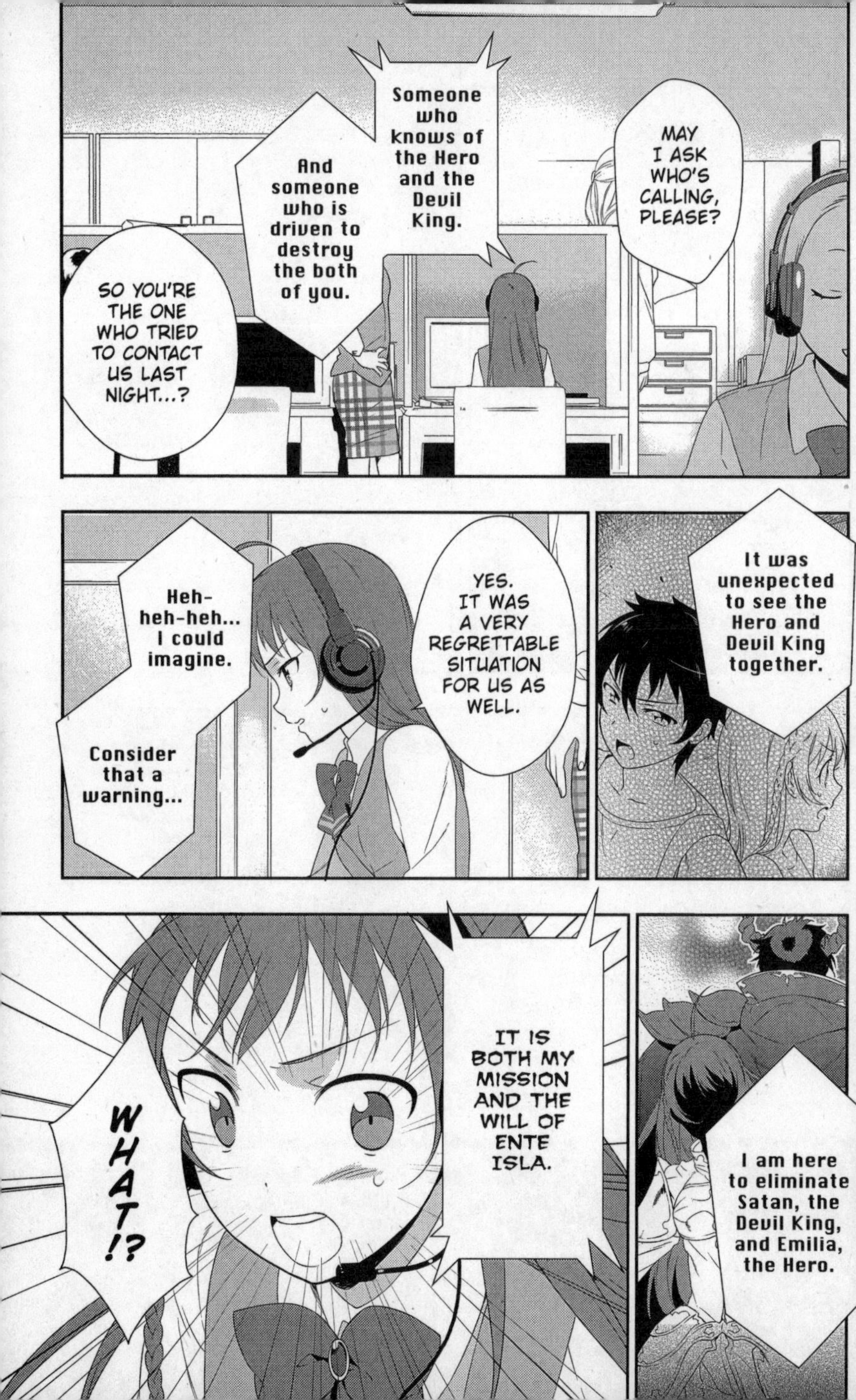
MAY I ASK WHO'S CALLING, PLEASE?
Someone who knows of the Hero and the Devil King.
And someone who is driven to destroy the both of you.
SO YOU'RE THE ONE WHO TRIED TO CONTACT US LAST NIGHT...?
It was unexpected to see the Hero and Devil King together.
YES. IT WAS A VERY REGRETTABLE SITUATION FOR US AS WELL.
Heh-heh-heh... I could imagine.
Consider that a warning...
I am here to eliminate Satan, the Devil King, and Emilia, the Hero.
IT IS BOTH MY MISSION AND THE WILL OF ENTE ISLA.
WHAT!?

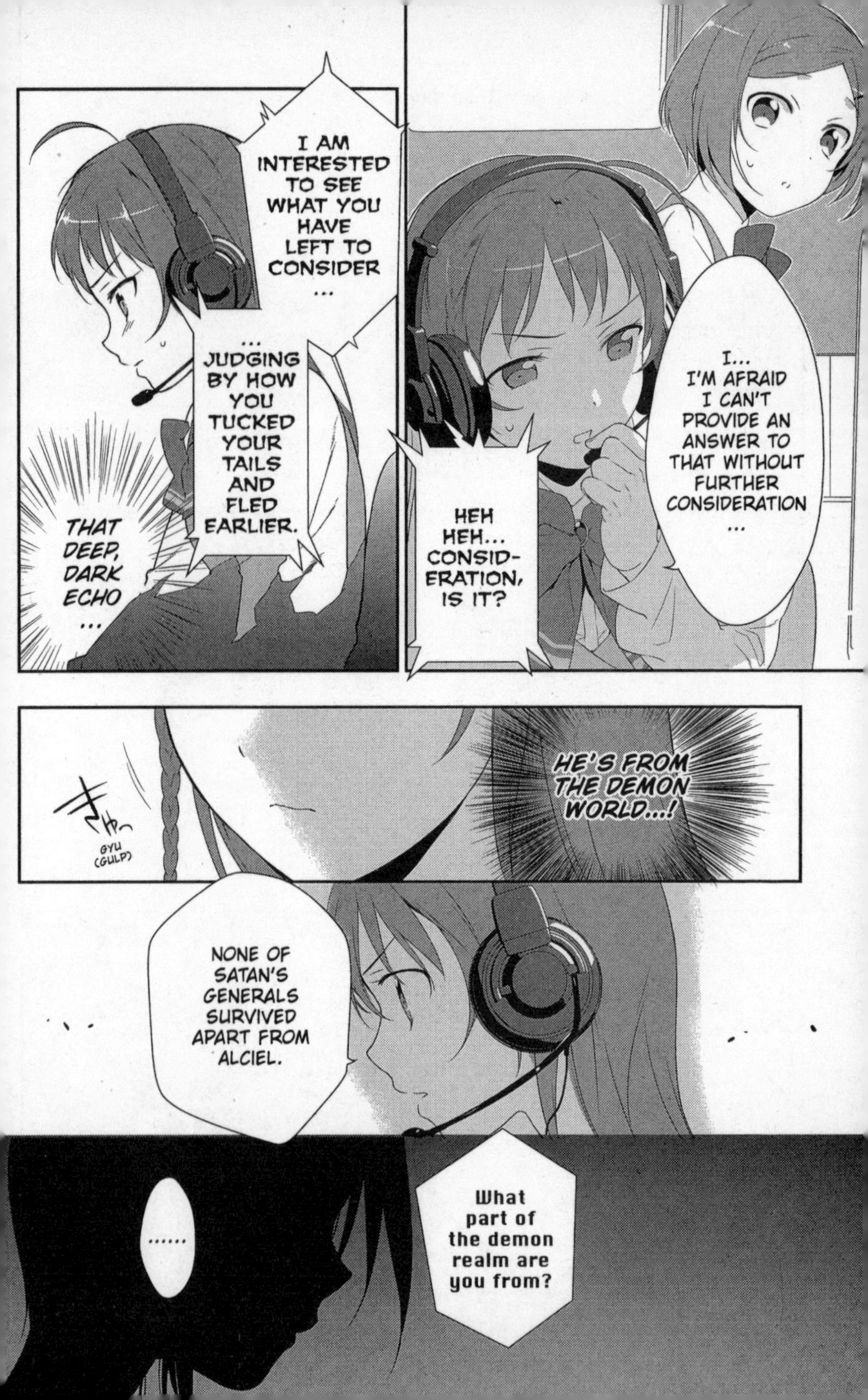
I... I'M AFRAID I CAN'T PROVIDE AN ANSWER TO THAT WITHOUT FURTHER CONSIDERATION ...
HEH HEH... CONSID-ERATION, IS IT?
I AM INTERESTED TO SEE WHAT YOU HAVE LEFT TO CONSIDER ...
... JUDGING BY HOW YOU TUCKED YOUR TAILS AND FLED EARLIER.
THAT DEEP, DARK ECHO ...
HE'S FROM THE DEMON WORLD...!
GYU (GULP)
NONE OF SATAN'S GENERALS SURVIVED APART FROM ALCIEL.
What part of the demon realm are you from?
......

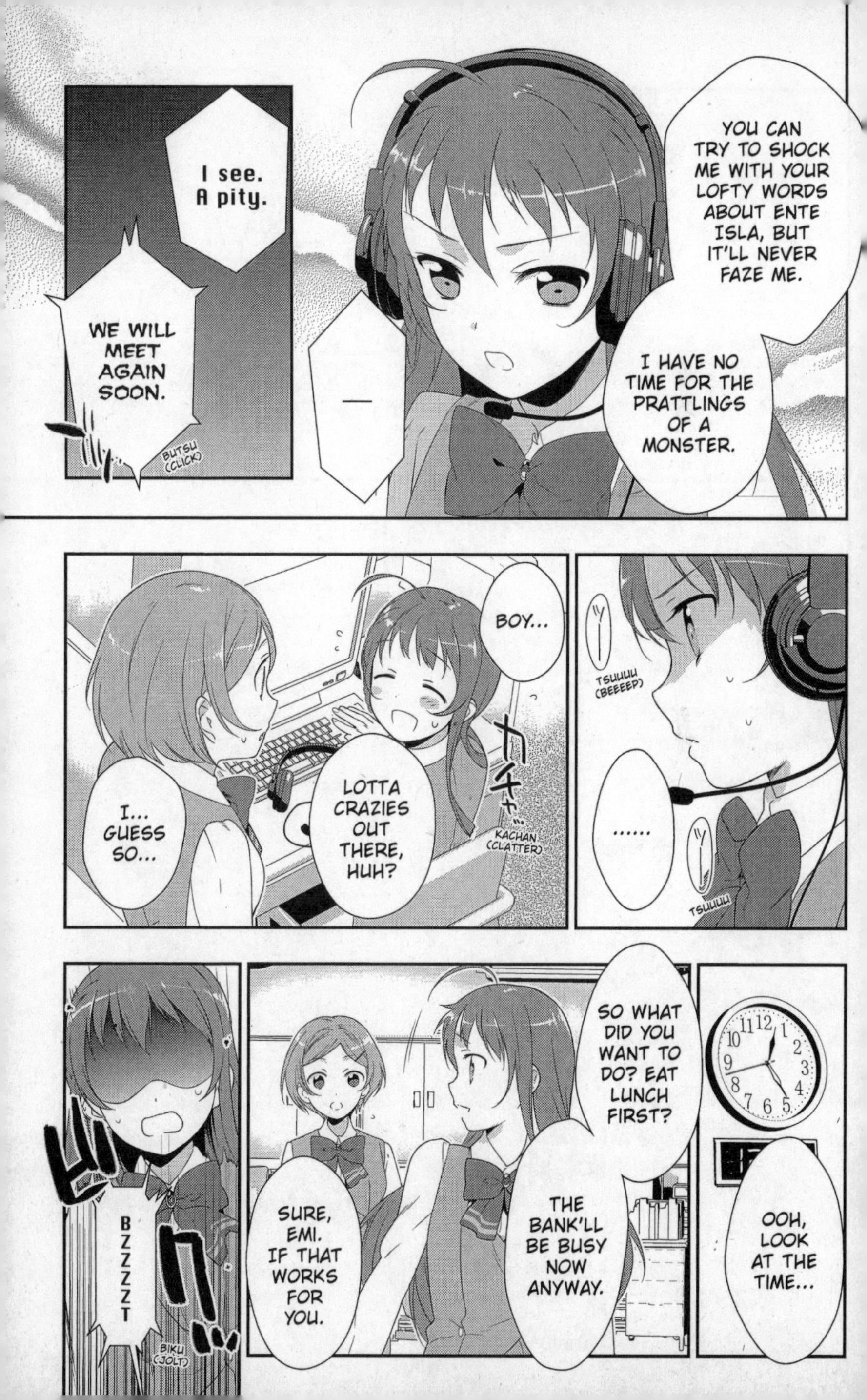
YOU CAN TRY TO SHOCK ME WITH YOUR LOFTY WORDS ABOUT ENTE ISLA, BUT IT'LL NEVER FAZE ME.
I HAVE NO TIME FOR THE PRATTLINGS OF A MONSTER.
—
I see. A pity.
WE WILL MEET AGAIN SOON.
BUTSU (CLICK)
TSUUUU (BEEEEP)
......
TSUUUU
BOY...
LOTTA CRAZIES OUT THERE, HUH?
KACHAN (CLATTER)
I... GUESS SO...
OOH, LOOK AT THE TIME...
SO WHAT DID YOU WANT TO DO? EAT LUNCH FIRST?
THE BANK'LL BE BUSY NOW ANYWAY.
SURE, EMI. IF THAT WORKS FOR YOU.
BZZZZT
BIKU (JOLT)

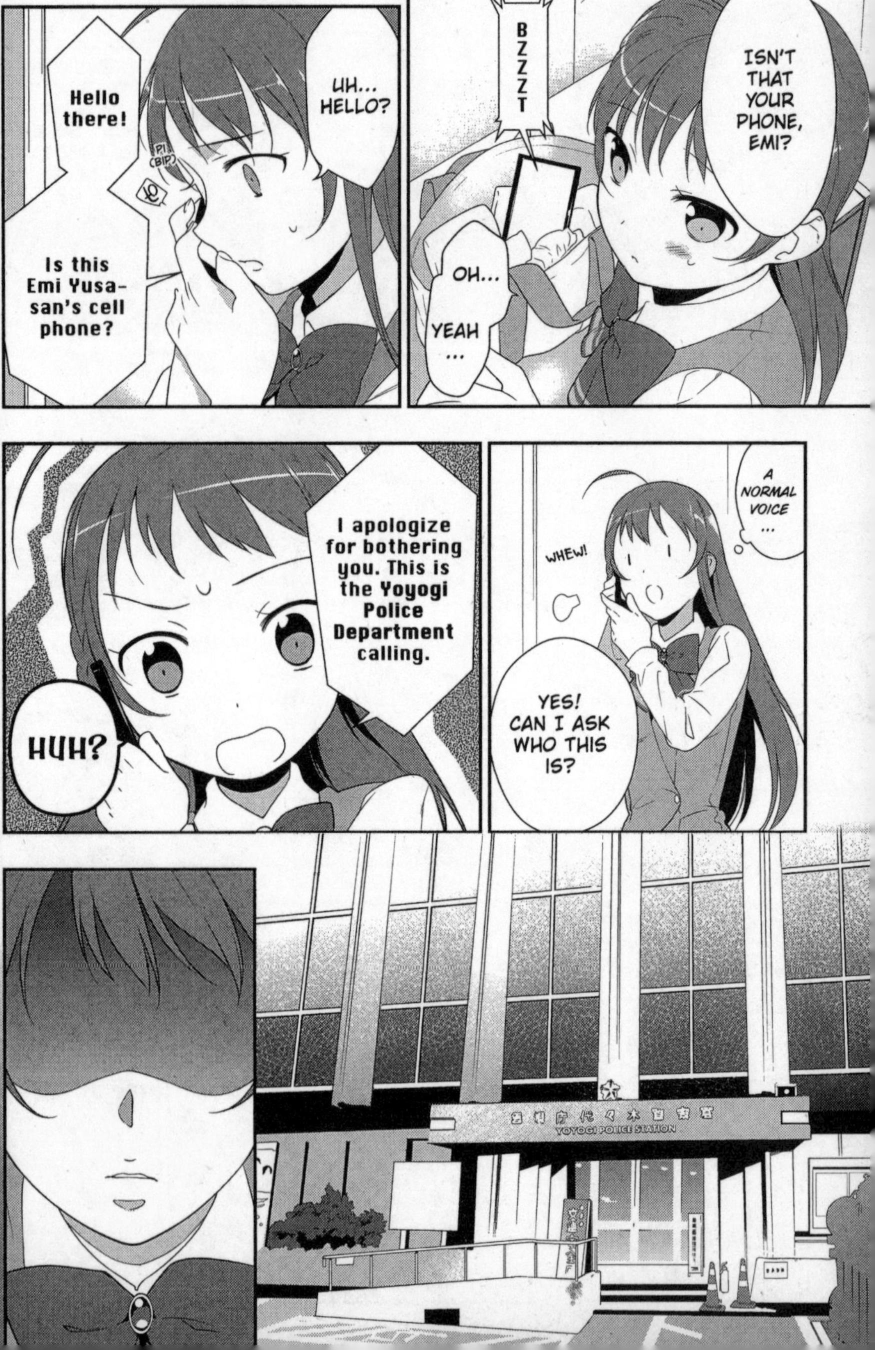
ISN'T THAT YOUR PHONE, EMI?
BZZZT
OH... YEAH...
UH... HELLO?
Hello there!
PI (BIP)
Is this Emi Yusa-san's cell phone?
A NORMAL VOICE...
WHEW!
YES! CAN I ASK WHO THIS IS?
I apologize for bothering you. This is the Yoyogi Police Department calling.
HUH?
YOYOGI POLICE STATION

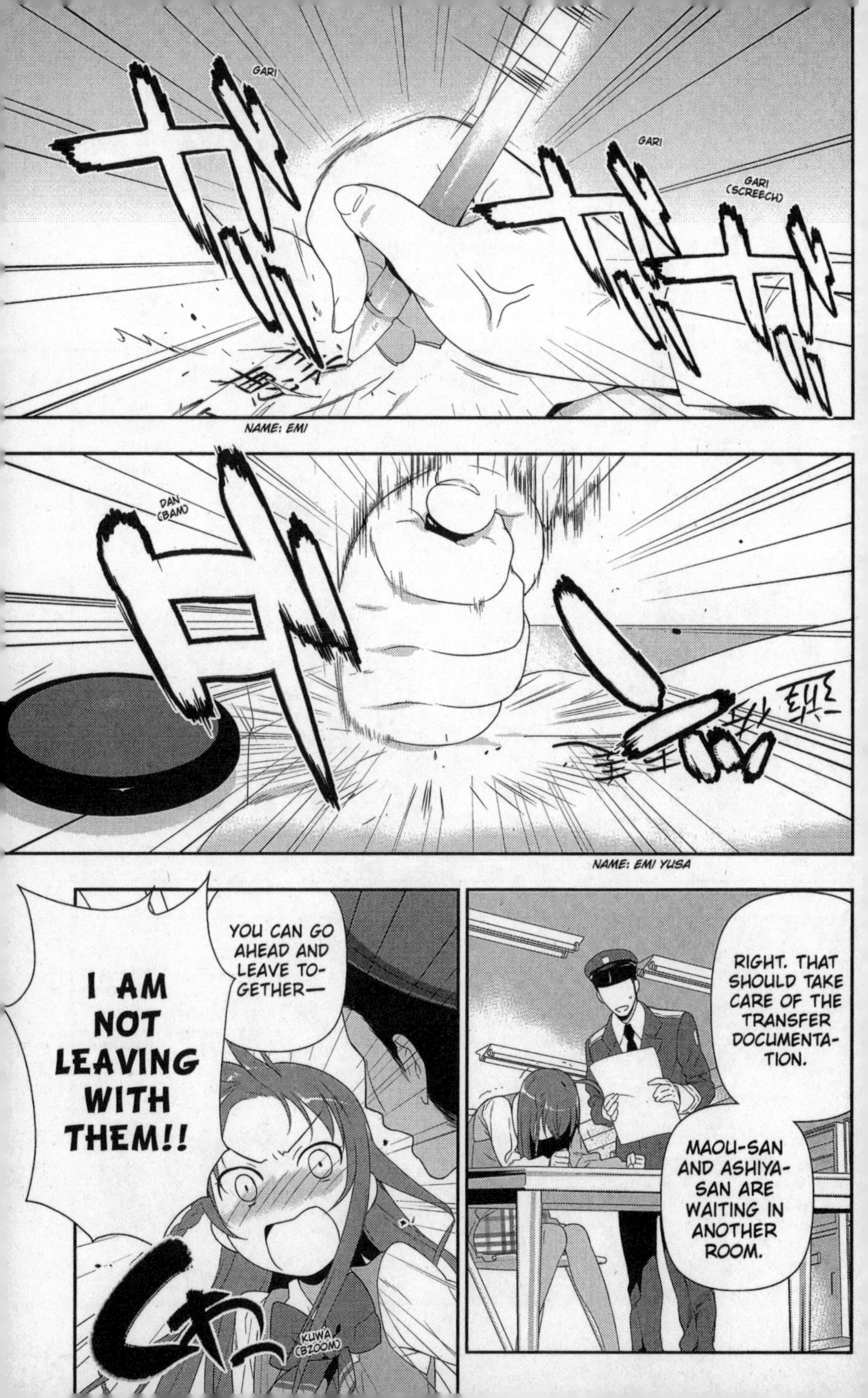
GARI (SCREECH)
GARI
GARI
NAME: EMI
DAN (BAM)
NAME: EMI YUSA
RIGHT. THAT SHOULD TAKE CARE OF THE TRANSFER DOCUMENTA-TION.
MAOU-SAN AND ASHIYA-SAN ARE WAITING IN ANOTHER ROOM.
YOU CAN GO AHEAD AND LEAVE TO-GETHER—
I AM NOT LEAVING WITH THEM!!
KUWA (BZOOM)

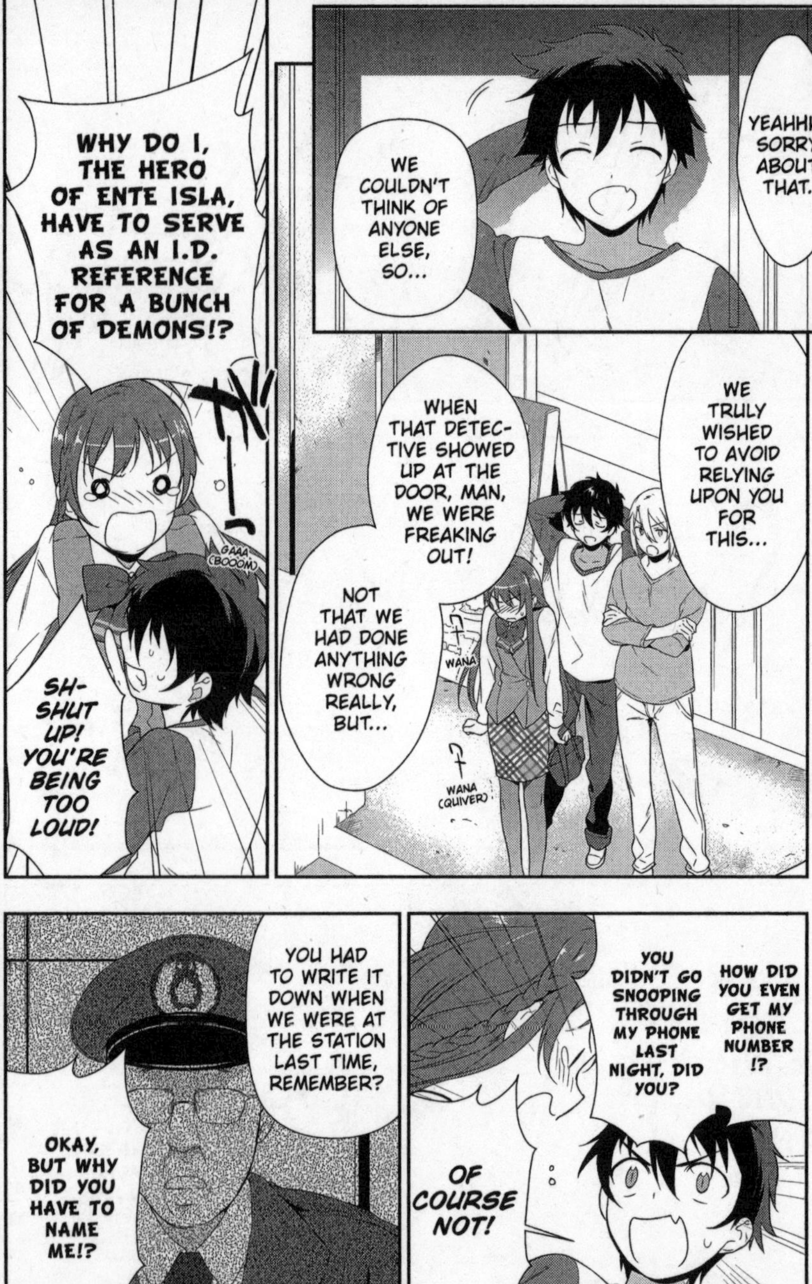
YEAHHH, SORRY ABOUT THAT.
WE COULDN'T THINK OF ANYONE ELSE, SO...
WE TRULY WISHED TO AVOID RELYING UPON YOU FOR THIS...
WHEN THAT DETECTIVE SHOWED UP AT THE DOOR, MAN, WE WERE FREAKING OUT!
NOT THAT WE HAD DONE ANYTHING WRONG REALLY, BUT...
WANA
WANA (QUIVER)
WHY DO I, THE HERO OF ENTE ISLA, HAVE TO SERVE AS AN I.D. REFERENCE FOR A BUNCH OF DEMONS!?
GAAA (BOOOM)
SH-SHUT UP! YOU'RE BEING TOO LOUD!
HOW DID YOU EVEN GET MY PHONE NUMBER!?
YOU DIDN'T GO SNOOPING THROUGH MY PHONE LAST NIGHT, DID YOU?
OF COURSE NOT!
YOU HAD TO WRITE IT DOWN WHEN WE WERE AT THE STATION LAST TIME, REMEMBER?
OKAY, BUT WHY DID YOU HAVE TO NAME ME!?

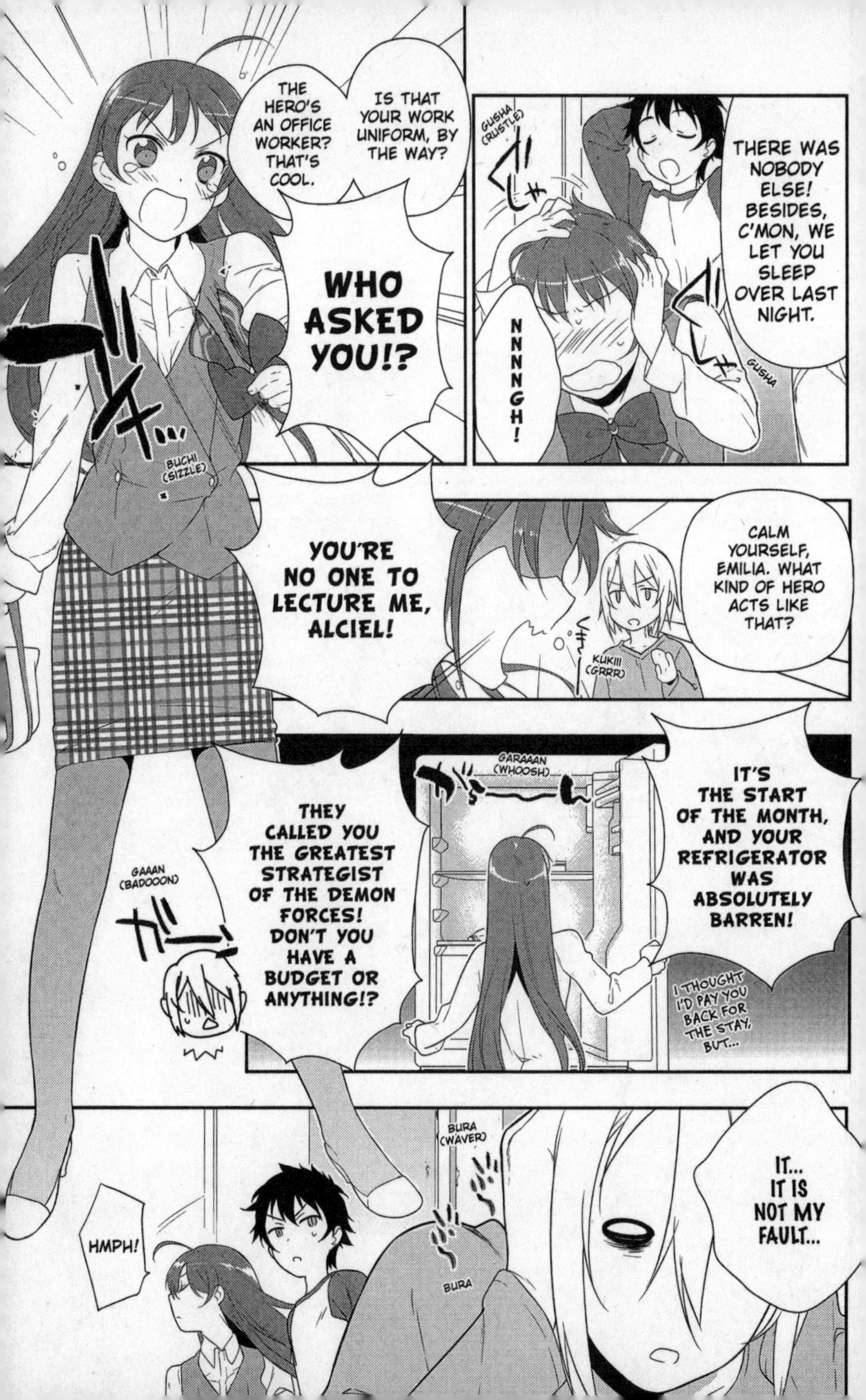
GUSHA (RUSTLE)
THERE WAS NOBODY ELSE! BESIDES, C'MON, WE LET YOU SLEEP OVER LAST NIGHT.
GUSHA
NNNNGH!
IS THAT YOUR WORK UNIFORM, BY THE WAY?
THE HERO'S AN OFFICE WORKER? THAT'S COOL.
WHO ASKED YOU!?
BUCHI (SIZZLE)
CALM YOURSELF, EMILIA. WHAT KIND OF HERO ACTS LIKE THAT?
KUKIII (GRRR)
YOU'RE NO ONE TO LECTURE ME, ALCIEL!
GARAAAN (WHOOSH)
IT'S THE START OF THE MONTH, AND YOUR REFRIGERATOR WAS ABSOLUTELY BARREN!
I THOUGHT I'D PAY YOU BACK FOR THE STAY, BUT...
THEY CALLED YOU THE GREATEST STRATEGIST OF THE DEMON FORCES! DON'T YOU HAVE A BUDGET OR ANYTHING!?
GAAAN (BADOOON)
IT... IT IS NOT MY FAULT...
BURA (WAVER)
BURA
HMPH!

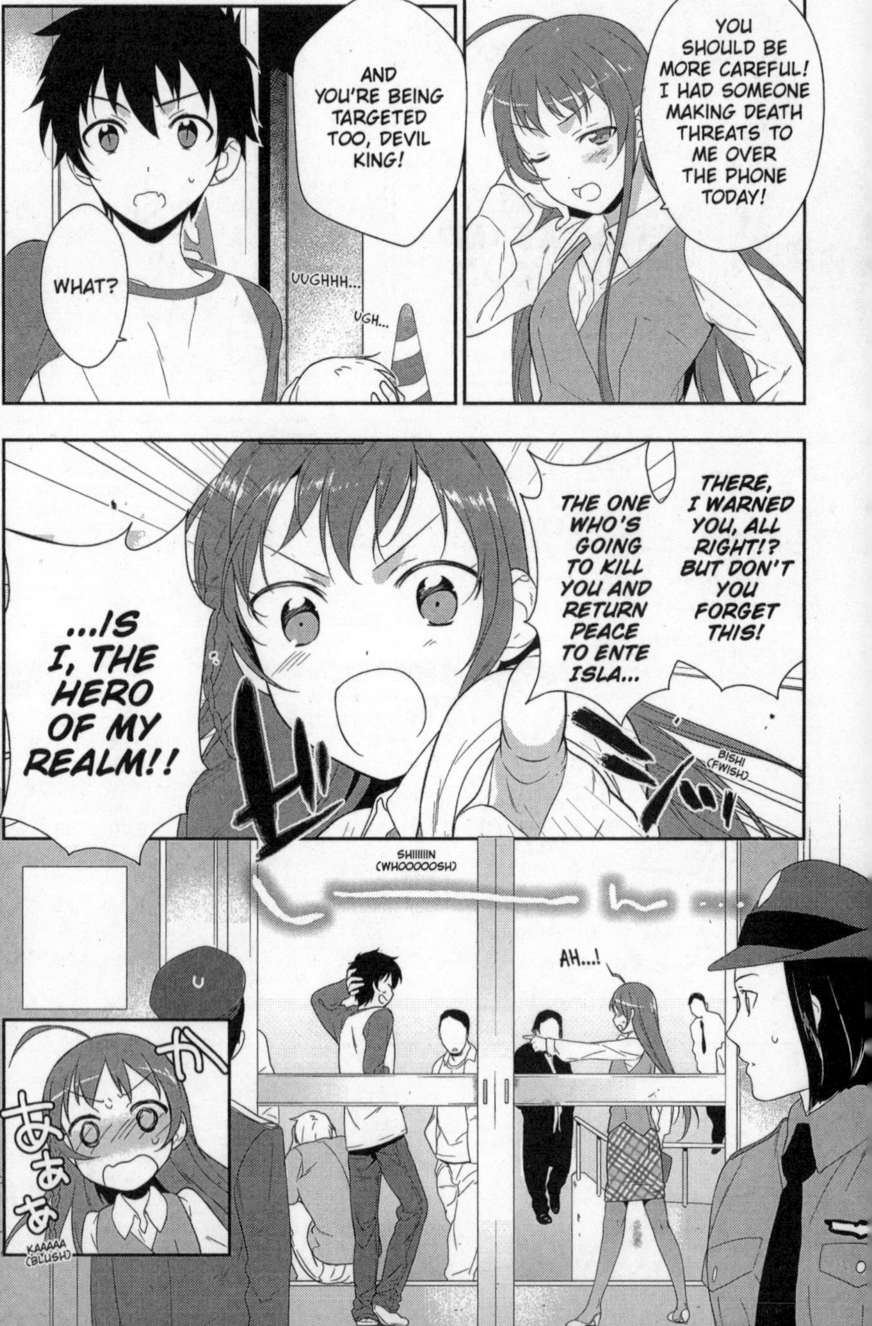
YOU SHOULD BE MORE CAREFUL! I HAD SOMEONE MAKING DEATH THREATS TO ME OVER THE PHONE TODAY!
AND YOU'RE BEING TARGETED TOO, DEVIL KING!
WHAT?
UUGHHH...
UGH...
THERE, I WARNED YOU, ALL RIGHT!? BUT DON'T YOU FORGET THIS!
THE ONE WHO'S GOING TO KILL YOU AND RETURN PEACE TO ENTE ISLA...
...IS I, THE HERO OF MY REALM!!
BISHI (FWISH)
SHIIIIIN (WHOOOOOSH)
AH...!
KAAAAA (BLUSH)

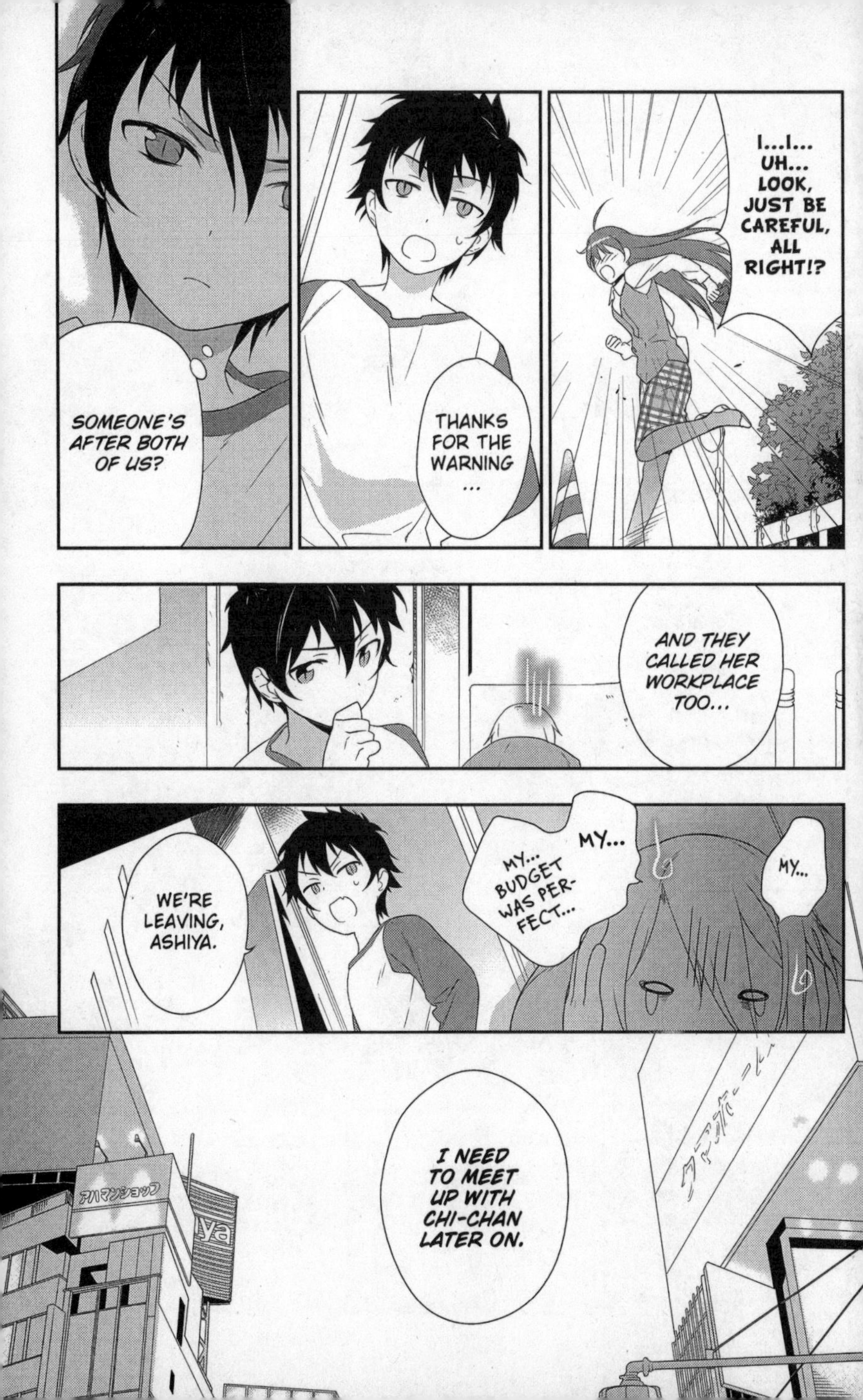
I...I... UH... LOOK, JUST BE CAREFUL, ALL RIGHT!?
THANKS FOR THE WARNING ...
SOMEONE'S AFTER BOTH OF US?
AND THEY CALLED HER WORKPLACE TOO...
MY...
MY...
MY... BUDGET WAS PER-FECT...
WE'RE LEAVING, ASHIYA.
I NEED TO MEET UP WITH CHI-CHAN LATER ON.

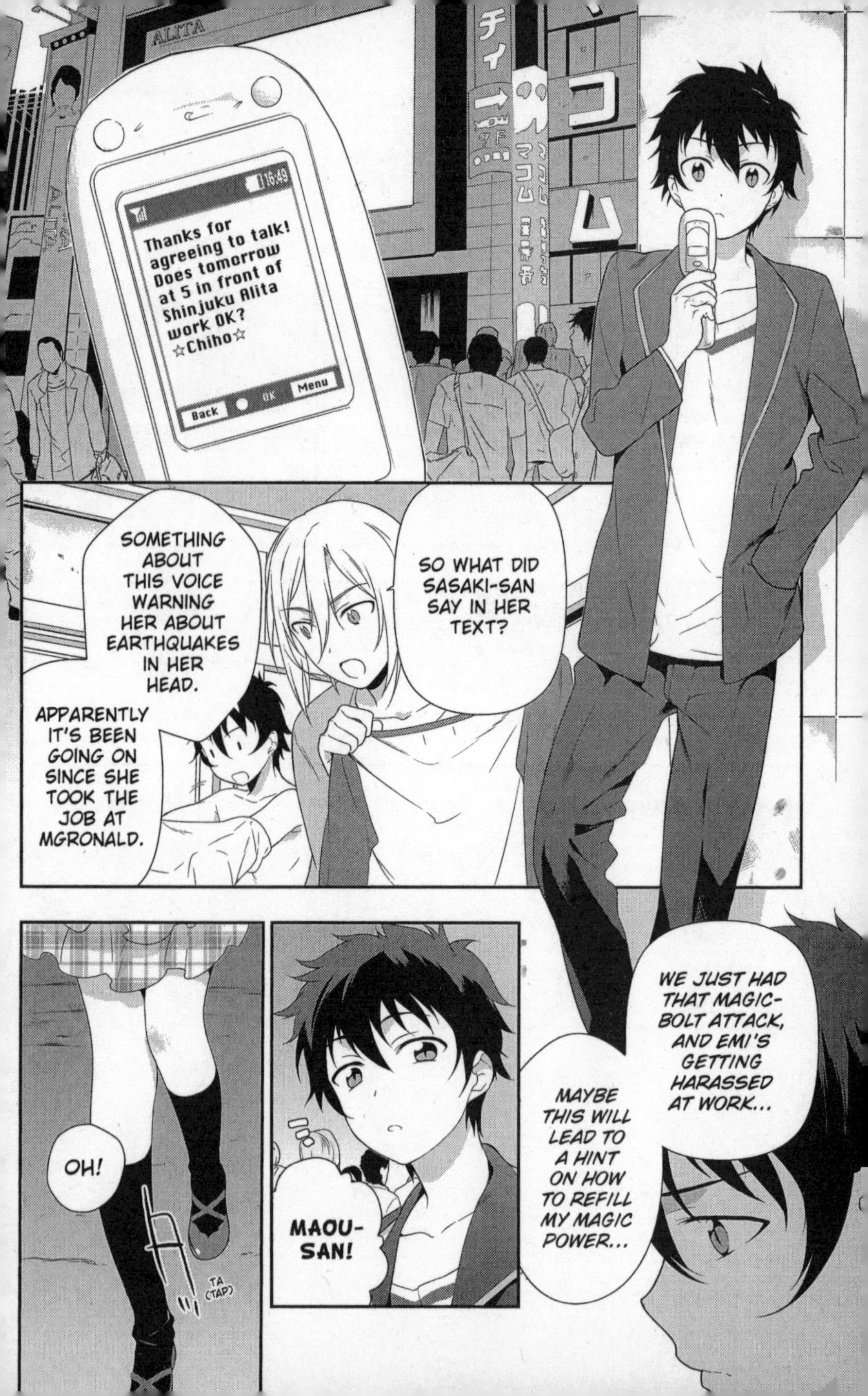

ALITA
16:49
Thanks for agreeing to talk! Does tomorrow at 5 in front of Shinjuku Alita work OK? ☆Chiho☆
Back
OK
Menu
SO WHAT DID SASAKI-SAN SAY IN HER TEXT?
SOMETHING ABOUT THIS VOICE WARNING HER ABOUT EARTHQUAKES IN HER HEAD.
APPARENTLY IT'S BEEN GOING ON SINCE SHE TOOK THE JOB AT MGRONALD.
WE JUST HAD THAT MAGIC-BOLT ATTACK, AND EMI'S GETTING HARASSED AT WORK...
MAYBE THIS WILL LEAD TO A HINT ON HOW TO REFILL MY MAGIC POWER...
MAOU-SAN!
OH!
TA (TAP)

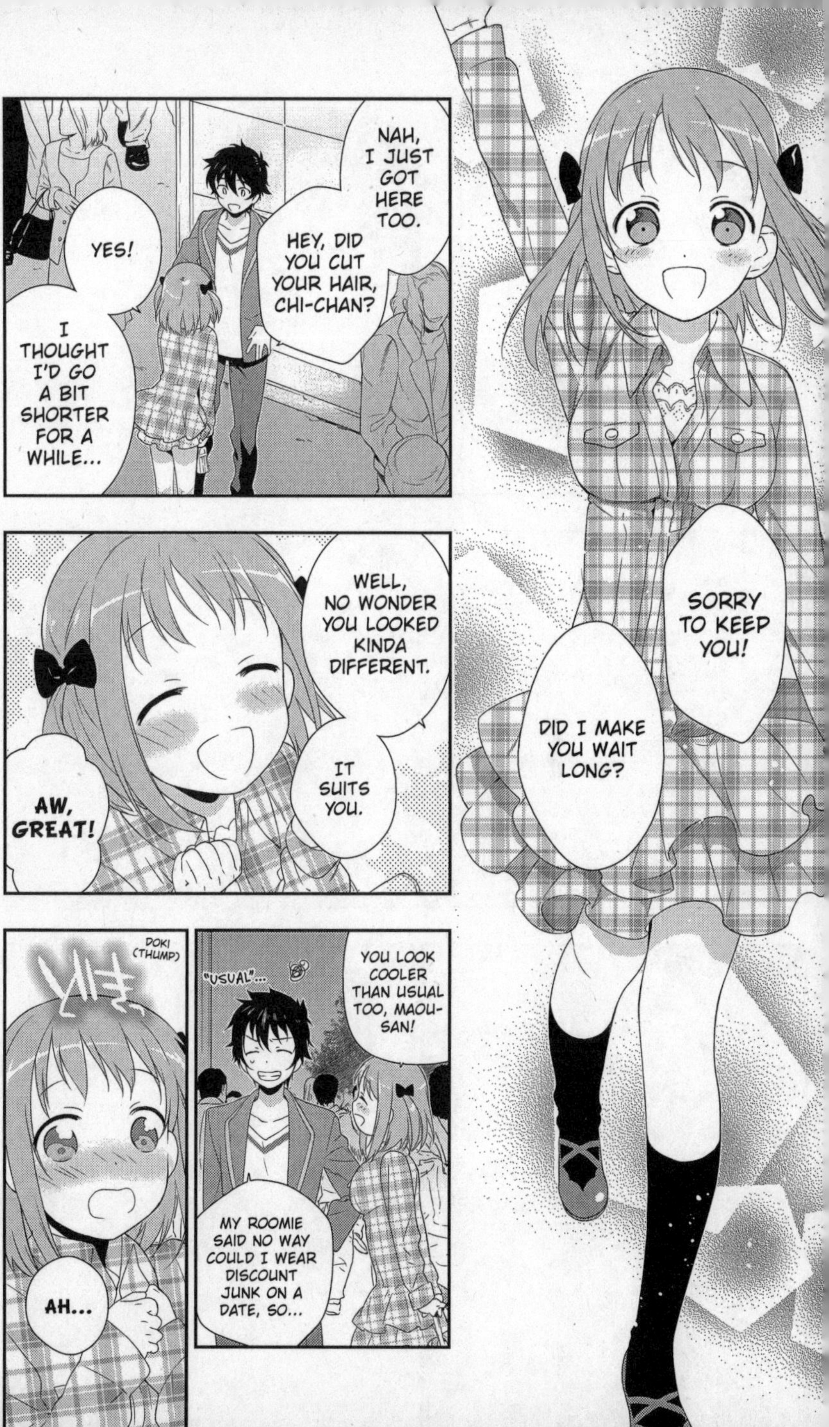
SORRY TO KEEP YOU!
DID I MAKE YOU WAIT LONG?
NAH, I JUST GOT HERE TOO.
HEY, DID YOU CUT YOUR HAIR, CHI-CHAN?
YES!
I THOUGHT I'D GO A BIT SHORTER FOR A WHILE...
WELL, NO WONDER YOU LOOKED KINDA DIFFERENT.
IT SUITS YOU.
AW, GREAT!
YOU LOOK COOLER THAN USUAL TOO, MAOU-SAN!
"USUAL"...
MY ROOMIE SAID NO WAY COULD I WEAR DISCOUNT JUNK ON A DATE, SO...
DOKI (THUMP)
AH...

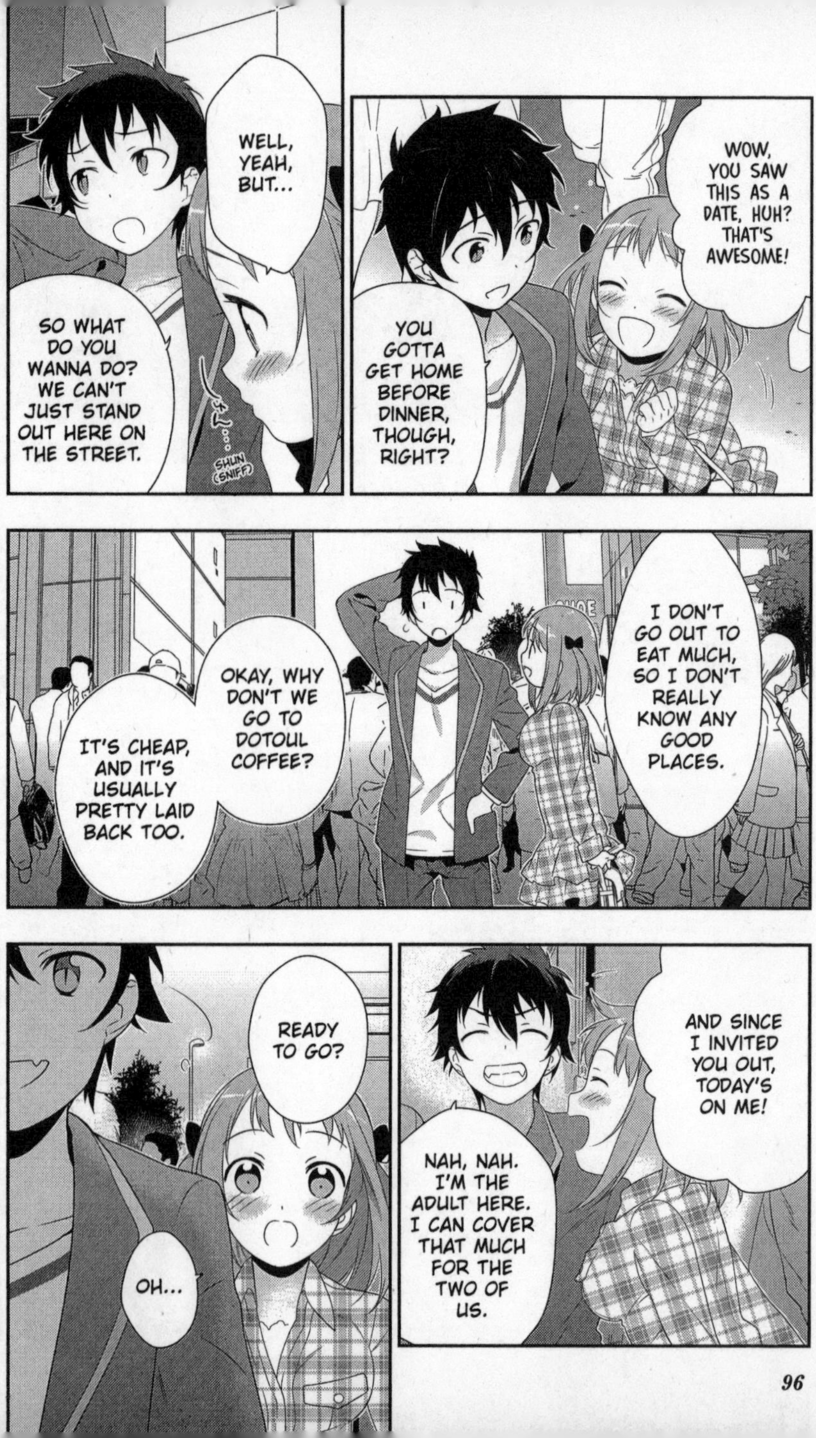
WOW, YOU SAW THIS AS A DATE, HUH? THAT'S AWESOME!
YOU GOTTA GET HOME BEFORE DINNER, THOUGH, RIGHT?
WELL, YEAH, BUT...
SHUN (SNIFF)
SO WHAT DO YOU WANNA DO? WE CAN'T JUST STAND OUT HERE ON THE STREET.
I DON'T GO OUT TO EAT MUCH, SO I DON'T REALLY KNOW ANY GOOD PLACES.
OKAY, WHY DON'T WE GO TO DOTOUL COFFEE?
IT'S CHEAP, AND IT'S USUALLY PRETTY LAID BACK TOO.
AND SINCE I INVITED YOU OUT, TODAY'S ON ME!
NAH, NAH. I'M THE ADULT HERE. I CAN COVER THAT MUCH FOR THE TWO OF US.
READY TO GO?
OH...

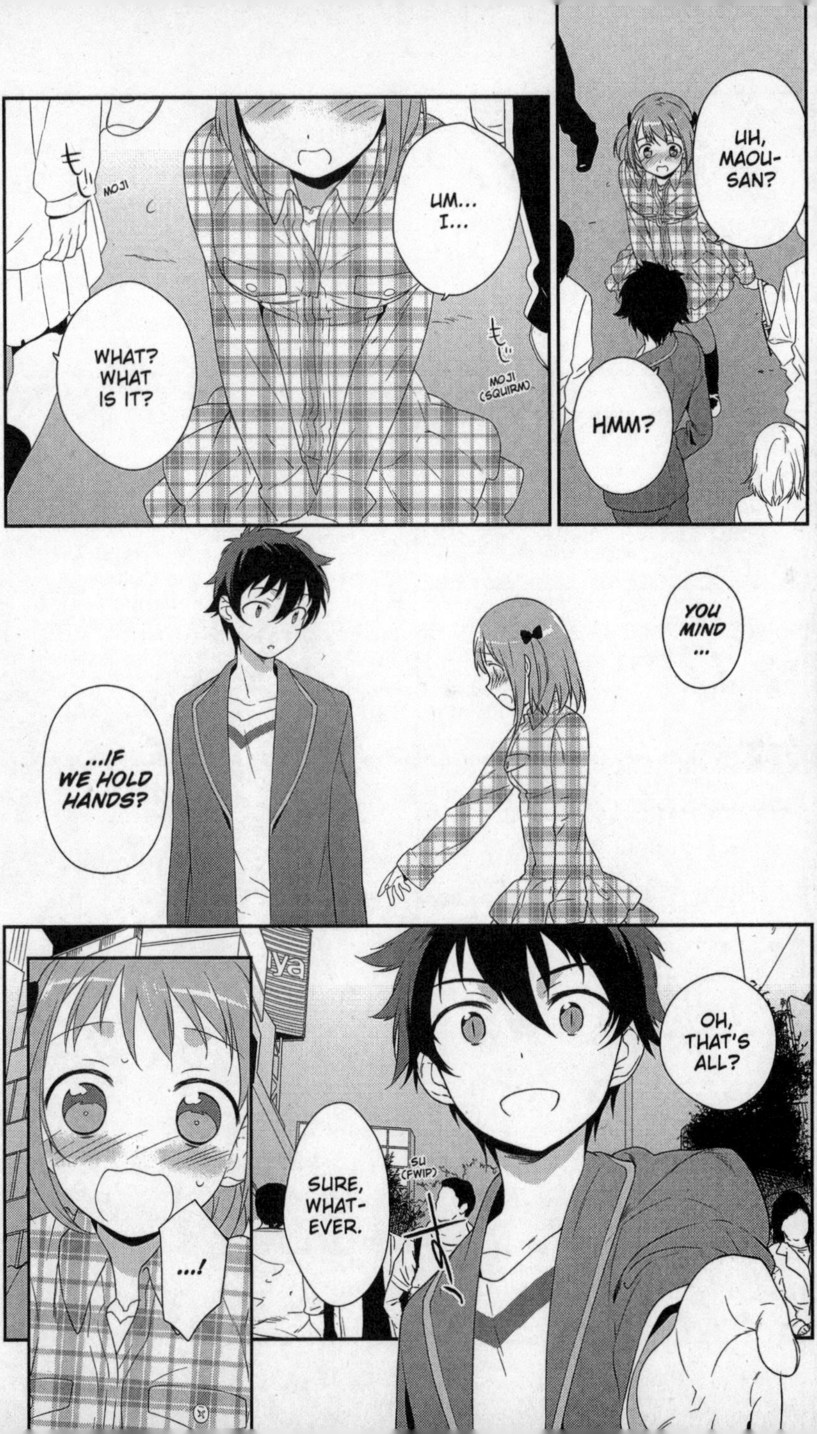
UH, MAOU-SAN?
HMM?
UM... I...
もじ
MOJI (SQUIRM)
WHAT? WHAT IS IT?
もじ
MOJI
YOU MIND...
...IF WE HOLD HANDS?
OH, THAT'S ALL?
SURE, WHATEVER.
SU (FWIP)
ya
...!

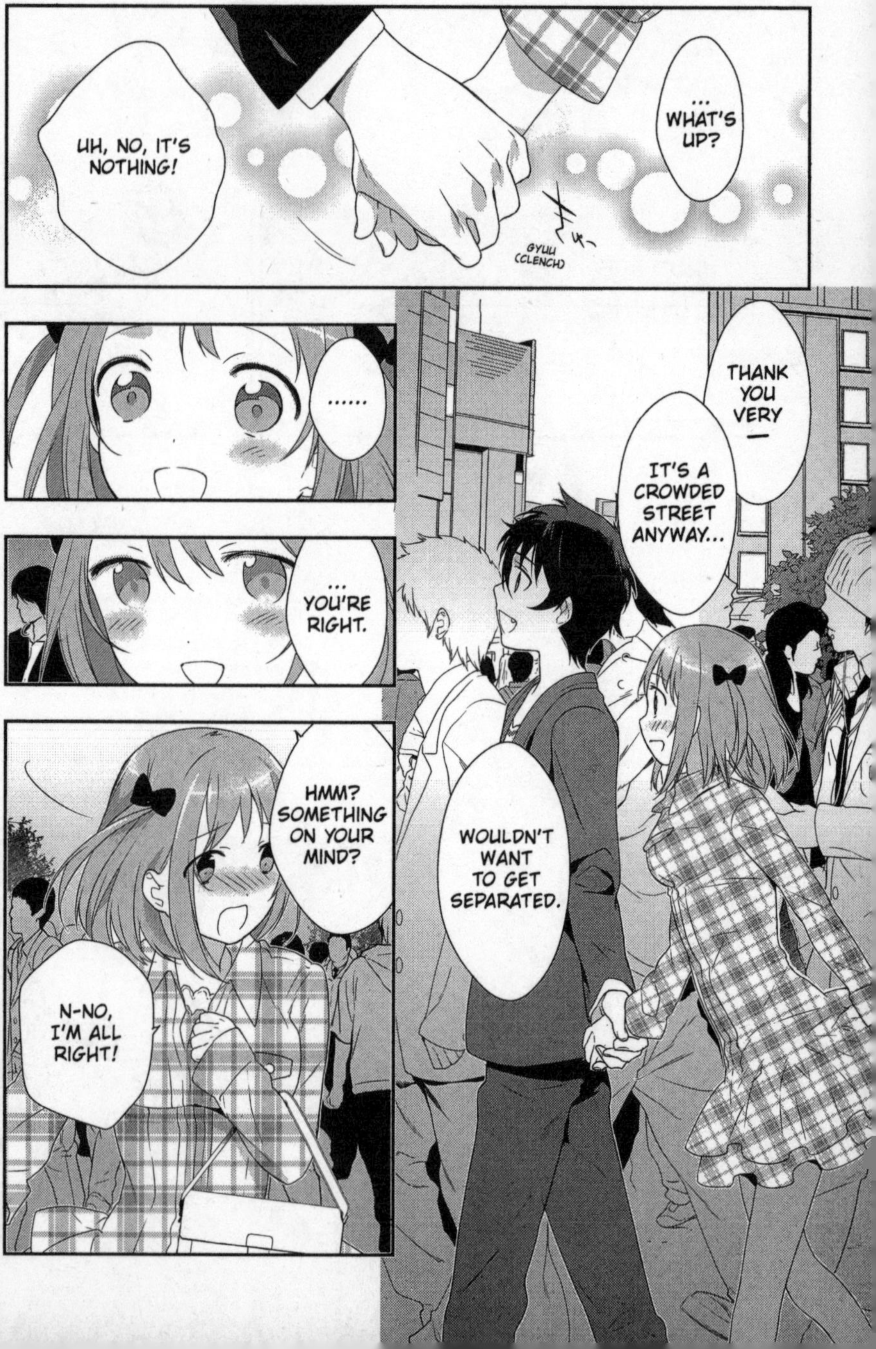
... WHAT'S UP?
UH, NO, IT'S NOTHING!
GYUU (CLENCH)
THANK YOU VERY —
IT'S A CROWDED STREET ANYWAY...
WOULDN'T WANT TO GET SEPARATED.
......
... YOU'RE RIGHT.
HMM? SOMETHING ON YOUR MIND?
N-NO, I'M ALL RIGHT!

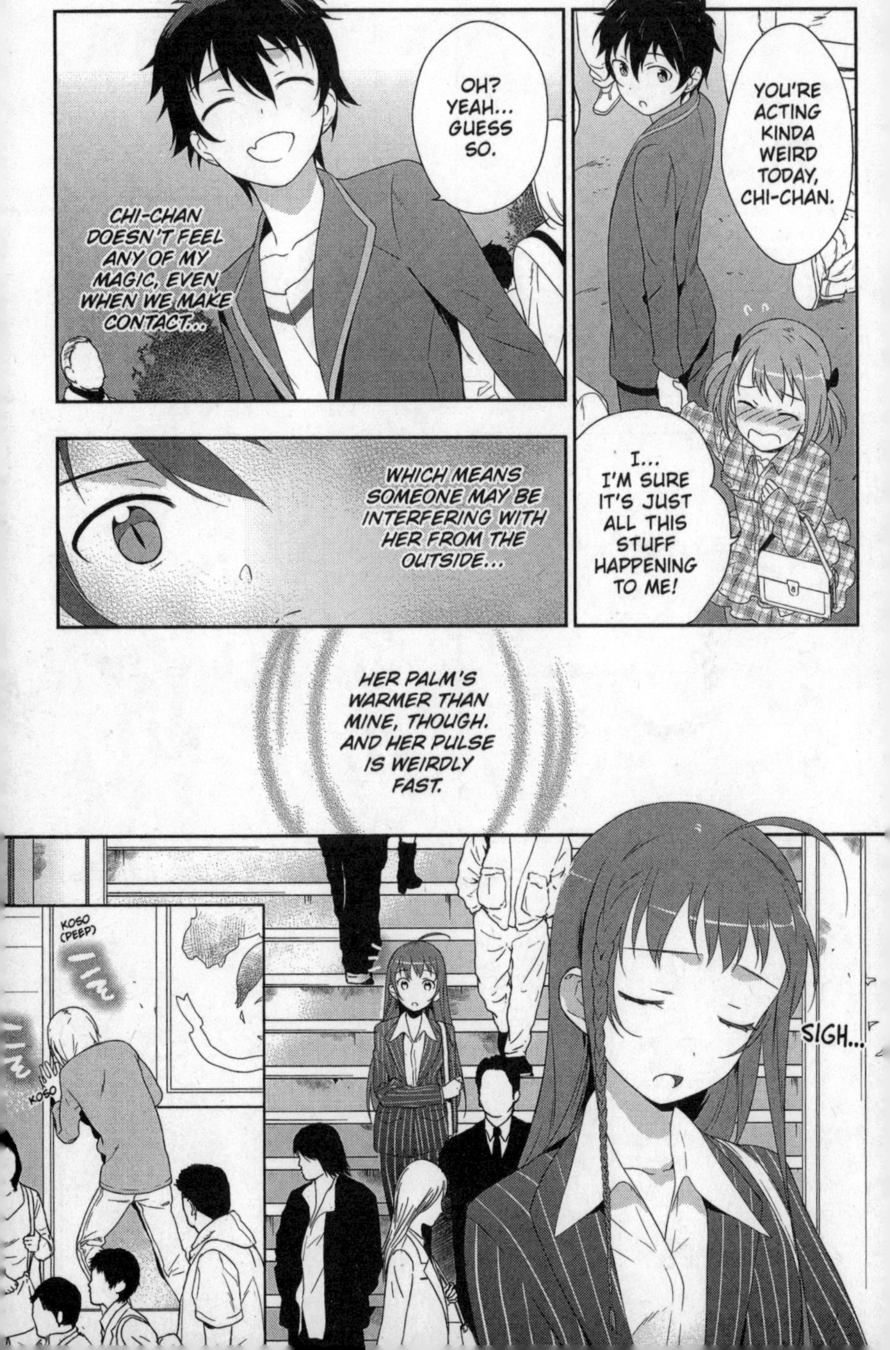
YOU'RE ACTING KINDA WEIRD TODAY, CHI-CHAN.
I... I'M SURE IT'S JUST ALL THIS STUFF HAPPENING TO ME!
OH? YEAH... GUESS SO.
CHI-CHAN DOESN'T FEEL ANY OF MY MAGIC, EVEN WHEN WE MAKE CONTACT...
WHICH MEANS SOMEONE MAY BE INTERFERING WITH HER FROM THE OUTSIDE...
HER PALM'S WARMER THAN MINE, THOUGH. AND HER PULSE IS WEIRDLY FAST.
SIGH...
KOSO (PEEP)
KOSO

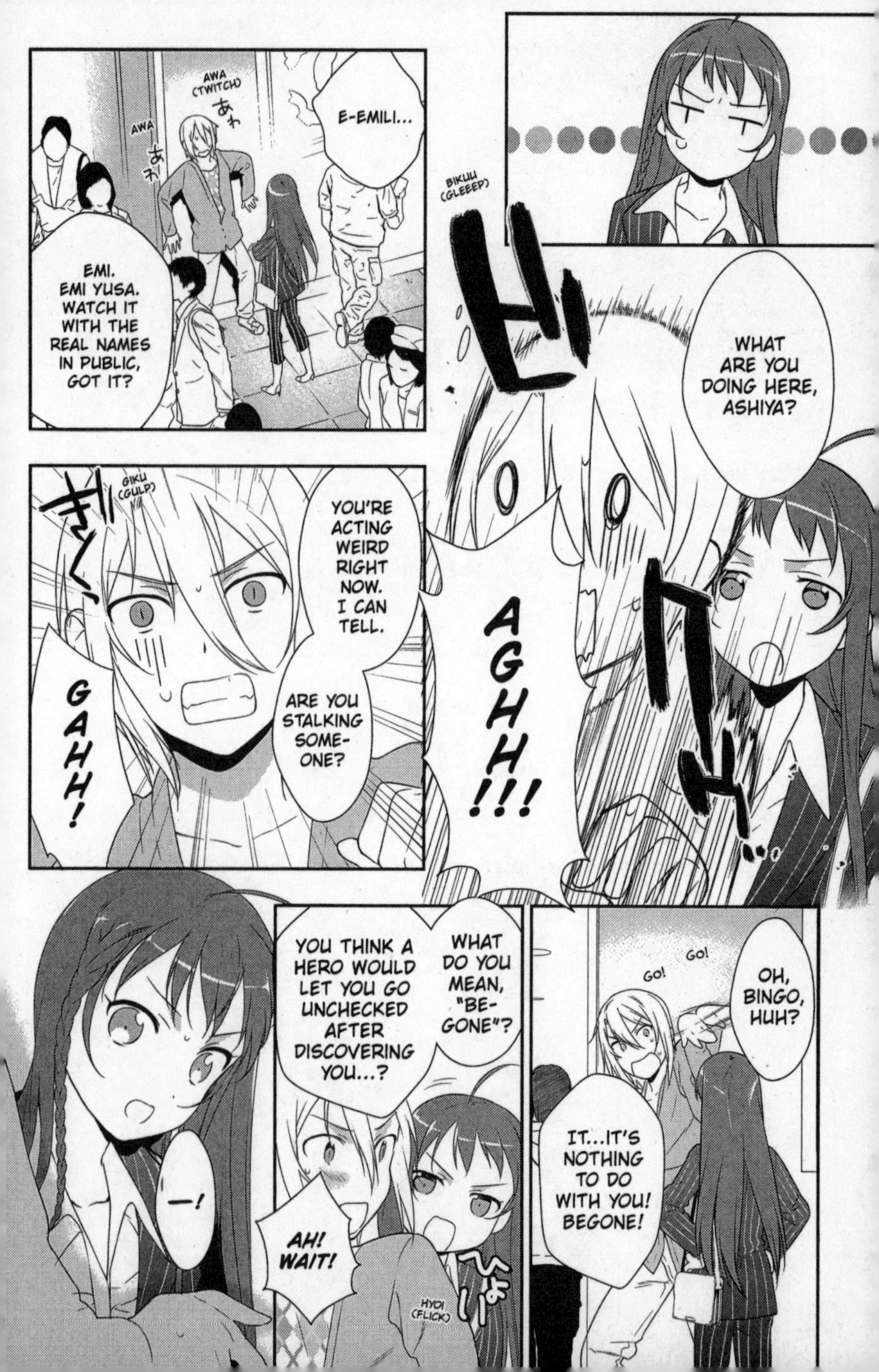
E-EMILI...
AWA (TWITCH)
あわ
AWA
あわ
EMI. EMI YUSA. WATCH IT WITH THE REAL NAMES IN PUBLIC, GOT IT?
BIKUU (GLEEEP)
WHAT ARE YOU DOING HERE, ASHIYA?
AGHH!!!
GIKU (GULP)
YOU'RE ACTING WEIRD RIGHT NOW. I CAN TELL.
ARE YOU STALKING SOME-ONE?
GAHH!
OH, BINGO, HUH?
GO!
GO!
IT...IT'S NOTHING TO DO WITH YOU! BEGONE!
WHAT DO YOU MEAN, "BE-GONE"?
YOU THINK A HERO WOULD LET YOU GO UNCHECKED AFTER DISCOVERING YOU...?
AH! WAIT!
HYOI (FLICK)
—!

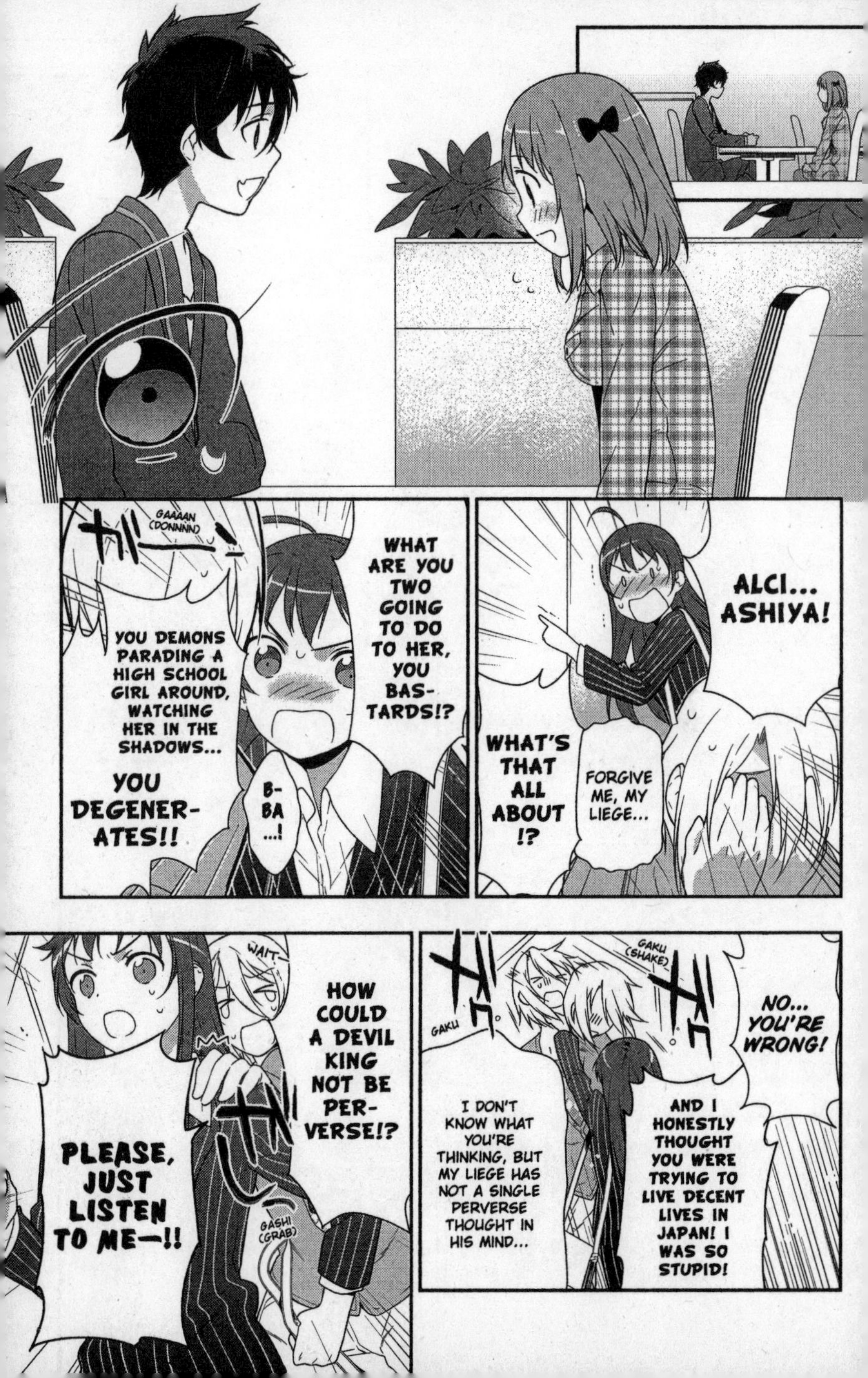
ALCI... ASHIYA!
FORGIVE ME, MY LIEGE...
WHAT'S THAT ALL ABOUT!?
GAAAAN (DONNNN)
WHAT ARE YOU TWO GOING TO DO TO HER, YOU BASTARDS!?
YOU DEMONS PARADING A HIGH SCHOOL GIRL AROUND, WATCHING HER IN THE SHADOWS...
YOU DEGENERATES!!
B-BA...!
GAKU (SHAKE)
NO... YOU'RE WRONG!
AND I HONESTLY THOUGHT YOU WERE TRYING TO LIVE DECENT LIVES IN JAPAN! I WAS SO STUPID!
GAKU
I DON'T KNOW WHAT YOU'RE THINKING, BUT MY LIEGE HAS NOT A SINGLE PERVERSE THOUGHT IN HIS MIND...
WAIT
HOW COULD A DEVIL KING NOT BE PERVERSE!?
PLEASE, JUST LISTEN TO ME—!!
GASHI (GRAB)

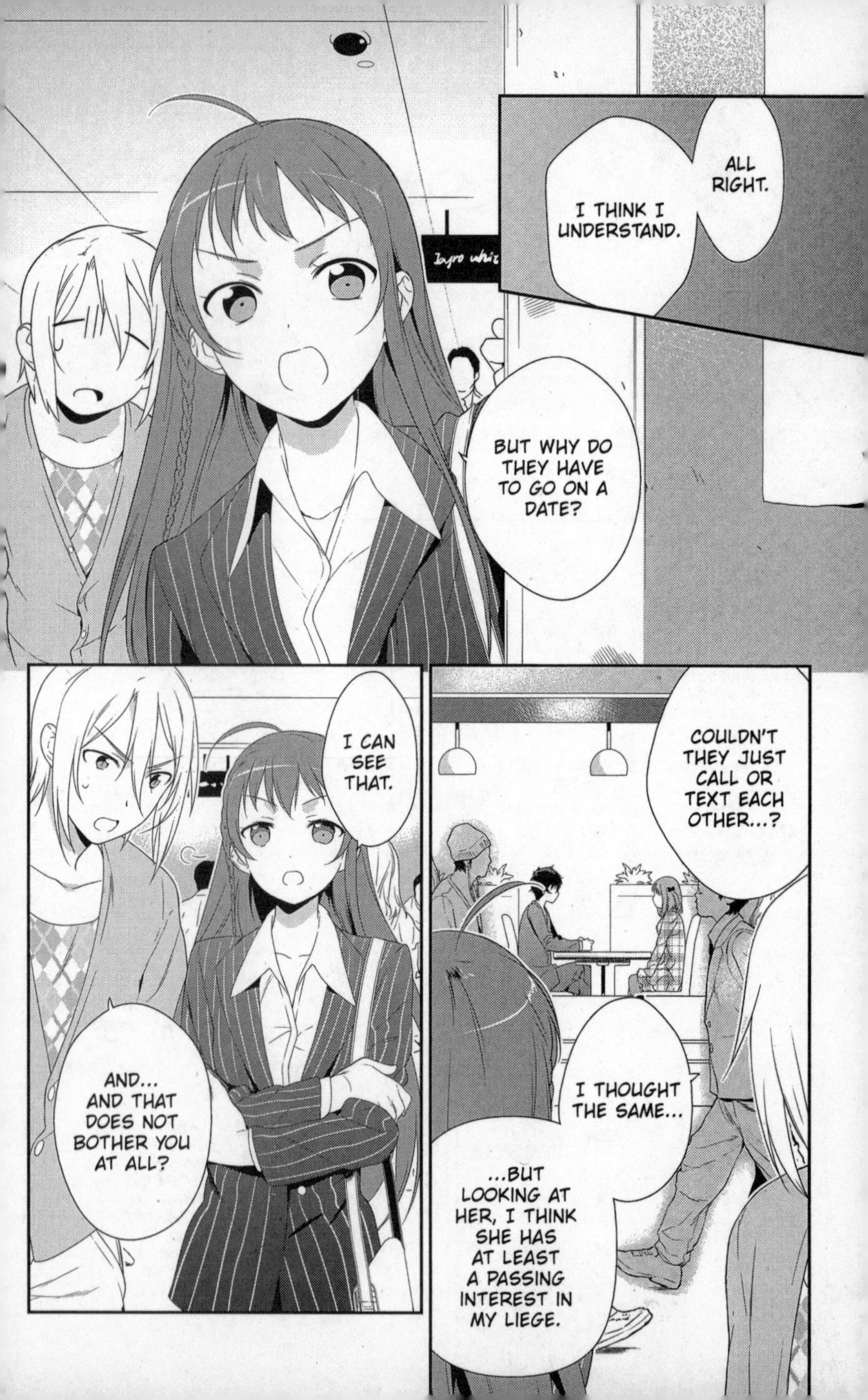
ALL RIGHT.
I THINK I UNDERSTAND.
BUT WHY DO THEY HAVE TO GO ON A DATE?
COULDN'T THEY JUST CALL OR TEXT EACH OTHER...?
I THOUGHT THE SAME...
...BUT LOOKING AT HER, I THINK SHE HAS AT LEAST A PASSING INTEREST IN MY LIEGE.
I CAN SEE THAT.
AND... AND THAT DOES NOT BOTHER YOU AT ALL?

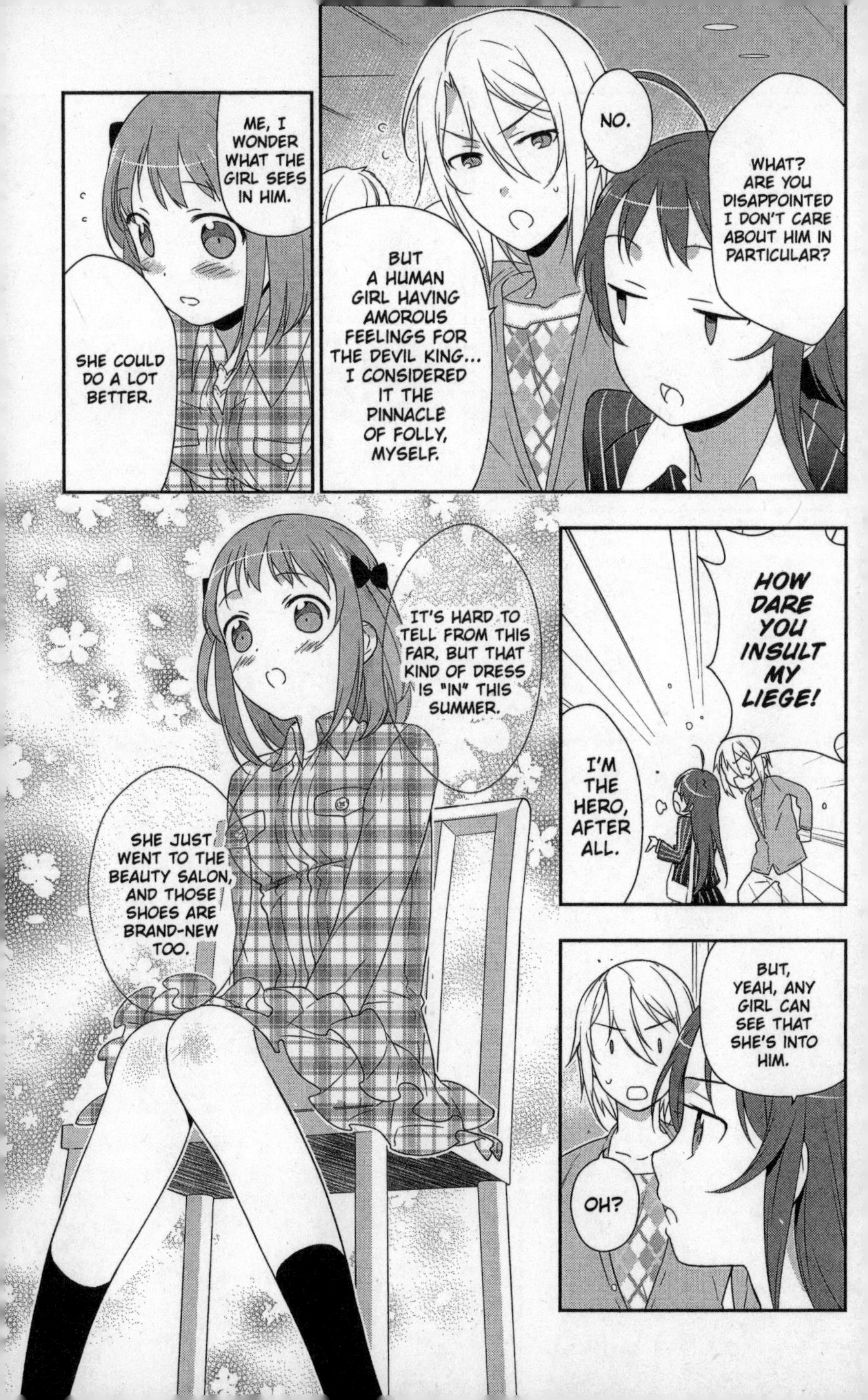
WHAT? ARE YOU DISAPPOINTED I DON'T CARE ABOUT HIM IN PARTICULAR?
NO.
BUT A HUMAN GIRL HAVING AMOROUS FEELINGS FOR THE DEVIL KING... I CONSIDERED IT THE PINNACLE OF FOLLY, MYSELF.
ME, I WONDER WHAT THE GIRL SEES IN HIM.
SHE COULD DO A LOT BETTER.
HOW DARE YOU INSULT MY LIEGE!
I'M THE HERO, AFTER ALL.
BUT, YEAH, ANY GIRL CAN SEE THAT SHE'S INTO HIM.
OH?
IT'S HARD TO TELL FROM THIS FAR, BUT THAT KIND OF DRESS IS "IN" THIS SUMMER.
SHE JUST WENT TO THE BEAUTY SALON, AND THOSE SHOES ARE BRAND-NEW TOO.

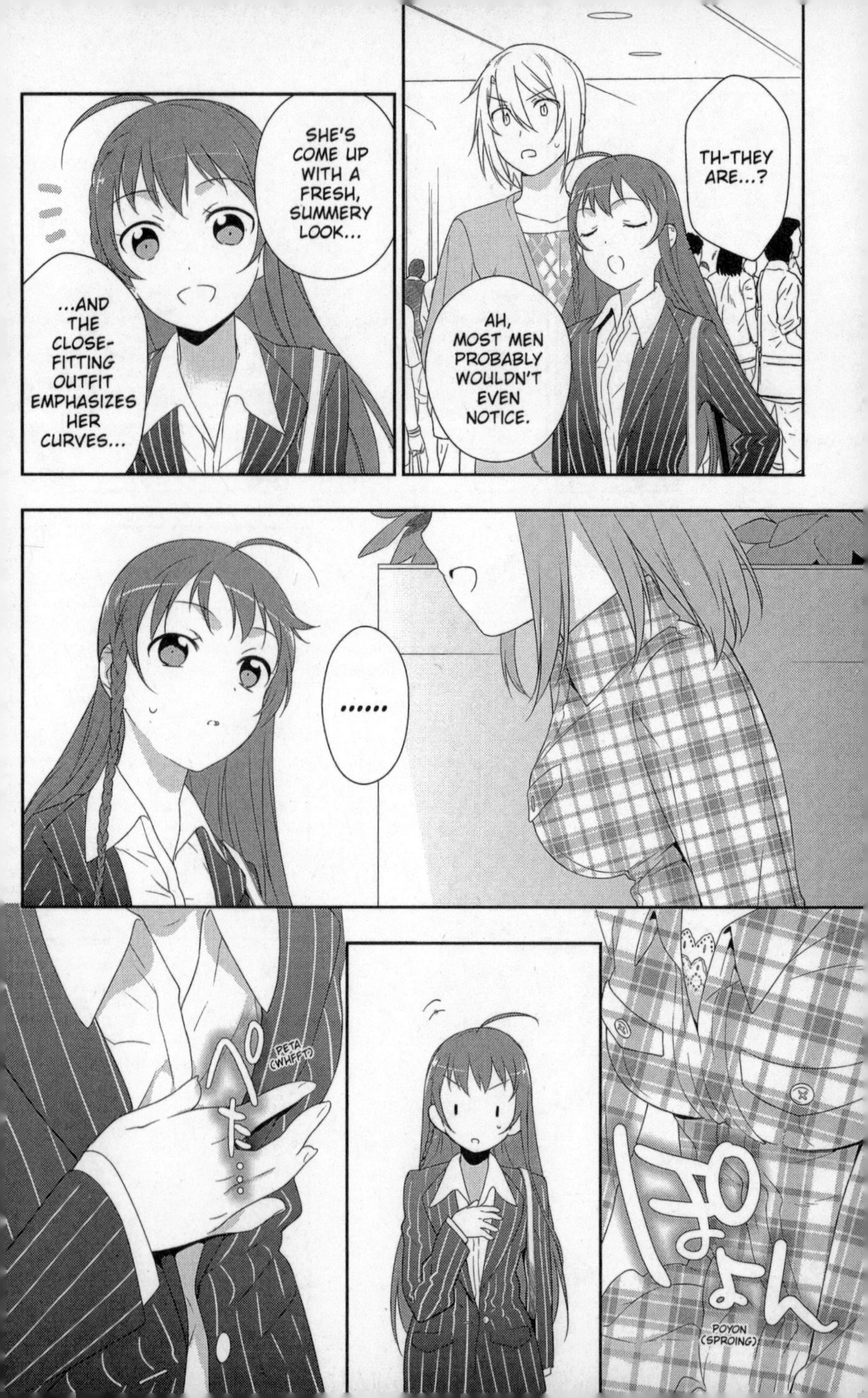
TH-THEY ARE...?
AH, MOST MEN PROBABLY WOULDN'T EVEN NOTICE.
SHE'S COME UP WITH A FRESH, SUMMERY LOOK...
...AND THE CLOSE-FITTING OUTFIT EMPHASIZES HER CURVES...
......
ぽよん
POYON (SPROING)
PETA (WHFFT)

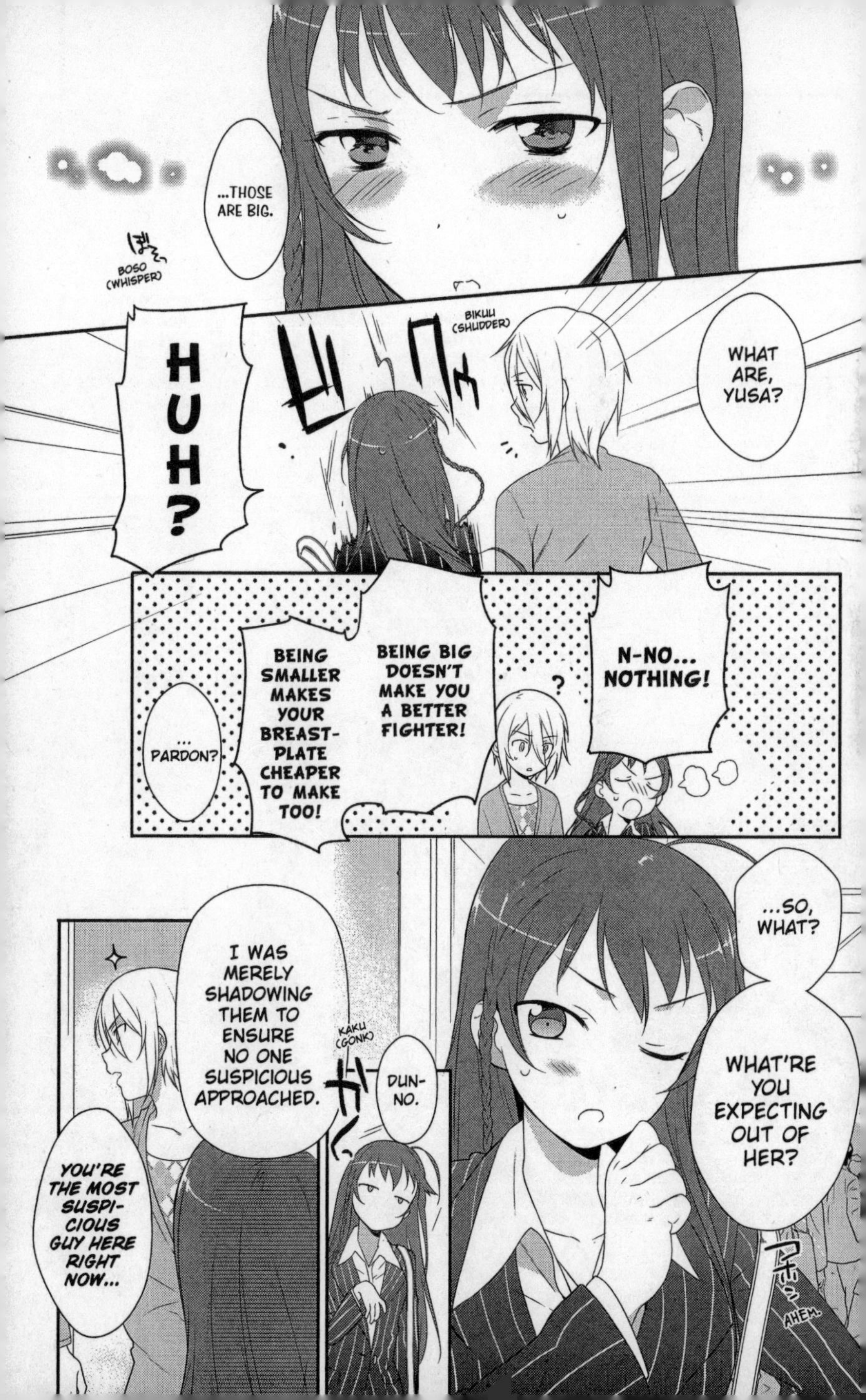
...THOSE ARE BIG.
BOSO (WHISPER)
WHAT ARE, YUSA?
BIKUU (SHUDDER)
HUH?
N-NO... NOTHING!
?
BEING BIG DOESN'T MAKE YOU A BETTER FIGHTER!
BEING SMALLER MAKES YOUR BREAST-PLATE CHEAPER TO MAKE TOO!
... PARDON?
...SO, WHAT?
WHAT'RE YOU EXPECTING OUT OF HER?
AHEM.
DUN-NO.
KAKU (GONK)
I WAS MERELY SHADOWING THEM TO ENSURE NO ONE SUSPICIOUS APPROACHED.
YOU'RE THE MOST SUSPI-CIOUS GUY HERE RIGHT NOW...

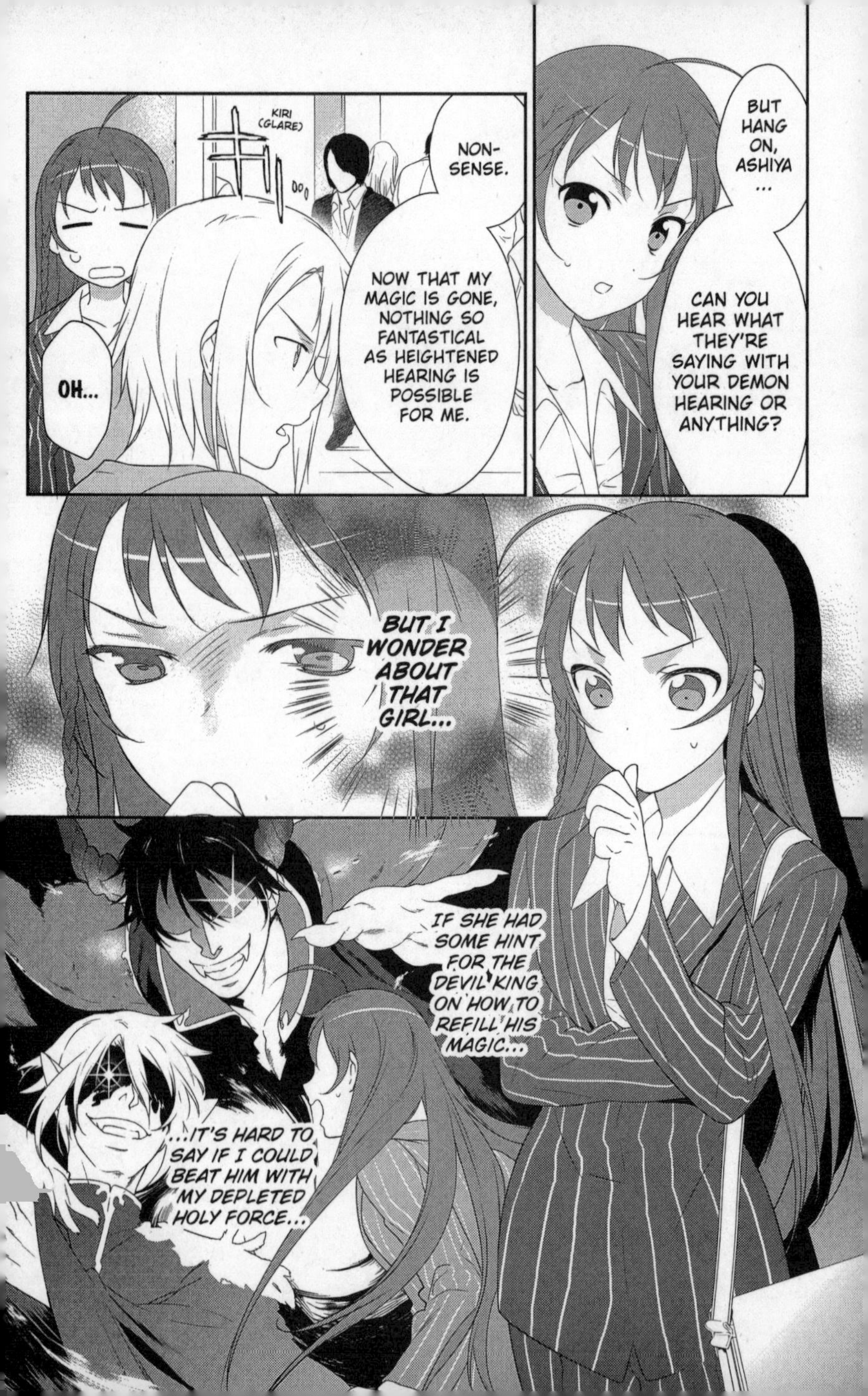
BUT HANG ON, ASHIYA...
CAN YOU HEAR WHAT THEY'RE SAYING WITH YOUR DEMON HEARING OR ANYTHING?
NON-SENSE.
KIRI (GLARE)
NOW THAT MY MAGIC IS GONE, NOTHING SO FANTASTICAL AS HEIGHTENED HEARING IS POSSIBLE FOR ME.
OH...
BUT I WONDER ABOUT THAT GIRL...
IF SHE HAD SOME HINT FOR THE DEVIL KING ON HOW TO REFILL HIS MAGIC...
...IT'S HARD TO SAY IF I COULD BEAT HIM WITH MY DEPLETED HOLY FORCE...

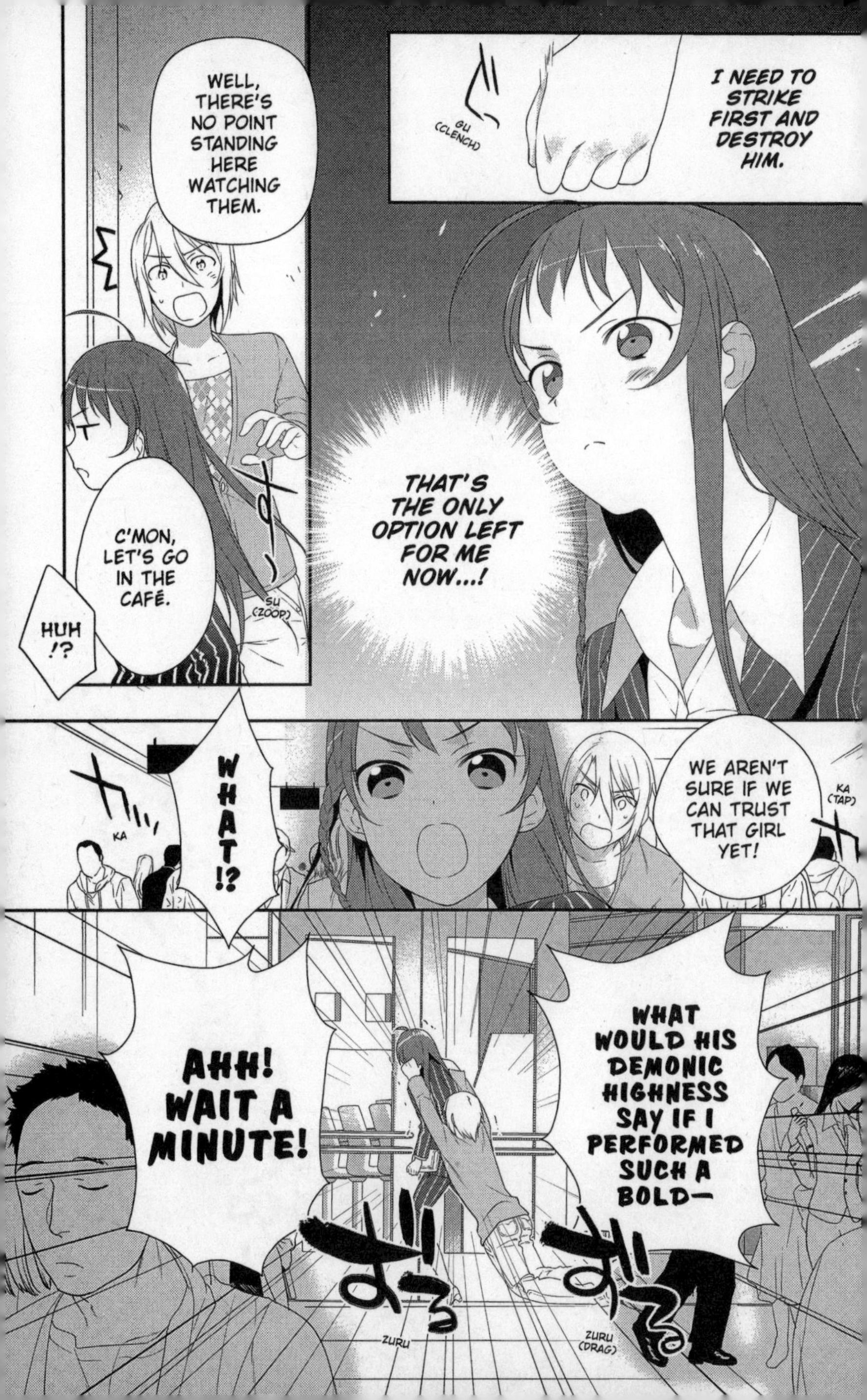
GU (CLENCH)
I NEED TO STRIKE FIRST AND DESTROY HIM.
THAT'S THE ONLY OPTION LEFT FOR ME NOW...!
WELL, THERE'S NO POINT STANDING HERE WATCHING THEM.
C'MON, LET'S GO IN THE CAFÉ.
SU (ZOOP)
HUH!?
KA (TAP)
WE AREN'T SURE IF WE CAN TRUST THAT GIRL YET!
WHAT!?
KA
WHAT WOULD HIS DEMONIC HIGHNESS SAY IF I PERFORMED SUCH A BOLD—
AHH! WAIT A MINUTE!
ZURU (DRAG)
ZURU

THE DEVIL IS A PART-TIMER!

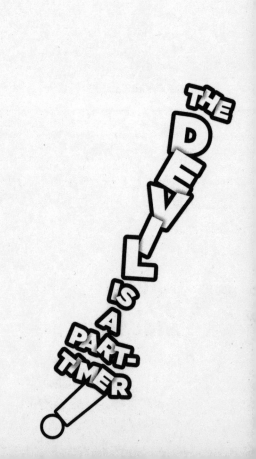

Emi
Yusa

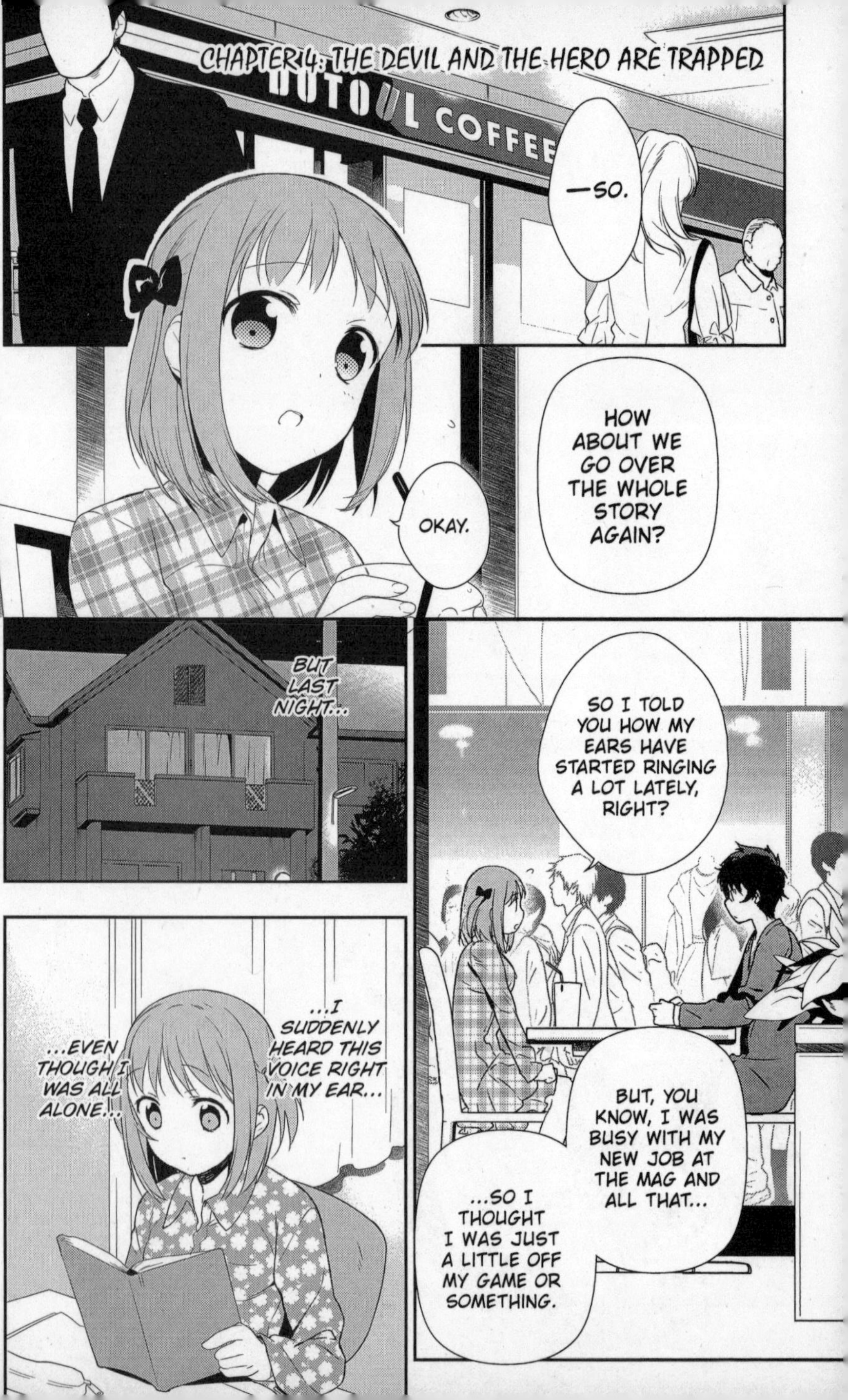
CHAPTER 4: THE DEVIL AND THE HERO ARE TRAPPED
—SO.
HOW ABOUT WE GO OVER THE WHOLE STORY AGAIN?
OKAY.
SO I TOLD YOU HOW MY EARS HAVE STARTED RINGING A LOT LATELY, RIGHT?
BUT, YOU KNOW, I WAS BUSY WITH MY NEW JOB AT THE MAG AND ALL THAT...
...SO I THOUGHT I WAS JUST A LITTLE OFF MY GAME OR SOMETHING.
BUT LAST NIGHT...
...I SUDDENLY HEARD THIS VOICE RIGHT IN MY EAR...
...EVEN THOUGH I WAS ALL ALONE...

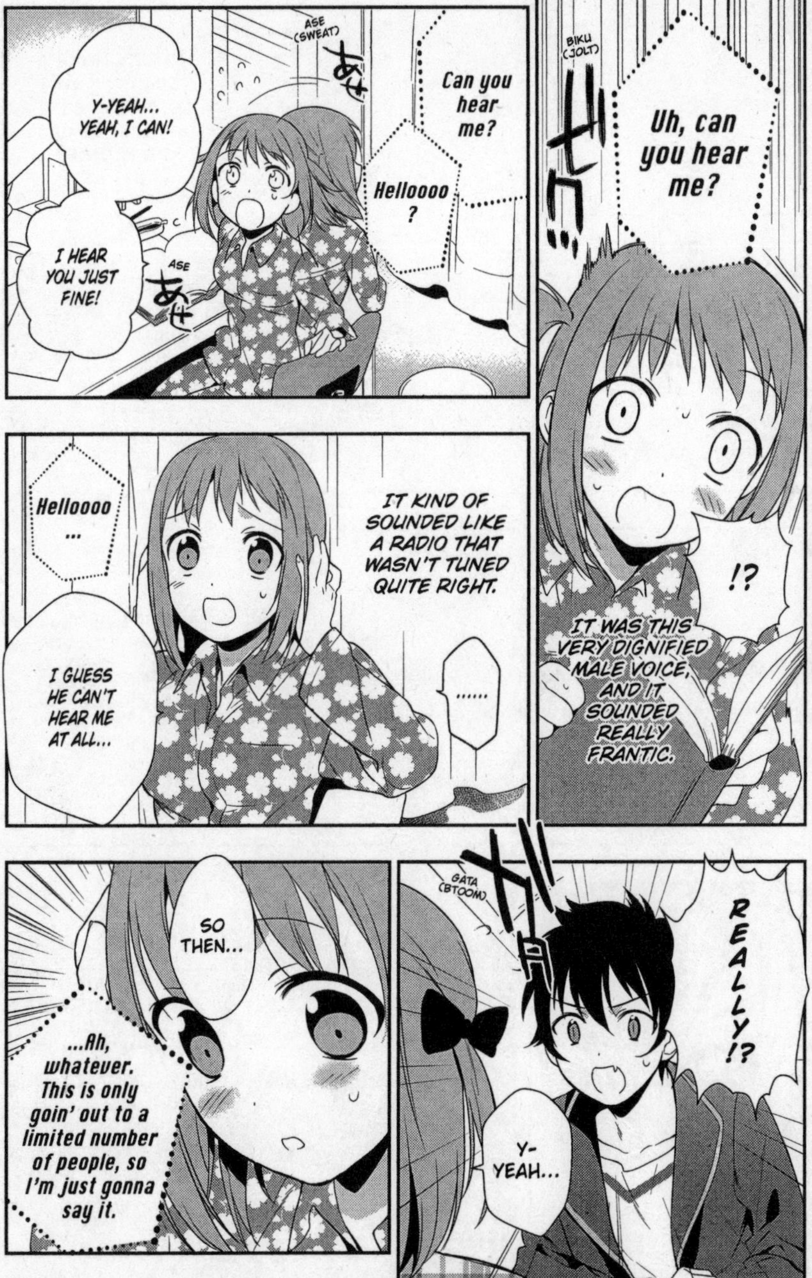
BIKU (JOLT)
Uh, can you hear me?
!?
IT WAS THIS VERY DIGNIFIED MALE VOICE, AND IT SOUNDED REALLY FRANTIC.
Can you hear me?
ASE (SWEAT)
Helloooo?
Y-YEAH... YEAH, I CAN!
ASE
I HEAR YOU JUST FINE!
IT KIND OF SOUNDED LIKE A RADIO THAT WASN'T TUNED QUITE RIGHT.
Helloooo...
......
I GUESS HE CAN'T HEAR ME AT ALL...
REALLY!?
GATA (BTOOM)
Y-YEAH...
SO THEN...
...Ah, whatever. This is only goin' out to a limited number of people, so I'm just gonna say it.

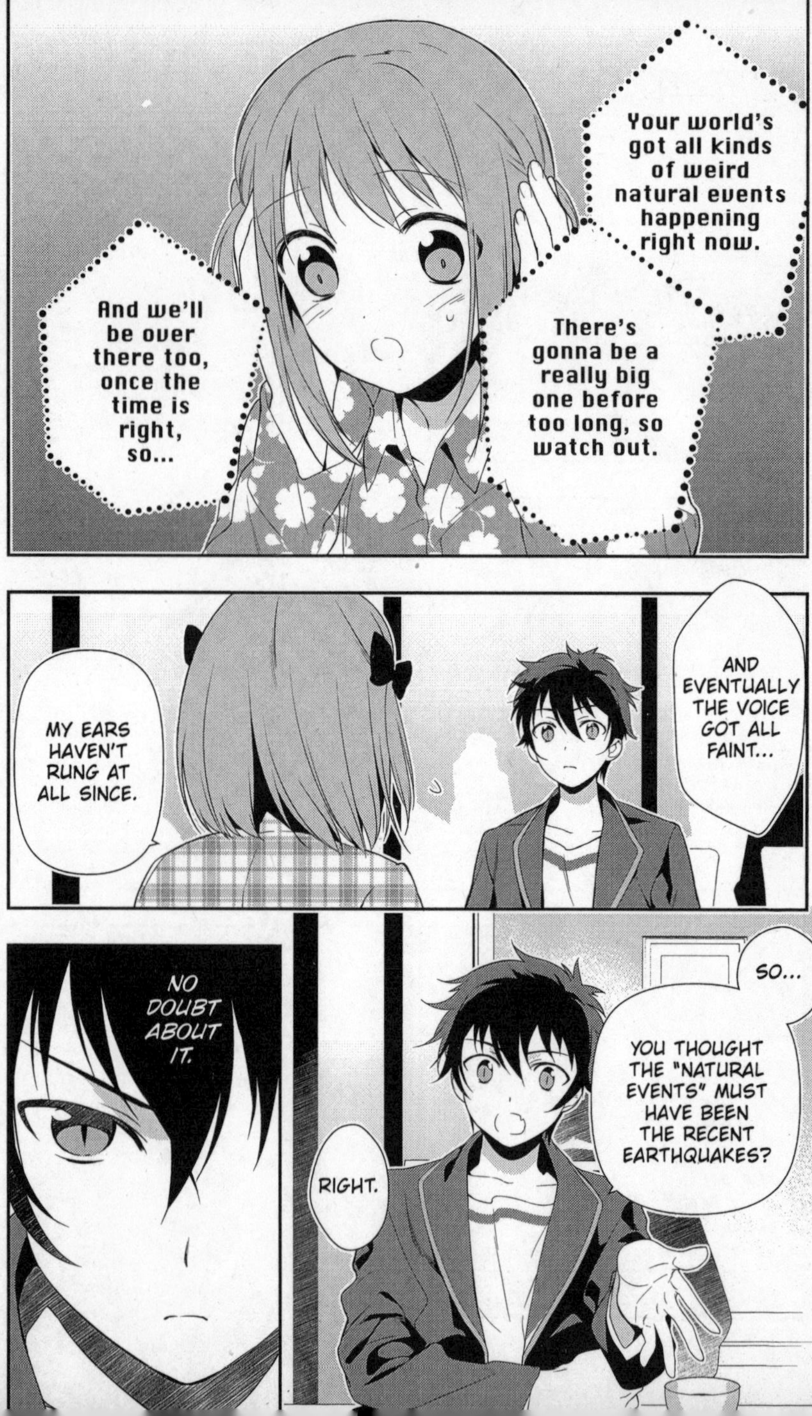
Your world's got all kinds of weird natural events happening right now.
There's gonna be a really big one before too long, so watch out.
And we'll be over there too, once the time is right, so...
AND EVENTUALLY THE VOICE GOT ALL FAINT...
MY EARS HAVEN'T RUNG AT ALL SINCE.
SO...
YOU THOUGHT THE "NATURAL EVENTS" MUST HAVE BEEN THE RECENT EARTHQUAKES?
RIGHT.
NO DOUBT ABOUT IT.

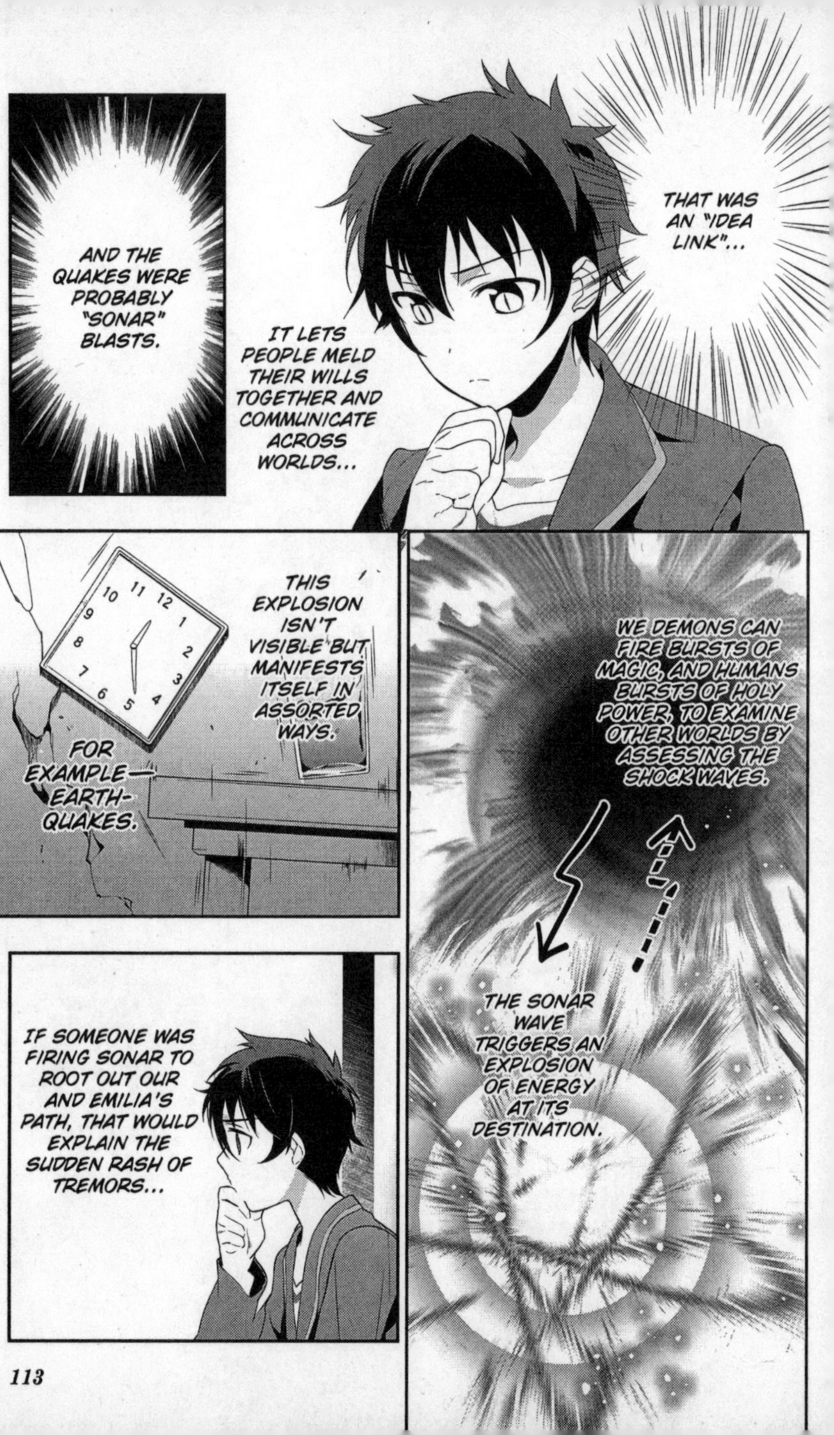
THAT WAS AN "IDEA LINK"...
IT LETS PEOPLE MELD THEIR WILLS TOGETHER AND COMMUNICATE ACROSS WORLDS...
AND THE QUAKES WERE PROBABLY "SONAR" BLASTS.
WE DEMONS CAN FIRE BURSTS OF MAGIC, AND HUMANS BURSTS OF HOLY POWER, TO EXAMINE OTHER WORLDS BY ASSESSING THE SHOCK WAVES.
THE SONAR WAVE TRIGGERS AN EXPLOSION OF ENERGY AT ITS DESTINATION.
THIS EXPLOSION ISN'T VISIBLE BUT MANIFESTS ITSELF IN ASSORTED WAYS.
FOR EXAMPLE—EARTHQUAKES.
IF SOMEONE WAS FIRING SONAR TO ROOT OUT OUR AND EMILIA'S PATH, THAT WOULD EXPLAIN THE SUDDEN RASH OF TREMORS...

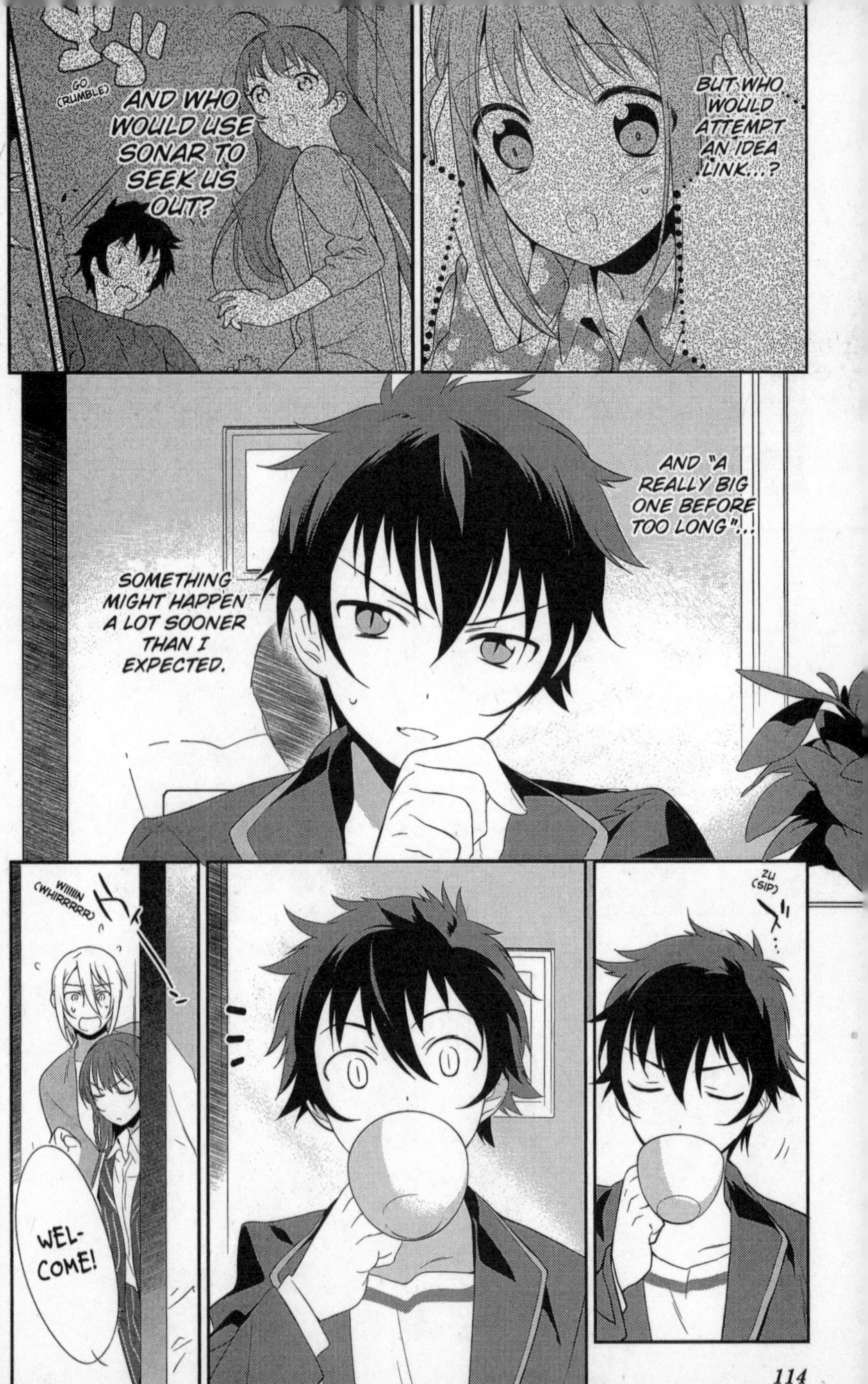
BUT WHO WOULD ATTEMPT AN IDEA LINK...?
GO (RUMBLE)
AND WHO WOULD USE SONAR TO SEEK US OUT?
AND "A REALLY BIG ONE BEFORE TOO LONG"...
SOMETHING MIGHT HAPPEN A LOT SOONER THAN I EXPECTED.
ZU (SIP)
WIIIIN (WHIRRRRR)
WEL-COME!

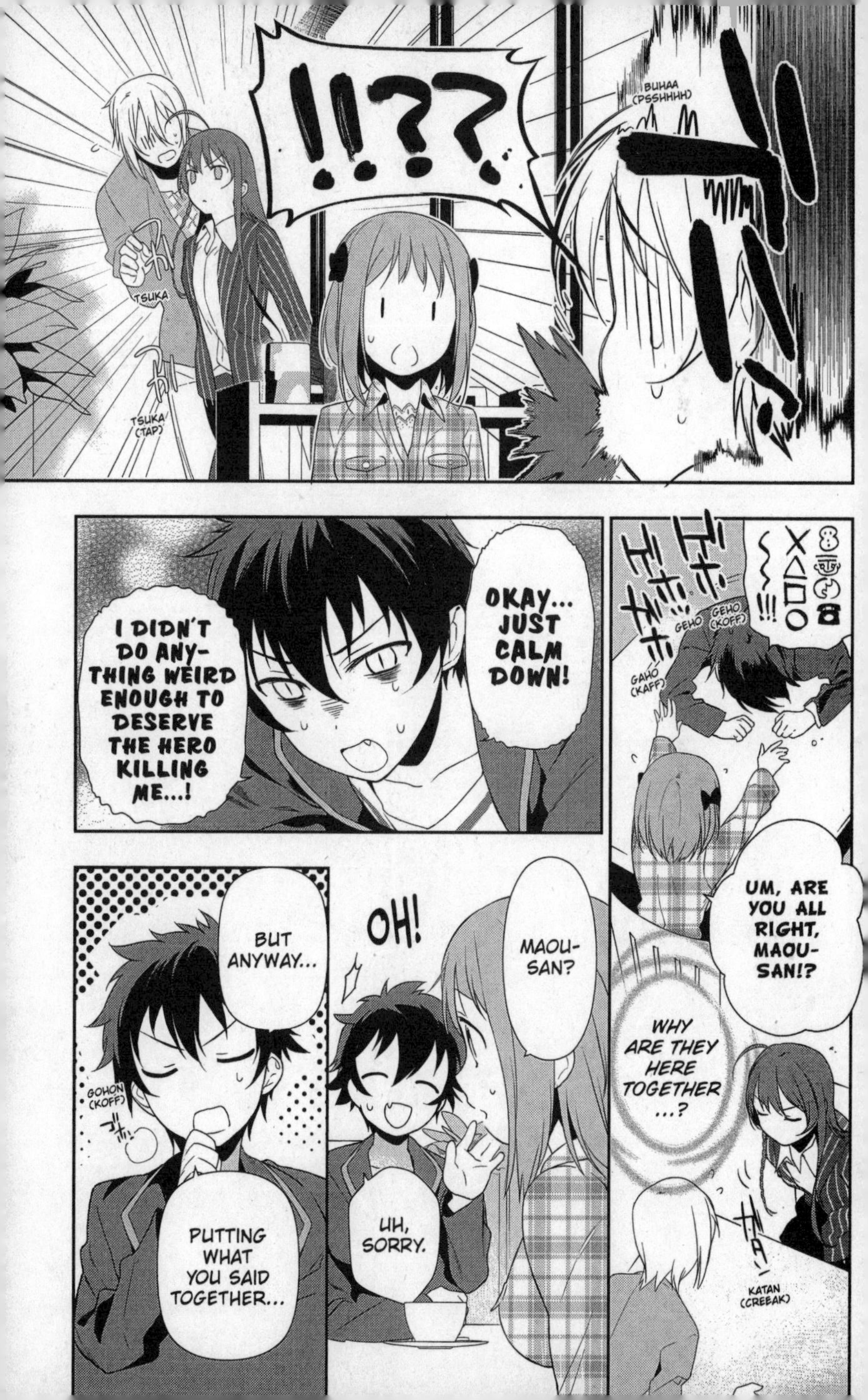
BUHAA (PSSHHHH)
!!??
TSUKA
TSUKA (TAP)
GEHO (KOFF)
GEHO
GAHO (KAFF)
UM, ARE YOU ALL RIGHT, MAOU-SAN!?
WHY ARE THEY HERE TOGETHER ...?
KATAN (CREEAK)
OKAY... JUST CALM DOWN!
I DIDN'T DO ANY-THING WEIRD ENOUGH TO DESERVE THE HERO KILLING ME...!
MAOU-SAN?
OH!
UH, SORRY.
BUT ANYWAY...
GOHON (KOFF)
PUTTING WHAT YOU SAID TOGETHER...

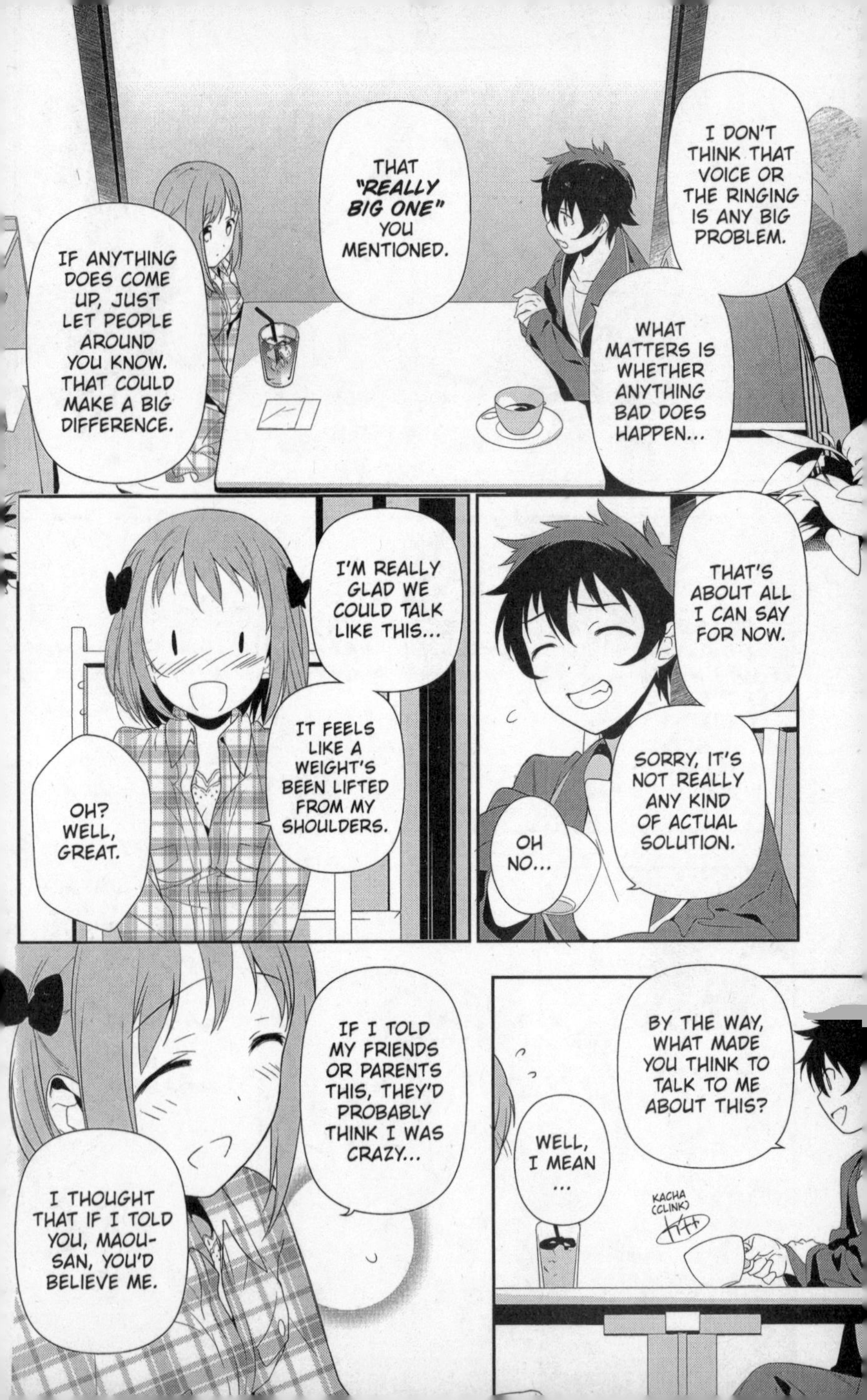
I DON'T THINK THAT VOICE OR THE RINGING IS ANY BIG PROBLEM.
WHAT MATTERS IS WHETHER ANYTHING BAD DOES HAPPEN...
THAT ***"REALLY BIG ONE"*** YOU MENTIONED.
IF ANYTHING DOES COME UP, JUST LET PEOPLE AROUND YOU KNOW. THAT COULD MAKE A BIG DIFFERENCE.
THAT'S ABOUT ALL I CAN SAY FOR NOW.
SORRY, IT'S NOT REALLY ANY KIND OF ACTUAL SOLUTION.
OH NO...
I'M REALLY GLAD WE COULD TALK LIKE THIS...
IT FEELS LIKE A WEIGHT'S BEEN LIFTED FROM MY SHOULDERS.
OH? WELL, GREAT.
BY THE WAY, WHAT MADE YOU THINK TO TALK TO ME ABOUT THIS?
KACHA (CLINK)
WELL, I MEAN ...
IF I TOLD MY FRIENDS OR PARENTS THIS, THEY'D PROBABLY THINK I WAS CRAZY...
I THOUGHT THAT IF I TOLD YOU, MAOU-SAN, YOU'D BELIEVE ME.

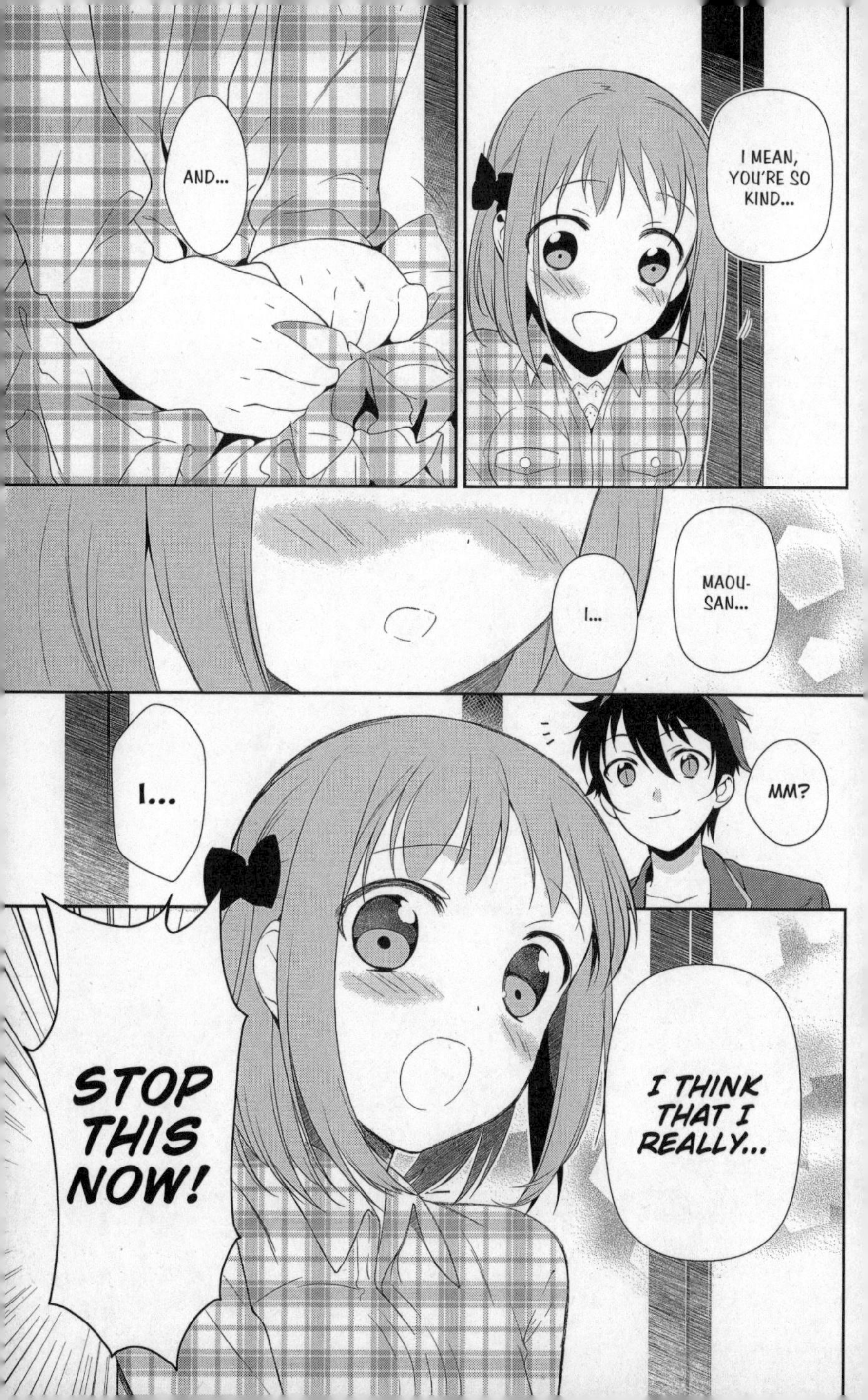
I MEAN, YOU'RE SO KIND...
AND...
MAOU-SAN...
I...
I...
MM?
I THINK THAT I REALLY...
STOP THIS NOW!

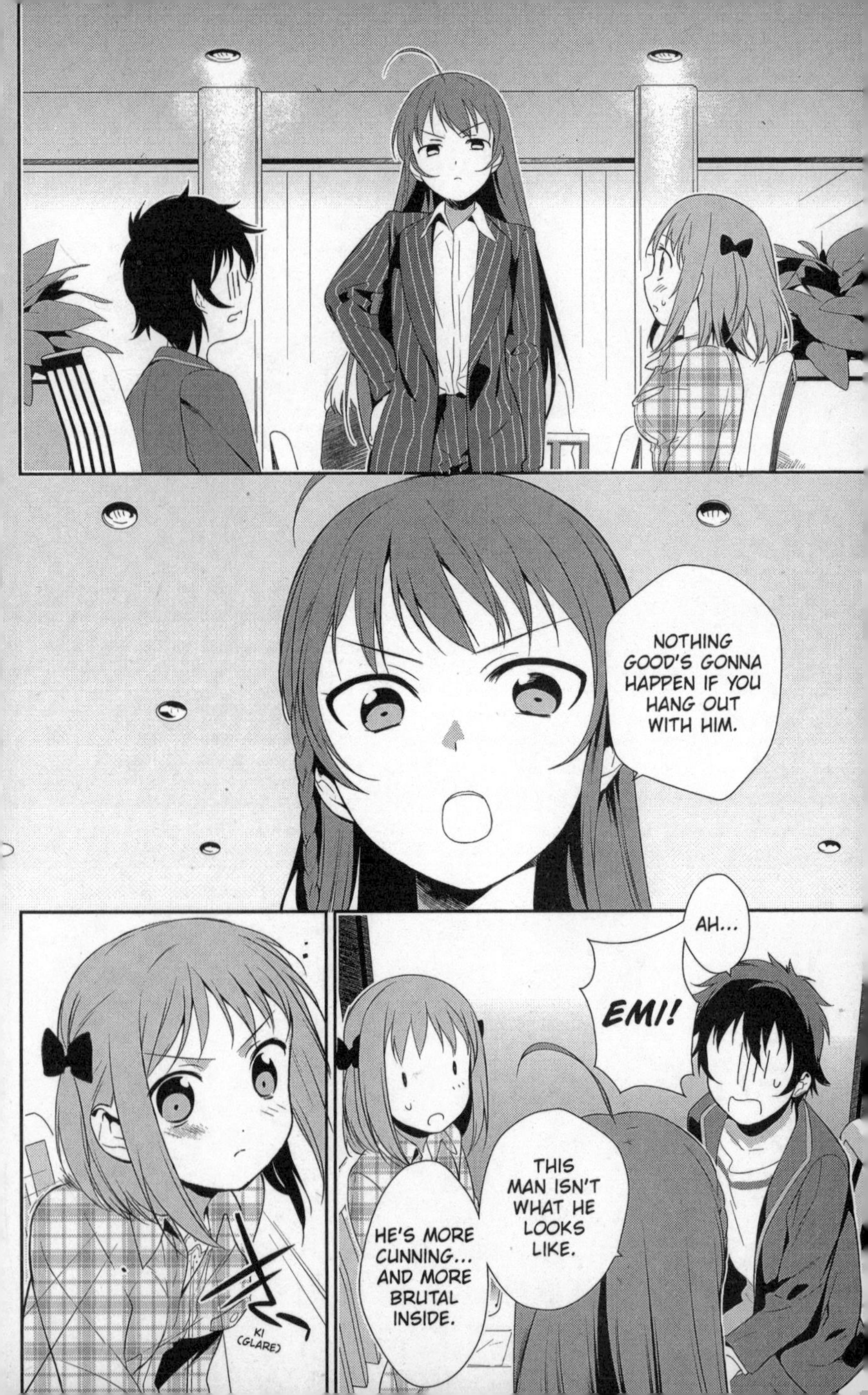
NOTHING GOOD'S GONNA HAPPEN IF YOU HANG OUT WITH HIM.
AH...
EMI!
THIS MAN ISN'T WHAT HE LOOKS LIKE.
HE'S MORE CUNNING... AND MORE BRUTAL INSIDE.
KI (GLARE)

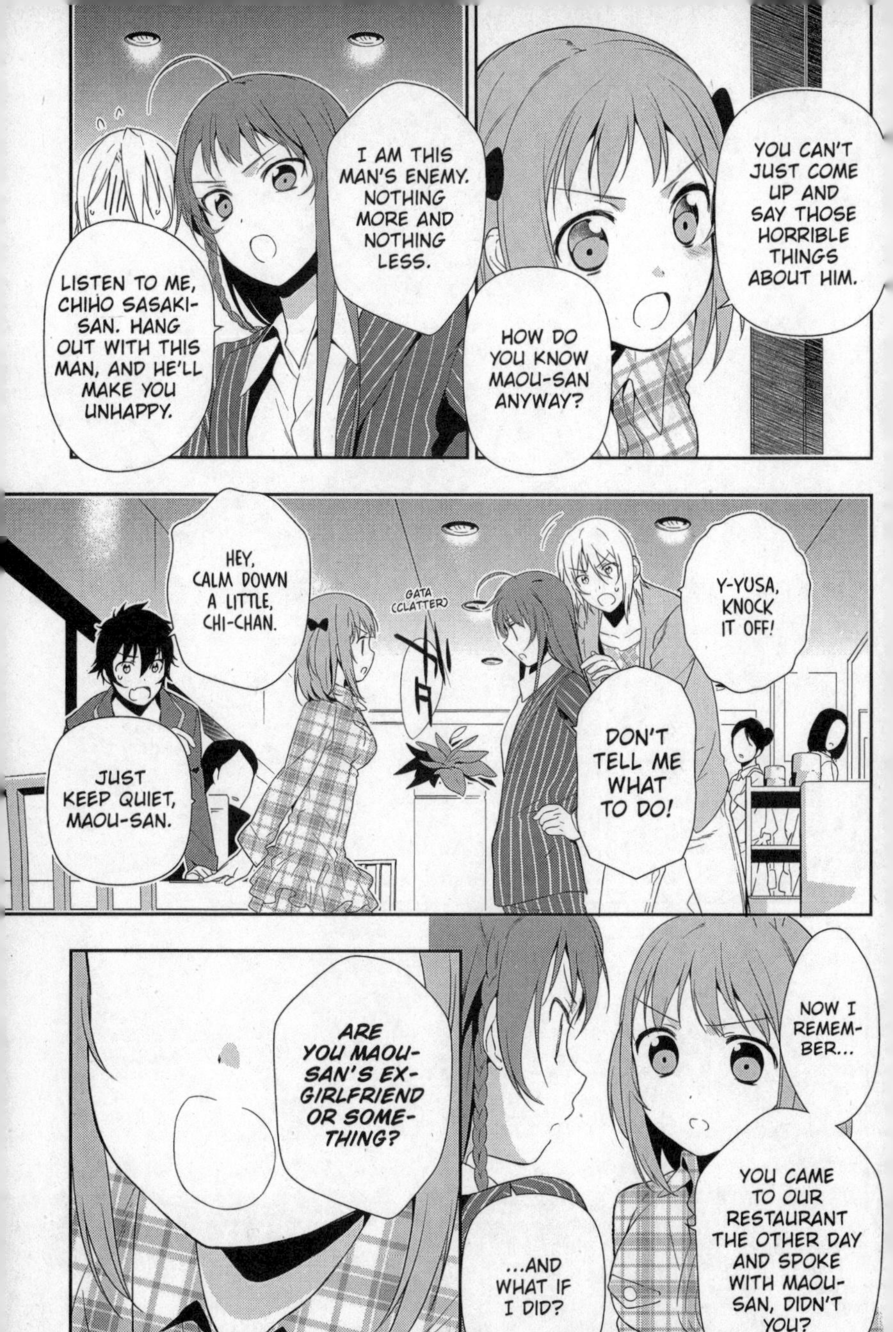
YOU CAN'T JUST COME UP AND SAY THOSE HORRIBLE THINGS ABOUT HIM.
HOW DO YOU KNOW MAOU-SAN ANYWAY?
I AM THIS MAN'S ENEMY. NOTHING MORE AND NOTHING LESS.
LISTEN TO ME, CHIHO SASAKI-SAN. HANG OUT WITH THIS MAN, AND HE'LL MAKE YOU UNHAPPY.
Y-YUSA, KNOCK IT OFF!
DON'T TELL ME WHAT TO DO!
GATA (CLATTER)
HEY, CALM DOWN A LITTLE, CHI-CHAN.
JUST KEEP QUIET, MAOU-SAN.
NOW I REMEMBER...
YOU CAME TO OUR RESTAURANT THE OTHER DAY AND SPOKE WITH MAOU-SAN, DIDN'T YOU?
...AND WHAT IF I DID?
ARE YOU MAOU-SAN'S EX-GIRLFRIEND OR SOMETHING?

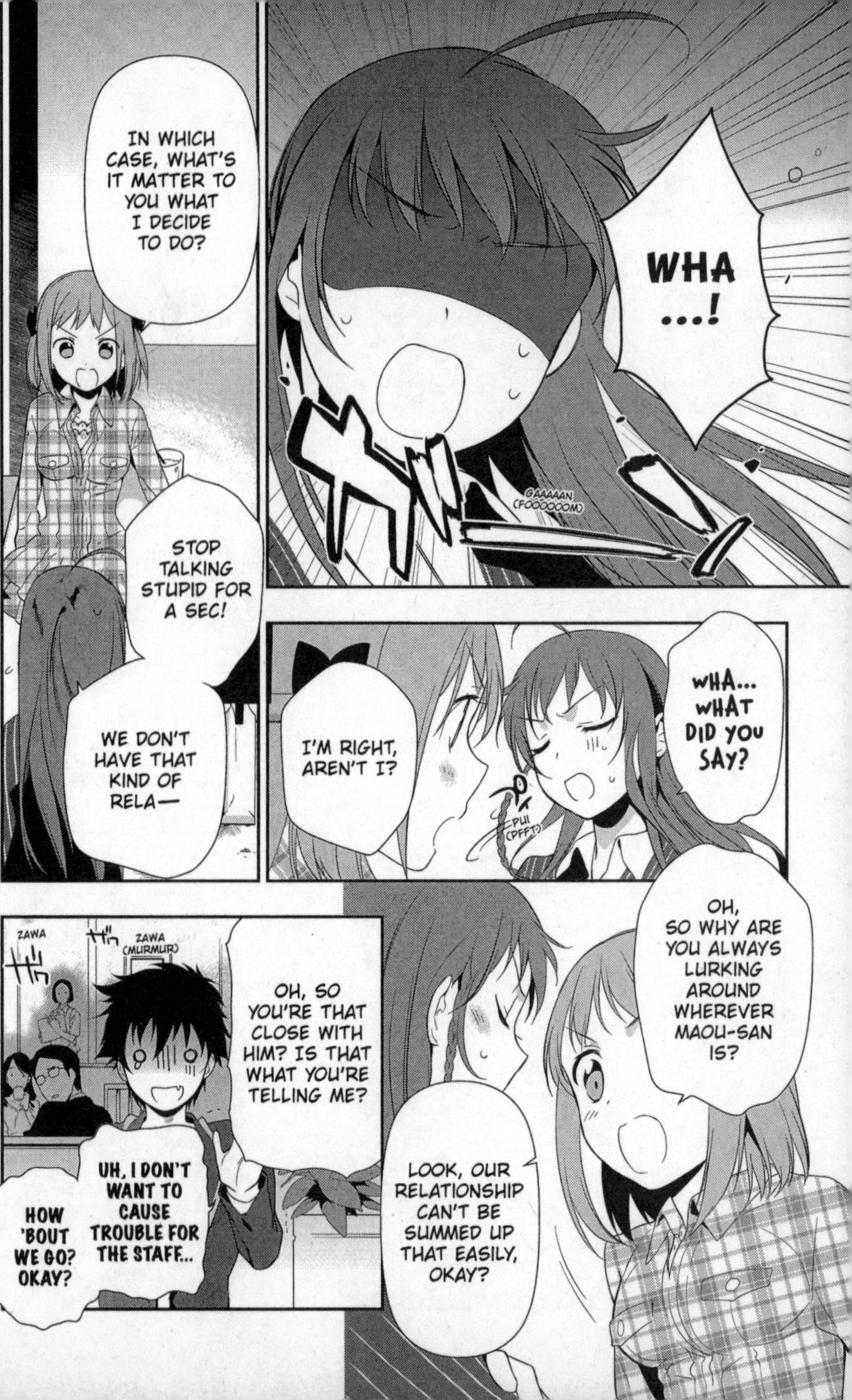
WHA ...!
GAAAAAN (FOOOOOOM)
WHA... WHAT DID YOU SAY?
PUI (PFFT)
I'M RIGHT, AREN'T I?
IN WHICH CASE, WHAT'S IT MATTER TO YOU WHAT I DECIDE TO DO?
STOP TALKING STUPID FOR A SEC!
WE DON'T HAVE THAT KIND OF RELA—
OH, SO WHY ARE YOU ALWAYS LURKING AROUND WHEREVER MAOU-SAN IS?
LOOK, OUR RELATIONSHIP CAN'T BE SUMMED UP THAT EASILY, OKAY?
OH, SO YOU'RE THAT CLOSE WITH HIM? IS THAT WHAT YOU'RE TELLING ME?
ZAWA (MURMUR)
ZAWA
UH, I DON'T WANT TO CAUSE TROUBLE FOR THE STAFF...
HOW 'BOUT WE GO? OKAY?

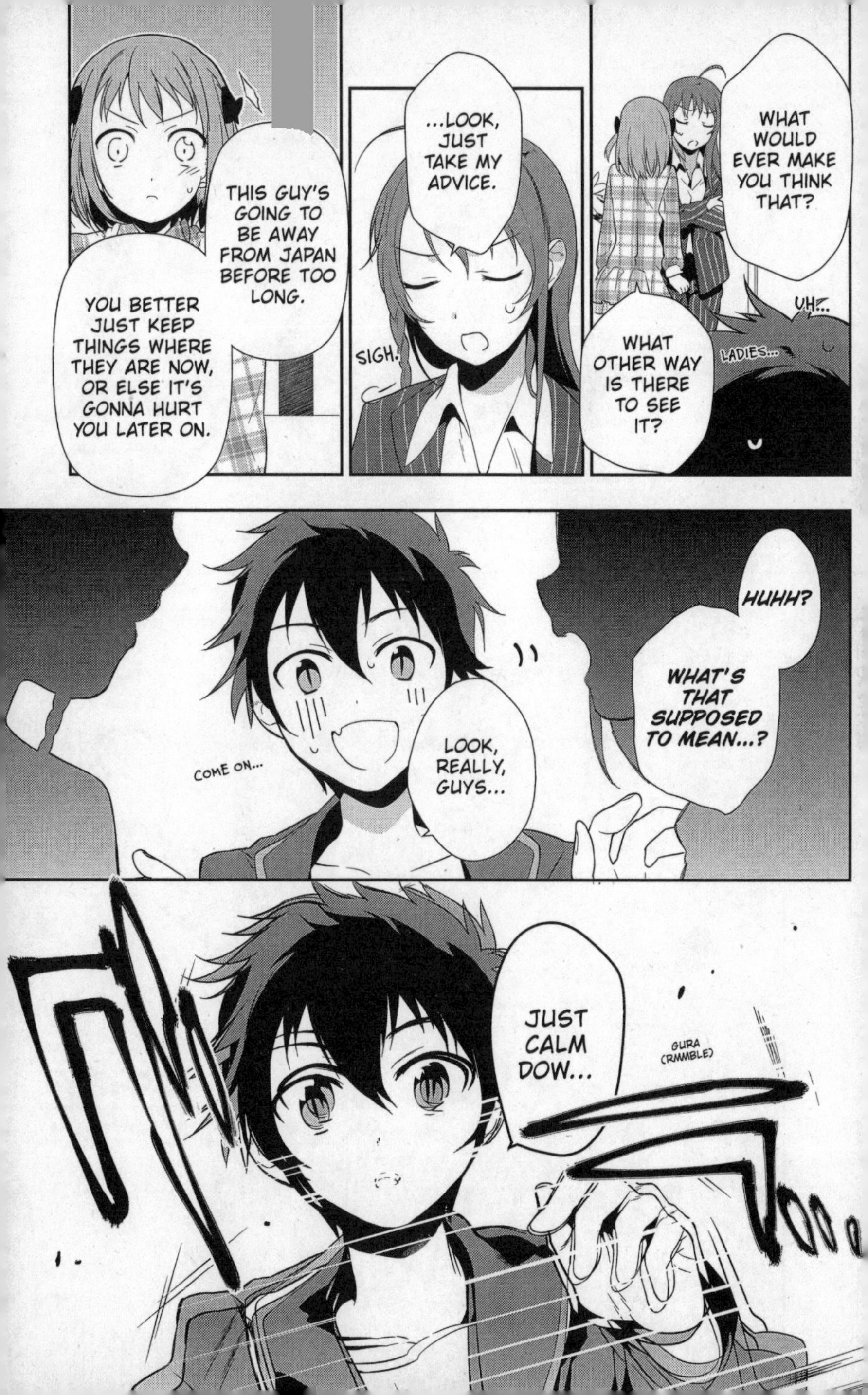
WHAT WOULD EVER MAKE YOU THINK THAT?
UH... LADIES...
WHAT OTHER WAY IS THERE TO SEE IT?
...LOOK, JUST TAKE MY ADVICE.
SIGH.
THIS GUY'S GOING TO BE AWAY FROM JAPAN BEFORE TOO LONG.
YOU BETTER JUST KEEP THINGS WHERE THEY ARE NOW, OR ELSE IT'S GONNA HURT YOU LATER ON.
HUHH?
WHAT'S THAT SUPPOSED TO MEAN...?
LOOK, REALLY, GUYS...
COME ON...
JUST CALM DOW...
GURA (RMMBLE)

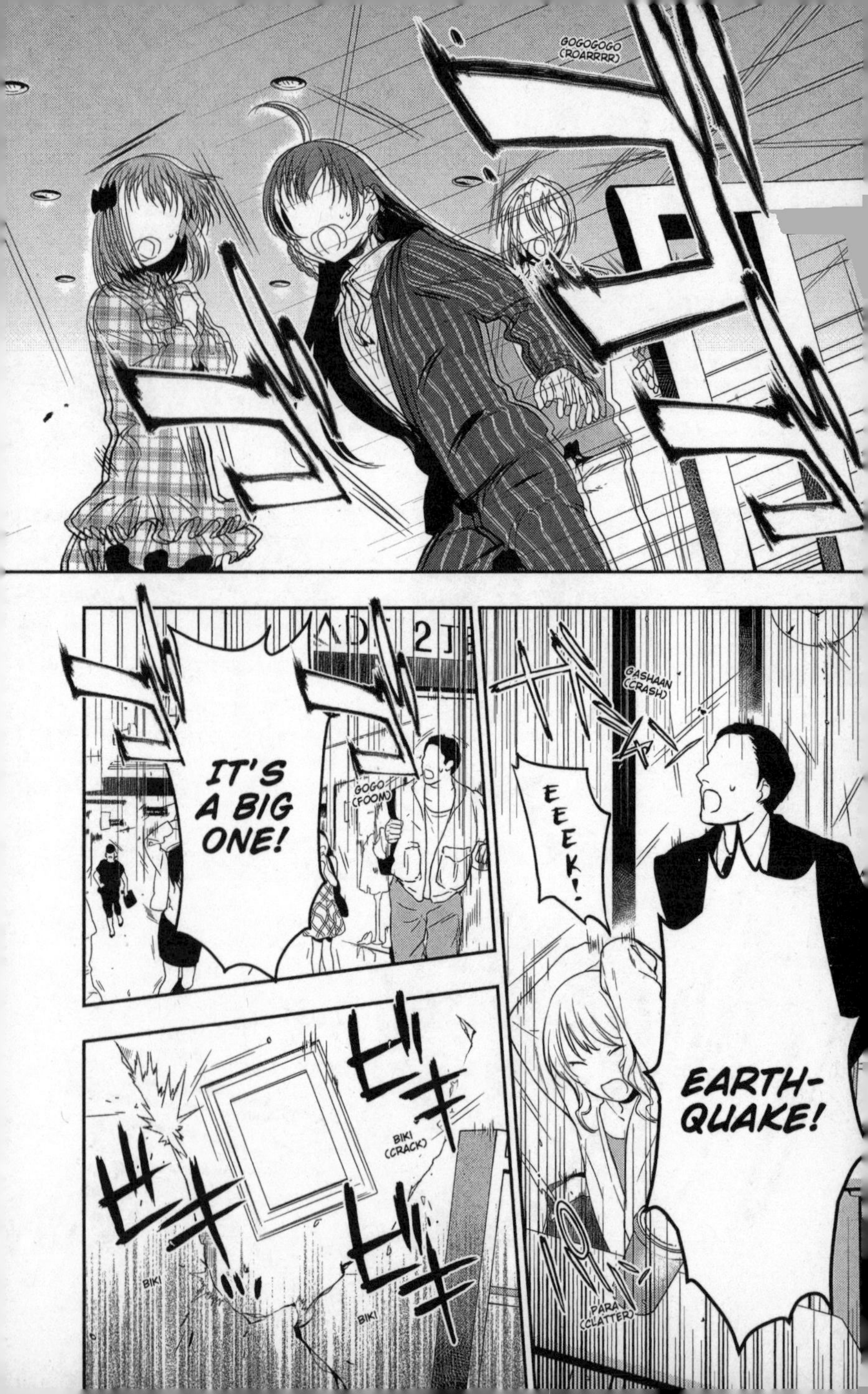
GOGOGOGO (ROARRRR)
GASHAAN (CRASH)
EEEK!
EARTH-QUAKE!
PARA (CLATTER)
IT'S A BIG ONE!
GOGO (FOOM)
BIKI (CRACK)
BIKI
BIKI

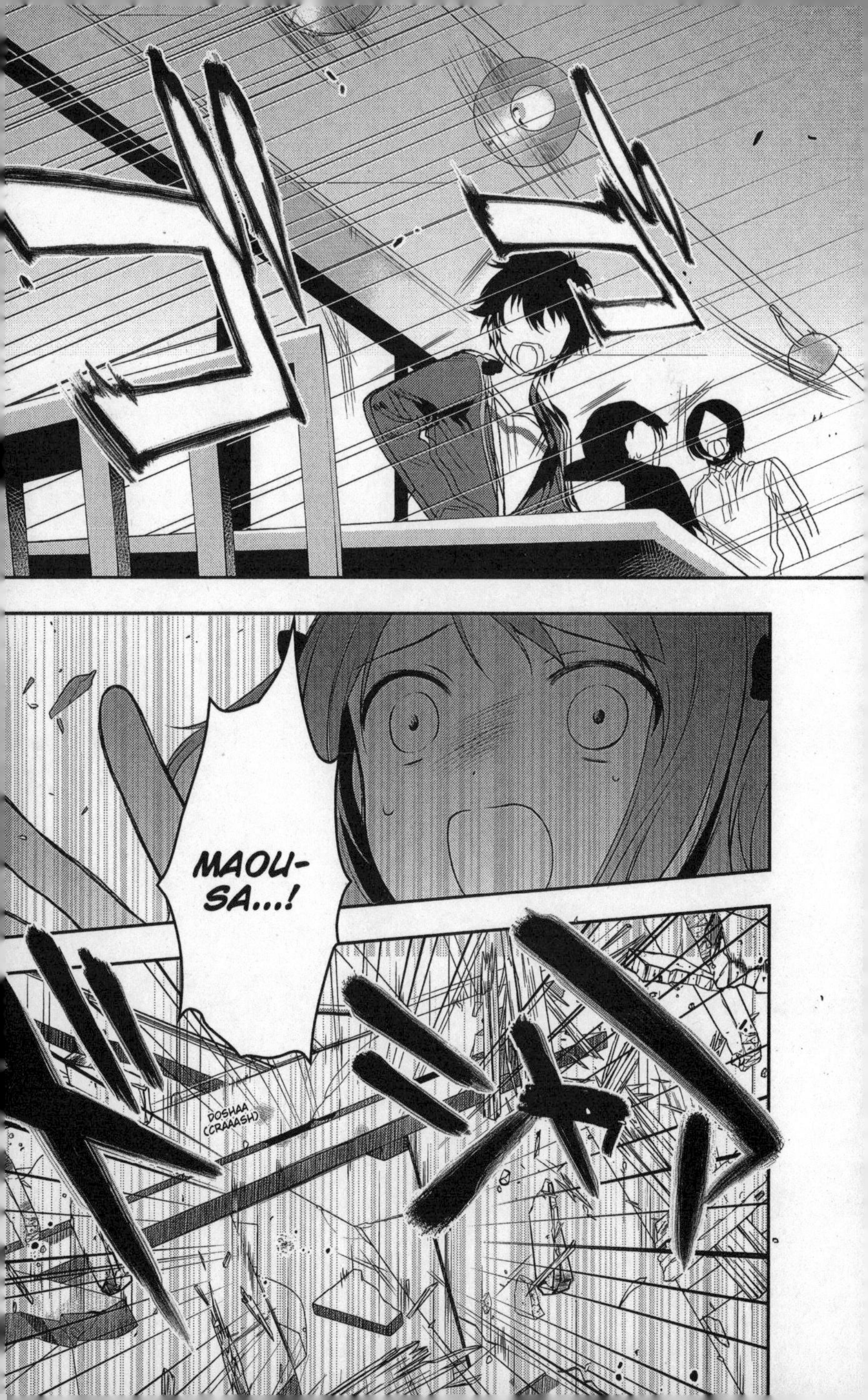
MAOU-SA...!
DOSHAA (CRAAASH)

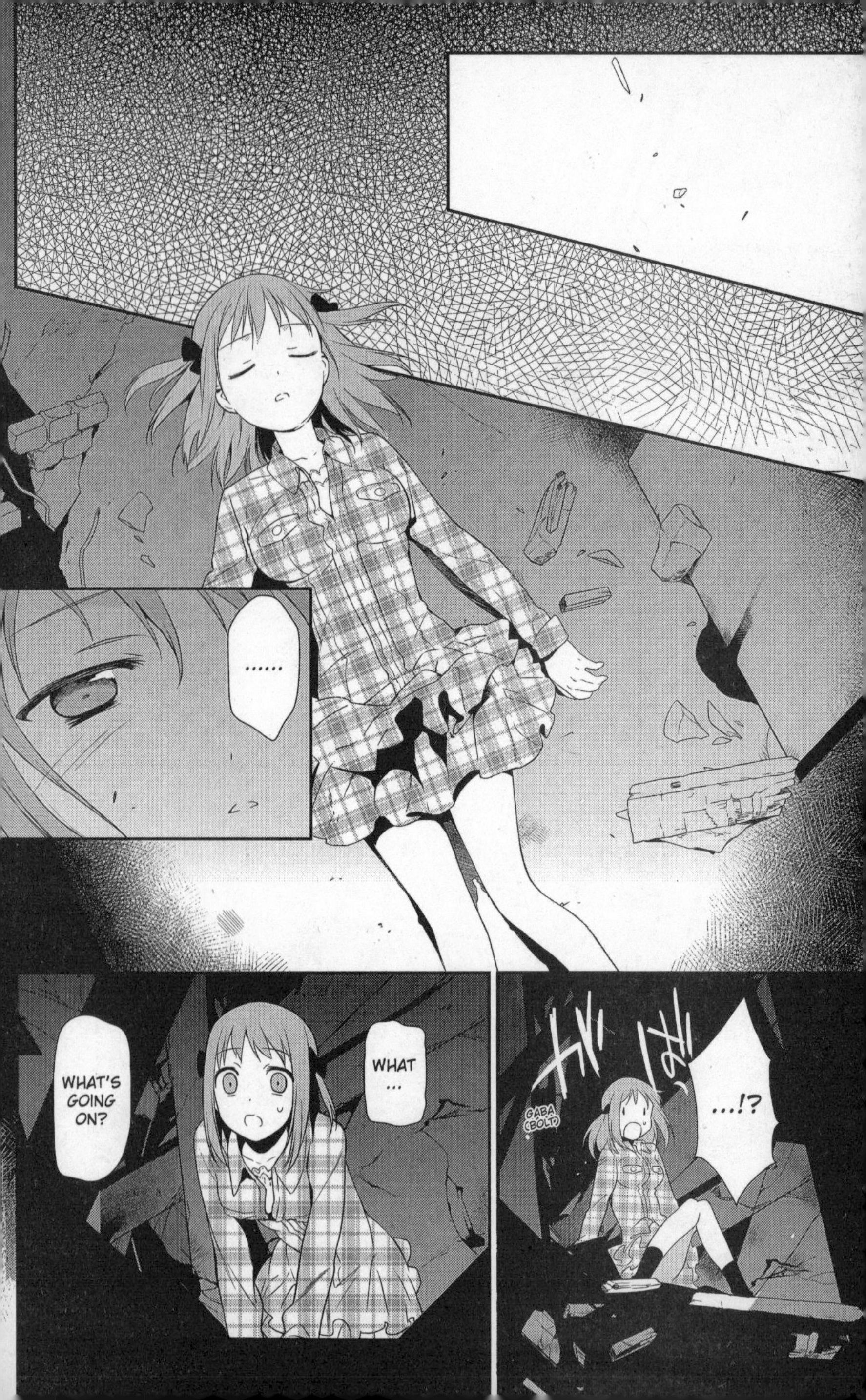

......
GABA (BOLT)
...!?
WHAT ...
WHAT'S GOING ON?

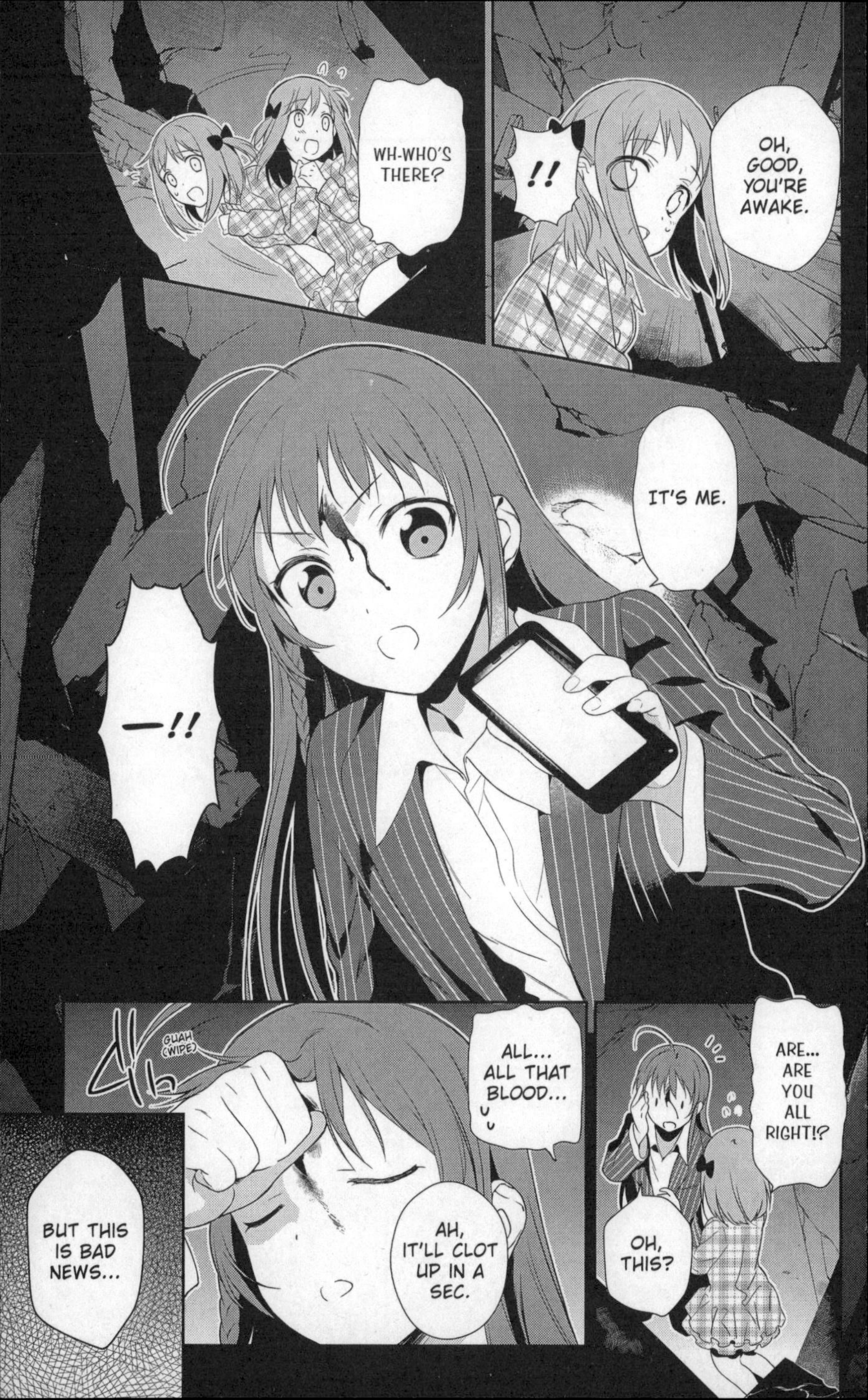
!!
OH, GOOD, YOU'RE AWAKE.
WH-WHO'S THERE?
IT'S ME.
—!!
ARE... ARE YOU ALL RIGHT!?
OH, THIS?
ALL... ALL THAT BLOOD...
GUAH (WIPE)
AH, IT'LL CLOT UP IN A SEC.
BUT THIS IS BAD NEWS...

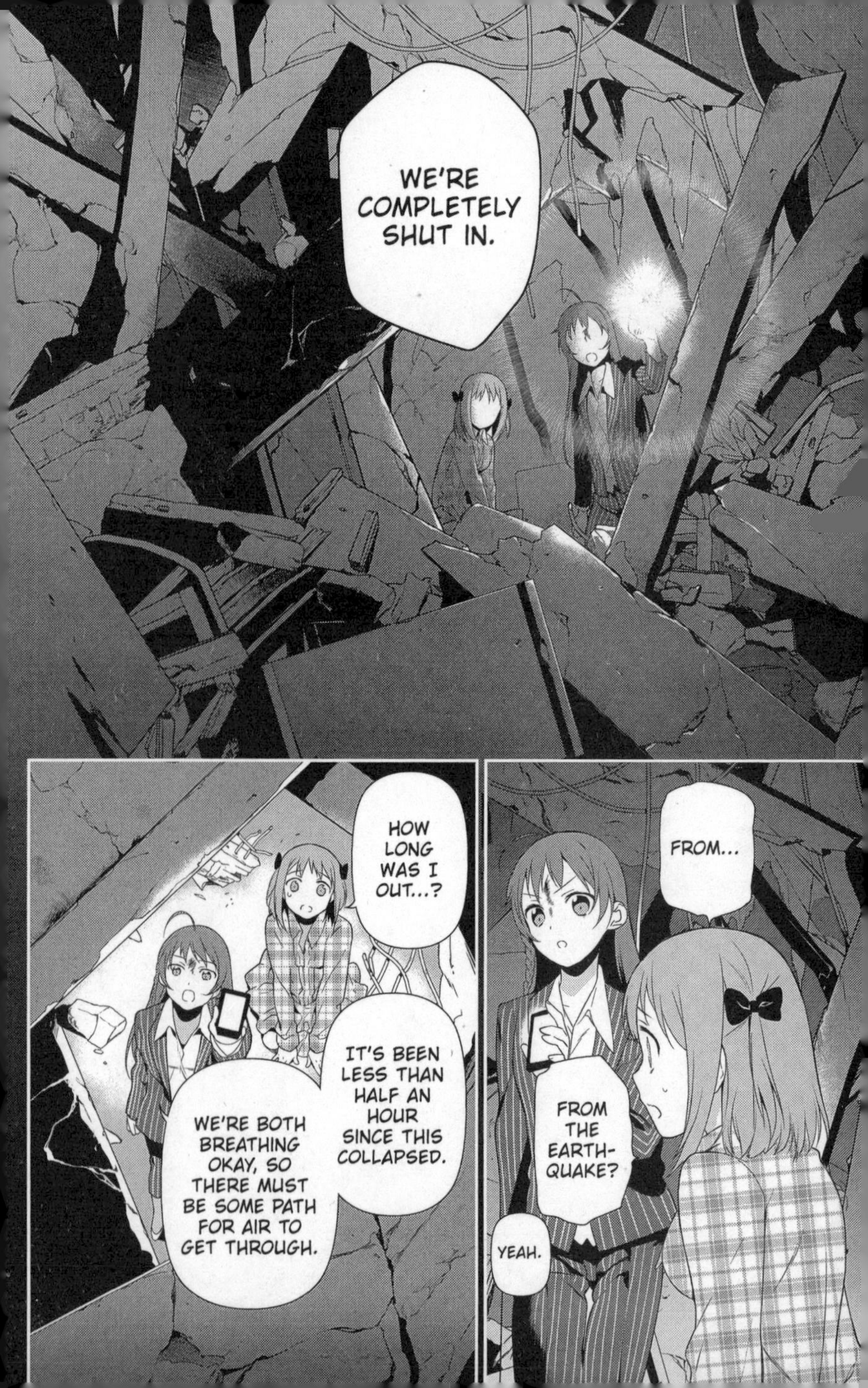
WE'RE COMPLETELY SHUT IN.
FROM...
FROM THE EARTH-QUAKE?
YEAH.
HOW LONG WAS I OUT...?
IT'S BEEN LESS THAN HALF AN HOUR SINCE THIS COLLAPSED.
WE'RE BOTH BREATHING OKAY, SO THERE MUST BE SOME PATH FOR AIR TO GET THROUGH.

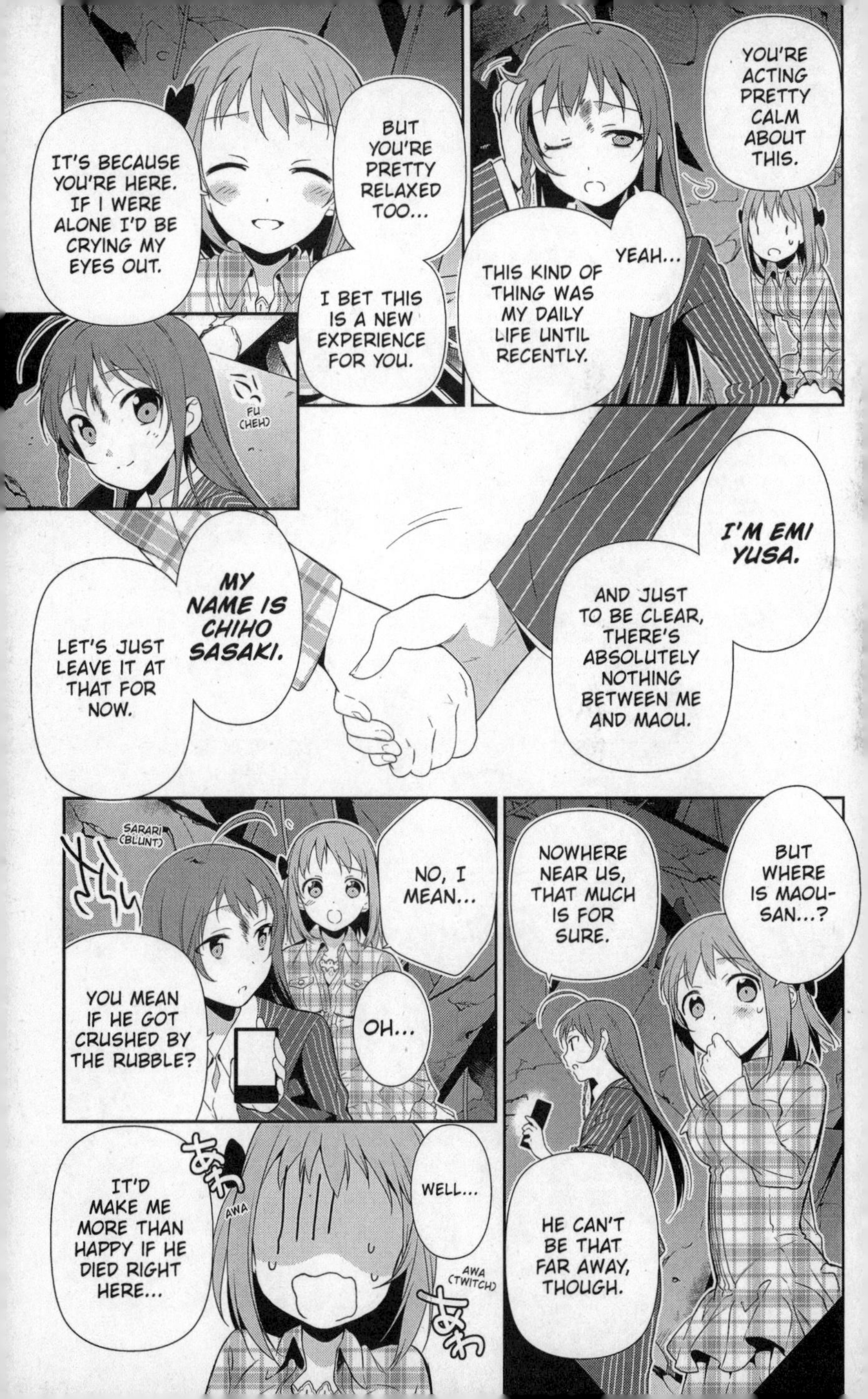
YOU'RE ACTING PRETTY CALM ABOUT THIS.
YEAH...
THIS KIND OF THING WAS MY DAILY LIFE UNTIL RECENTLY.
BUT YOU'RE PRETTY RELAXED TOO...
IT'S BECAUSE YOU'RE HERE. IF I WERE ALONE I'D BE CRYING MY EYES OUT.
FU (HEH)
I BET THIS IS A NEW EXPERIENCE FOR YOU.
I'M EMI YUSA.
AND JUST TO BE CLEAR, THERE'S ABSOLUTELY NOTHING BETWEEN ME AND MAOU.
MY NAME IS CHIHO SASAKI.
LET'S JUST LEAVE IT AT THAT FOR NOW.
BUT WHERE IS MAOU-SAN...?
NOWHERE NEAR US, THAT MUCH IS FOR SURE.
HE CAN'T BE THAT FAR AWAY, THOUGH.
NO, I MEAN...
SARARI (BLUNT)
YOU MEAN IF HE GOT CRUSHED BY THE RUBBLE?
OH...
WELL...
IT'D MAKE ME MORE THAN HAPPY IF HE DIED RIGHT HERE...
AWA
AWA (TWITCH)

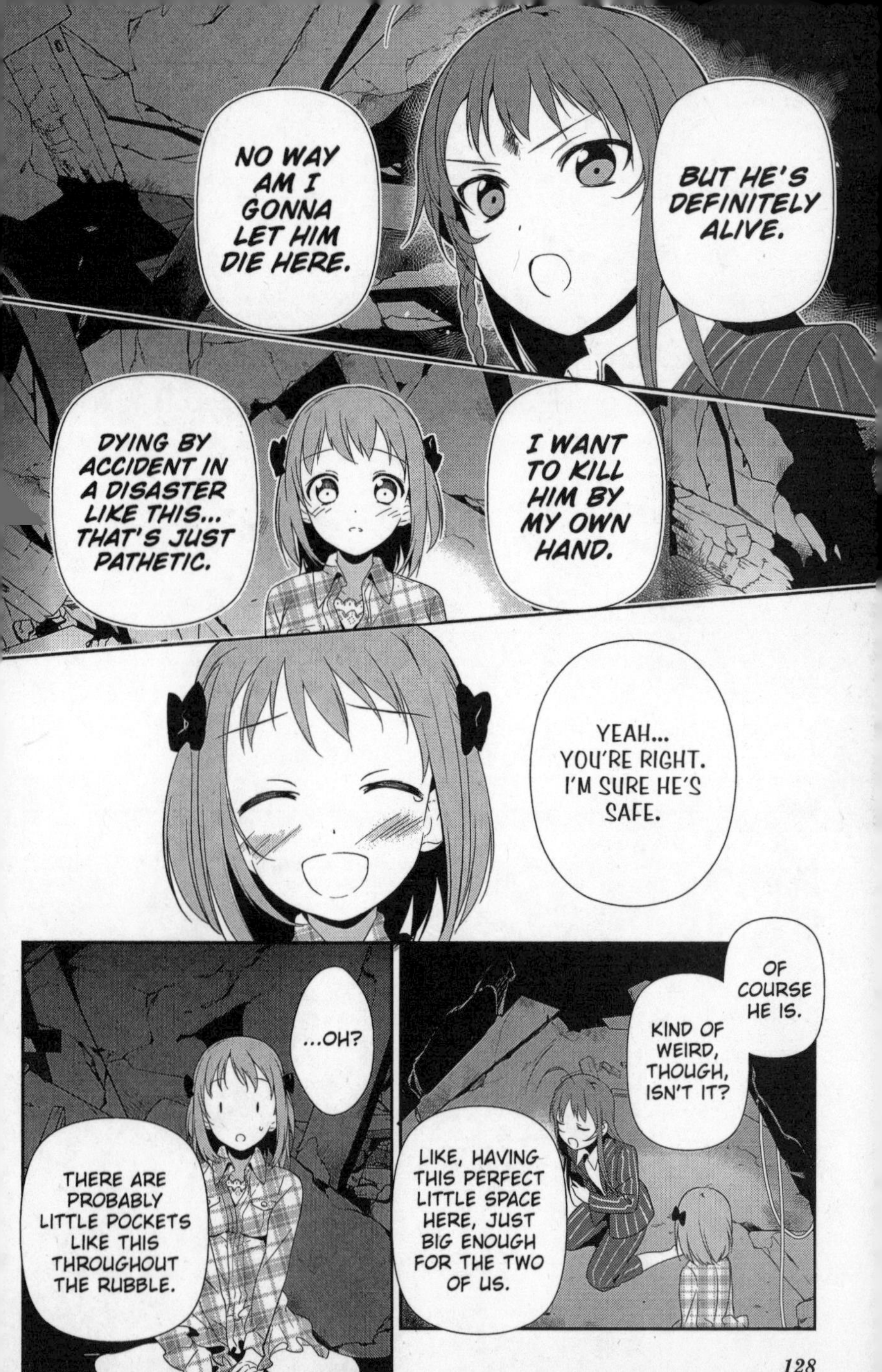
BUT HE'S DEFINITELY ALIVE.
NO WAY AM I GONNA LET HIM DIE HERE.
I WANT TO KILL HIM BY MY OWN HAND.
DYING BY ACCIDENT IN A DISASTER LIKE THIS... THAT'S JUST PATHETIC.
YEAH... YOU'RE RIGHT. I'M SURE HE'S SAFE.
OF COURSE HE IS.
KIND OF WEIRD, THOUGH, ISN'T IT?
LIKE, HAVING THIS PERFECT LITTLE SPACE HERE, JUST BIG ENOUGH FOR THE TWO OF US.
...OH?
THERE ARE PROBABLY LITTLE POCKETS LIKE THIS THROUGHOUT THE RUBBLE.

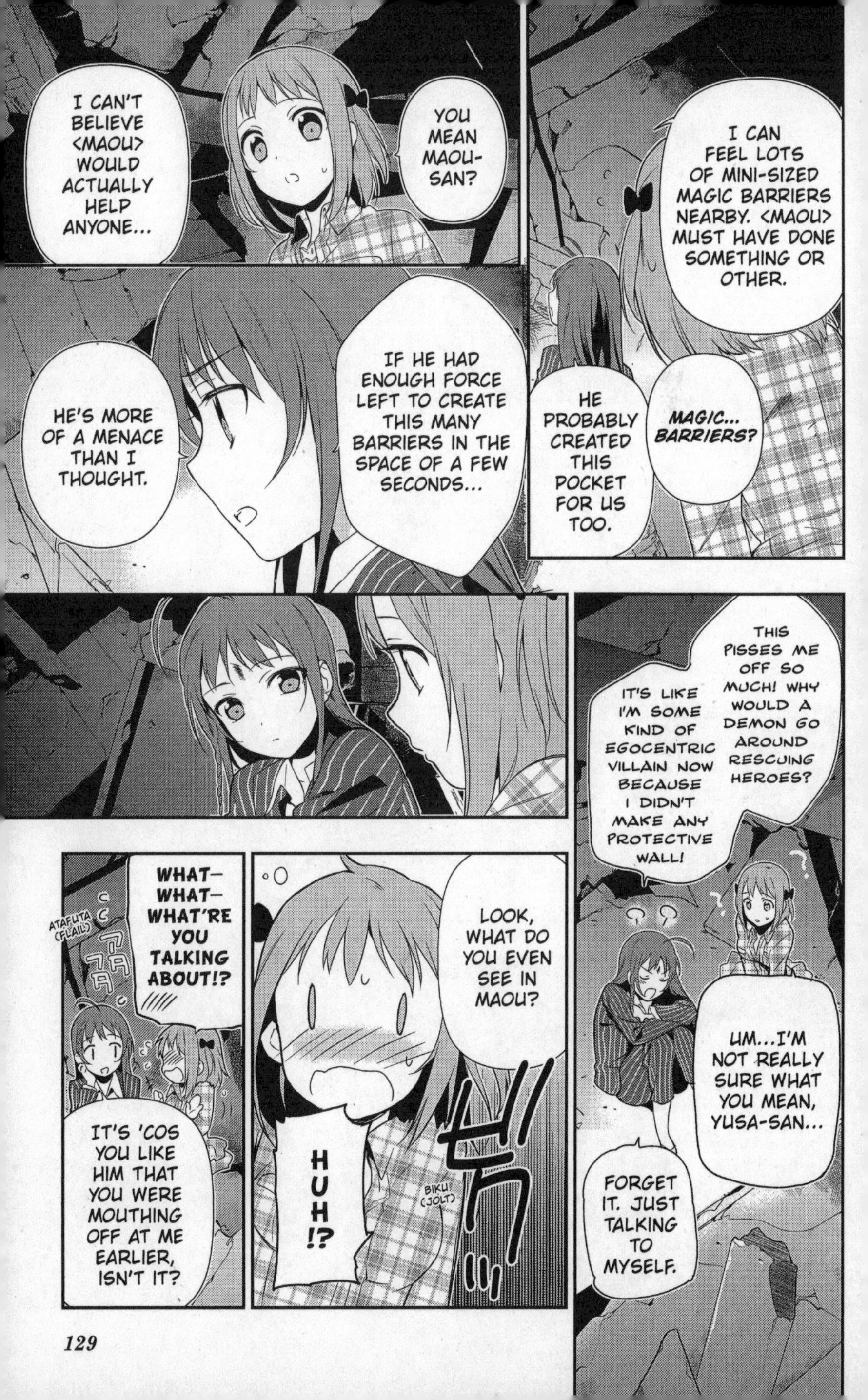
I CAN FEEL LOTS OF MINI-SIZED MAGIC BARRIERS NEARBY. <MAOU> MUST HAVE DONE SOMETHING OR OTHER.
MAGIC... BARRIERS?
HE PROBABLY CREATED THIS POCKET FOR US TOO.
YOU MEAN MAOU-SAN?
I CAN'T BELIEVE <MAOU> WOULD ACTUALLY HELP ANYONE...
IF HE HAD ENOUGH FORCE LEFT TO CREATE THIS MANY BARRIERS IN THE SPACE OF A FEW SECONDS...
HE'S MORE OF A MENACE THAN I THOUGHT.
THIS PISSES ME OFF SO MUCH! WHY WOULD A DEMON GO AROUND RESCUING HEROES?
IT'S LIKE I'M SOME KIND OF EGOCENTRIC VILLAIN NOW BECAUSE I DIDN'T MAKE ANY PROTECTIVE WALL!
UM...I'M NOT REALLY SURE WHAT YOU MEAN, YUSA-SAN...
FORGET IT. JUST TALKING TO MYSELF.
LOOK, WHAT DO YOU EVEN SEE IN MAOU?
HUH!?
BIKU (JOLT)
WHAT—WHAT—WHAT'RE YOU TALKING ABOUT!?
ATAFUTA (FLAIL)
IT'S 'COS YOU LIKE HIM THAT YOU WERE MOUTHING OFF AT ME EARLIER, ISN'T IT?

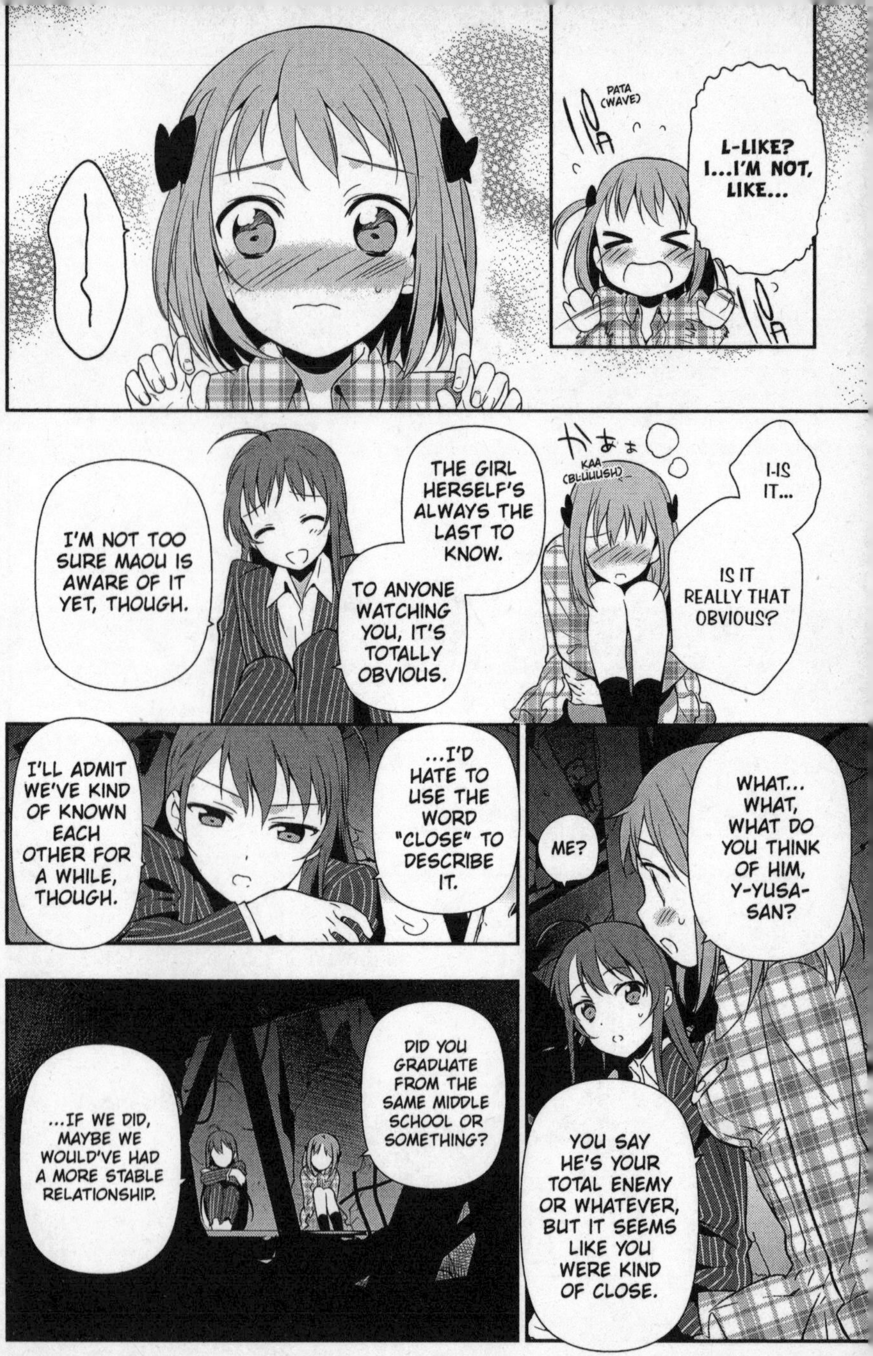
PATA (WAVE)
L-LIKE? I...I'M NOT, LIKE...
KAA (BLUUUSH)
I-IS IT...
IS IT REALLY THAT OBVIOUS?
THE GIRL HERSELF'S ALWAYS THE LAST TO KNOW.
TO ANYONE WATCHING YOU, IT'S TOTALLY OBVIOUS.
I'M NOT TOO SURE MAOU IS AWARE OF IT YET, THOUGH.
WHAT... WHAT, WHAT DO YOU THINK OF HIM, Y-YUSA-SAN?
ME?
YOU SAY HE'S YOUR TOTAL ENEMY OR WHATEVER, BUT IT SEEMS LIKE YOU WERE KIND OF CLOSE.
...I'D HATE TO USE THE WORD "CLOSE" TO DESCRIBE IT.
I'LL ADMIT WE'VE KIND OF KNOWN EACH OTHER FOR A WHILE, THOUGH.
DID YOU GRADUATE FROM THE SAME MIDDLE SCHOOL OR SOMETHING?
...IF WE DID, MAYBE WE WOULD'VE HAD A MORE STABLE RELATIONSHIP.

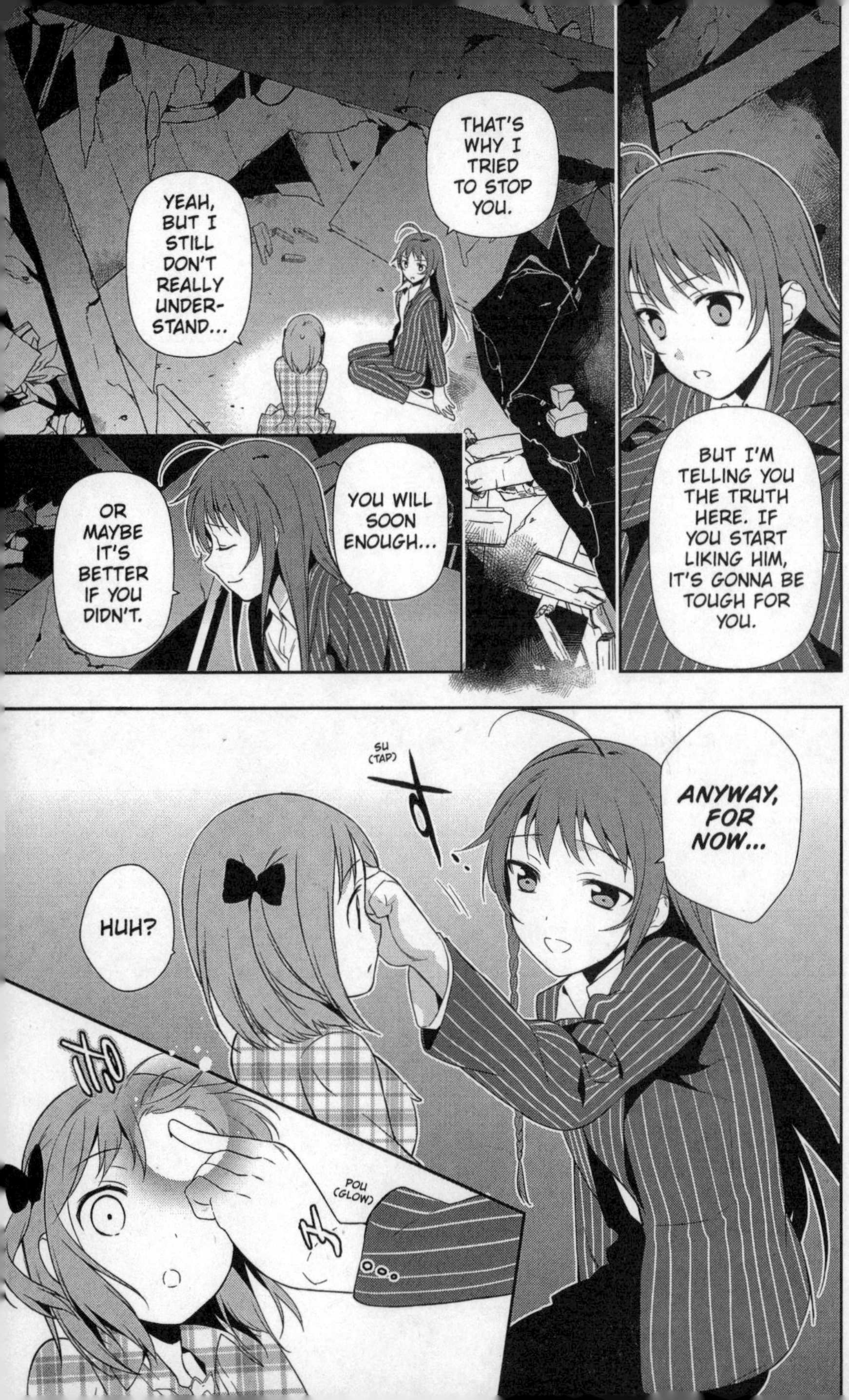
BUT I'M TELLING YOU THE TRUTH HERE. IF YOU START LIKING HIM, IT'S GONNA BE TOUGH FOR YOU.
THAT'S WHY I TRIED TO STOP YOU.
YEAH, BUT I STILL DON'T REALLY UNDER-STAND...
YOU WILL SOON ENOUGH...
OR MAYBE IT'S BETTER IF YOU DIDN'T.
ANYWAY, FOR NOW...
SU (TAP)
HUH?
POU (GLOW)

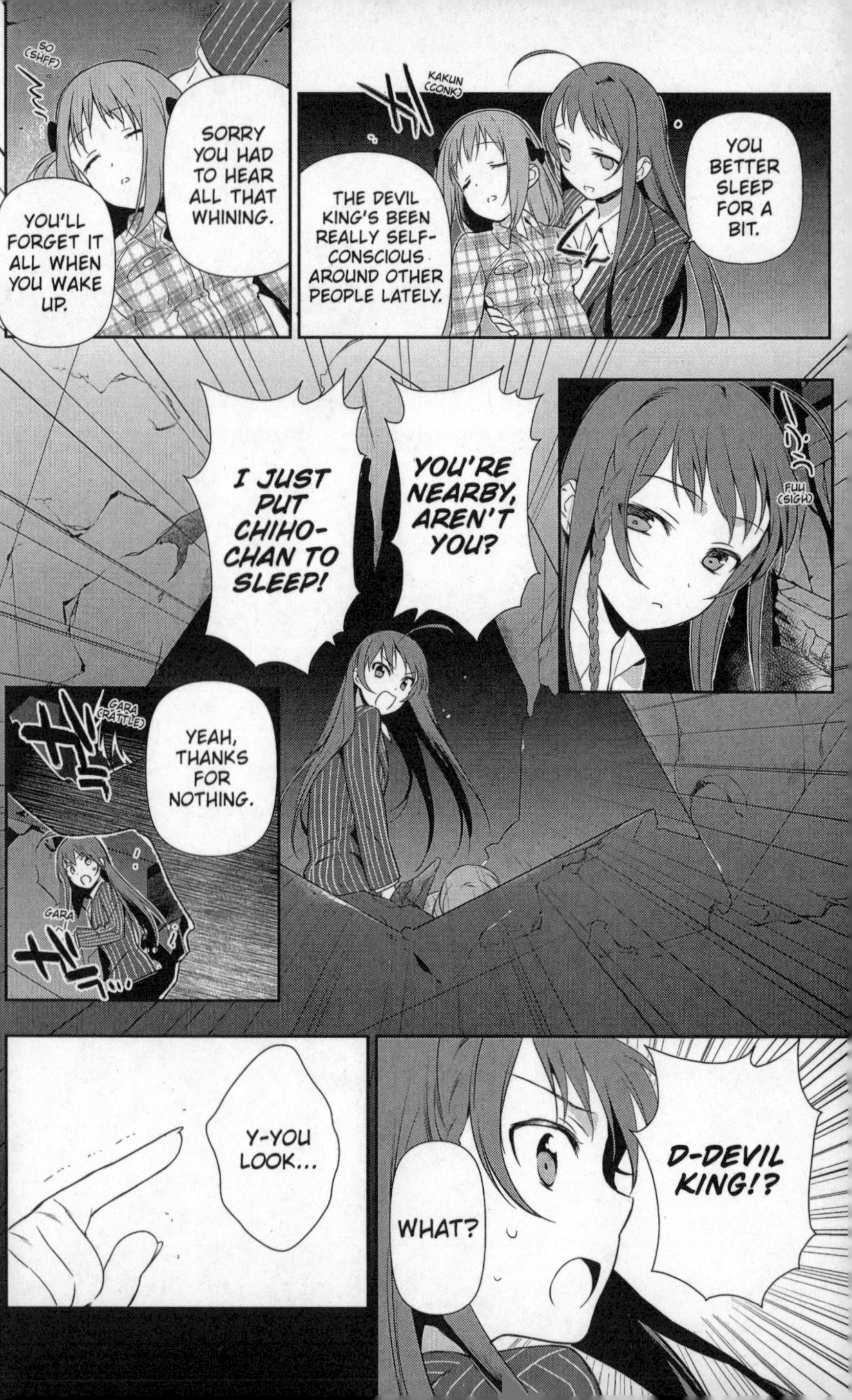
YOU BETTER SLEEP FOR A BIT.
KAKUN (CONK)
THE DEVIL KING'S BEEN REALLY SELF-CONSCIOUS AROUND OTHER PEOPLE LATELY.
SO (SHFF)
SORRY YOU HAD TO HEAR ALL THAT WHINING.
YOU'LL FORGET IT ALL WHEN YOU WAKE UP.
FUU (SIGH)
YOU'RE NEARBY, AREN'T YOU?
I JUST PUT CHIHO-CHAN TO SLEEP!
GARA (RATTLE)
YEAH, THANKS FOR NOTHING.
GARA
D-DEVIL KING!?
WHAT?
Y-YOU LOOK...

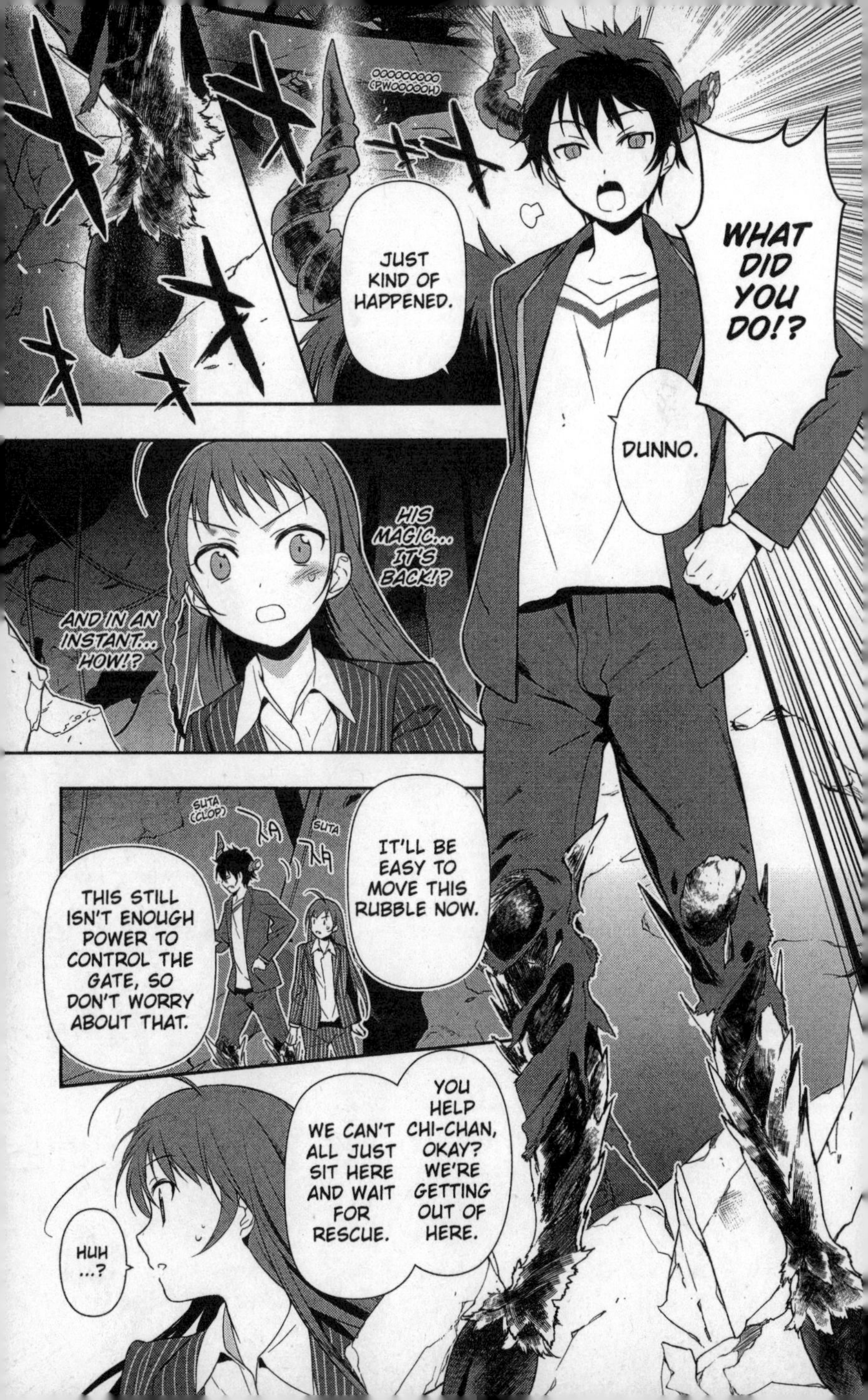
WHAT DID YOU DO!?
DUNNO.
OOOOOOOOO (PWOOOOOH)
JUST KIND OF HAPPENED.
HIS MAGIC... IT'S BACK!?
AND IN AN INSTANT... HOW!?
SUTA (CLOP)
SUTA
IT'LL BE EASY TO MOVE THIS RUBBLE NOW.
THIS STILL ISN'T ENOUGH POWER TO CONTROL THE GATE, SO DON'T WORRY ABOUT THAT.
YOU HELP CHI-CHAN, OKAY? WE'RE GETTING OUT OF HERE.
WE CAN'T ALL JUST SIT HERE AND WAIT FOR RESCUE.
HUH ...?

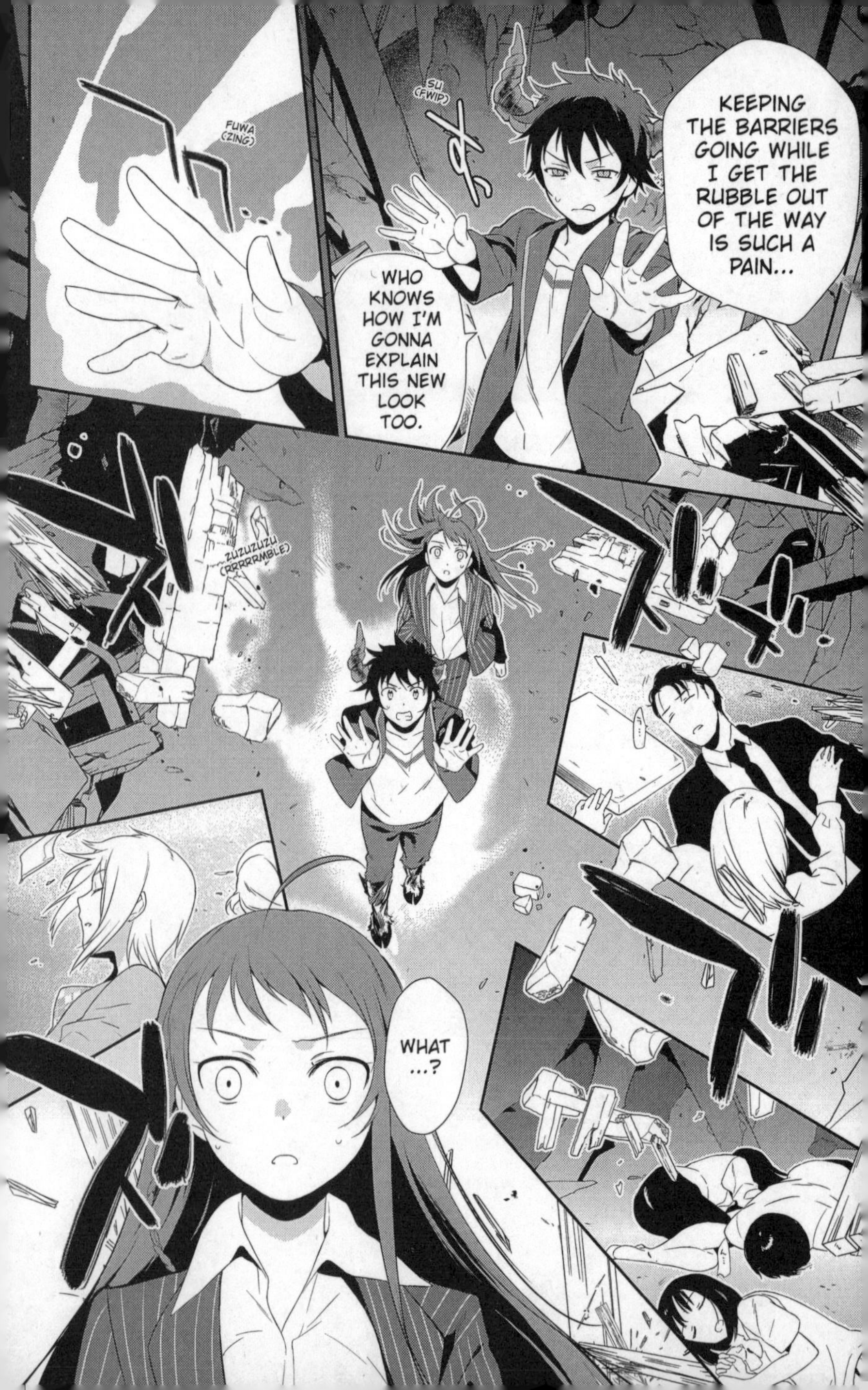
KEEPING THE BARRIERS GOING WHILE I GET THE RUBBLE OUT OF THE WAY IS SUCH A PAIN...
SU (FWIP)
WHO KNOWS HOW I'M GONNA EXPLAIN THIS NEW LOOK TOO.
FUWA (ZING)
ZUZUZUZU (RRRRRMBLE)
WHAT ...?

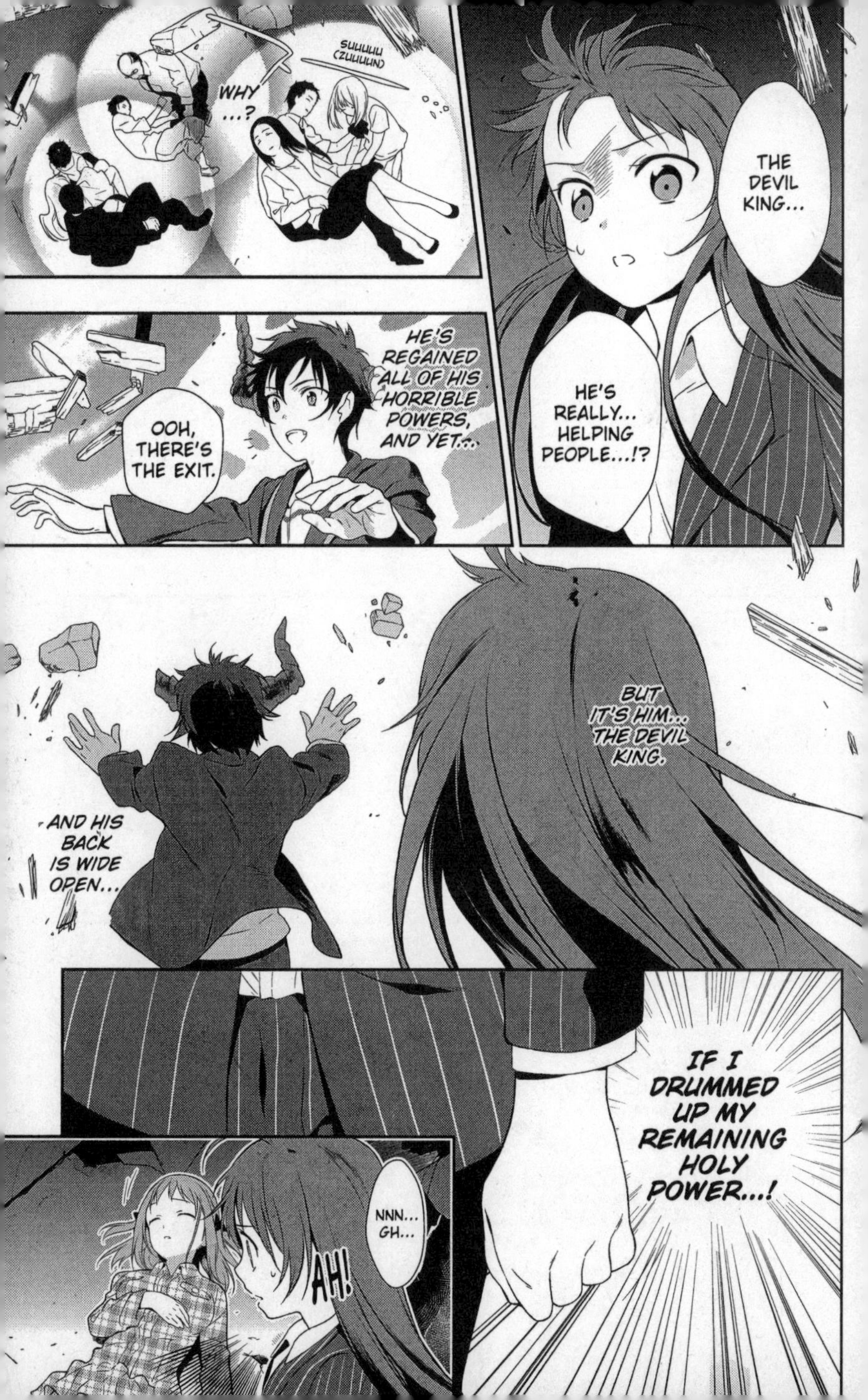
THE DEVIL KING...
HE'S REALLY... HELPING PEOPLE...!?
SUUUUU (ZUUUUUN)
WHY ...?
HE'S REGAINED ALL OF HIS HORRIBLE POWERS, AND YET...
OOH, THERE'S THE EXIT.
BUT IT'S HIM... THE DEVIL KING.
AND HIS BACK IS WIDE OPEN...
IF I DRUMMED UP MY REMAINING HOLY POWER...!
NNN... GH...
AH!

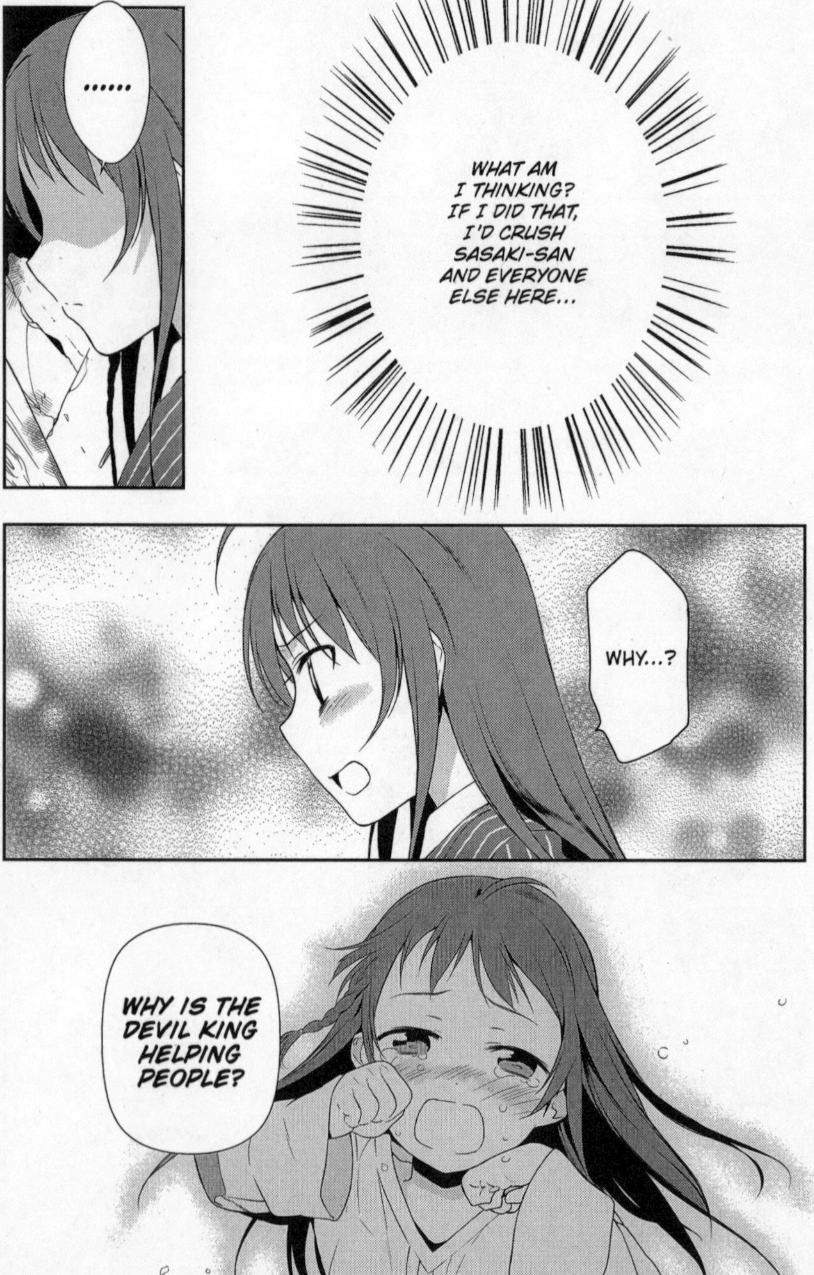
WHAT AM I THINKING? IF I DID THAT, I'D CRUSH SASAKI-SAN AND EVERYONE ELSE HERE...
......
WHY...?
WHY IS THE DEVIL KING HELPING PEOPLE?

Chiho
Sasaki

THE DEVIL IS A PART-TIMER!

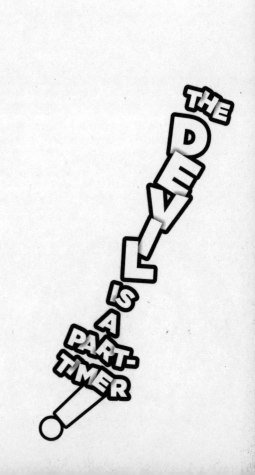

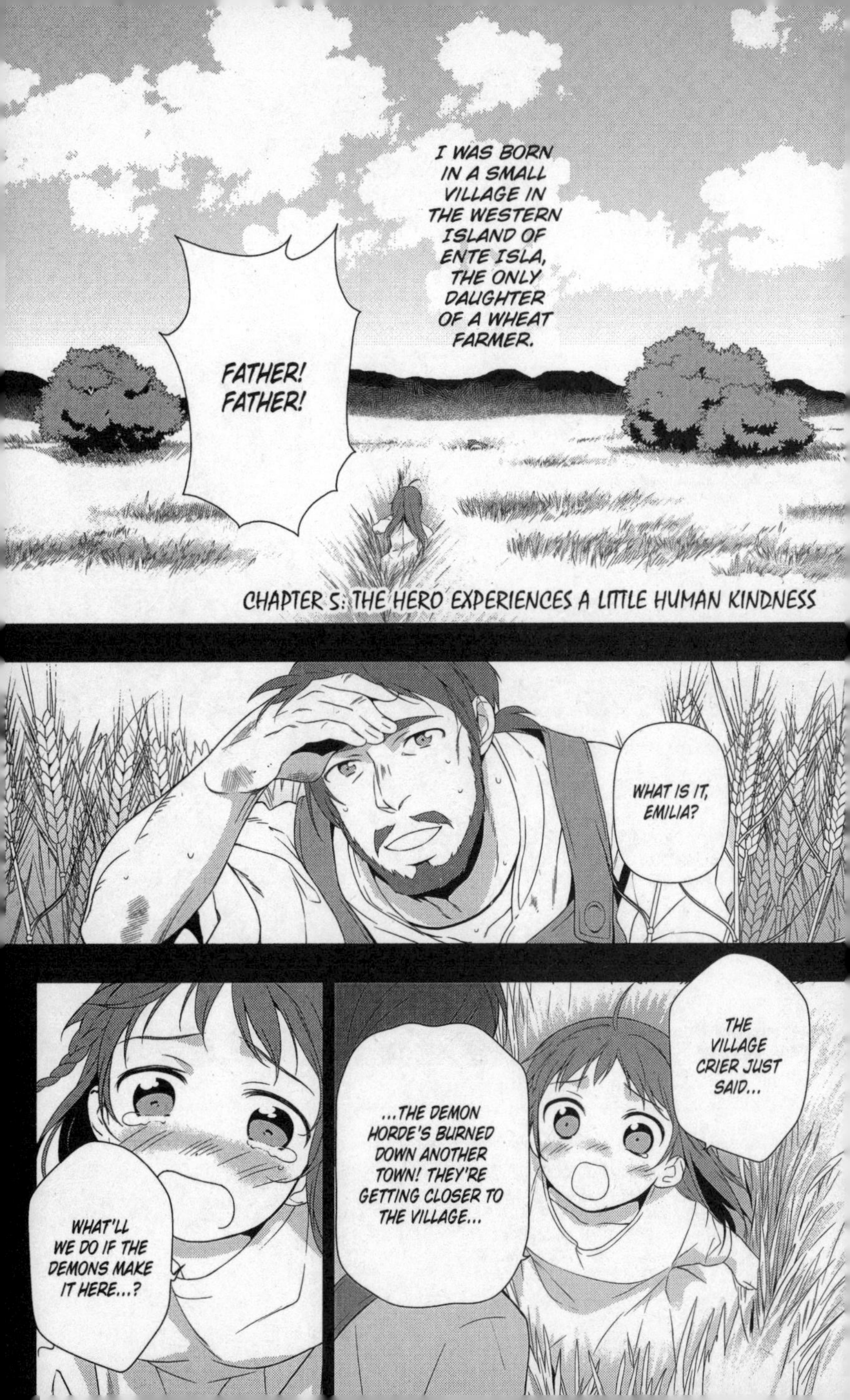
I WAS BORN IN A SMALL VILLAGE IN THE WESTERN ISLAND OF ENTE ISLA, THE ONLY DAUGHTER OF A WHEAT FARMER.
FATHER! FATHER!
CHAPTER 5: THE HERO EXPERIENCES A LITTLE HUMAN KINDNESS
WHAT IS IT, EMILIA?
THE VILLAGE CRIER JUST SAID...
...THE DEMON HORDE'S BURNED DOWN ANOTHER TOWN! THEY'RE GETTING CLOSER TO THE VILLAGE...
WHAT'LL WE DO IF THE DEMONS MAKE IT HERE...?

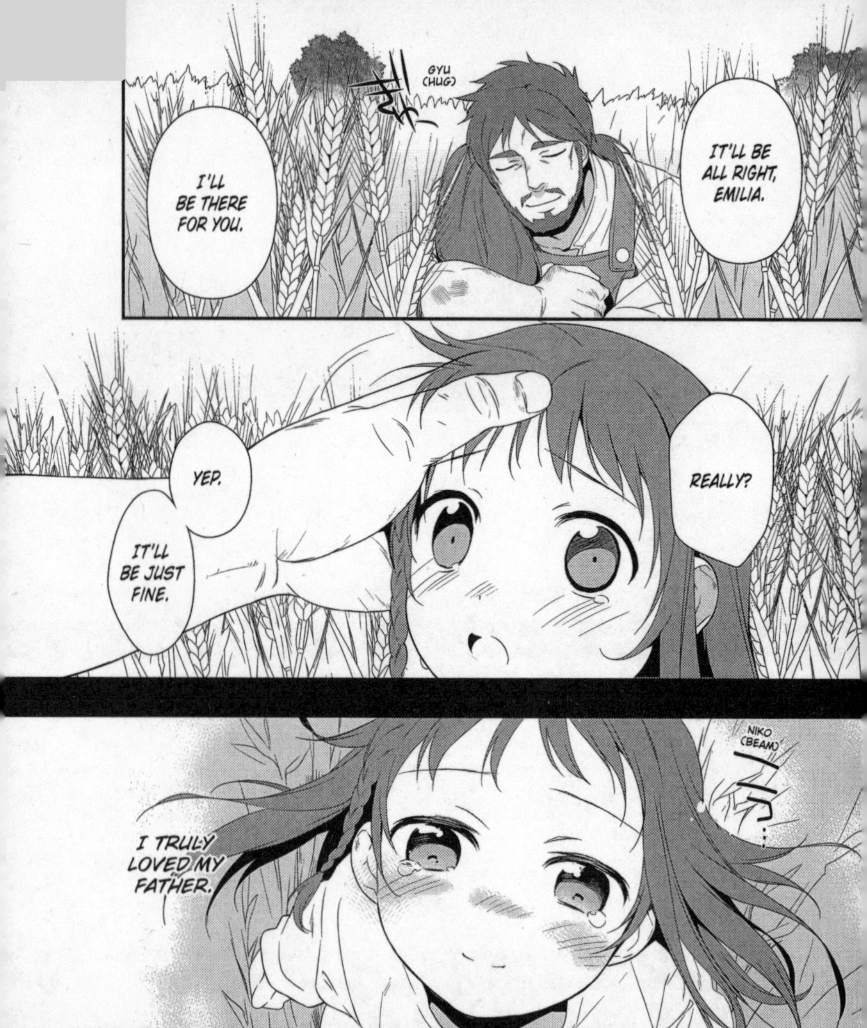
IT'LL BE ALL RIGHT, EMILIA.
GYU (HUG)
I'LL BE THERE FOR YOU.
REALLY?
YEP.
IT'LL BE JUST FINE.
NIKO (BEAM)
I TRULY LOVED MY FATHER.

ALL HE KNEW ABOUT WAS TENDING TO THE WHEAT FIELDS...

...BUT I RELIED ON HIM MORE THAN ANYONE ELSE. HE WAS THE GREATEST HERO IN THE WORLD.

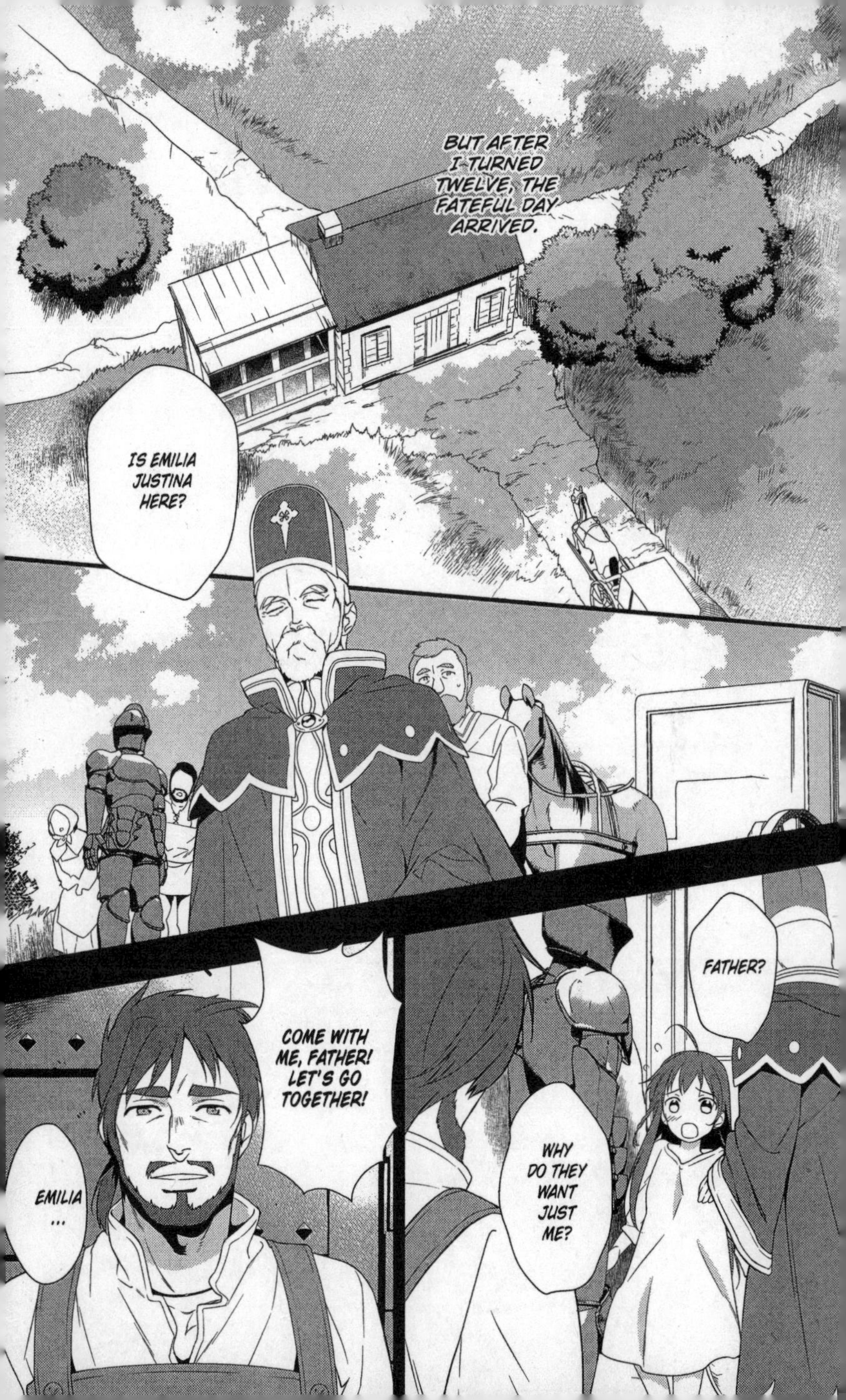
BUT AFTER I TURNED TWELVE, THE FATEFUL DAY ARRIVED.
IS EMILIA JUSTINA HERE?
FATHER?
WHY DO THEY WANT JUST ME?
COME WITH ME, FATHER! LET'S GO TOGETHER!
EMILIA ...

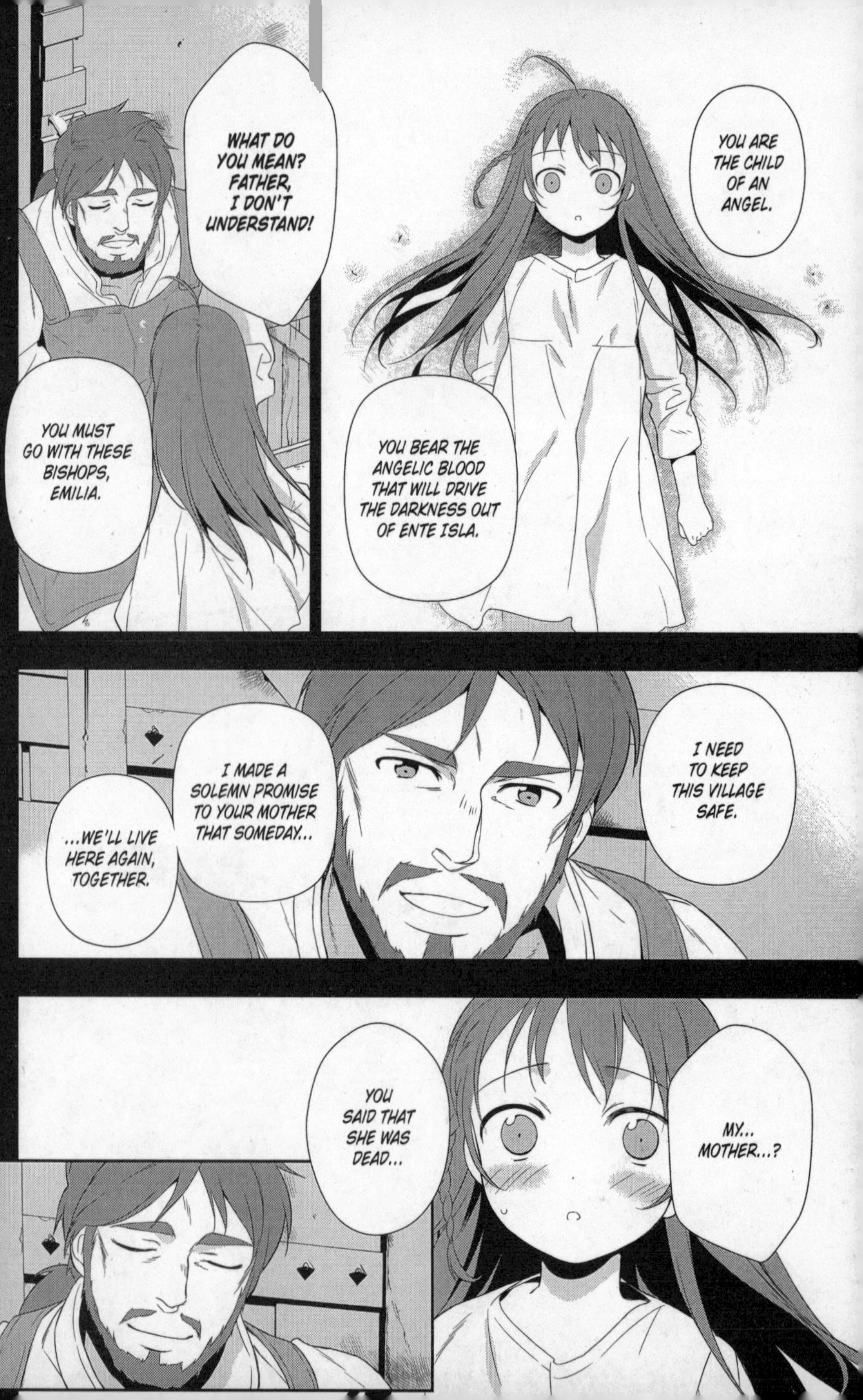
YOU ARE THE CHILD OF AN ANGEL.
YOU BEAR THE ANGELIC BLOOD THAT WILL DRIVE THE DARKNESS OUT OF ENTE ISLA.
WHAT DO YOU MEAN? FATHER, I DON'T UNDERSTAND!
YOU MUST GO WITH THESE BISHOPS, EMILIA.
I NEED TO KEEP THIS VILLAGE SAFE.
I MADE A SOLEMN PROMISE TO YOUR MOTHER THAT SOMEDAY...
...WE'LL LIVE HERE AGAIN, TOGETHER.
MY... MOTHER...?
YOU SAID THAT SHE WAS DEAD...

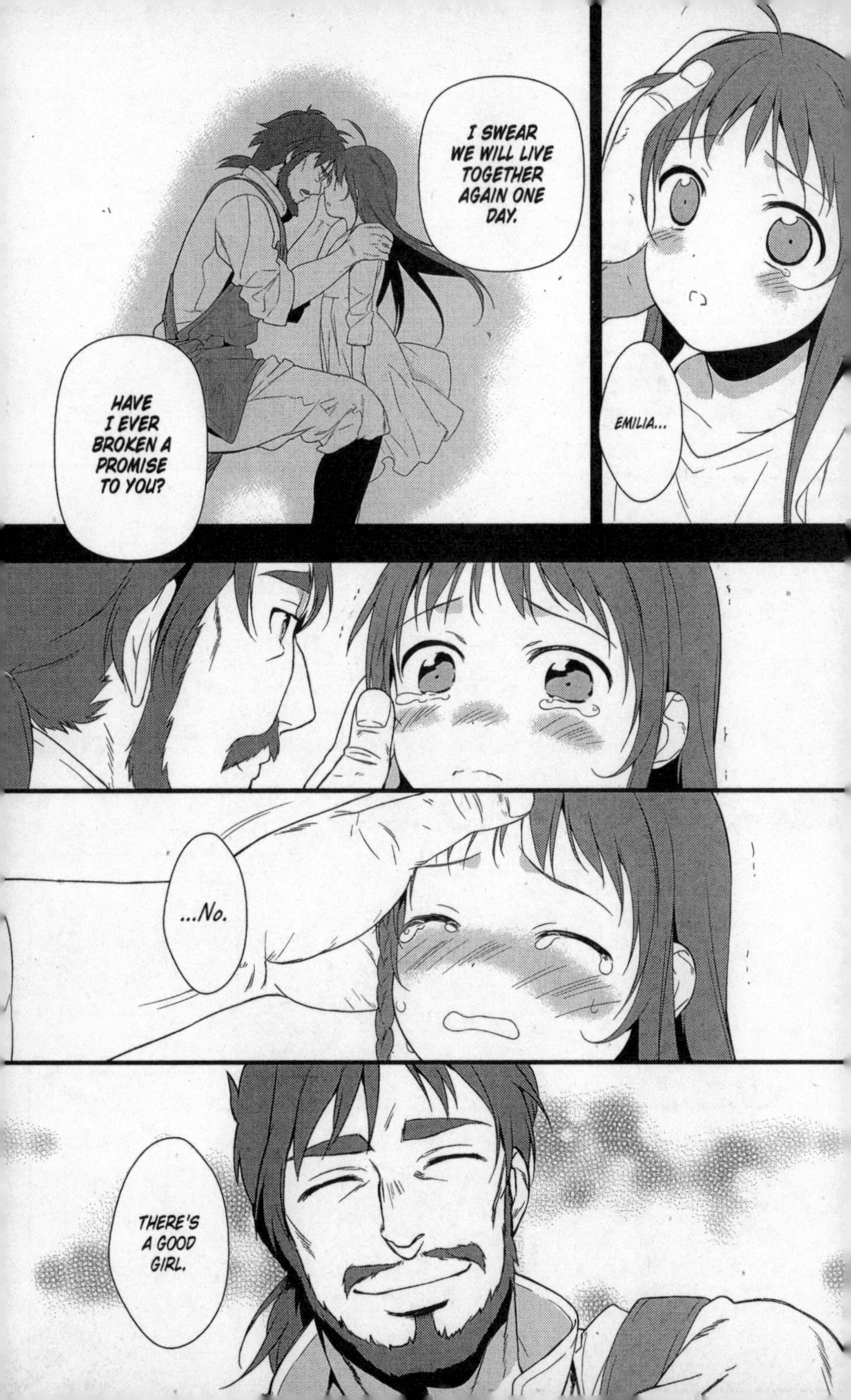
EMILIA...
I SWEAR WE WILL LIVE TOGETHER AGAIN ONE DAY.
HAVE I EVER BROKEN A PROMISE TO YOU?
...No.
THERE'S A GOOD GIRL.

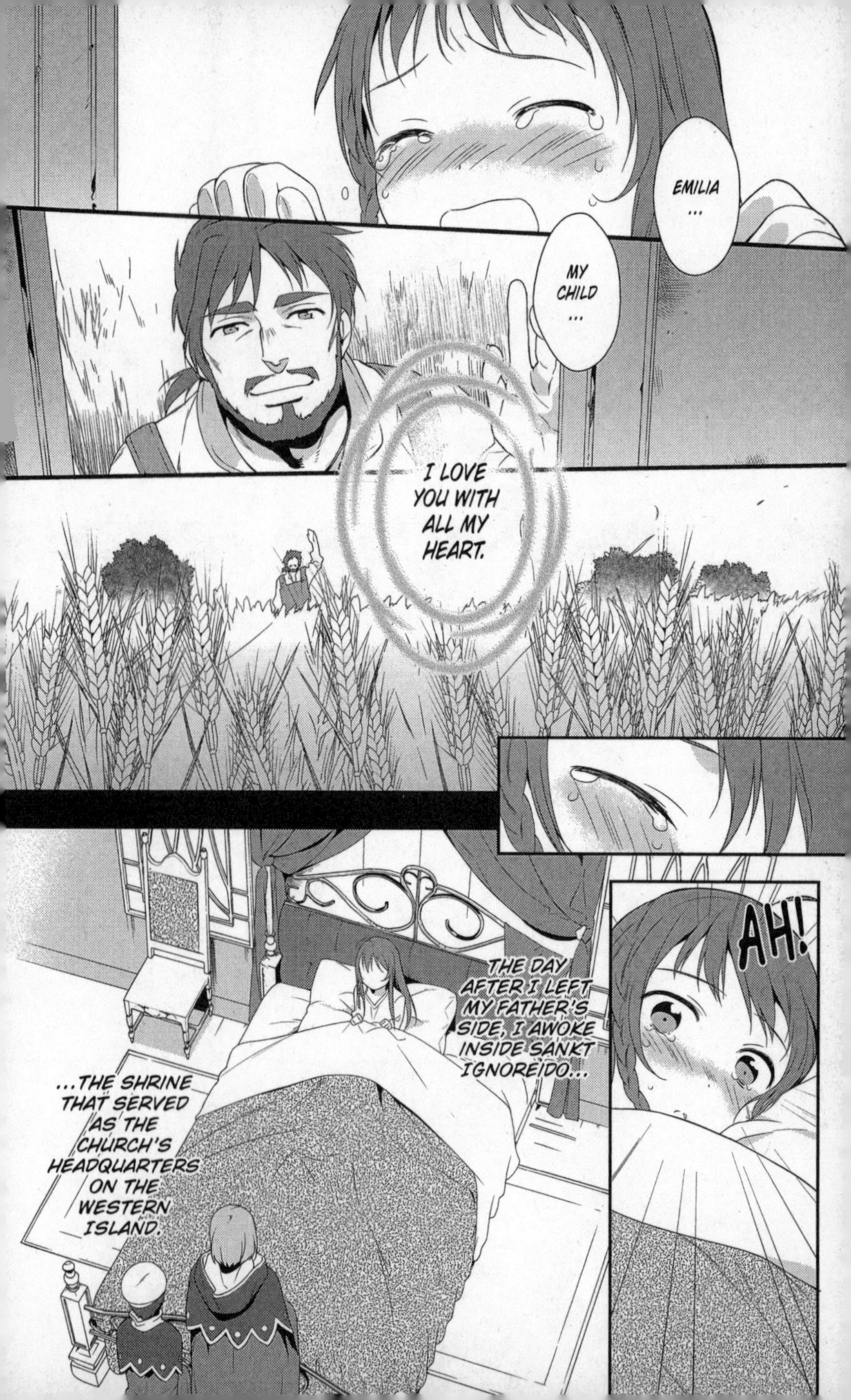
EMILIA ...
MY CHILD ...
I LOVE YOU WITH ALL MY HEART.
AH!
THE DAY AFTER I LEFT MY FATHER'S SIDE, I AWOKE INSIDE SANKT IGNOREIDO...
...THE SHRINE THAT SERVED AS THE CHURCH'S HEADQUARTERS ON THE WESTERN ISLAND.

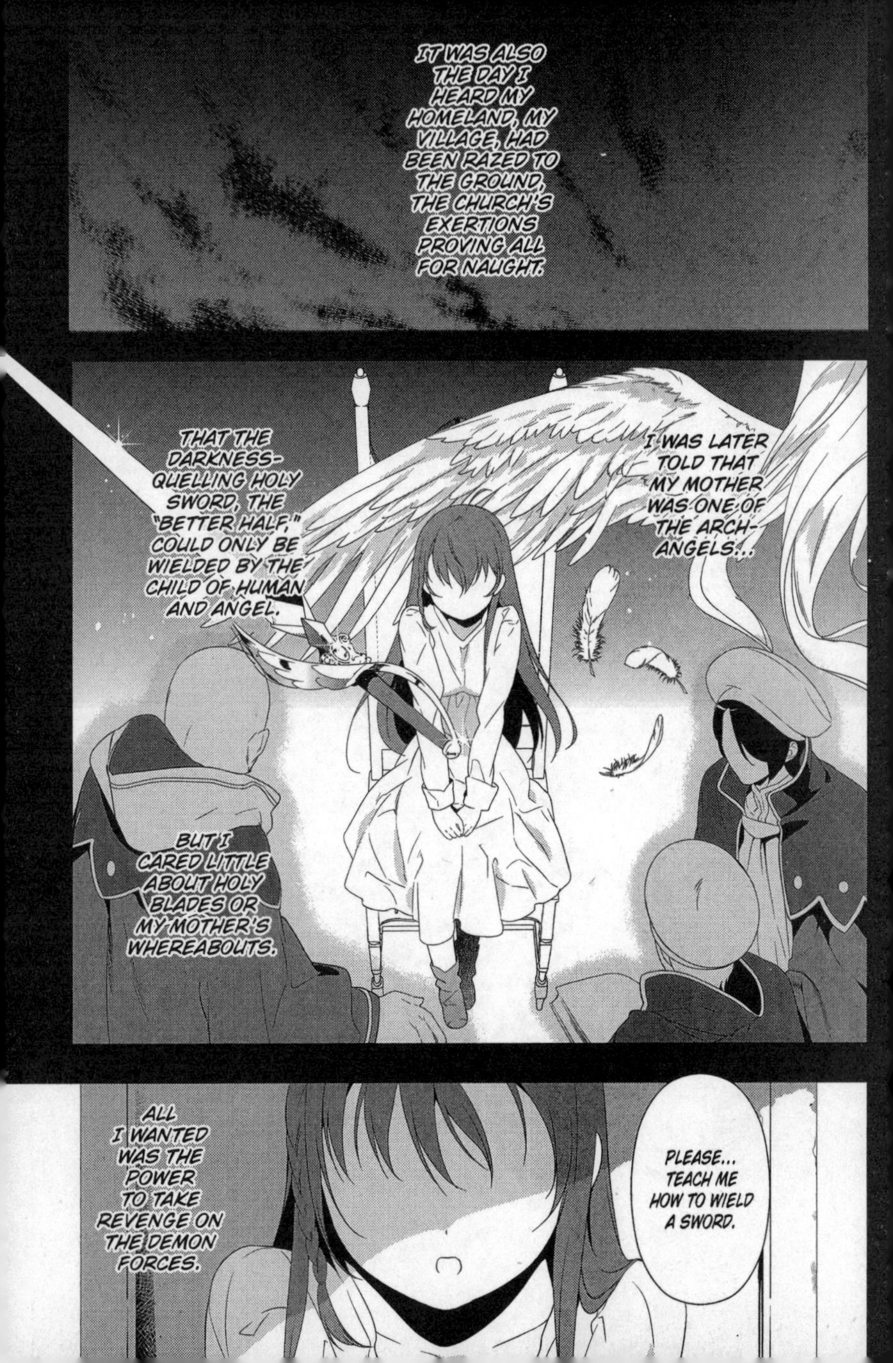
IT WAS ALSO THE DAY I HEARD MY HOMELAND, MY VILLAGE, HAD BEEN RAZED TO THE GROUND, THE CHURCH'S EXERTIONS PROVING ALL FOR NAUGHT.
I WAS LATER TOLD THAT MY MOTHER WAS ONE OF THE ARCH-ANGELS...
THAT THE DARKNESS-QUELLING HOLY SWORD, THE "BETTER HALF," COULD ONLY BE WIELDED BY THE CHILD OF HUMAN AND ANGEL.
BUT I CARED LITTLE ABOUT HOLY BLADES OR MY MOTHER'S WHEREABOUTS.
PLEASE... TEACH ME HOW TO WIELD A SWORD.
ALL I WANTED WAS THE POWER TO TAKE REVENGE ON THE DEMON FORCES.

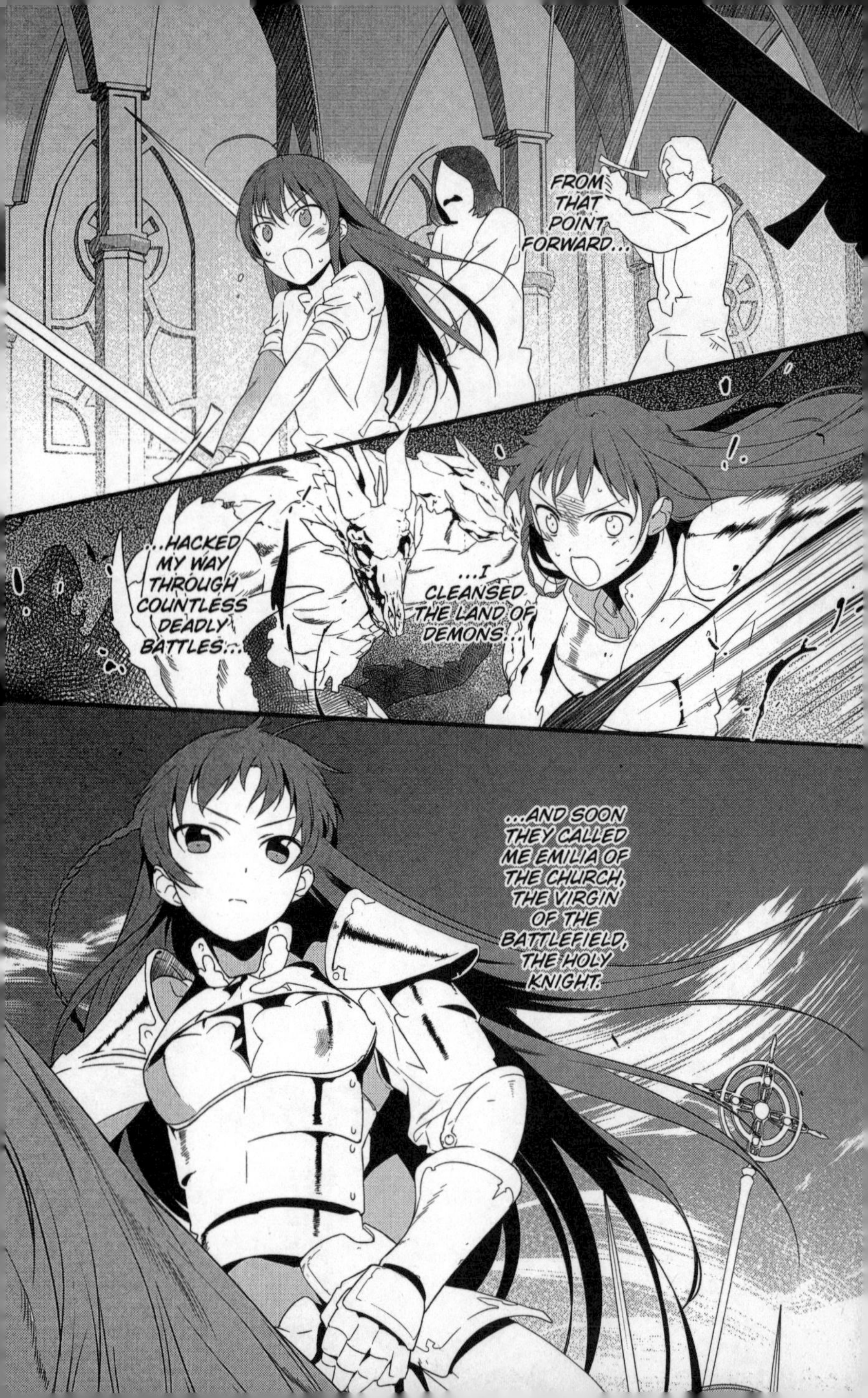
FROM THAT POINT FORWARD...
...I CLEANSED THE LAND OF DEMONS...
...HACKED MY WAY THROUGH COUNTLESS DEADLY BATTLES...
...AND SOON THEY CALLED ME EMILIA OF THE CHURCH, THE VIRGIN OF THE BATTLEFIELD, THE HOLY KNIGHT.

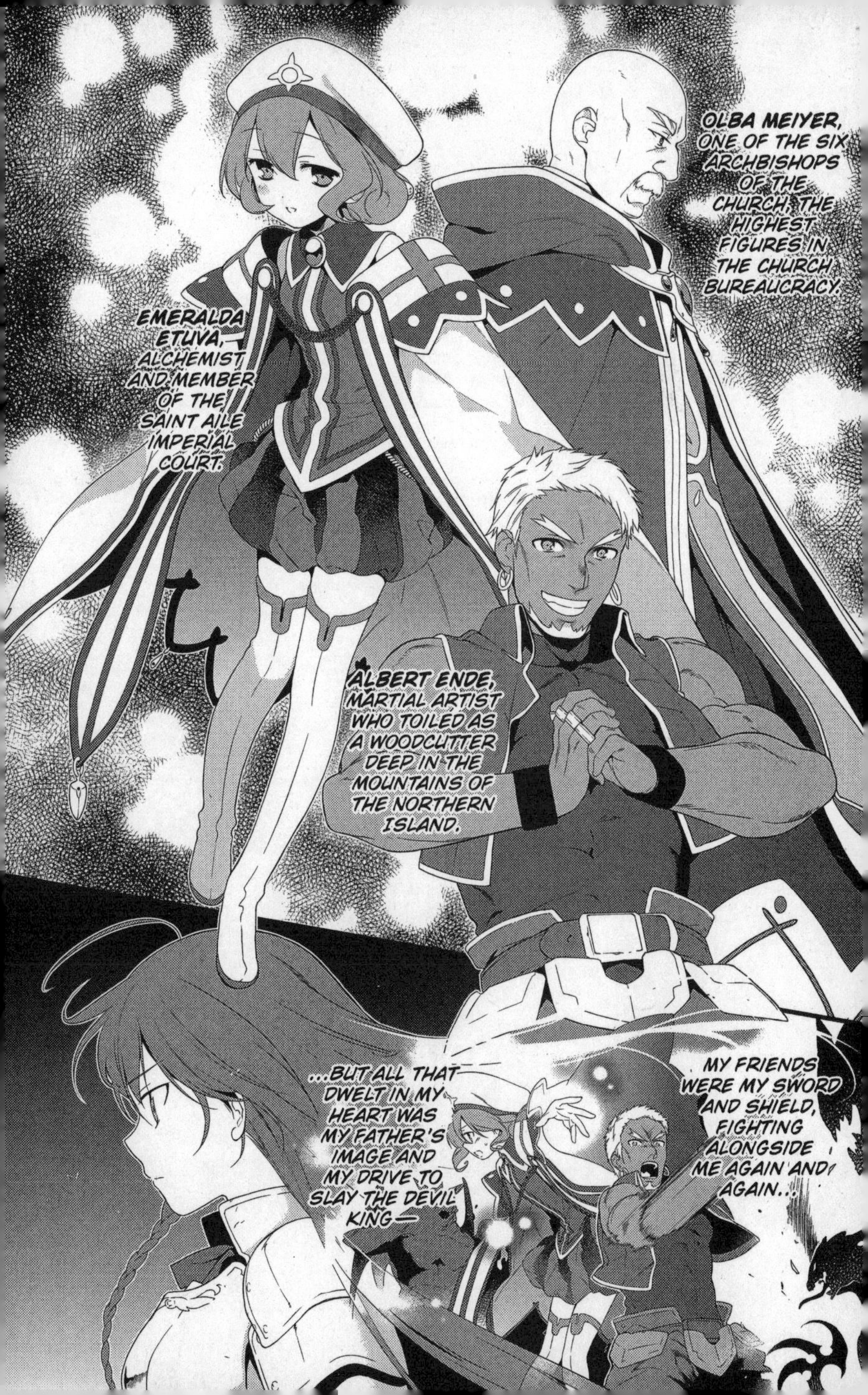
OLBA MEIYER, ONE OF THE SIX ARCHBISHOPS OF THE CHURCH, THE HIGHEST FIGURES IN THE CHURCH BUREAUCRACY.
EMERALDA ETUVA, ALCHEMIST AND MEMBER OF THE SAINT AILE IMPERIAL COURT.
ALBERT ENDE, MARTIAL ARTIST WHO TOILED AS A WOODCUTTER DEEP IN THE MOUNTAINS OF THE NORTHERN ISLAND.
MY FRIENDS WERE MY SWORD AND SHIELD, FIGHTING ALONGSIDE ME AGAIN AND AGAIN...
...BUT ALL THAT DWELT IN MY HEART WAS MY FATHER'S IMAGE AND MY DRIVE TO SLAY THE DEVIL KING—

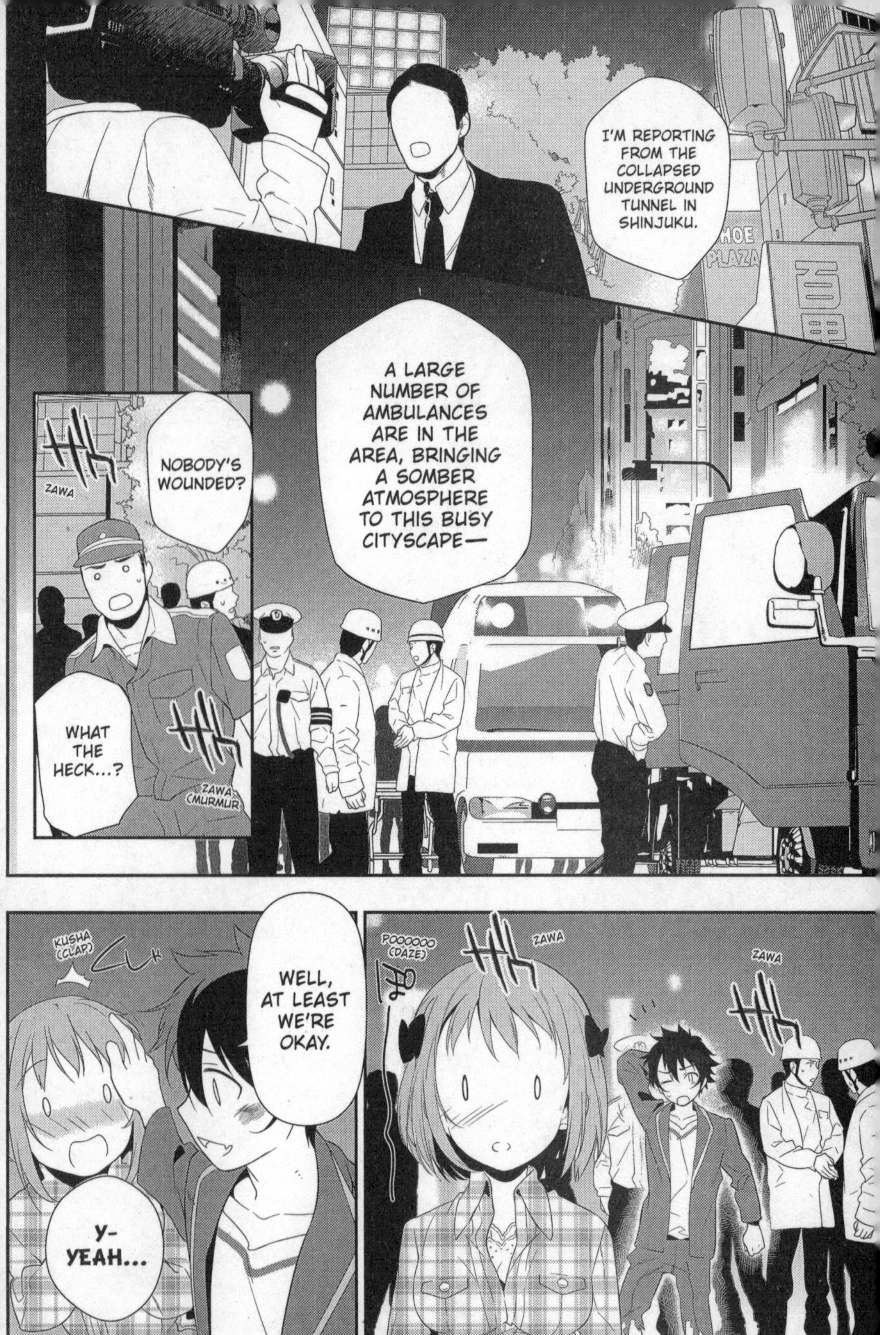
I'M REPORTING FROM THE COLLAPSED UNDERGROUND TUNNEL IN SHINJUKU.
A LARGE NUMBER OF AMBULANCES ARE IN THE AREA, BRINGING A SOMBER ATMOSPHERE TO THIS BUSY CITYSCAPE—
NOBODY'S WOUNDED?
ZAWA
WHAT THE HECK...?
ZAWA (MURMUR)
POOOOOO (DAZE)
ZAWA
ZAWA
WELL, AT LEAST WE'RE OKAY.
KUSHA (CLAP)
Y-YEAH...

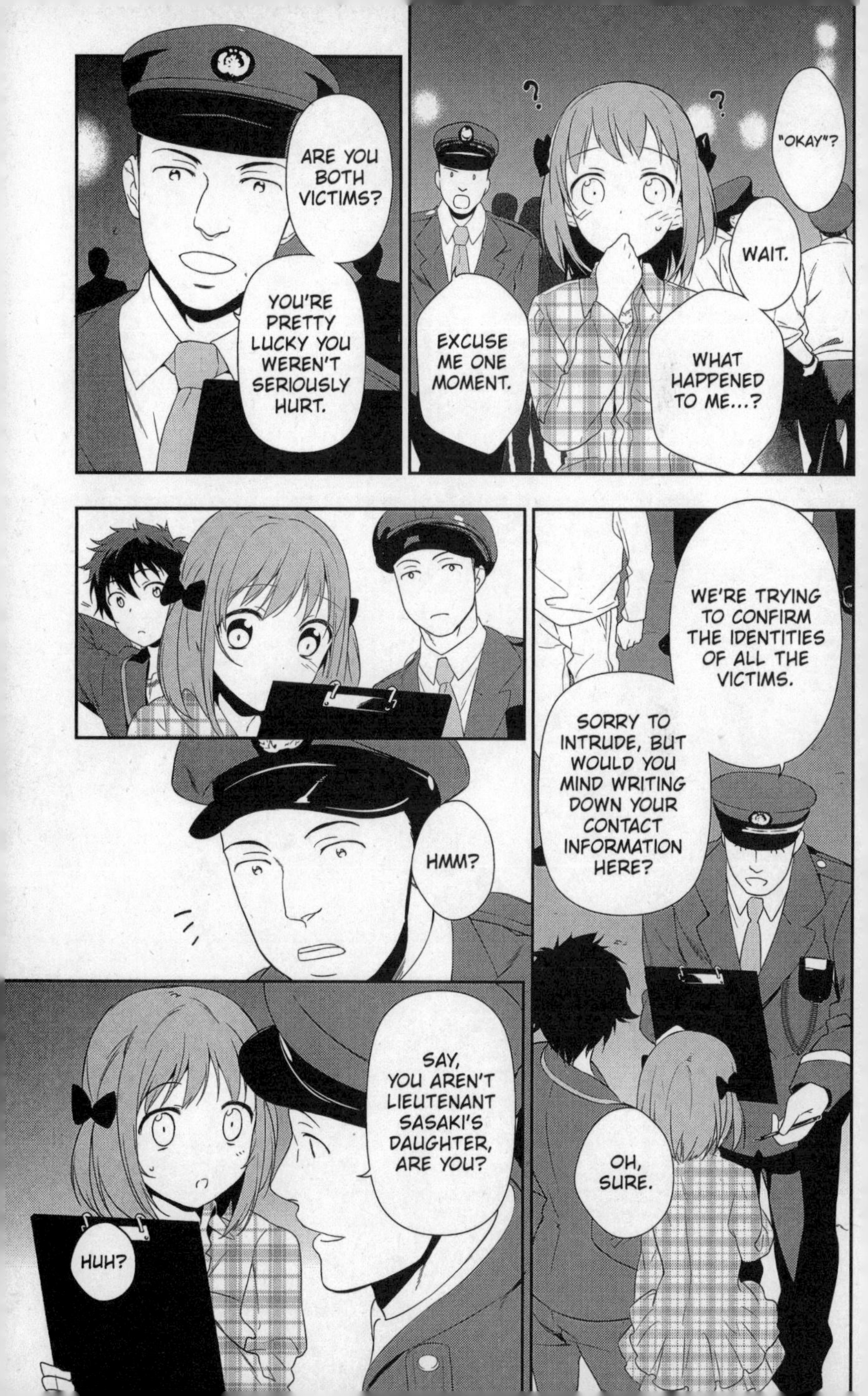
"OKAY"?
WAIT.
WHAT HAPPENED TO ME...?
EXCUSE ME ONE MOMENT.
ARE YOU BOTH VICTIMS?
YOU'RE PRETTY LUCKY YOU WEREN'T SERIOUSLY HURT.
WE'RE TRYING TO CONFIRM THE IDENTITIES OF ALL THE VICTIMS.
SORRY TO INTRUDE, BUT WOULD YOU MIND WRITING DOWN YOUR CONTACT INFORMATION HERE?
OH, SURE.
HMM?
SAY, YOU AREN'T LIEUTENANT SASAKI'S DAUGHTER, ARE YOU?
HUH?

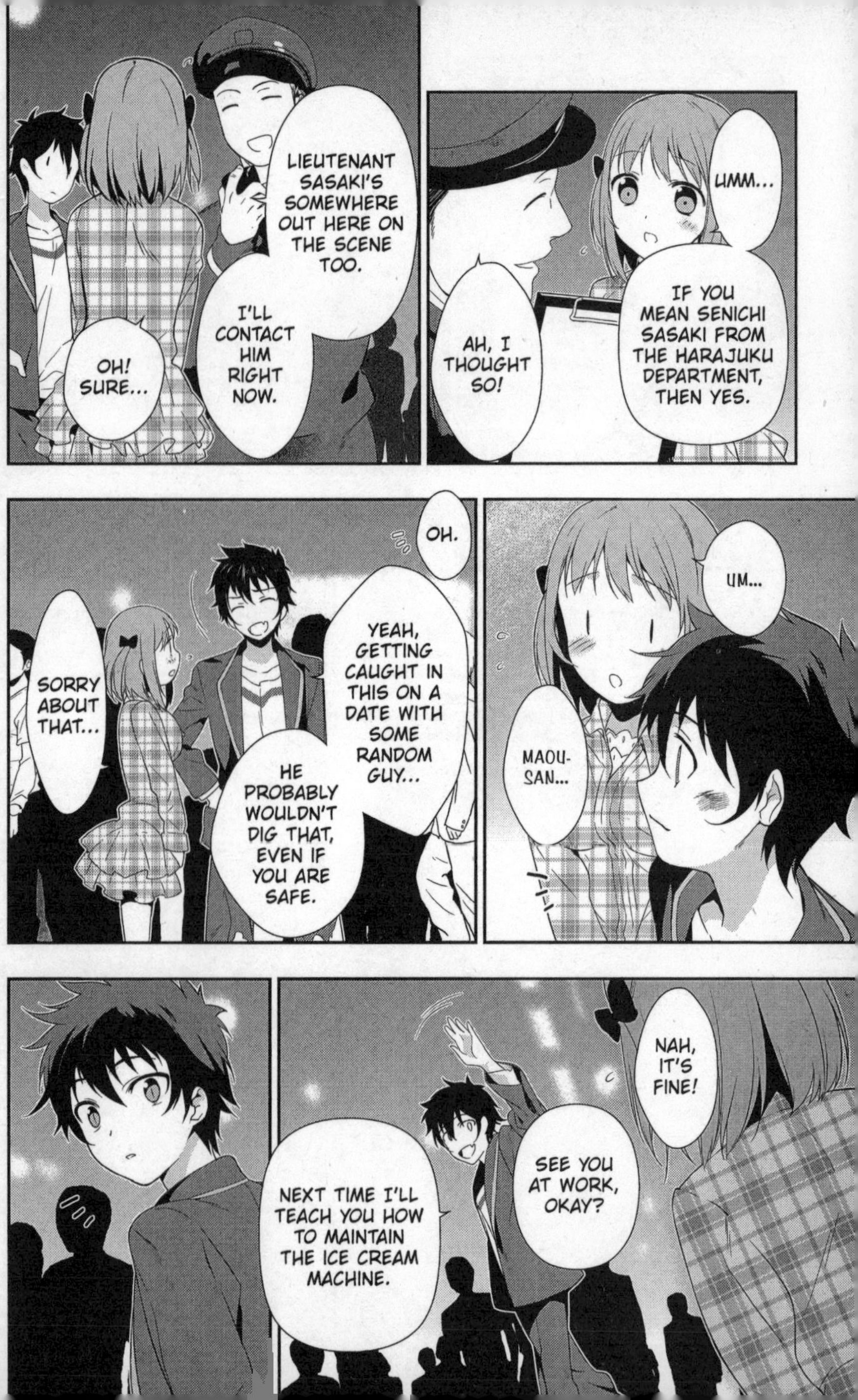
UMM...
IF YOU MEAN SENICHI SASAKI FROM THE HARAJUKU DEPARTMENT, THEN YES.
AH, I THOUGHT SO!
LIEUTENANT SASAKI'S SOMEWHERE OUT HERE ON THE SCENE TOO.
I'LL CONTACT HIM RIGHT NOW.
OH! SURE...
UM...
MAOU-SAN...
OH.
YEAH, GETTING CAUGHT IN THIS ON A DATE WITH SOME RANDOM GUY...
HE PROBABLY WOULDN'T DIG THAT, EVEN IF YOU ARE SAFE.
SORRY ABOUT THAT...
NAH, IT'S FINE!
SEE YOU AT WORK, OKAY?
NEXT TIME I'LL TEACH YOU HOW TO MAINTAIN THE ICE CREAM MACHINE.

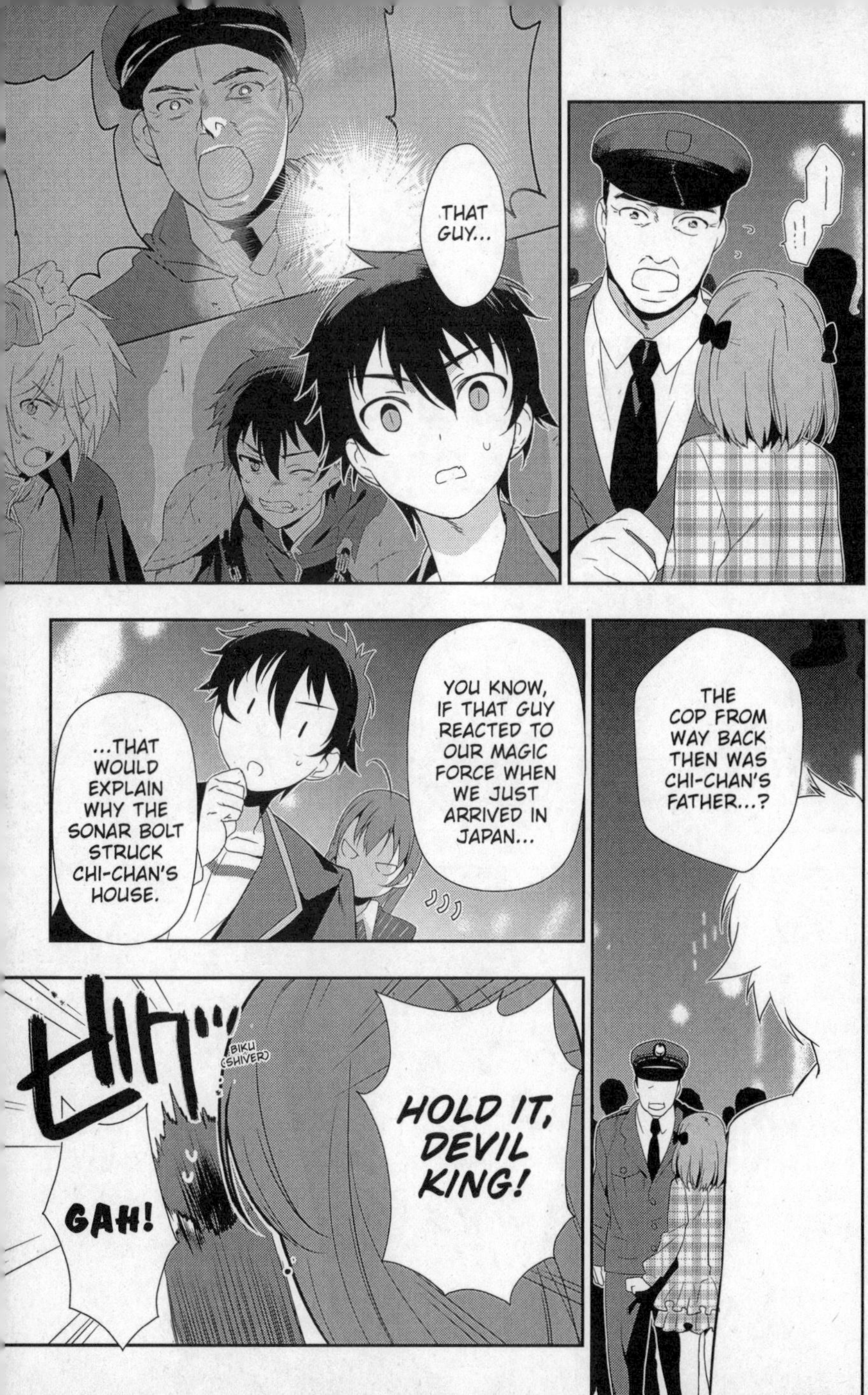
THAT GUY...
THE COP FROM WAY BACK THEN WAS CHI-CHAN'S FATHER...?
YOU KNOW, IF THAT GUY REACTED TO OUR MAGIC FORCE WHEN WE JUST ARRIVED IN JAPAN...
...THAT WOULD EXPLAIN WHY THE SONAR BOLT STRUCK CHI-CHAN'S HOUSE.
HOLD IT, DEVIL KING!
BIKU (SHIVER)
GAH!

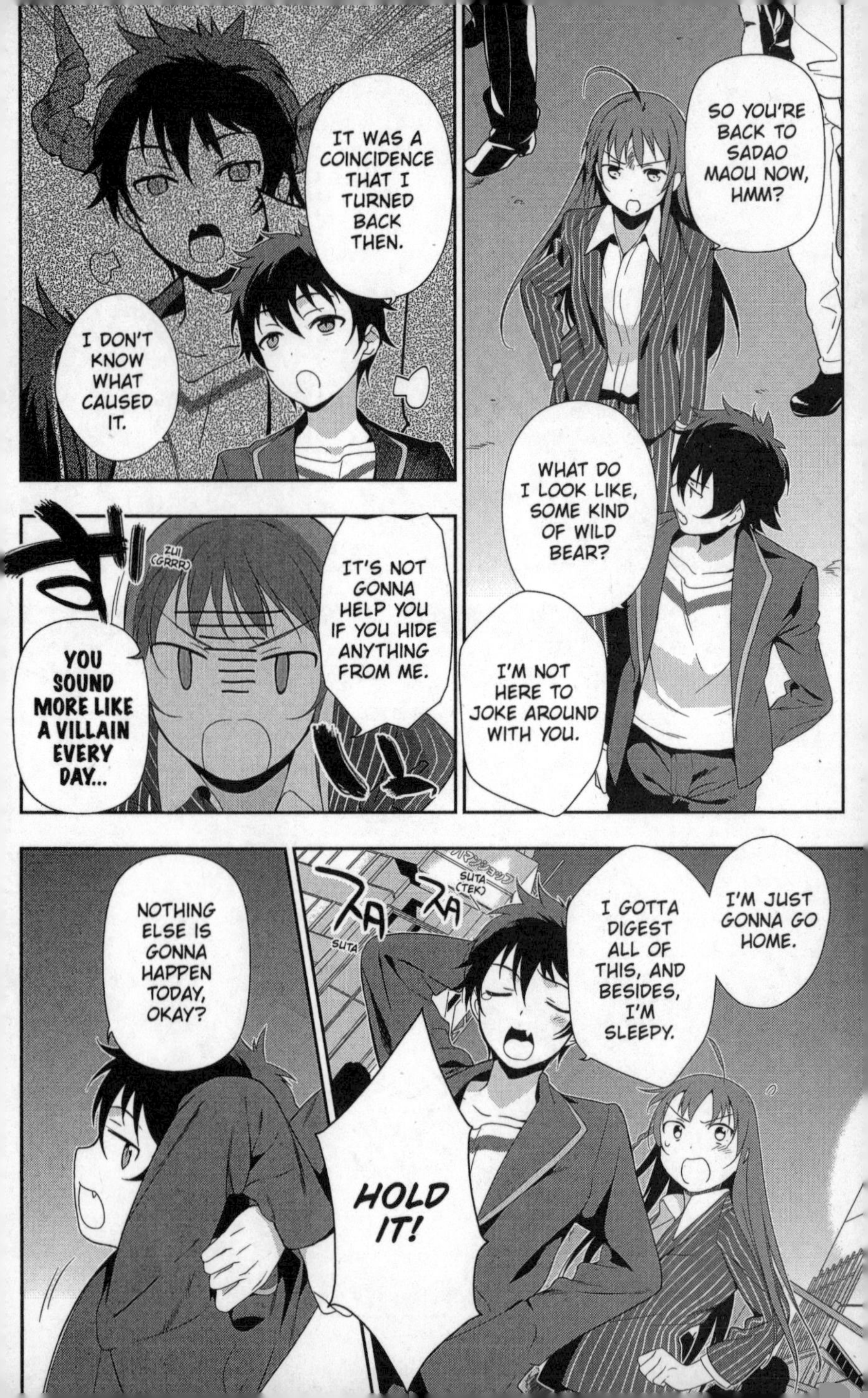
SO YOU'RE BACK TO SADAO MAOU NOW, HMM?
WHAT DO I LOOK LIKE, SOME KIND OF WILD BEAR?
I'M NOT HERE TO JOKE AROUND WITH YOU.
IT WAS A COINCIDENCE THAT I TURNED BACK THEN.
I DON'T KNOW WHAT CAUSED IT.
IT'S NOT GONNA HELP YOU IF YOU HIDE ANYTHING FROM ME.
ZUI (GRRR)
YOU SOUND MORE LIKE A VILLAIN EVERY DAY...
I'M JUST GONNA GO HOME.
I GOTTA DIGEST ALL OF THIS, AND BESIDES, I'M SLEEPY.
SUTA (TEK)
SUTA
HOLD IT!
NOTHING ELSE IS GONNA HAPPEN TODAY, OKAY?

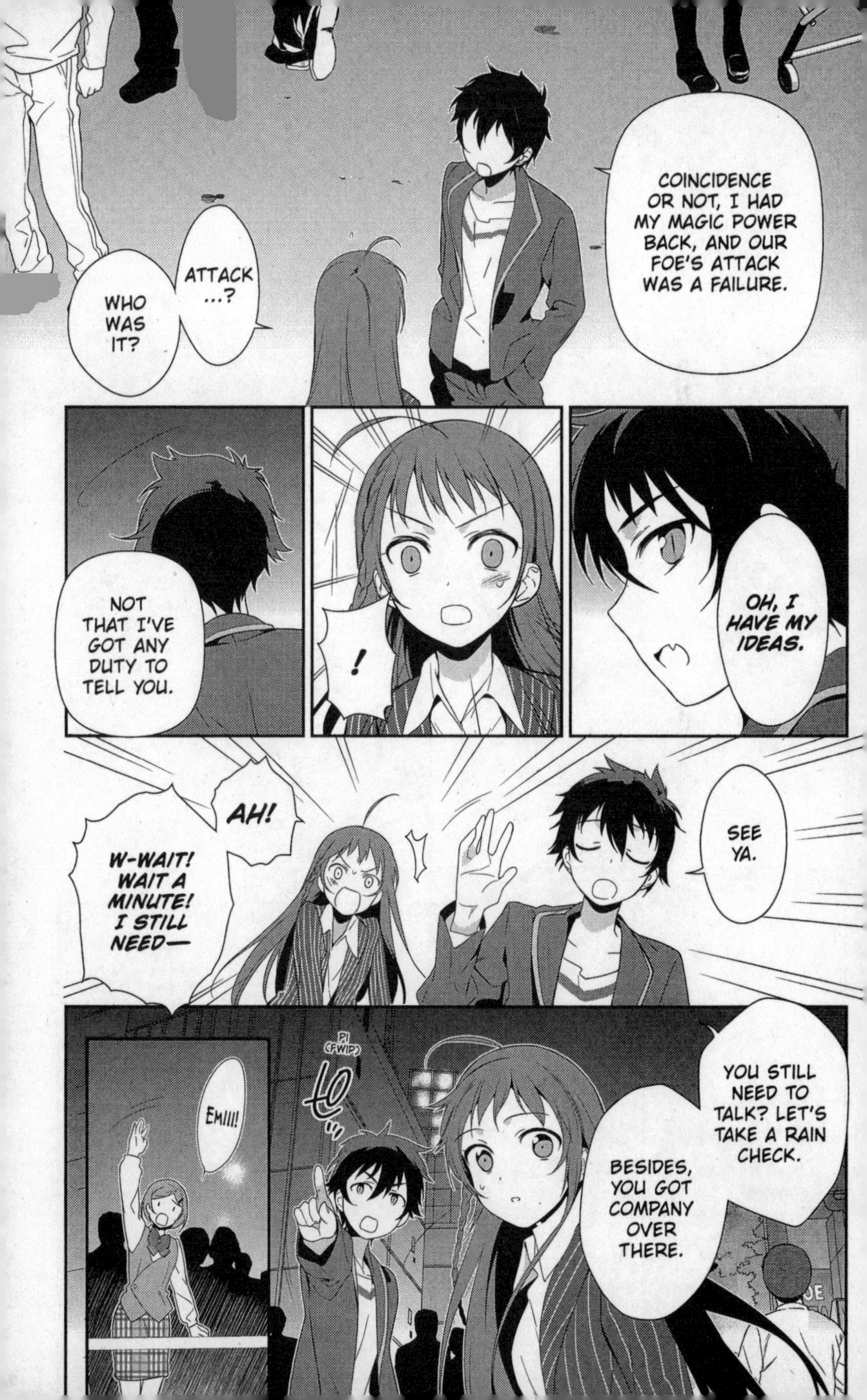
COINCIDENCE OR NOT, I HAD MY MAGIC POWER BACK, AND OUR FOE'S ATTACK WAS A FAILURE.
ATTACK ...?
WHO WAS IT?
OH, I HAVE MY IDEAS.
!
NOT THAT I'VE GOT ANY DUTY TO TELL YOU.
SEE YA.
AH!
W-WAIT! WAIT A MINUTE! I STILL NEED—
YOU STILL NEED TO TALK? LET'S TAKE A RAIN CHECK.
BESIDES, YOU GOT COMPANY OVER THERE.
P! (FWIP)
EMIII!

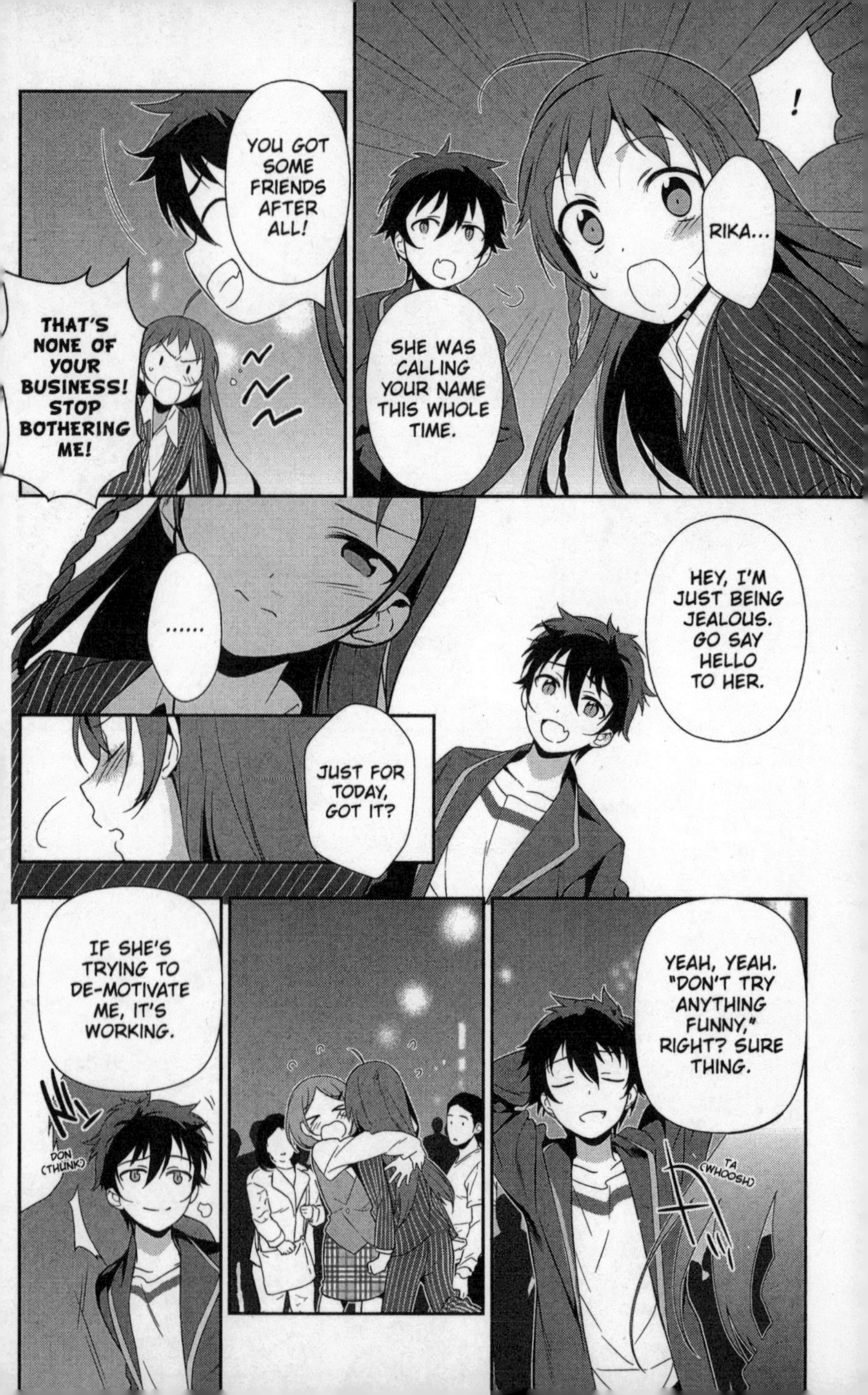
!
RIKA...
SHE WAS CALLING YOUR NAME THIS WHOLE TIME.
YOU GOT SOME FRIENDS AFTER ALL!
THAT'S NONE OF YOUR BUSINESS! STOP BOTHERING ME!
HEY, I'M JUST BEING JEALOUS. GO SAY HELLO TO HER.
......
JUST FOR TODAY, GOT IT?
YEAH, YEAH. "DON'T TRY ANYTHING FUNNY," RIGHT? SURE THING.
TA (WHOOSH)
IF SHE'S TRYING TO DE-MOTIVATE ME, IT'S WORKING.
DON (THUNK)

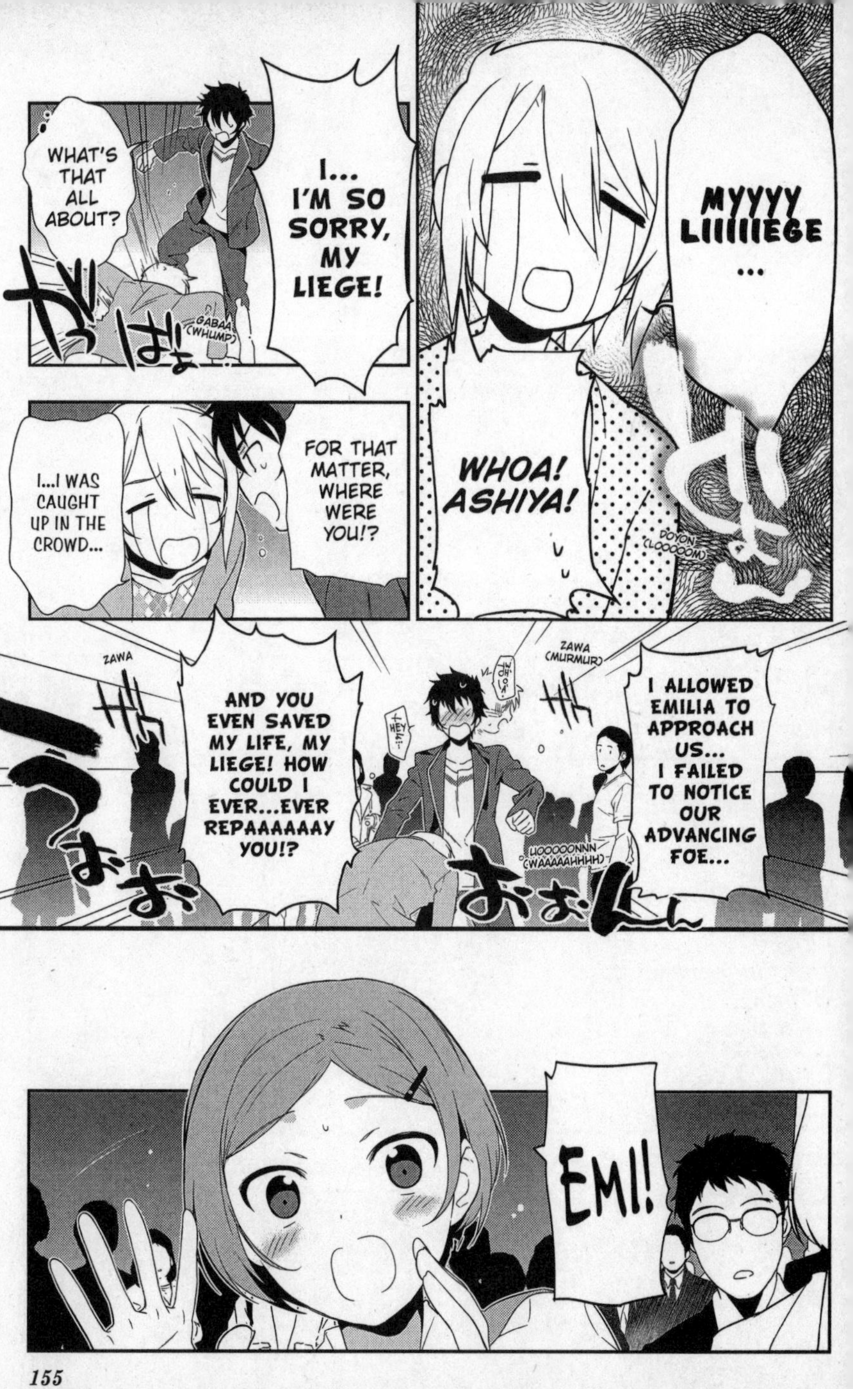
MYYYY LIIIIIEGE ...
DOYON (LOOOOOM)
WHOA! ASHIYA!
I... I'M SO SORRY, MY LIEGE!
GABAA (WHUMP)
WHAT'S THAT ALL ABOUT?
FOR THAT MATTER, WHERE WERE YOU!?
I...I WAS CAUGHT UP IN THE CROWD...
I ALLOWED EMILIA TO APPROACH US... I FAILED TO NOTICE OUR ADVANCING FOE...
ZAWA (MURMUR)
UOOOOONNN (WAAAAAHHHH)
HEY
AND YOU EVEN SAVED MY LIFE, MY LIEGE! HOW COULD I EVER...EVER REPAAAAAAY YOU!?
ZAWA
EMI!

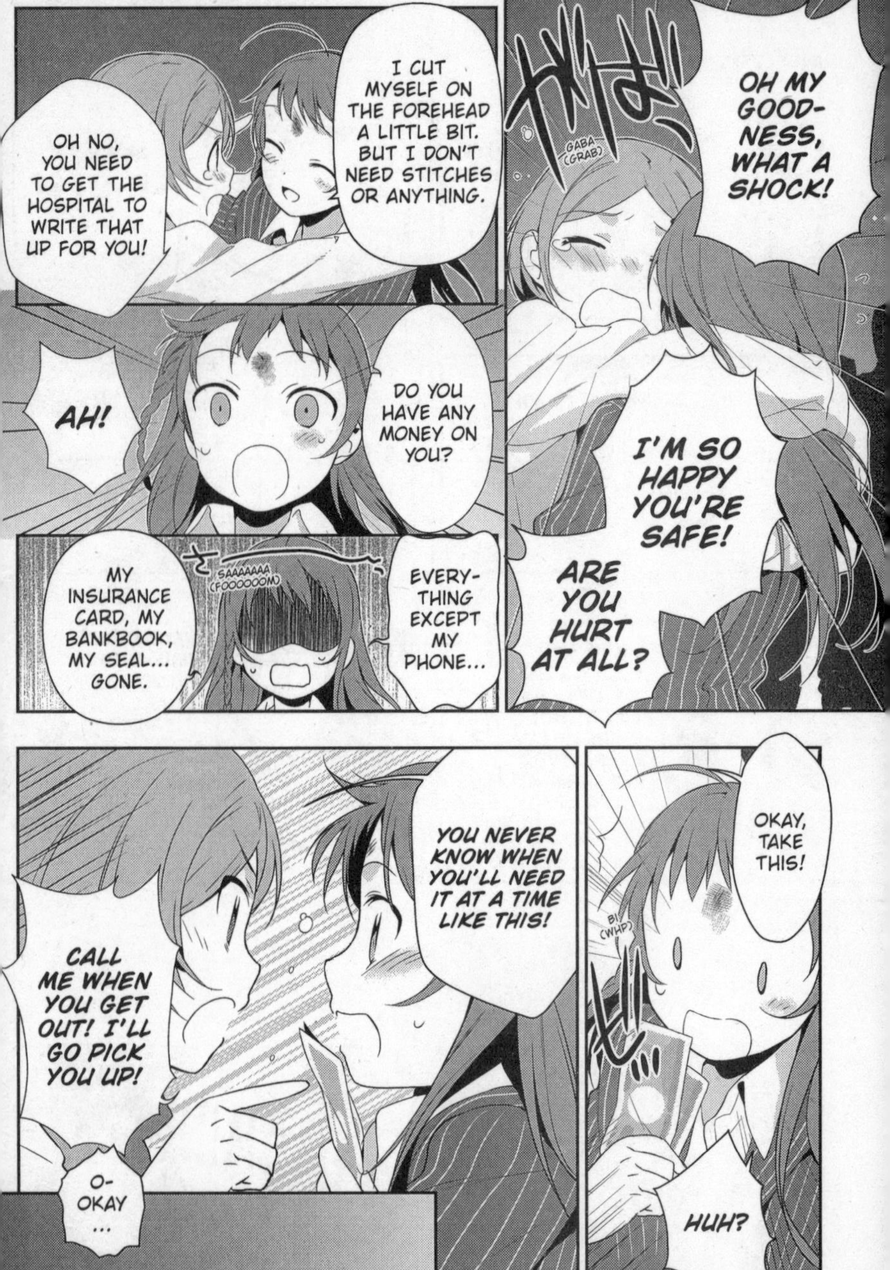
OH MY GOODNESS, WHAT A SHOCK!
GABA (GRAB)
I'M SO HAPPY YOU'RE SAFE!
ARE YOU HURT AT ALL?
I CUT MYSELF ON THE FOREHEAD A LITTLE BIT. BUT I DON'T NEED STITCHES OR ANYTHING.
OH NO, YOU NEED TO GET THE HOSPITAL TO WRITE THAT UP FOR YOU!
DO YOU HAVE ANY MONEY ON YOU?
AH!
EVERYTHING EXCEPT MY PHONE...
SAAAAAAA (FOOOOOOM)
MY INSURANCE CARD, MY BANKBOOK, MY SEAL... GONE.
OKAY, TAKE THIS!
BI (WHP)
HUH?
YOU NEVER KNOW WHEN YOU'LL NEED IT AT A TIME LIKE THIS!
CALL ME WHEN YOU GET OUT! I'LL GO PICK YOU UP!
O-OKAY...

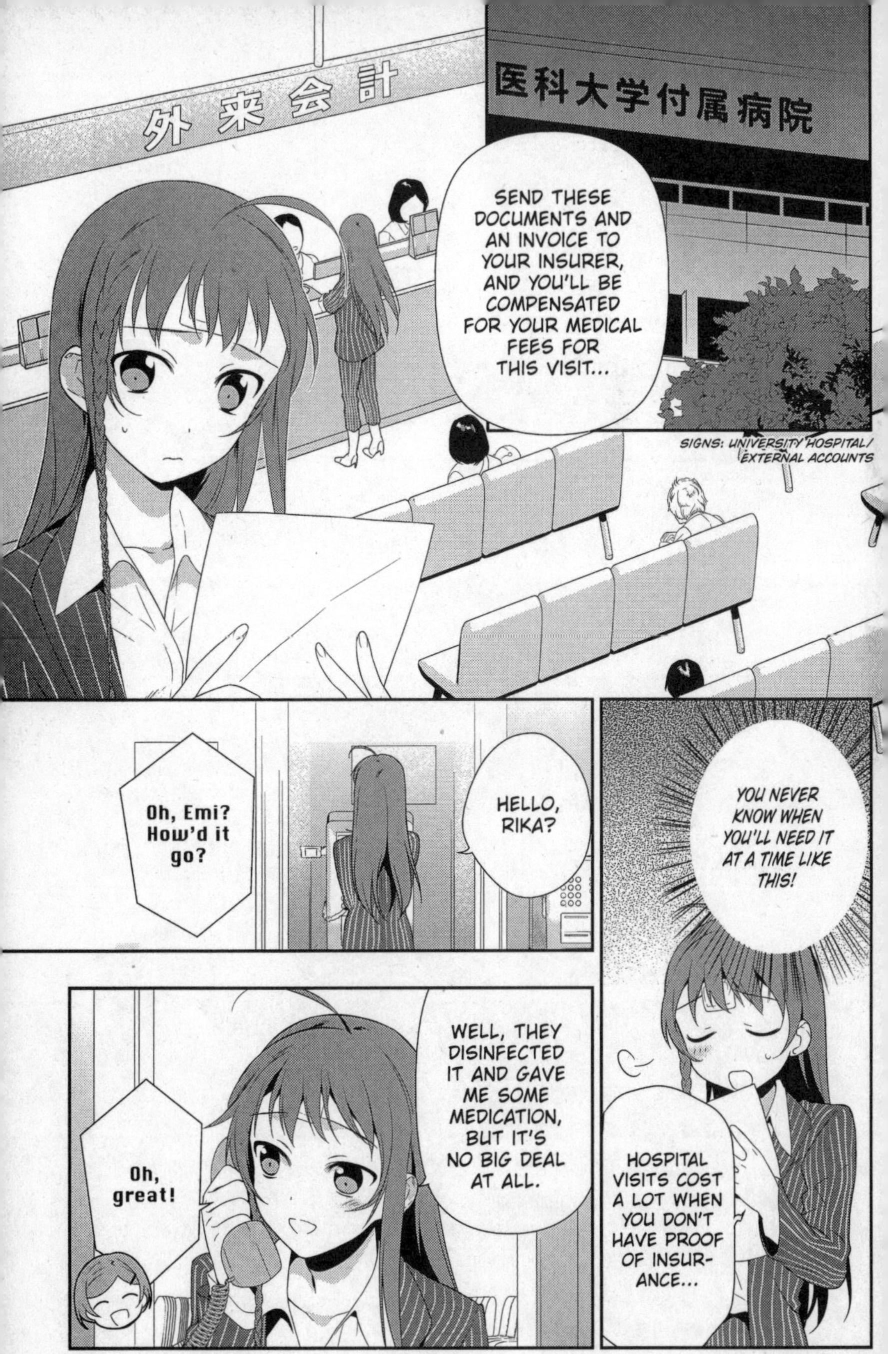
医科大学付属病院
外来会計
SEND THESE DOCUMENTS AND AN INVOICE TO YOUR INSURER, AND YOU'LL BE COMPENSATED FOR YOUR MEDICAL FEES FOR THIS VISIT...
SIGNS: UNIVERSITY HOSPITAL/ EXTERNAL ACCOUNTS
YOU NEVER KNOW WHEN YOU'LL NEED IT AT A TIME LIKE THIS!
HOSPITAL VISITS COST A LOT WHEN YOU DON'T HAVE PROOF OF INSUR-ANCE...
HELLO, RIKA?
Oh, Emi? How'd it go?
WELL, THEY DISINFECTED IT AND GAVE ME SOME MEDICATION, BUT IT'S NO BIG DEAL AT ALL.
Oh, great!

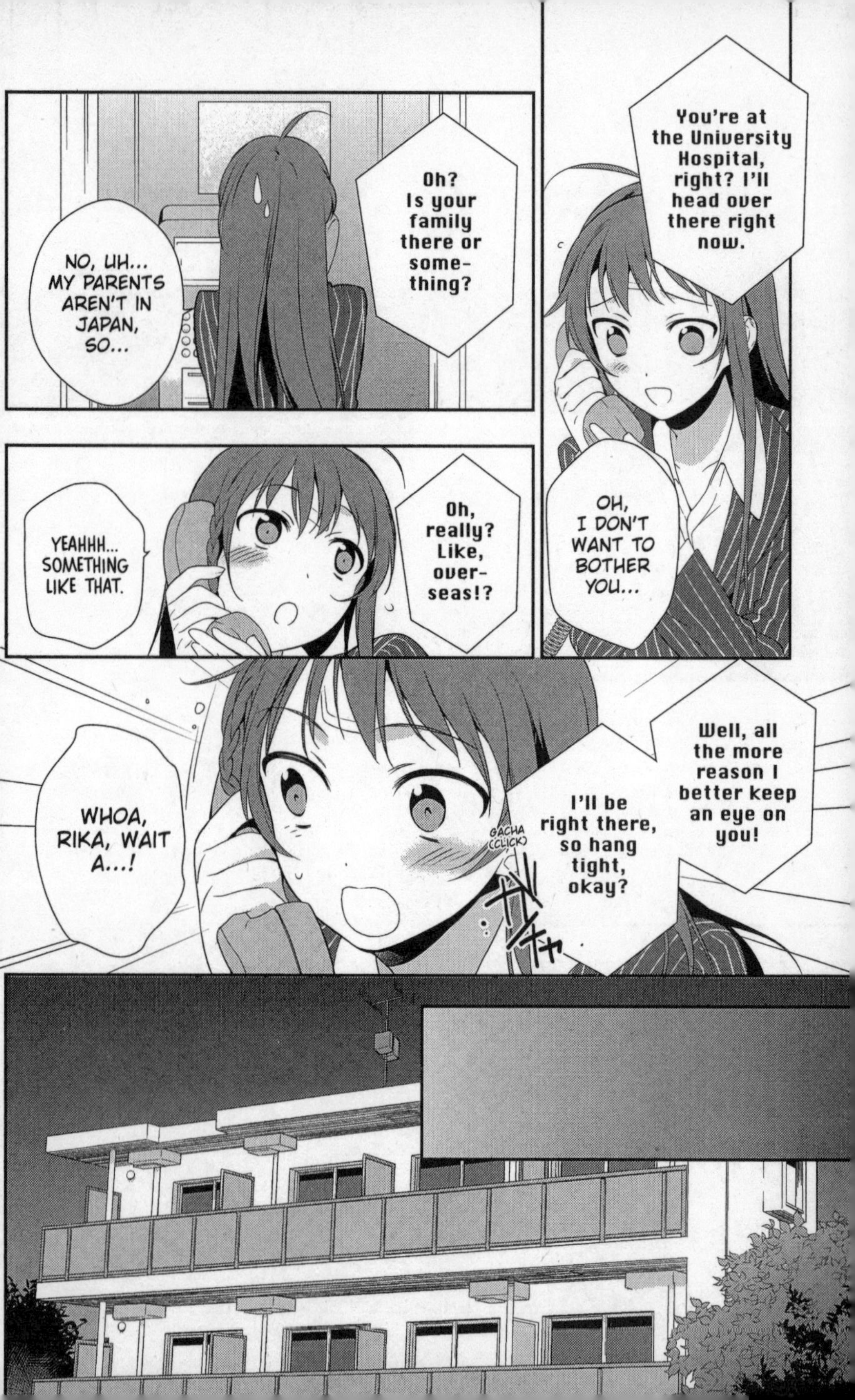
You're at the University Hospital, right? I'll head over there right now.
OH, I DON'T WANT TO BOTHER YOU...
Oh? Is your family there or some-thing?
NO, UH... MY PARENTS AREN'T IN JAPAN, SO...
Oh, really? Like, over-seas!?
YEAHHH... SOMETHING LIKE THAT.
Well, all the more reason I better keep an eye on you!
I'll be right there, so hang tight, okay?
GACHA (CLICK)
WHOA, RIKA, WAIT A...!

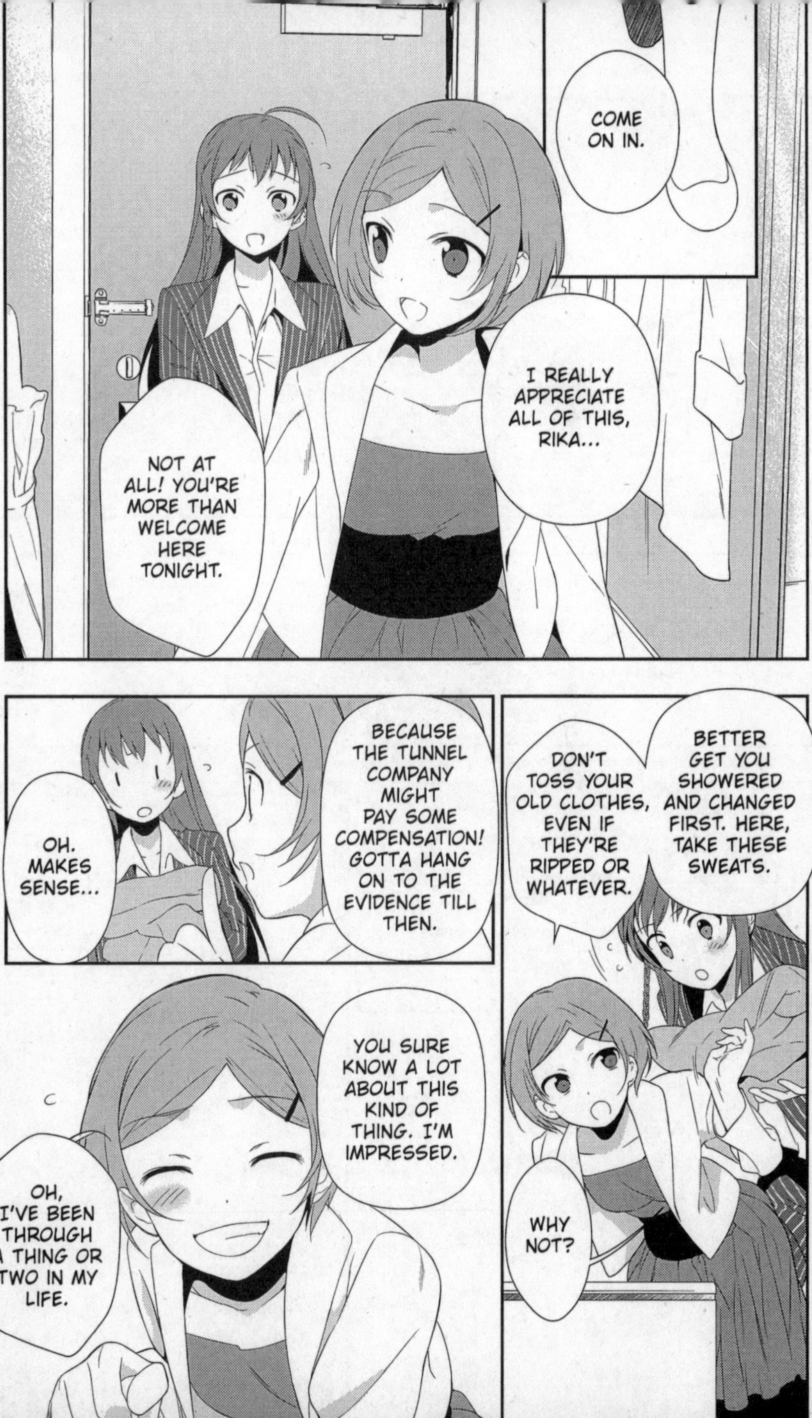
COME ON IN.
I REALLY APPRECIATE ALL OF THIS, RIKA...
NOT AT ALL! YOU'RE MORE THAN WELCOME HERE TONIGHT.
BETTER GET YOU SHOWERED AND CHANGED FIRST. HERE, TAKE THESE SWEATS.
DON'T TOSS YOUR OLD CLOTHES, EVEN IF THEY'RE RIPPED OR WHATEVER.
WHY NOT?
BECAUSE THE TUNNEL COMPANY MIGHT PAY SOME COMPENSATION! GOTTA HANG ON TO THE EVIDENCE TILL THEN.
OH. MAKES SENSE...
YOU SURE KNOW A LOT ABOUT THIS KIND OF THING. I'M IMPRESSED.
OH, I'VE BEEN THROUGH A THING OR TWO IN MY LIFE.

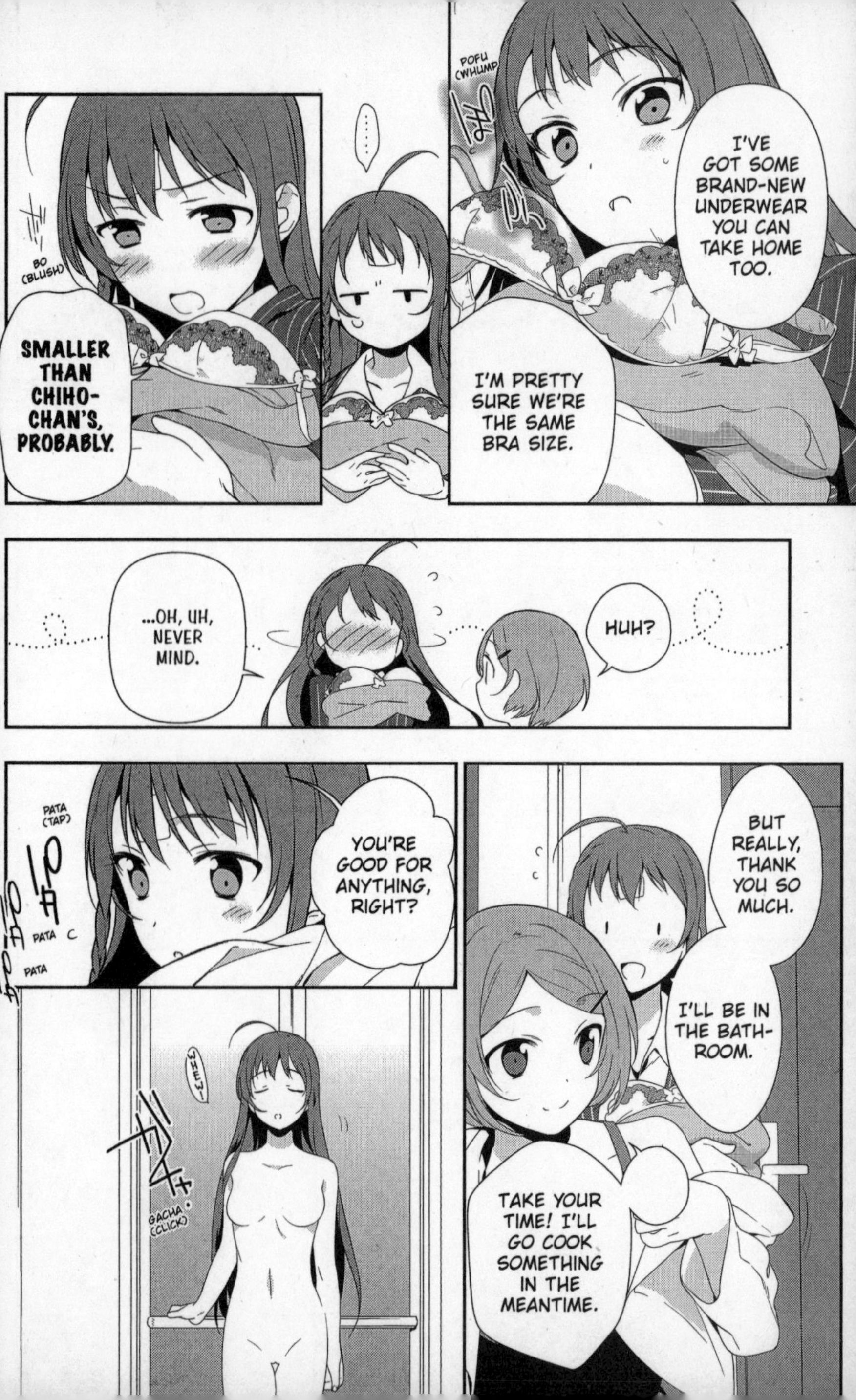
POFU (WHUMP)
I'VE GOT SOME BRAND-NEW UNDERWEAR YOU CAN TAKE HOME TOO.
I'M PRETTY SURE WE'RE THE SAME BRA SIZE.
......
BO (BLUSH)
SMALLER THAN CHIHO-CHAN'S, PROBABLY.
HUH?
...OH, UH, NEVER MIND.
BUT REALLY, THANK YOU SO MUCH.
I'LL BE IN THE BATH-ROOM.
TAKE YOUR TIME! I'LL GO COOK SOMETHING IN THE MEANTIME.
PATA (TAP)
PATA
PATA
YOU'RE GOOD FOR ANYTHING, RIGHT?
WHEW!
GACHA (CLICK)

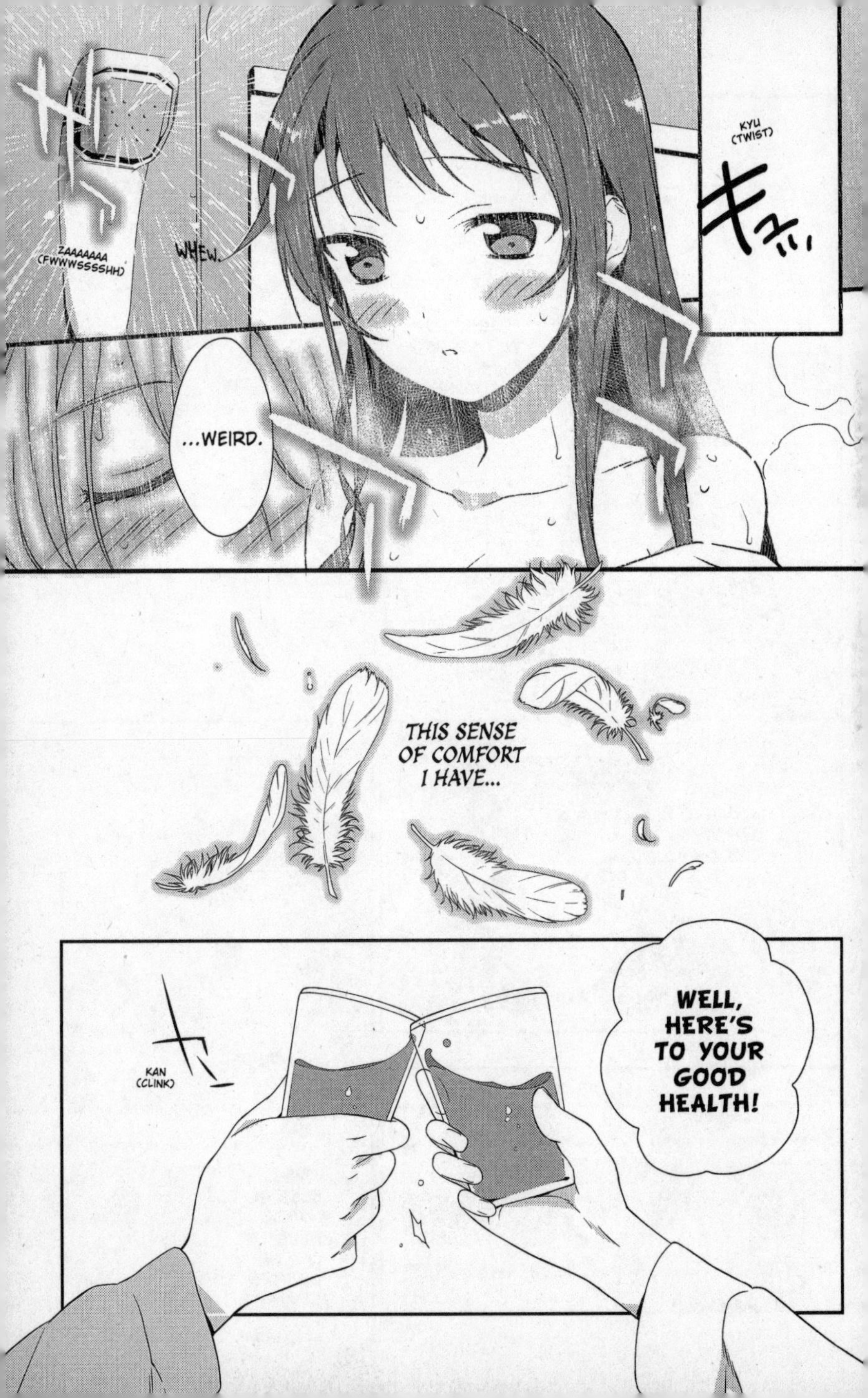
KYU (TWIST)
ZAAAAAAA (FWWWSSSSHH)
WHEW.
...WEIRD.
THIS SENSE OF COMFORT I HAVE...
WELL, HERE'S TO YOUR GOOD HEALTH!
KAN (CLINK)

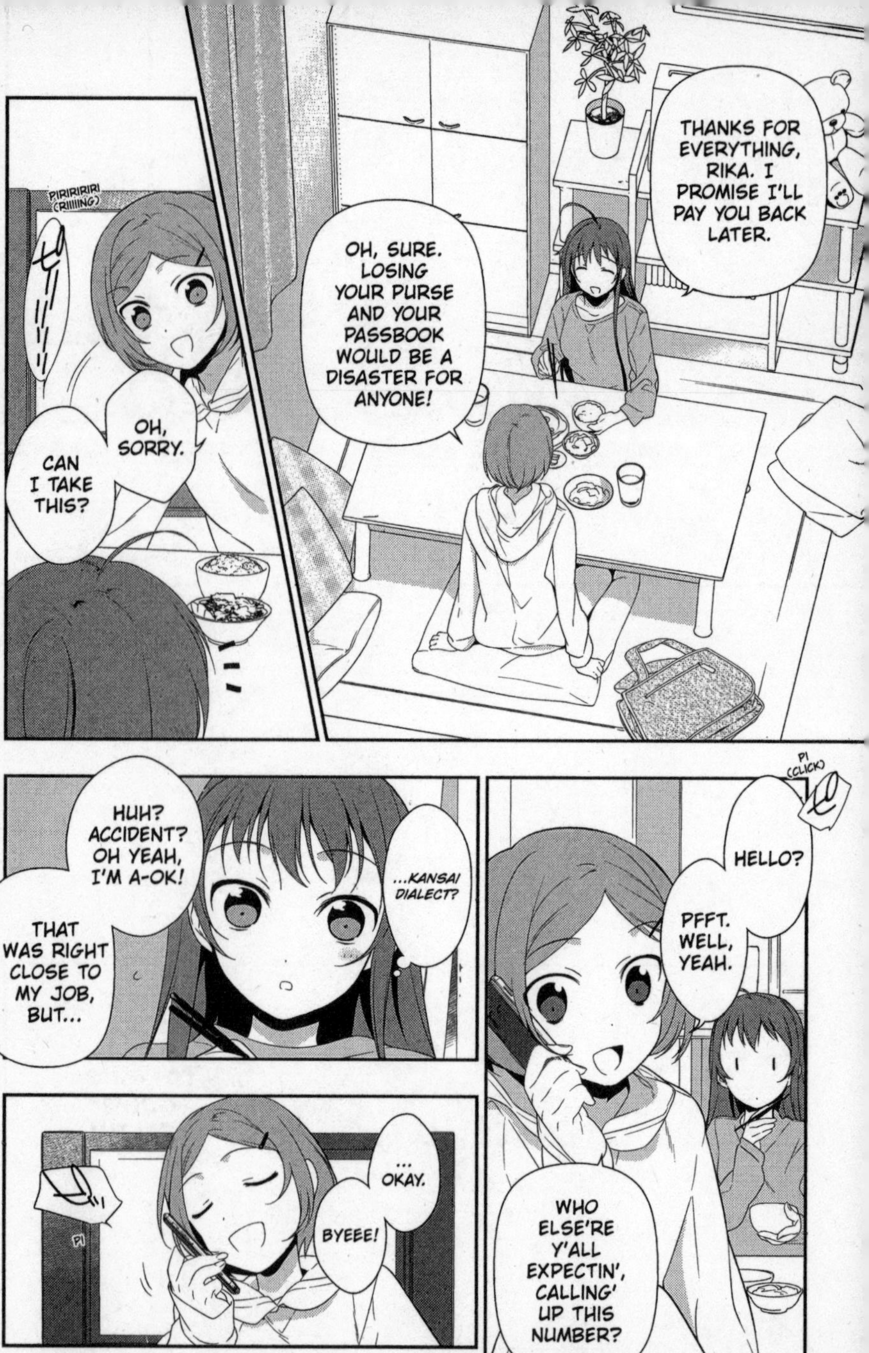
THANKS FOR EVERYTHING, RIKA. I PROMISE I'LL PAY YOU BACK LATER.
OH, SURE. LOSING YOUR PURSE AND YOUR PASSBOOK WOULD BE A DISASTER FOR ANYONE!
PIRIRIRIRI (RIIIIING)
OH, SORRY.
CAN I TAKE THIS?
PI (CLICK)
HELLO?
PFFT. WELL, YEAH.
WHO ELSE'RE Y'ALL EXPECTIN', CALLING' UP THIS NUMBER?
HUH? ACCIDENT? OH YEAH, I'M A-OK!
THAT WAS RIGHT CLOSE TO MY JOB, BUT...
...KANSAI DIALECT?
...OKAY.
BYEEE!
PI

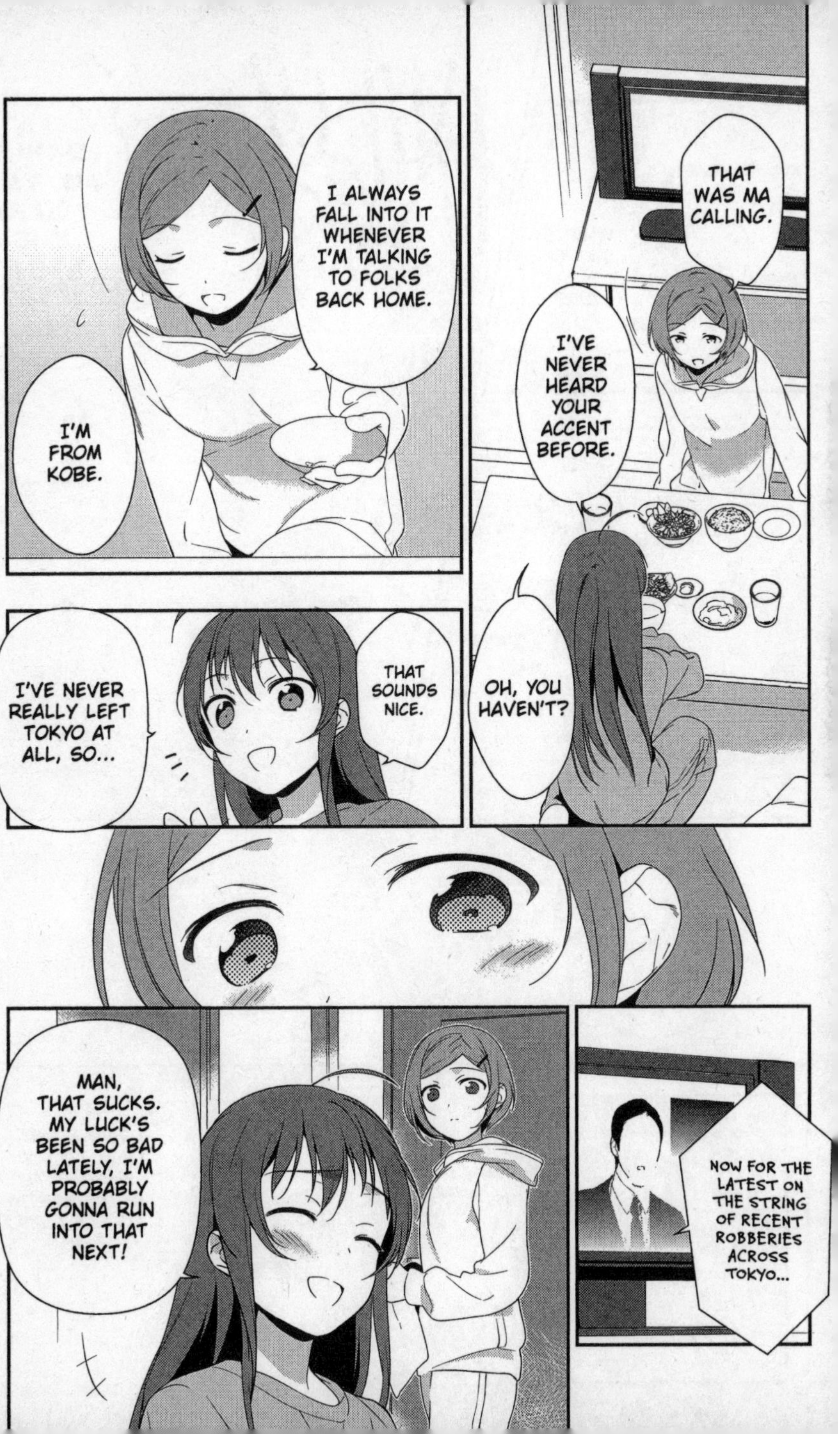
THAT WAS MA CALLING.
I'VE NEVER HEARD YOUR ACCENT BEFORE.
OH, YOU HAVEN'T?
I ALWAYS FALL INTO IT WHENEVER I'M TALKING TO FOLKS BACK HOME.
I'M FROM KOBE.
THAT SOUNDS NICE.
I'VE NEVER REALLY LEFT TOKYO AT ALL, SO...
NOW FOR THE LATEST ON THE STRING OF RECENT ROBBERIES ACROSS TOKYO...
MAN, THAT SUCKS. MY LUCK'S BEEN SO BAD LATELY, I'M PROBABLY GONNA RUN INTO THAT NEXT!

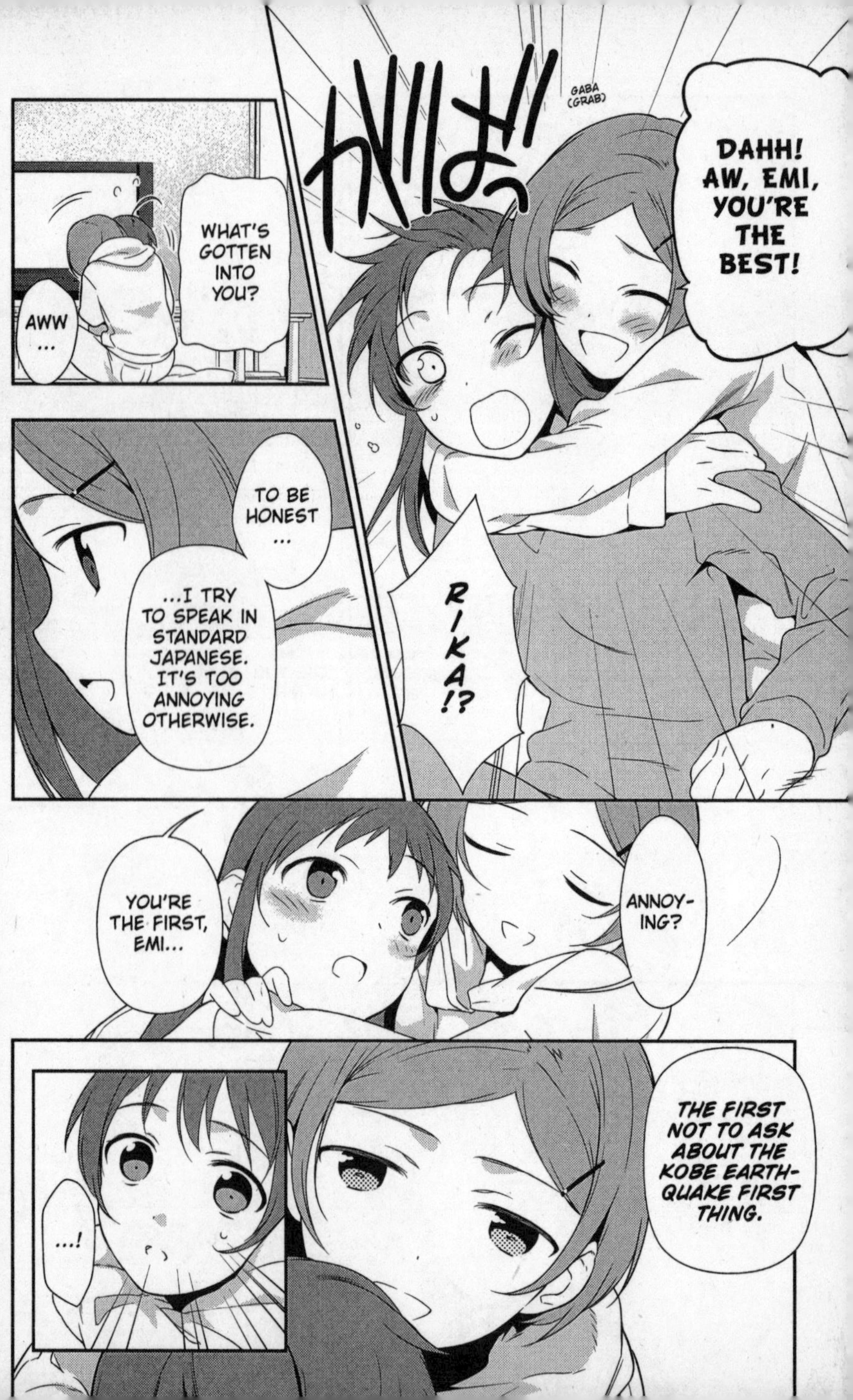
DAHH! AW, EMI, YOU'RE THE BEST!
GABA (GRAB)
かばっ
RIKA!?
WHAT'S GOTTEN INTO YOU?
AWW ...
TO BE HONEST ...
...I TRY TO SPEAK IN STANDARD JAPANESE. IT'S TOO ANNOYING OTHERWISE.
ANNOY-ING?
YOU'RE THE FIRST, EMI...
THE FIRST NOT TO ASK ABOUT THE KOBE EARTH-QUAKE FIRST THING.
...!

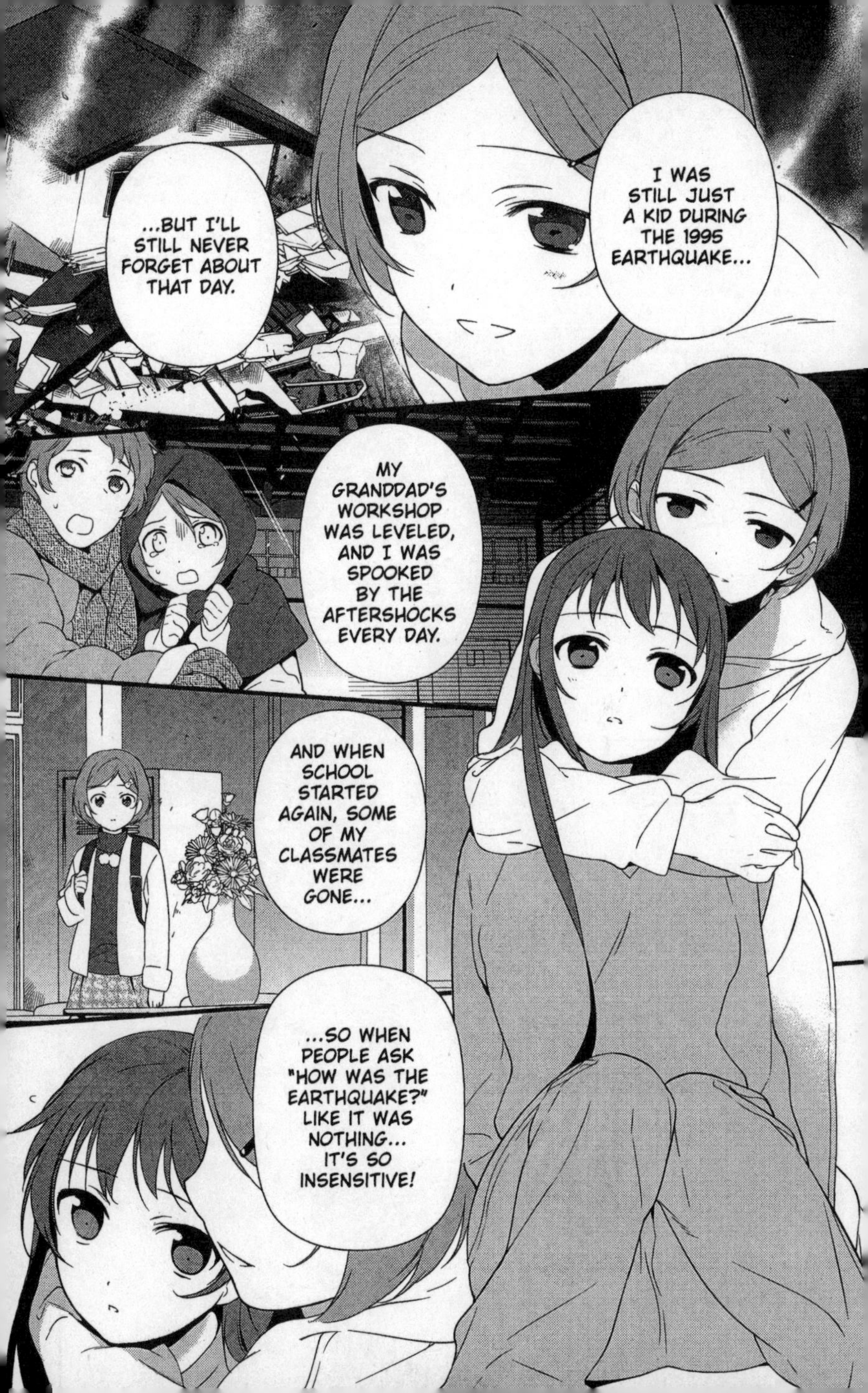
I WAS STILL JUST A KID DURING THE 1995 EARTHQUAKE...
...BUT I'LL STILL NEVER FORGET ABOUT THAT DAY.
MY GRANDDAD'S WORKSHOP WAS LEVELED, AND I WAS SPOOKED BY THE AFTERSHOCKS EVERY DAY.
AND WHEN SCHOOL STARTED AGAIN, SOME OF MY CLASSMATES WERE GONE...
...SO WHEN PEOPLE ASK "HOW WAS THE EARTHQUAKE?" LIKE IT WAS NOTHING... IT'S SO INSENSITIVE!

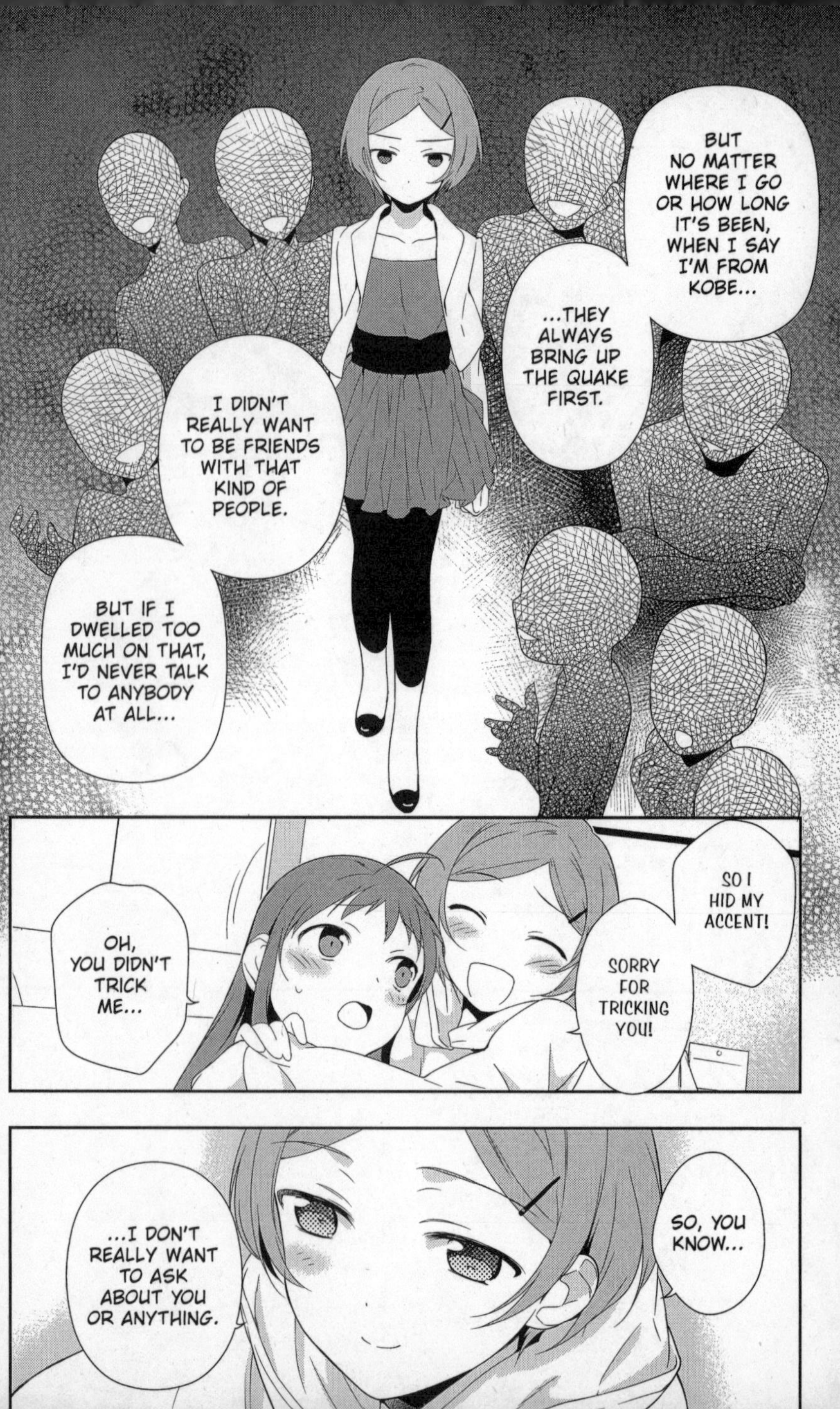
BUT NO MATTER WHERE I GO OR HOW LONG IT'S BEEN, WHEN I SAY I'M FROM KOBE...
...THEY ALWAYS BRING UP THE QUAKE FIRST.
I DIDN'T REALLY WANT TO BE FRIENDS WITH THAT KIND OF PEOPLE.
BUT IF I DWELLED TOO MUCH ON THAT, I'D NEVER TALK TO ANYBODY AT ALL...
SO I HID MY ACCENT!
SORRY FOR TRICKING YOU!
OH, YOU DIDN'T TRICK ME...
SO, YOU KNOW...
...I DON'T REALLY WANT TO ASK ABOUT YOU OR ANYTHING.

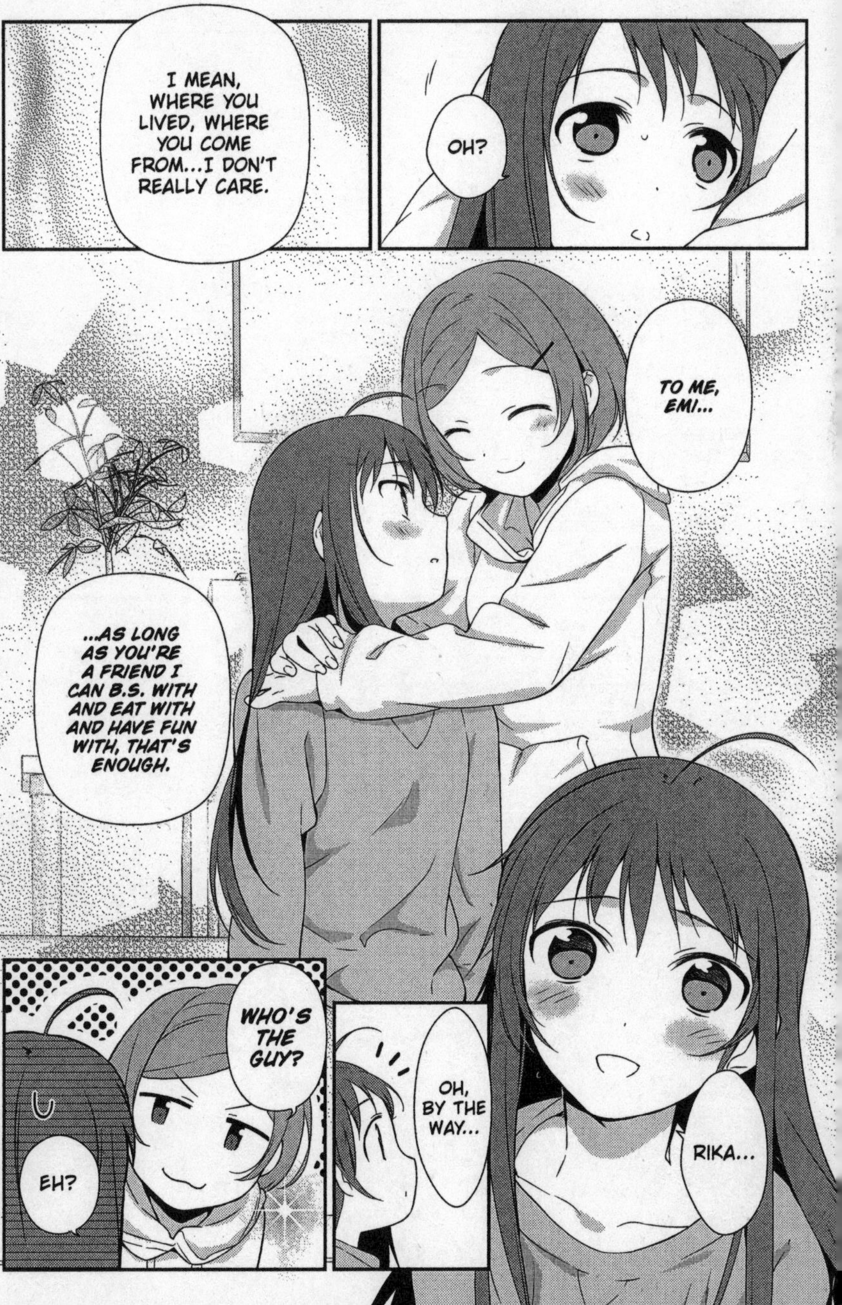
OH?
I MEAN, WHERE YOU LIVED, WHERE YOU COME FROM...I DON'T REALLY CARE.
TO ME, EMI...
...AS LONG AS YOU'RE A FRIEND I CAN B.S. WITH AND EAT WITH AND HAVE FUN WITH, THAT'S ENOUGH.
RIKA...
OH, BY THE WAY...
WHO'S THE GUY?
EH?

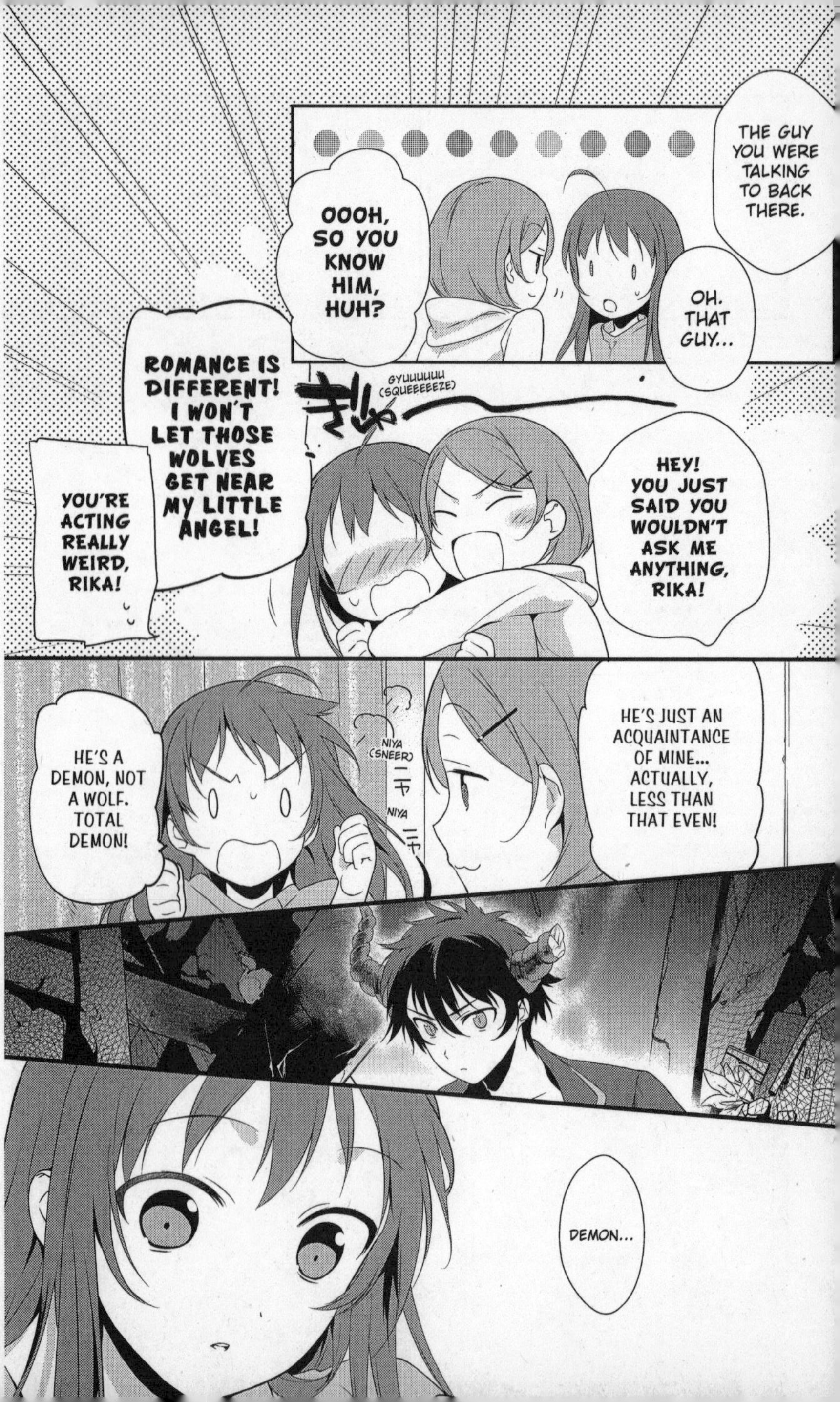
THE GUY YOU WERE TALKING TO BACK THERE.
OH. THAT GUY...
OOOH, SO YOU KNOW HIM, HUH?
HEY! YOU JUST SAID YOU WOULDN'T ASK ME ANYTHING, RIKA!
GYUUUUUU (SQUEEEEEZE)
ROMANCE IS DIFFERENT! I WON'T LET THOSE WOLVES GET NEAR MY LITTLE ANGEL!
YOU'RE ACTING REALLY WEIRD, RIKA!
HE'S JUST AN ACQUAINTANCE OF MINE... ACTUALLY, LESS THAN THAT EVEN!
NIYA (SNEER)
NIYA
HE'S A DEMON, NOT A WOLF. TOTAL DEMON!
DEMON...

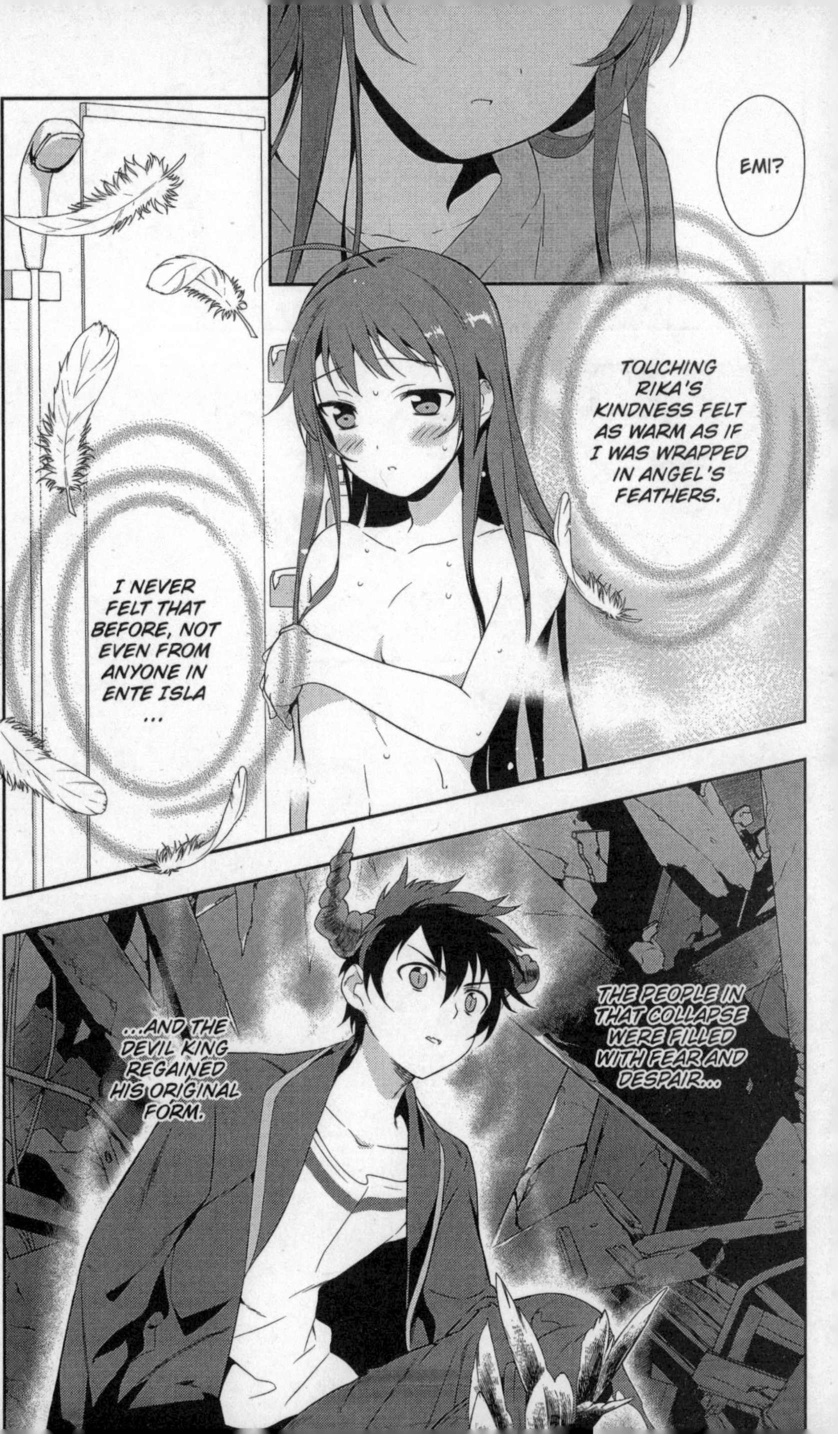
EMI?
TOUCHING RIKA'S KINDNESS FELT AS WARM AS IF I WAS WRAPPED IN ANGEL'S FEATHERS.
I NEVER FELT THAT BEFORE, NOT EVEN FROM ANYONE IN ENTE ISLA ...
THE PEOPLE IN THAT COLLAPSE WERE FILLED WITH FEAR AND DESPAIR...
...AND THE DEVIL KING REGAINED HIS ORIGINAL FORM.

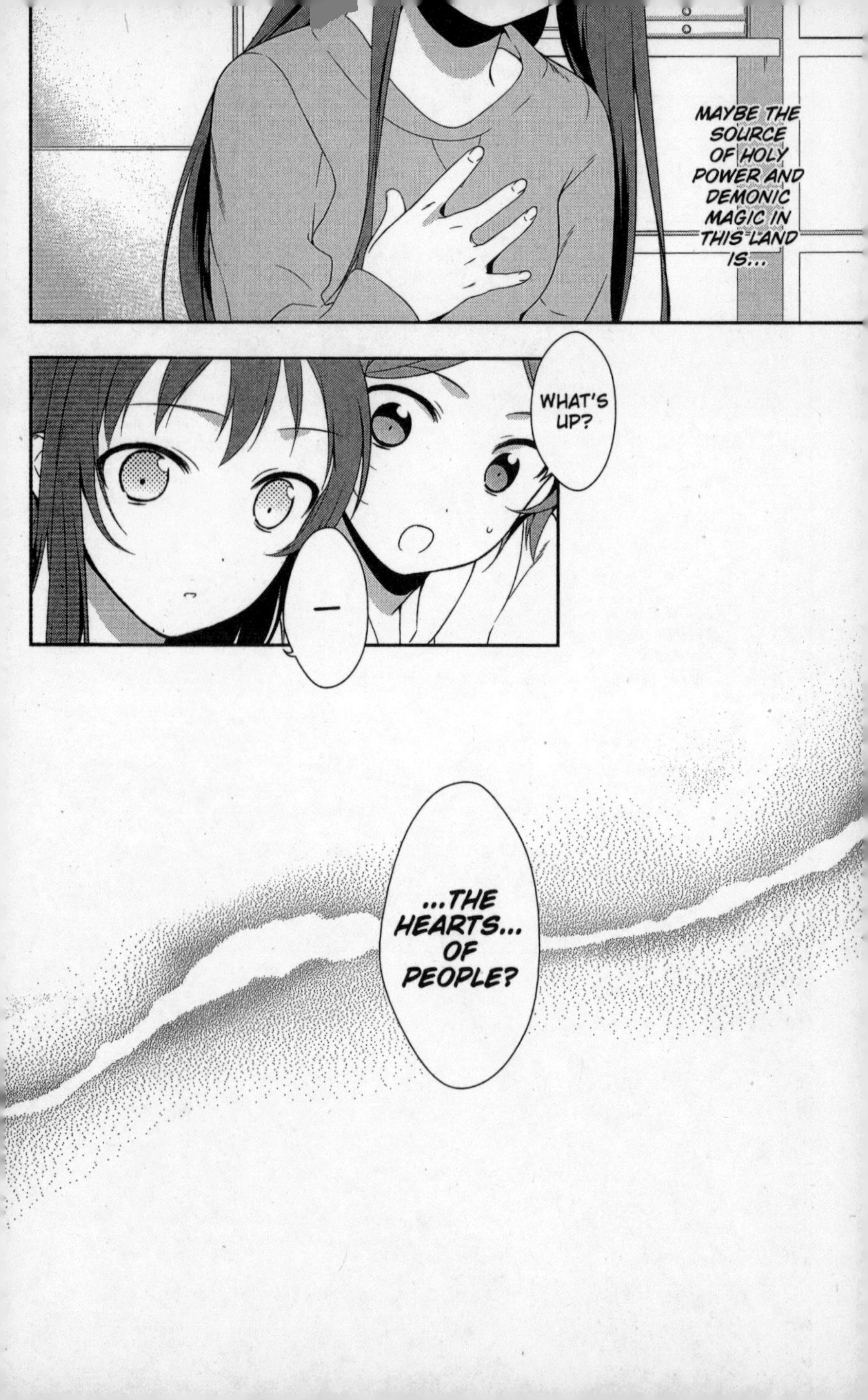
MAYBE THE SOURCE OF HOLY POWER AND DEMONIC MAGIC IN THIS LAND IS...
WHAT'S UP?
—
...THE HEARTS... OF PEOPLE?

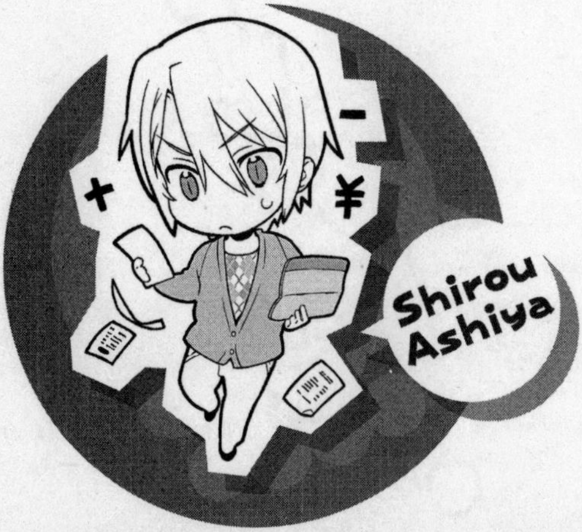
Shirou
Ashiya

TRANSLATION NOTES

COMMON HONORIFICS

No honorific: indicates familiarity or closeness; if used without permission or reason, addressing someone in this manner would constitute an insult.
-san: the japanese equivalent of mr./Mrs./Miss. If a situation calls for politeness, this is the fail-safe honorific.
-sama: conveys great respect; may also indicate that the social status of the speaker is lower than that of the addressee.
-kun: used most often when referring to boys, this indicates affection or familiarity. Occasionally used by older men among their peers, but it may also be used by anyone referring to a person of lower standing.
-chan: an affectionate honorific indicating familiarity used mostly in reference to girls; also used in reference to cute persons or animals of either gender.

PAGE 14

Mikitty: This is also the nickname of a famous idol in Japan, Miki Fujimoto.

PAGE 14

MHK Guy: A reference to the NHK TV network employees who go door-to-door in order to collect the yearly fee that anyone who owns a TV is obligated to pay.

PAGE 15

Maou: The kanji written for Sadao Maou's Japanese surname means "true middle," but sounds exactly the same as the kanji for "Devil King"—so everyone in modern Japan is basically calling Maou by his true title as the "Devil King"!

PAGE 129

Maou/<Maou>: When Emi says "<Maou>," she's actually referring to him with the kanji for "Devil King," hence Chi-chan's confusion.

THE DEVIL IS A PART-TIMER!

CHAPTER X: THE DEMON LORD IS BLESSED BY SOME PORK

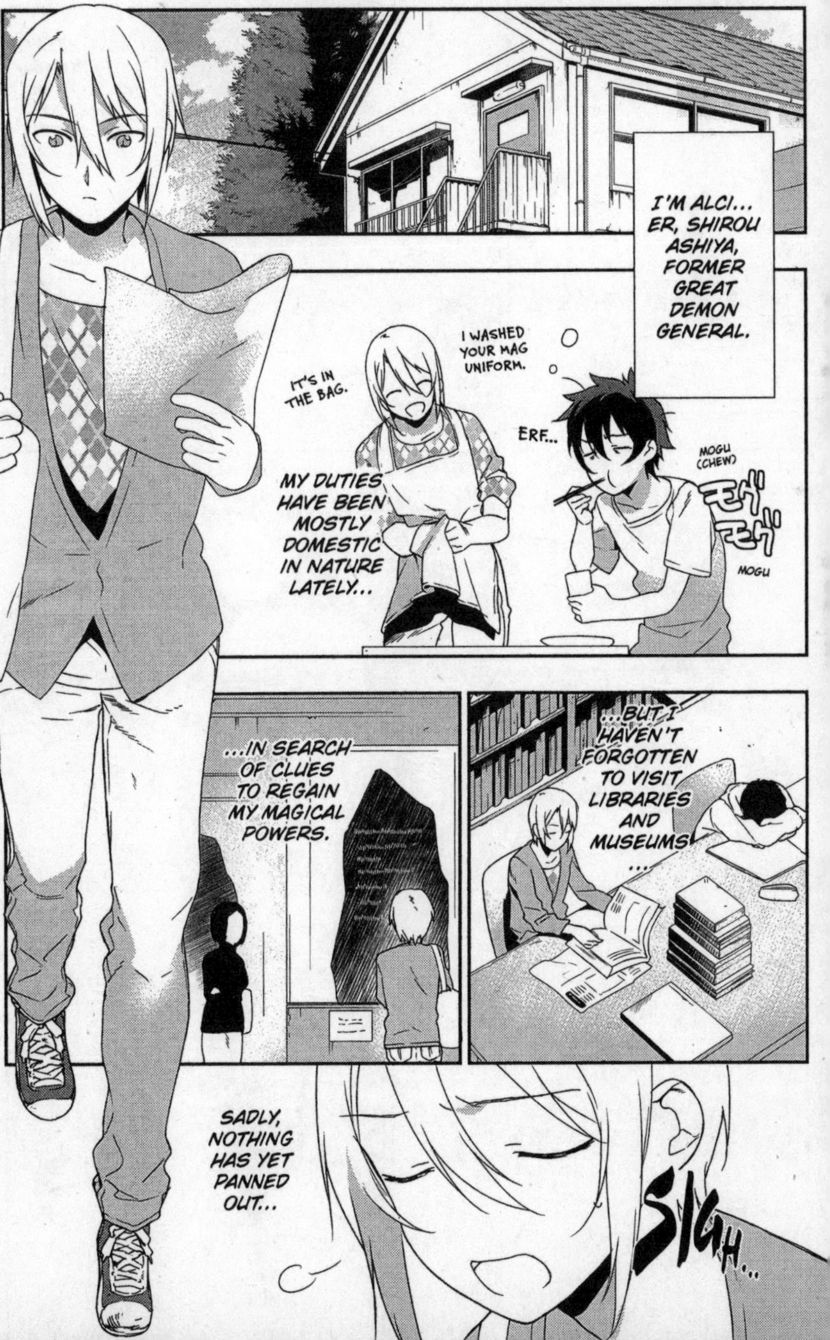

I'M ALCI... ER, SHIROU ASHIYA, FORMER GREAT DEMON GENERAL.
MOGU (CHEW)
モグモグ
MOGU
ERF...
I WASHED YOUR MAG UNIFORM.
IT'S IN THE BAG.
MY DUTIES HAVE BEEN MOSTLY DOMESTIC IN NATURE LATELY...
...BUT I HAVEN'T FORGOTTEN TO VISIT LIBRARIES AND MUSEUMS...
...IN SEARCH OF CLUES TO REGAIN MY MAGICAL POWERS.
SIGH...
SADLY, NOTHING HAS YET PANNED OUT...

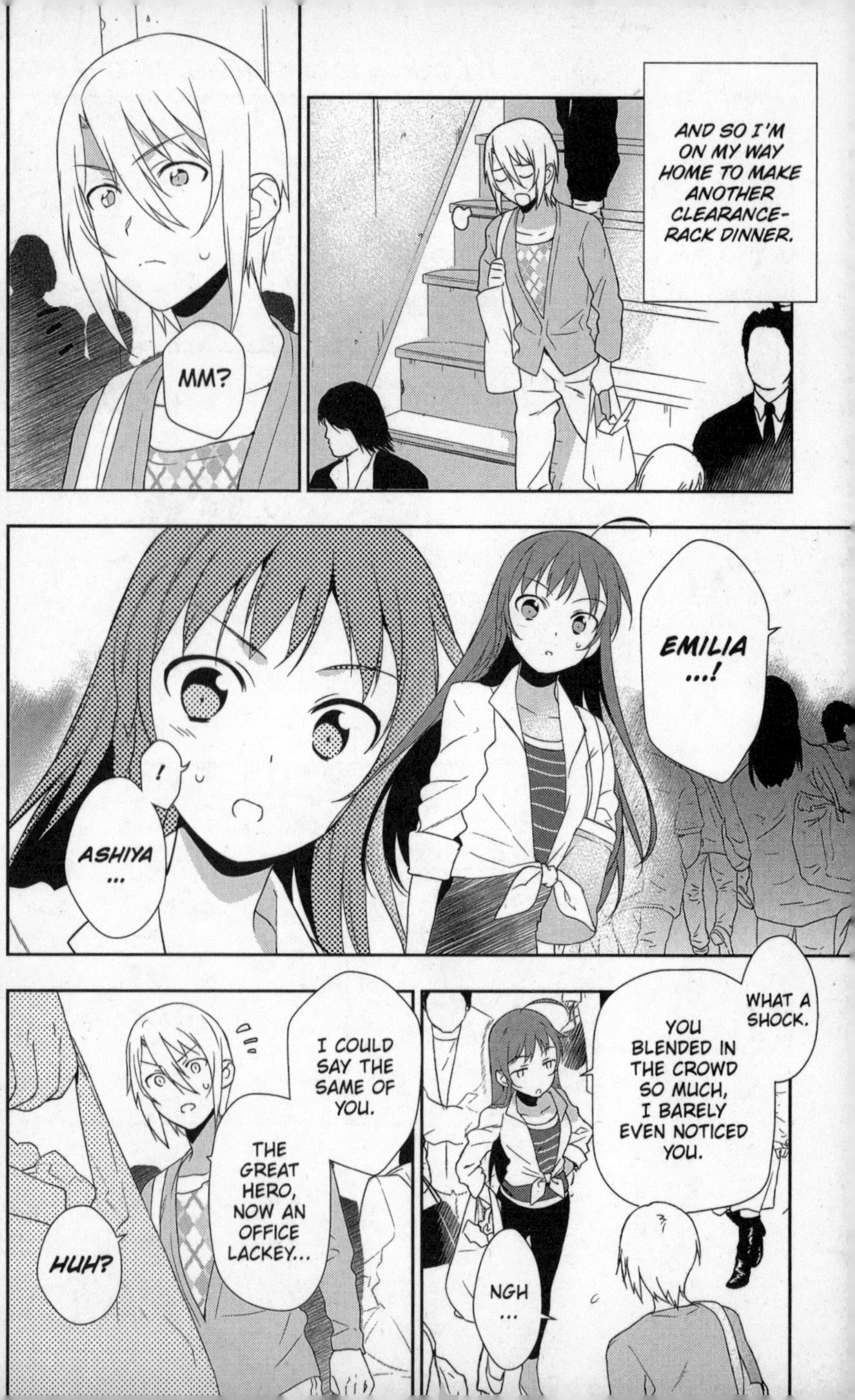
AND SO I'M ON MY WAY HOME TO MAKE ANOTHER CLEARANCE-RACK DINNER.
MM?
EMILIA ...!
!
ASHIYA ...
WHAT A SHOCK.
YOU BLENDED IN THE CROWD SO MUCH, I BARELY EVEN NOTICED YOU.
NGH ...
I COULD SAY THE SAME OF YOU.
THE GREAT HERO, NOW AN OFFICE LACKEY...
HUH?

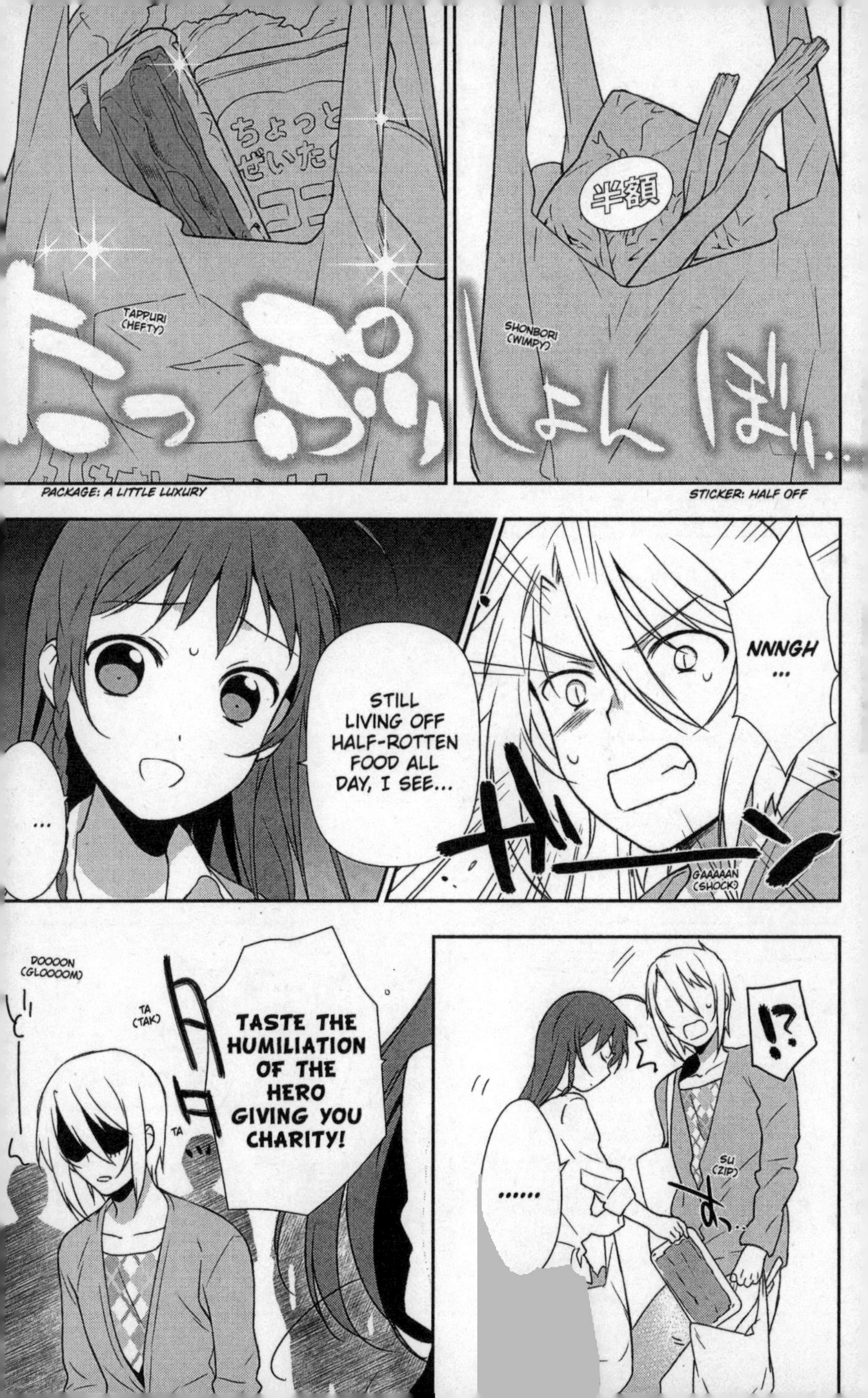
半額
SHONBORI (WIMPY)
STICKER: HALF OFF
TAPPURI (HEFTY)
PACKAGE: A LITTLE LUXURY
NNNGH...
GAAAAAN (SHOCK)
STILL LIVING OFF HALF-ROTTEN FOOD ALL DAY, I SEE...
...
!?
SU (ZIP)
......
TASTE THE HUMILIATION OF THE HERO GIVING YOU CHARITY!
TA (TAK)
TA
DOOOON (GLOOOOM)

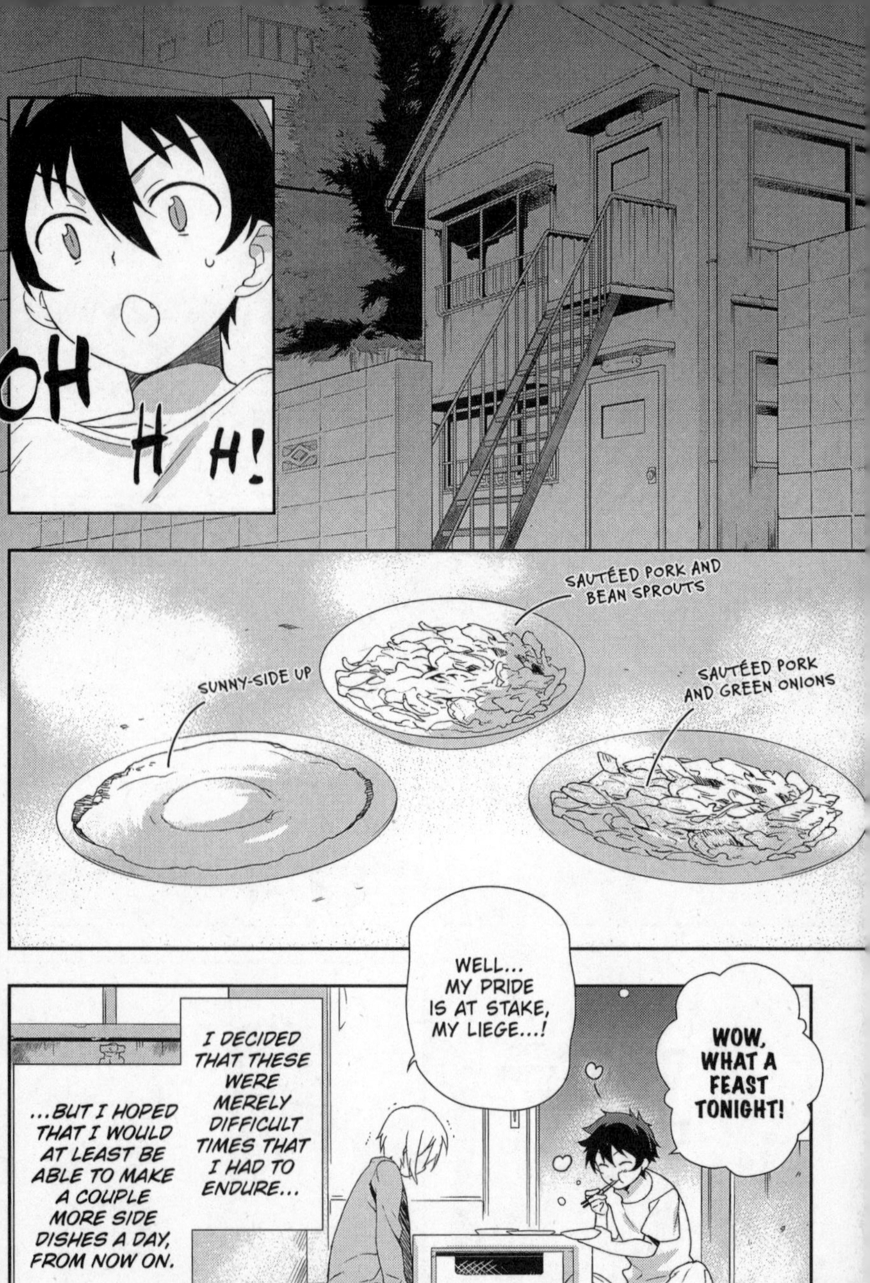
OHHH!
SAUTÉED PORK AND BEAN SPROUTS
SAUTÉED PORK AND GREEN ONIONS
SUNNY-SIDE UP
WOW, WHAT A FEAST TONIGHT!
WELL... MY PRIDE IS AT STAKE, MY LIEGE...!
I DECIDED THAT THESE WERE MERELY DIFFICULT TIMES THAT I HAD TO ENDURE...
...BUT I HOPED THAT I WOULD AT LEAST BE ABLE TO MAKE A COUPLE MORE SIDE DISHES A DAY, FROM NOW ON.

AFTERWORD

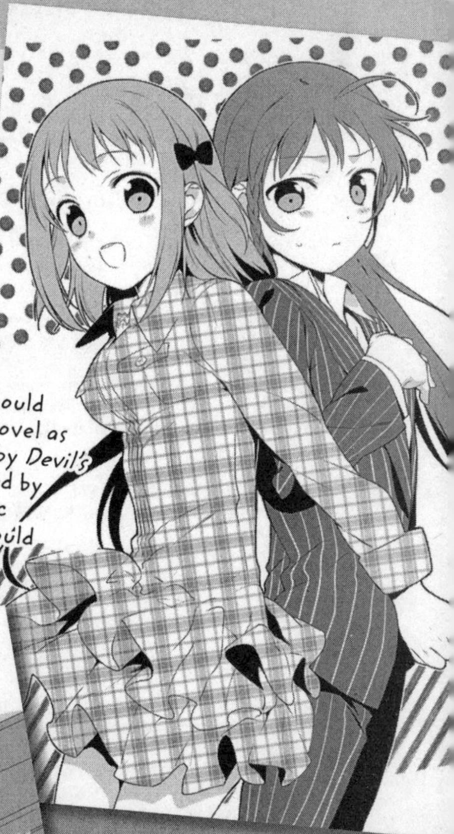

Hello to everyone. This is Akio Hiiragi.

I drew this manga in the hopes that I could recreate the feel of the original light novel as best I could, from the humble lives led by *Devil's* cast to the fetching characters designed by 029-san (Oniku). If you enjoy this comic alongside the original novels, nothing would make me happier!

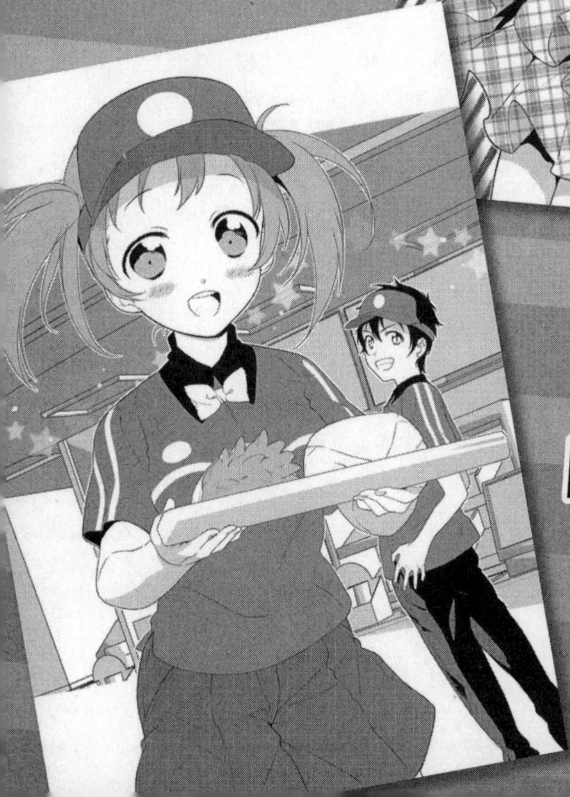

AKIO HIIRAGI

THE DEVIL IS A PART-TIMER! ①

Art: Akio Hiiragi
Original Story: Satoshi Wagahara
Character Design: 029 (Oniku)

Translation: Kevin Gifford

Lettering: Brndn Blakeslee & Lys Blakeslee

This book is a work of fiction. Names, characters, places, and incidents are the product of the author's imagination or are used fictitiously. Any resemblance to actual events, locales, or persons, living or dead, is coincidental.

HATARAKU MAOUSAMA! Vol. 1
© SATOSHI WAGAHARA / AKIO HIIRAGI 2012
All rights reserved.
Edited by ASCII MEDIA WORKS
First published in Japan in 2012 by KADOKAWA CORPORATION, Tokyo.
English translation rights arranged with KADOKAWA CORPORATION, Tokyo, through Tuttle-Mori Agency, Inc., Tokyo.

Translation © 2015 by Hachette Book Group, Inc.

Yen Press
Hachette Book Group
1290 Avenue of the Americas
New York, NY 10104

www.HachetteBookGroup.com
www.YenPress.com

Yen Press is an imprint of Hachette Book Group, Inc. The Yen Press name and logo are trademarks of Hachette Book Group, Inc.

The publisher is not responsible for websites (or their content) that are not owned by the publisher.

First Yen Press Edition: March 2015

ISBN: 978-0-316-38313-4

10 9 8 7 6 5 4 3 2

BVG

Printed in the United States of America